EARLY MODERN ENGLAND

A Social History 1550–1760

Second Edition

J A SHARPE

Professor of History,
University of York, England

A member of the Hodder Headline Group
LONDON • NEW YORK • SYDNEY • AUCKLAND

First published in Great Britain 1987
Second edition published in 1997 by
Arnold, a member of the Hodder Headline Group
338 Euston Road, London NW1 3BH

Co-published in the United States of America by
Oxford University Press Inc.,
198 Madison Avenue, New York NY10016

Whilst the advice and information in this book is believed to be true
and accurate at the date of going to press, neither the author nor
the publisher can accept any legal responsibility or liability for
any errors or omissions that may be made.

British Library Cataloguing in Publication Data
A catalogue record for this book is available from the British Library

Library of Congress Cataloging-in-Publication Data
A catalog record for this book is available from the Library of Congress

ISBN 0 340 57752 5

2 3 4 5 6 7 8 9 10

Composition by Scribe Design, Gillingham, Kent, UK
Printed and bound in Great Britain by J W Arrowsmith Ltd, Bristol

Contents

List of figures, maps and tables

Preface to the first edition

Thirteen years ago I took up employment at the University of York, and found that the first teaching I was required to do was a second-year seminar on English society 1550–1750. Over the intervening years, quite apart from my research interest, I have found myself teaching in and around that subject area and, more generally, in early modern European history. This book is in large measure the product of the questions I have had to answer, the problems I have tried to raise, and the speculations I have put forward in that process.

It is probably that experience to which the work owes its peculiarities. This is not, perhaps, the best place in which to set out my views on what social history is: I would contend, however, that it is most certainly not history with the politics (a word amenable in any case to wide definition) left out. It is mainly for this reason that I have chosen to begin and conclude with narrative chapters exploring the interplay between politics and society. These chapters will, I hope, have additional benefits. Narrative history of this type does provide an accessible chronological framework, and readers coming new to the period via this book will at least gain an impression of what events followed what. They will also, I hope, become convinced that 'political' and 'social' history are not subjects tucked away into separate boxes. My hostility to such notions has also led me to devote a third of the main body of the book to religion, education, culture and ideas: if the social must take account of the political, so it must of the interaction between the material and the intellectual.

I must also emphasize that my subject is England. The Scots, Irish and Welsh have derived a number of disadvantages and benefits from their proximity to the English, but I am confident that any attempt on my part to write their history would be numbered with the former. Their cultures were, and in many ways still are, separate, and so should their history be. Similarly, the decision to write over the period between the mid-sixteenth and the mid-eighteenth centuries was a very conscious one. Both my teaching and my earlier research on crime and punishment have convinced me that this timespan constitutes a useful period of study. I am certainly profoundly unconvinced of the viability of writing English social history by centuries: from the coming of the Black Death in the fourteenth century to the creation of the Welfare State in the twentieth the really significant historical watersheds have tended to come in the middle of centuries rather than at their beginnings or ends, and I am confident that this is true of the two centuries or so covered by this book. As its readers will discover, I see this period as falling into two distinct halves, bisected across the middle of the seventeenth century.

Writing this book, like any enterprise of the kind, has led me to incur a number of debts. The decision to have minimal recourse to footnotes has meant that I have not always been able to acknowledge the sources of my statements as directly as may have been desirable, although I have done my best to make these explicit either in the text or in the suggestions for further reading. More specifically, Professor Anthony Fletcher, Dr Dwyryd Jones, Dr Jonathan Powis, Dr Bill Sheils, Professor William Speck and Dr Keith Wrightson have all commented on earlier drafts of sections of this book. It has benefited from these comments, and I am happy to accept responsibility for any errors of fact or interpretation which remain. As I have hinted, this book also owes a great deal to my experience of having worked in the History Department of the University of York. Although, as my colleagues will confirm, my attitude to this Department is not totally uncritical, it is a very good place for an early modernist to be. This situation has been strengthened, in recent years, by the experience of supervising research students: discussing their work with Sarah Barbour-Mercer, Nigel Bruen, Pete Darman, Jane Holmes, Mick Riley and John Smail has done a great deal more to broaden my view of early modern England than they realize.

J. A. Sharpe
Park Grove, York
November 1986

Preface to the second edition

Writing a second edition of this book has allowed me to give more space to some issues, such as gender and cultural history, whose importance was only dimly recognized when the initial edition of this book was being put together, to incorporate the findings of a number of recent works in the text, to adapt some areas in the light of the comments of reviewers, and to update the bibliography. I hope that these alterations and additions, within an unchanged overall structure, will continue to make the second edition of this book as useful to students and their teachers as the first apparently has been.

A number of further debts have been incurred while the necessary thinking through problems for this second edition have been taking place. Both undergraduate and graduate students have continued to force me to reassess and refine my views, while, among friends and colleagues, I should like to thank Mark Jenner for frequent discussions about early modern England, and also for the frequent loan of his books, and Roger Dickinson and Penny Wilson for their help with getting the text of the first edition scanned on to disc.

J.A. Sharpe
Park Grove, York
February 1997

PROLOGUE:
TOWARDS THE DAYS OF SHAKING

Politics and society, 1550–1653

John Okey died at Bolton in Lancashire on 29 April 1684. Born in London in 1608, he moved north when he was 21, and, as his friends and relatives recorded in the inscription they composed for his funeral memorial, married a local girl who bore him 10 children. Less conventionally, they also added a brief description of the world in which he lived his adult life:

> In his time there were many great changes, and terrible alterations, 18 yeares civil warres in England, besides many dreadful sea-fights, the crown or command of England changed 8 times, episcopacy laid aside 14 years, London burnt by papists, and more stately built again, Germany wasted 300 miles, 200,000 protestants murdered by papists in Ireland, this town thrice stormed, he went through many troubles and divers conditions.

In such an uncertain world Okey, like many of his contemporaries, 'found rest, joy and happiness only in holiness, the faith, fear and love of God in Jesus Christ'. For most people life in the early modern period was insecure enough. Relative helplessness in the face of disease, of the vicissitudes of economic uncertainty, of the disasters attendant upon such uncontrollable phenomena as a bad harvest or a house-fire, all ensured that even the modest degree of comfort and stability which might be achieved in the normal run of things was inherently precarious. To those living in mid-seventeenth-century England the hazards of life seemed unusually pressing. As Okey's funeral inscription pointed out, civil warfare wracked the nation and might come to any small town in the form of savage plundering by hostile troops. This civil warfare was compounded by the threat of popery, that alien and threatening ideology whose agents, so the inhabitants of Bolton deluded themselves, were likely to be responsible for such national disasters as the Great Fire of London. Internationally, England's troubles were dwarfed by the endemic warfare

which ravaged central Europe from 1618 and which, as even those
dwelling in this small provincial town were aware, left much of Germany
in ruins: 'great changes and terrible alterations' indeed.

Others besides John Okey's friends in Bolton thought of the mid-seventeenth century as an especially fraught era, and a wide range of evidence
attests that contemporaries were convinced that they lived in unusually
difficult times. The philosopher Thomas Hobbes, contemplating the Civil
Wars, declared that 'if in time, as in place, there were degrees of high and
low, I verily believe that the highest of time would be that which passed
between the years of 1640 and 1660'. Ralph Josselin, an Essex clergyman
whose 250,000 word diary is especially full for the 20 years singled out
by Hobbes, was equally aware of the instability of the times. As well as
recording his reactions to the Civil Wars, the political upheavals which
followed them, and the prospects of Christ's Second Coming, Josselin cast
a worried eye abroad. Thus on 25 January 1652 his diary entry pondered
the Fronde in France, the Catalan Revolt, Polish fears of warfare against
the Cossacks, the uneasy peace between Denmark and Sweden and in
Germany, the decline of the military efforts of the Ottoman Empire against
Venice, floods in Spain and Italy, and an earthquake in the Scilly Islands.
It was not just England, seemingly, but most of the civilized world which
was experiencing warfare, political change and general insecurity. Another
clergyman, Jeremiah Whittaker, was emphatic on this point when he
preached before parliament in January 1643: 'These are the days of
shaking ... and this shaking is universal, the Palatinate, Bohemia,
Germanie, Catalonia, Portugall, Ireland, England. There are shaking
sinnes, judgements, sorrowes, feares all Christendom over.'

Three centuries later, a number of historians became convinced that the
turmoils of the mid-seventeenth century, if not quite universal, were at
least very far-reaching. In 1954 Eric Hobsbawm published two scholarly
articles which introduced a new concept to historical discourse: the
General Crisis of the Seventeenth Century. As a Marxist, Hobsbawm
explained this phenomenon by economic change rather than the will of
the Almighty, and argued that the General Crisis was a symptom of a
decisive phase in the transition from feudalism to capitalism. A wider
debate was opened when Hugh Trevor-Roper responded by claiming that
if a General Crisis had existed, its essence lay not in economics, but in
the relationship between state and society. The state apparatus, especially
under the impetus of warfare, outgrew the capacity of economy or society
to sustain it, and in consequence most western European powers experienced political crisis. The subsequent efforts of historians have made the
General Crisis a lot more general, both geographically and conceptually.
Political instability and revolts have been traced as far afield as China and
Japan, while in Europe fundamental changes have been discerned in such
areas as the family, political theory, scientific thought, art, crime and
punishment, even the weather. Although many historians might shy away

from using the term 'General Crisis', it is nevertheless clear that a number of important, and perhaps decisive, changes took place over the second third of the seventeenth century.

For historians of England, the most striking, and certainly the most studied, of the problems besetting mid-seventeenth-century Europe is that series of military and political events known variously as the English Civil War, the English Revolution, the Great Rebellion or the Puritan Revolution. The first major historian of these events, the Earl of Clarendon, was insistent that their origins could be traced back no further than the accession of Charles 1 in 1625: 'I am not so sharp-sighted,' he wrote, 'as those who have discerned this rebellion contriving from (if not before) the death of Queen Elizabeth.' More recent historians have been less cautious. To Marxists, the crisis in England which began in 1640 was the first great bourgeois revolution, the replacement of a feudal past by a capitalist future, the replacement of an old feudal ruling class by a new bourgeois one. Thus to Hobsbawm 'the English Revolution, with all its far-reaching results, is therefore in a real sense the most decisive product of the seventeenth century.'[1] To Christopher Hill, writing on the tercentenary of its outbreak, the result of the struggle was that 'an old order that was essentially feudal was destroyed by violence, and a new and capitalist order created in its place.'[2] The interpretation of the Civil War offered by historians working within the Whig–Liberal tradition is in many ways similar. Their rising middle class is the same animal as the Marxist's rising bourgeoisie. Even the slow progress towards parliamentary sovereignty, a basic theme of Whig history, locates the Civil War firmly in a context of long-term social change and, in many respects, is connected to the notion of a rising middle class. This emphasis on long-term causes has proved attractive to historians who are neither Whig nor Marxist: thus Lawrence Stone has produced books variously tracing the origins of the war back to the calling of the Reformation Parliament in 1529, a process of social change beginning in 1540, and a crisis of the aristocracy commencing in 1558.

However much it may complicate things, the writer of a book on early modern social history has to confront the challenge of interpreting this crowded and much debated series of events which lie across the middle of the seventeenth century. If nothing else, the willingness of so many historians to attribute these events to fundamental changes in economy and society makes this desirable. Moreover, as we have argued in the preface to the first edition of this book, social history is not history with the politics left out: the social and political spheres are not separate, but frequently interact. We will therefore address three problems in this introductory chapter. First comes·that of providing a narrative framework of English political history from the middle of the sixteenth century to the appointment of Oliver Cromwell as Lord Protector in 1653. Second, we will examine the main institutions of government, and show how they connected with society. And third, we will examine the alleged links between the coming of the Civil War and socioeconomic change. Most surveys of the political history of this period begin with a chapter describing the social context. The main aim here is to return the compliment, and open a work on social history with a sketch of political developments over the first half of the period it covers. Let us, accordingly, turn to our starting point, the middle of the sixteenth century.

From Tudor crisis to Gloriana

Seeing ourselves as others see us is sometimes a chastening experience. A number of foreign visitors left their impressions of England around 1550, many of them Venetian diplomats or Spanish attendants of Philip II. Once these inhabitants of more cultured and more important states had recovered from a sense of being on the edge of the familiar world ('I had always heard that the marvels described in books of chivalry fell far short of what was to be seen here') their reports generally agreed on a number of points. First, the English were seen as being different. The Venetian Ambassador commented in 1555 upon 'what strange fancies prevail amongst this people, and how much their ideas differ from those of other nations'. One of their salient features was their xenophobia. The English were 'most hostile by their nature to foreigners', or were 'naturally the enemies of all aliens, but they hate the French and Spaniards most of all'. Another peculiarity was the disturbing freedom which the English allowed their women, who had 'a handsome presence, fine complexion, and a great liberty of action', and dressed in 'a manner which I am unable to approve of, and I do not think any Spaniard would differ from me'. The English were a courageous race, 'the more so in the difficulty of the undertaking', although given to ease and gluttony ('there is plenty of beer here, and they drink more than would fill the Vallodolid River'). They were also dangerous, unpredictable and untrustworthy, 'said to be naturally very obstinate ... but they are also fickle and most inconsiderate in their actions', 'not to be trusted by anyone'. 'The man who said that England was a paradise inhabited by devils,' wrote a correspondent to the Duke of Mantua in 1557, 'did not deceive himself.' 'The country, it is true, is a good one,' wrote a Spanish gentleman to a friend at about the same time, 'but we are surrounded by the worst people that ever lived, at any rate in a Christian land.'

Such a people obviously presented a number of difficulties for their rulers. A Venetian diplomat writing at the beginning of Elizabeth I's reign was insistent about this. Not only did the English hate foreigners, he reported, but they were 'not very friendly among themselves'. He felt that 'a greater number of insurrections have broken out in this country than in all the rest of the world', causing

Many depositions of great men and promotions of the unworthy, many imprisonments, exiles and deaths. It is also a fact, incredible though true, namely, that during the last twenty years three Princes of the Blood, four Dukes, forty Earls, and more than three thousand other persons have died by violent death.

The English, 'inconstant, rash, vainglorious, light and deceiving', as a Fleming characterized them later in the reign, were evidently a violent and unpredictable lot.

Reports from foreign observers should not always be accepted at face value, yet events in the middle of the sixteenth century supported their contentions that the English were politically unstable. Historians are cautious about applying such labels as 'The Mid-Tudor Crisis' to this period, yet it remains clear that the two decades after 1540, like those after 1640, were difficult and at times dangerous ones. In 1540 Thomas Cromwell, Henry VIII's able but low-born minister, was ousted by an aristocratic coup. From that point Henry exercised rule without dependence on any single minister, a rule which became increasingly capricious as the monarch waxed older and sicker. On his death in 1547 he was followed by his son, the young Edward VI, and those problems of noble faction which normally accompanied a royal minority emerged rapidly. Protectorship of the realm passed from Edward Seymour, Duke of Somerset, to John Dudley, Duke of Northumberland. On the death of the monarch in 1553 Northumberland attempted to engineer a coup by marrying his son to Lady Jane Grey, grand-daughter of Henry VIII's sister, to whom he had persuaded Edward to bequeath the crown. Henry's elder daughter, Mary, declared herself Queen and rallied enough support to defeat Northumberland, partly thanks to inherent respect for her stronger claim to the throne, partly because Northumberland was too transparently a self-seeking crook. England narrowly escaped that dynastic instability which was to precipitate civil warfare in France within a decade, but there remained troubles enough. England's imperfect Reformation left much uncertainty in matters of religion. The economy, burdened with financing warfare against Scotland, and with such dubious governmental expedients as the debasement of the coinage, was in a poor condition. A society familiar with a number of fatal diseases now confronted a new one, the 'sweating sickness' or 'English sweat' (probably a very violent form of influenza) which was to reach epidemic proportions by the late 1550s. Most frightening of all for the government, peasant revolt had broken out on a large scale in 1549, with two whole regions, East Anglia and the south-west, in danger of passing under rebel control, and with abortive or less serious revolts occurring from Yorkshire in the north down to Sussex.

The reign of Mary Tudor (1553–58) was obviously too short to solve any outstanding problems. Recent research has revised the old caricature of Mary's reign as an era of sterility, and there is little doubt that had she lived she would have achieved a stable regime which might well have been capable of implementing her most cherished policy, the reimposition of Roman Catholicism. Her early death, however, left this process barely begun, while memories of 300 Protestant martyrs, allied to the unpopularity of her marriage to Philip II, King of Spain, meant that the end product of her reign was, ironically, to discredit the two things most dear to her: the Roman faith and the Anglo–Habsburg alliance. Yet her younger sister Elizabeth, 25 when she came to the throne in November 1558, faced a difficult situation. Religious affairs were in chaos, with the barely started thrust towards further reformation of Edward VI followed by Mary's equally incomplete efforts at re-catholicization. In foreign affairs, England had suffered the shock of losing Calais, her last continental possession, to the French, who were creating further problems by their intervention in the civil war then occurring in Scotland. French presence in the British Isles at least made Philip II tread carefully, but it was obvious that he would watch developments in England very attentively. At home, the prospect of noble faction and internecine warfare could not be discounted. Many of those working to construct a viable regime around Elizabeth must have thought the exercise a very uncertain one.

In the event Elizabeth's reign was to be long and, in the opinion of many historians, exceptionally glorious. In 1558 she had three factors working in her favour. First, in an age when such things mattered a great deal, she was the most direct claimant to the throne. Second, there were few viable dynastic rivals to her. Indeed, there were few people around with much Tudor blood in their veins: accordingly, rebels, potential rebels and plotters could find few convincing rival claimants to the throne who might serve as a figurehead for their designs. Fifteenth-century England and France from the 1560s provided contemporary observers and modern historians with examples of the grim consequences of the combination of ambitious princes of the blood with an uncertain central authority. Third, most influential people believed in order, legitimacy and social hierarchy. The pulpit, the stage, royal proclamations, even the increasingly fashionable Neo-Platonic science, all emphasized the importance of these entities. The creation of a viable regime in early modern England depended on at least the acquiescence, and at best the active co-operation, of those peers, country gentry and urban oligarchs upon whom rule in the localities effectively depended. These people, the 'political nation', fell into line behind the new Queen as she assembled her team of loyal magnates, trusted administrators, and Protestant ecclesiastics at Westminster. Members of local élites had experienced rapid changes in central authority in the recent past, and perhaps saw no reason why this monarch should last any longer than her three predecessors. Those of broadly Catholic sympathies were doubtlessly unhappy with what was, with every week that passed, more manifestly a Protestant regime. Nevertheless, the political nation was more worried about the probable consequences of civil warfare and large-scale disorder than it was about any inadequacies of the new monarch.

There were a number of central institutions through which the holders of local power might come into contact with the central government. The least important of these was parliament. The tendency to view political events in the century before the Civil Wars mainly, and often purely, in terms of the developing power of parliament, or of the House of Commons, would have seemed very odd to Elizabethans. Before 1558 parliament had, undoubtedly, become more active. The Reformation Parliament of 1529–36, remarkable for its longevity, was followed by frequent sessions in the later years of Henry VIII and in the reigns of Edward VI and Mary. Money had to be raised for warfare, the frequent religious changes had to be endorsed by legislation, newly arrived and potentially unpopular regimes had to attempt to broaden the basis of their support and demonstrate their legitimacy. The more frequent meetings of parliament, together with the sense that the institution was participating in momentous changes, created an increased sense of identity and self-importance among parliament men. The number of members of the House of Commons rose over the sixteenth century, from 296 to 462, and these members came to be drawn increasingly from the ever more wealthy and ever more educated gentry. Yet the idea that the Commons was a constant arena of conflict between members and monarch is a nonsense. To the Crown, parliament meant money, and in Elizabeth's reign votes of taxation were forthcoming without any real trouble. To members, of both Lords and Commons, parliament meant a number of things. Professor Elton has recently stressed the importance of legislation, and especially of private Acts, and it is probable that a large number of members saw the institution, in part at least, as a place where local, sectional, or even personal interests might be furthered. Membership of the lower House was also thought desirable by the politically ambitious, or by those who simply wished to show that they had arrived politically. Lawyers considered membership a handy means of attracting attention, and hence lucrative office, while the House served more generally as one of a number of dimensions of patronage networks. Broad changes in concepts of what constituted state service, perhaps even the classical education to which the élite was increasingly exposed, encouraged gentry to enter the House. Members did not see themselves as stalwart constitutionalists crusading against royal prerogative: rather, they were a mixture of representatives of their localities or of their patrons, of the leading men of the realm giving loyal advice to their sovereign, and of Cato addressing the Senate.

Far more important was the Privy Council. This had its origins in the medieval royal council, and by 1550 had become a formalized body with a bureaucratic ethos and an established administrative procedure. Its membership depended upon the will of the monarch (although there were always some men that it would be unwise to exclude from membership) and tended to fluctuate in size and composition. Mary, anxious to incorporate all factions into her political system, favoured a large Privy Council, Elizabeth a much smaller one. There were never more than 20 privy councillors during her reign, and in the 1590s membership went down to 13. Whatever its size, the Privy Council was responsible for central decision-making. It met frequently, and despatched a wide range of business. On 10 March 1599, to take a typical day, eight councillors met and attended to the normal variety of matters: the evasion of taxes and other public responsibilities in the Home Counties and the City of Coventry; unsatisfactory and mutinous recruits for the army from Wales and London; the enforcement of regulations about meat-eating in Lent; the fate of English captives in Algiers; troop movements in Ireland; and the issuing of warrants of arrest. The Privy Council was the recipient of an endless flow of correspondence: from county administrators, from mayors and town corporations, from ambassadors and travellers abroad, from senior churchmen, from interested individuals. The information thus gathered was sifted, evaluated and discussed, and executive decisions concerning most aspects of government would be reached and transmitted back to the localities.

The third major institution bringing members of local élites to the centre was the court. The royal court had probably existed as long as there had been monarchs, but in the sixteenth century it became more important and more elaborate. The early Tudor court, modelled as it was on the Burgundian and French examples, was splendid enough, but it was totally eclipsed in Elizabeth's reign. Culturally, the royal court was now firmly established as a major centre for artistic performance and patronage, for the display of fashion, and for a constant flowering of the aristocratic way of life. Politically, it became established as the main arena for displays of political loyalty and as the centre for worldly advancement. The nobility regarded the court as the unique centre of patronage and of political life. It is significant that the prototype etiquette book for the Renaissance gentleman, written early in the sixteenth century by the Italian Baldessare Castiglione, should be entitled *The Book of the Courtier*. Even more significant, in England as elsewhere in Europe, was the willingness with which the Renaissance gentleman came to court. Once again, we find evidence of how far the political nation accepted royal authority, how willing it was to play the game of politics according to rules laid down by the monarch. But courtiers did not form a supine and undifferentiated mass: the court's role as a major political focal point meant that the most usual form which politics took in the period was faction – fighting between the great and famous.

The development of the court was connected with a massive promotion of the cult of monarchy. This trend, already well in motion in the reign of Henry VIII, received a substantial boost under Elizabeth. Sixteenth-century monarchs could normally expect a fair measure of flattery, but the levels of fawning sycophancy which surrounded Elizabeth were remarkable even by contemporary standards. As Christopher Haigh has commented, 'the selling of Elizabeth began as soon as she ascended the throne',[3] and the process expanded steadily thereafter. By the 1590s the official image of Elizabeth was fully developed. It was based upon two themes, that of imperial rule, and that of the Protestant heroine, so that by the end of her reign the Queen was being presented as a subtle mix of septuagenarian springtime goddess and Protestantism's answer to the Virgin Mary. 'Some call her Pandora,' declared a character in a play performed at court in 1599, 'some Cynthia, some Astrea, all by several names to express several loves. Yet all these names make but one celestial body, and all these loves meet to create one soul.' The outburst of posthumous eulogizing which followed Elizabeth's death has been well summarized by Roy Strong:

> The moon has gone into eclipse, the rose has withered on the briar, the maiden Astrea or Justice has fled once more from earth to heaven, Deborah, Hester, Judith, Solomon, David, Asa, the heroines and rulers of the Old Testament are no more, all have vanished with her demise.[4]

Once more, we are confronted by the persistent themes of order, security and hierarchy: the vision of Gloriana combined classical, biblical and Neo-Platonic imagery into a potent celebration of the stability which legitimate monarchy alone could offer.

Yet it is difficult not to conclude that the achievement of the reign was considerably less impressive than its image. Elizabeth has, generally speaking, been well treated by her biographers, and criticism of her reign has to be made in the face of a popular historical tradition which regards her as a successful and glorious monarch. In fact, the major lasting achievements of her reign number two, although each of them was, in its own way, very impressive. The first was the creation of the Church of England. The religious settlement of 1559 was, like most things Elizabeth did, essentially a bodged-up job, more Protestant than Elizabeth would have wished, not Protestant enough for some of her supporters, and initially at best barely tolerated by the bulk of the population, who still tended to write Protestantism off as 'the new religion'. But by the end of the reign the brand of Protestantism created by the Elizabethan Settlement was accepted as the true religion by most English men and women, and was to endure as a major force in English life for centuries to come. The second lasting achievement was the poor law. As the sixteenth century progressed, poverty increased both as an objective problem and as a cause of concern to central and local government. The great parliamentary Acts of 1598 and 1601 formalized two generations of experiment, and constructed a system of poor relief which was to survive, in its essentials, until 1834.

The reign produced little else that was lasting. Like that of most sixteenth-century monarchs, it was essentially an exercise in survival. Governments in this period did not formulate and follow policies in the modern fashion. They struggled from one crisis to the next, to a large extent keeping going through expedients and compromise. Concern for short-term problems always frustrated long-term objectives. The presence on the throne of a monarch like Elizabeth, who was chronically unable to reach decisions, did not help matters.

Nowhere is the contention that Elizabethan policy was largely a series of half-measures and short-term expedients undertaken indecisively within a more or less immutable set of parameters demonstrated more neatly than in foreign policy. Obviously England, on the fringe of Europe and at best a second-rate power, had to adapt to the situation in which it found itself. This was made difficult, however, by the post-Reformation reversal of the traditional guidelines of English foreign policy, hostility to France and friendship with the Burgundian dynasty and its Habsburg successor in The Netherlands. By the 1580s England was at war with Habsburg Spain and sending military assistance to French Huguenots. Yet the detailed study of Elizabethan foreign policy reveals not so much the consistent pursuit of aims through rational statesmanship as a succession of minor crises into which the Queen fell as a consequence of general dilatoriness compounded by her obsessions and her irrational fears and prejudices. Elizabeth's slow and unwilling drift to involvement in the Dutch Revolt illustrates this point. In January 1576, for example, the Queen was faced by the rare and unwelcome prospect of a united Privy Council determined to pursue military intervention on behalf of the Dutch. Elizabeth, hostile to this policy, reacted characteristically by falling into a rage of violent desperation. As Charles Wilson describes it:

> Gripped by one of those periodic fits of anger which were partly inherited from her father and partly perhaps attributable to her age (she was now 43), she locked herself away in her closet in parox-ysms of hysterical rage, emerging only now and then to visit her fury on the court and box the ears of those unfortunate ladies-in-waiting who happened to be nearest at hand.[5]

Most European observers would have agreed that the Revolt of The Netherlands presented immense diplomatic problems, but Elizabeth's reactions were hardly redolent of coherent and constructive statesmanship.

Given the currently popular interpretation of the reign, one of the most surprising features of Elizabeth's rule is that a fair number of her loyal subjects seem to have been more or less constantly afraid and insecure. They constantly reiterated their fears of disorder, and their conviction that the realm was secure against neither internal divisions nor external enemies. The greatest trauma was fear of Roman Catholicism. Foxe's

Book of Martyrs, with its image of the English as God's chosen people, had an important influence in forming English national consciousness, yet in so doing it created a clearly defined enemy. From the early years of Elizabeth until well into the eighteenth century there was a general belief in the existence of a united and monolithic conspiracy of popes, Jesuits, Spanish and French monarchs and domestic papists, a conspiracy which had the extirpation of English Protestantism close to the top of its agenda. Propagandists cast the war against papal antichrist in apocalyptic terms. This created a sense of purpose and a sense of identity, but also caused great tension. This tension linked with fears of domestic disorder: the English were a sinful nation, and national sinfulness might well bring down divine judgements. The medal commemorating the defeat of the Armada in 1588 attributed the salvation of the English to divine intervention: the enemy had been dispersed by tempests sent by the Lord. The fears that this divine intervention might not one day be forthcoming, even for the chosen nation, and that the forces of international Catholicism were always prepared to exploit such a situation, were very powerful.

The reality of Elizabeth's reign was therefore very different from its traditional portrayal as a self-confident and glorious period. The gulf between actuality and image was symbolized by an episode late in the reign, when an aged Queen presided over a political system which was showing signs of strain. In September 1599 Robert Devereux, Earl of Essex and royal favourite, was convinced that his position at court was crumbling while he commanded a military expedition in Ireland. He returned to England unannounced, bent on gaining access to the Queen, a move essential to restoring his fortunes. He burst into her bedroom at 10 o'clock in the morning, where he found Elizabeth dressing with the assistance of her ladies. What he saw before him was not the ageless and unfading beauty of official portraiture, the cosmic figure standing astride the world, banishing storms of uncertainty with the sunlight of royal authority. Instead, he was confronted by a scared old woman, toothless, a few wisps of grey hair hanging from her nearly bald head, her face wrinkled without its youthful cosmetic mask, her body clad in a dressing-gown rather than garments of imperial magnificence. The whole divergence between the Gloriana cult and the ramshackle reality of the Tudor state was symbolized in that moment. Students of Elizabeth's reign have succumbed all too easily to the Queen's propaganda and its subsequent extension into nationalist myth.

From Stuart accession to Civil War

Both the nation and the political system to which James I acceded in 1603 had recently experienced severe strains. The most serious of these arose from the costs of warfare. By the 1590s England was involved in fighting on the high seas, in the Low Countries, in France and, most costly of all, in Ireland. Together, these campaigns cost £3,500,000 in the last 12 years of Elizabeth's reign. Ordinary taxation was not able to meet this expense, and Elizabeth had resorted to such expedients as forced loans, benevolences, and the extension of ship money to the inland counties. The late 1590s also experienced a serious run of bad harvests which caused severe problems at the base of society: vagrancy, poverty, popular unrest and rising crime rates. Pressure was building up among the political élite. Elizabeth was parsimonious with honours, and it was felt that royal largesse was not being spread generously enough. In parliament, called frequently to grant taxes, members grumbled about the increasingly expensive and increasingly unsuccessful war. Above all, there was a continual juggling for position among courtiers and politicians, a natural consequence of the awareness that the Queen was old and that her death could not be postponed indefinitely. The tension between the Cecil faction and Essex, which boiled over into Essex's rebellion of 1601, was merely the most dramatic symptom of a growing instability. James I might be one of the most criticized monarchs in English history, but early in his reign at least many of his problems arose from having to clear up the mess which his predecessor had left him.

It is at least evident that James, whatever his later historical reputation, was widely welcomed by his new subjects in 1603. He had the necessary attributes of a monarch: he was adult, sane, Protestant, and he had an heir. He had also, by most accounts, been a successful King of Scotland. It is curious that James, whose kingship in England has been so much criticized by historians, seems to have done well in the less sophisticated but more robust arena of Scottish politics. Either he underwent a basic change when he came south (and it has been suggested that he regarded England as an easier realm to govern than Scotland) or English historians have been asking the wrong questions. The second of these possibilities seems the more likely. The reign of James I in England has been forced into the simple evolutionary model to which we have referred, rather than studied in its own terms. The fact that a civil war broke out under James's successor, Charles I, does not mean that there was necessarily anything wrong with the way James ruled: the sins of the son should not be visited upon the father.

Certainly religion, at least after the first years of the reign, was not a problem. James was a Calvinist intellectual of European standing, author of a tract against witchcraft, called in by the Dutch to help adjudicate their theological controversies of the 1610s. His credibility in Protestant circles was assured after 1605, when the papists attempted to add him to the list of assassinated rulers of the period. The Hampton Court Conference of 1604 may have left some of those seeking further reformation disappointed, the appointment of Richard Bancroft as Archbishop of Canterbury was unwelcome to Puritans, and a few sectaries were to leave the realm for Holland or New England. Yet mainstream Protestants, including moderate Puritans, could find little to complain about with James's religious policies, especially after the mildly Puritan George Abbot followed Bancroft in 1610. James was perhaps less adept at controlling faction. His early years were marred, at least for English courtiers, by his excessive favouring of Scots, while his penchant for personable young men (whether or not he was an active homosexual is still a matter of debate) complicated the normal functioning of patronage. Yet all monarchs of the period, not least Elizabeth, ruled through faction: it was one of the fundamental ways in which politics functioned, and James did not allow it to get out of hand until his dotage. Even James's lackadaisical attitude towards the minutiae of government can be overstated. He may not have been the most active monarch in Europe, but with Louis XIII on the French throne and Philip IV on the Spanish he was far from the laziest. As the well-kept local government records of the reign attest, his rule was essentially one in which things were kept ticking over as normal: this was roughly what most people in the political nation wanted.

Even the King's dealings with parliament must be reconsidered in the light of recent research. The theme of conflict is now played down, and it is clear that there was no 'high road to civil war' running through the parliamentary politics of the reign. Moreover, as Conrad Russell has pointed out, in early seventeenth-century England 'the majority of political events took place outside parliament'.[6] Major political and administrative decisions were taken at court or in the Privy Council, political attitudes were normally formed as a result of developments in the counties. Parliaments, to quote Professor Russell again, were essentially '*ad hoc* gatherings of men reacting to events taking place elsewhere'.[7] Recent research has also queried such notions as the 'winning of the initiative' by the House of Commons or the 'rise of a revolutionary party' there in James's reign. There were no parties in the modern sense, and it is difficult to trace any consistent 'opposition'. All members shared the same basic ideas about how the political system should operate, and although criticism might arise over specific issues, there was nothing very consistent or very threatening in either the attitudes expressed or the men expressing them. There were problems in parliament, but as the Addled Parliament of 1614, the impeachment of Francis Bacon in 1621, and the impeachment of Lionel Cranfield, Earl of Middlesex in 1624 demonstrate, these problems were at their most acute when aristocratic faction-fighting spilled over into the two Houses. The idea that James's relations with parliament involved an ever-deepening constitutional struggle is a myth, as is the idea that parliament was growing more important. England was governed perfectly well without any effective parliamentary presence between 1610 and 1621. This seems to have caused few difficulties and little adverse comment.

Things changed when James died in 1625, and Charles I came to the throne. In James's last years the Duke of Buckingham had achieved the difficult transition from being the favourite of the monarch to being that of the heir apparent. The first three years of Charles's reign were a joint rule between king and duke, but Buckingham's ascendancy undoubtedly had an adverse effect on politics, not least because of his almost exclusive control over patronage, favours and royal appointments. Two other developments were causing trouble. First, parliamentarians were becoming worried by the early manifestations of Charles's taste for a more relaxed form of Protestantism which was to become labelled as Arminianism. The usefulness of this term, and the adherence of individuals (Charles among them) to Arminianism, has recently caused some debate among historians, yet it remains clear that from the mid-1620s many English men and women regarded centrally directed innovations in religious matters a threat to Protestantism as they understood it. Second, England again became involved in warfare. The Thirty Years War began in 1618, and English opinion demanded armed intervention in support of the Protestant Cause in general, and James I's son-in-law, Frederick V of the Palatinate, in particular. James resisted precipitate action, but after his death Charles and Buckingham brought England into the war. Unfortunately, the war effort combined the maximum of disruption at home with the minimum of success abroad. People grumbled at high taxation, at forced loans, at the problems caused by raising and paying troops, at the spectre of the subversion of legal rights by martial law, at the inconvenience of billeting troops at free quarter, at such evidence of the military presence as the 70 bastards which the soldiery left behind when it left the Isle of Wight. Increasingly blame focused on Buckingham, leader of disastrous expeditions to Cadiz and the Isle of Rhe. His assassination at the hands of a disgruntled officer in 1628 removed a major political problem, but it did not defuse the growing tensions between Charles and the political nation. Real trouble broke out in parliament in late 1628 and early 1629. Tempers grew heated, and the celebrated scene which preceded parliament's dissolution, with the speaker of the House of Commons held down in his chair by the more hot-headed members, is redolent of political passion. Yet even at this stage it is difficult to sustain the argument that a total breakdown in relations between Charles and important sections of his subjects was inevitable: tempers can cool, and rash actions can be regretted in later contemplation.

From 1629 until 1640 Charles ruled England without parliament. The Personal Rule of Charles has now been analysed in a major work by Kevin Sharpe, and only some aspects of that period will be discussed here. Yet it remains evident that, once the dust raised at Westminster had settled, it began well. Charles returned to what was generally regarded as the normal form of government: rule through a Privy Council unobstructed by a dominant faction or overmighty favourite. A severe social crisis of 1629–31, engendered by industrial depression and bad harvests, elicited active co-operation from local élites, and the issue of the Book of Orders, a codification of poor law and other local administrative practices, formed the basis for a tighter control of local government throughout the 1630s. A self-confident tone was set at court. Masques celebrated royal authority, while royal and aristocratic patronage of the arts not only glorified monarchy but also made Charles's court one of the most cultured in Europe. There were, however, two nagging problems. The first was finance. Ruling without parliamentary subsidies led Charles to supplement indirect taxation with a number of financial expedients: fining under the forest laws, distraint of knighthood, a vigorous pursuit of royal rights of wardship. These measures were legal enough, but had not been systematically enforced for many generations and were therefore very irritating. Worse problems were caused from 1634 onwards when Charles decided to implement ship money, a tax for maintaining the Royal Navy traditionally paid only by coastal districts, on a national basis. The sums collected were substantial, but there were murmurings over both the heaviness of the tax and its legality. More seriously, Charles's alleged taste for Arminianism was creating a second major focus of discontent. Many feared that Protestantism as established in 1559, now part of the national identity, was being subverted from above. Dismay spread as the Arminian William Laud was made Archbishop of Canterbury, as predestinarian teaching was banned at the universities, as altars in parish churches were railed-in and as some clergymen introduced greater ceremonial into church services. All this smacked of popery, worry in this respect being heightened by the knowledge that the Queen, Henrietta Maria, was herself a Catholic and was attracting a papist coterie around her at court.

Many grumbled about these unwelcome innovations in taxation and religion, but there was little that they could actually do. After the decision in Hampden's case in 1637 ship money was legal. Disquiet at 'Arminian' innovations was widespread, but it lacked focus. The political nation may have found much that was distasteful in the Personal Rule, yet there is scant evidence that anybody was contemplating rebellion. Little could be done, apart from carrying on and hoping for better days. But Charles made a disastrous mistake. His rule in Scotland had also provoked discontent, but this, as in England, lacked focus. In 1637 his attempt to introduce the English prayer book into his northern kingdom provoked first a riot in Edinburgh, then a national rebellion. The book was unwelcome enough to the Calvinist Scots, but the manner of its imposition, by proclamation and with no serious consultation of representative bodies, made things worse. Charles negotiated, but it was soon obvious that he would have to raise troops. This in turn involved raising money. Various expedients were tried: loans were granted by the City of London, ship money was transferred to military purposes, courtiers and aristocrats raised troops at their own expense. This was not enough and, ultimately, in April 1640 Charles was forced to summon parliament. Sir Thomas Wentworth, whose regime in Ireland had been so successful, was raised to the earldom of Strafford and recalled to England to manage the English parliament. 'Never,' he commented, 'came man to so mightily lost a business.'

The parliament which met in April 1640, known to posterity as the Short Parliament, was a failure. Charles spent the summer trying to repair a deteriorating political situation without success, and was forced to call another parliament. This, the Long Parliament, met on 3 November 1640, Lords and Commons alike anxious to reverse those innovations in secular government and religion which they detested so much. Yet at this stage nobody within the political nation, either inside or outside parliament, wanted or even foresaw civil war. The story of how this conflict came a little less than two years after the Long Parliament sat is a complex one, a narrative of individual mistakes, of shifting groupings, of clashes of personality, of fears and suspicions. The basic problem can, however, be stated simply: how was it that Charles was virtually isolated in 1640, yet was supported by roughly half of those willing to involve themselves actively in warfare in the autumn of 1642?

For isolated, apart from a clique of courtiers, Charles was. When the Long Parliament sat perhaps 500 members were alienated from royal policy, leaving Charles with about 60 supporters in the Commons. The King's ministerial adherents were few in number, and lacked unity. Strafford had quarrelled with several magnates, and a number of prominent aristocrats, notably the Earls of Arundel and Newcastle, were his avowed enemies. The Queen had her own faction, composed for the most part of empty-headed courtiers, while at odd points matters were further complicated by the ill-considered actions of officers in the army facing the Scots. Parliament, on the other hand, was in the winter of 1640–41 united in the pursuit of what appeared to be very straightforward objectives: the overturning of innovations in church and state; the removal of the evil councillors who had misled the King into promoting these divisive policies; and the replacement of these evil councillors with men that could be trusted.

These objectives were conservative, could be achieved within the traditional frameworks of political theory and political practice, and were obtainable without civil war or social upheaval. The leaders of the opponents of royal policy, disgruntled peers and their allies in the Commons, made very unlikely social revolutionaries. At their head was the Earl of Bedford, boss of a large political connection in the West Country, while their other influential members included the Earls of Warwick, Essex and Manchester, and the Lords Brooke and Saye and Sele. In the winter of 1640–41 these peers, together with their associates in the Commons (it is worth noting that two leading oppositionists in the lower House, John Pym and Oliver St John, both sat for Bedford pocket boroughs) attacked the policies, institutions and chief contrivers of the Personal Rule, trying meanwhile to negotiate with the monarch a settlement which would prevent its recurrence. Men whom parliament could trust were placed around Charles in the Privy Council, and the trial of the man identified as the King's most wicked evil councillor, Strafford, proceeded apace. A Bill of Attainder, a simple legislative declaration that he was a traitor, was passed against Strafford (albeit only after some frantic manoeuvrings in the House of Lords) and on 12 May he went to the block. Bedford, the most likely architect of a lasting settlement, had died of natural causes three days earlier. John Pym, the member for Devizes, had clearly enjoyed considerable influence in the Commons since November: he now emerged as the leader of the parliamentarians.

By the summer of 1641 Strafford was dead, Laud was in the Tower of London, prerogative courts had been abolished, and extra-parliamentary taxation had gone. That unity of purpose which had existed in the early days of the Long Parliament began to dissolve once these objectives had been attained, and the choices before Lords and Commons became more complicated. Pym was convinced of the need to hold parliament together, partly because he thought there was still much to be done, partly because he realized the need for guarantees that what had been achieved would not be reversed when Charles's fortunes revived. But many members felt that enough had been done. Some, unused to the idea of lengthy sittings of parliament, simply wanted to go home. Others, previously convinced that the constitutional balance had swung too far in favour of the central administration in 1640, were now equally convinced that it was swinging too far against the King. Religion was proving an intractable problem. Arminianism had discredited episcopacy, but there was little consensus as to what to replace it with. Worst of all, members of both Houses were becoming increasingly aware that the lower orders, as many of their betters had feared, were getting restless as political uncertainty continued. Lower-class Londoners, orchestrated by Puritan preachers in and around the capital, and in contact with some of the Commons, supported reform with petitions and demonstration. Reports came in from outside London of enclosure riots, urban disturbances and attacks on royal deer-parks. Fear of the many-headed monster was an additional factor driving moderate gentry towards an accommodation with the traditional fount of social stability: the monarch.

The reassembly of the Long Parliament after the summer recess in the autumn of 1641 found Pym and his associates confronted by a decline in their support among moderate opinion. Events, however, took on a dramatic new turn. In that autumn, first reports reached England of a rebellion by the Irish. Soon Protestant refugees arrived, full of tales of atrocity and murder which confirmed the worst anxieties of God-fearing English men and women, brought up as they were convinced of the reality of the Catholic conspiracy. In a heightened atmosphere, Pym introduced the Grand Remonstrance into the Commons. This was a full and lengthy indictment of Charles's policy since his accession, and in particular alleged that he had attempted to rule with the aid of the 'popish and malignant party'. The Remonstrance passed the Commons with a majority of only 11 votes, proof of how far the House now was from its unity of a year previously. As the situation worsened, Charles decided to strike by arresting five members of the Commons, Pym, Hampden, Haselrigg, Holles and Strode, and one peer, Mandeville. In a massive miscalculation, Charles entered the Commons accompanied by soldiers on 3 January 1642, only to find that the members he had come to arrest had been forewarned and had fled. Those wishing that moderate support would swing back to Charles had their hopes dashed as a new wave of determination swept through parliament. This, together with a mood of militancy among the capital's population, convinced Charles that London was too dangerous: he went first to Hampton Court, and then left for the north in March. Had he not acted precipitately in attempting to arrest the five members, it is probable that opinion would have moved decisively in his favour by that time.

The next half year saw a slow drift towards war. Parliament, anxious to raise an army against the rebel Irish, issued a Militia Ordinance. Charles countered this with the Commission of Array, his own call to arms, and local government officials found themselves faced with the problem of deciding between two claimants to the right to raise troops. On 1 June 1642 parliament issued the Nineteen Propositions, virtually an assertion of parliamentary sovereignty. Charles's reply to these propositions, issued on 18 June, was a classic statement of the traditional concept of mixed monarchy, obviously aimed at wooing moderate opinion. In August Charles, who had been concentrating support at York, moved south to Nottingham, and on 22 August he formally declared war on parliament by unfurling his banner there. Small groups of activists on either side attempted to gain control of county militia magazines, or to launch pre-emptive strikes against the opposite party in their locality. But this activism took place against a background of general dismay at what was happening. Very few desired war. Gentry diaries and correspondence attest to this, as do the attempts in many areas, notably Yorkshire, Staffordshire, and (perhaps with better chance of success) the Isle of Wight to declare formal neutrality. These efforts proved fruitless: the English were sucked into the vortex of civil warfare.

Hopes now fixed on the possibility of a quick decisive victory for one of the two parties, which would lead to a negotiated settlement with a minimum of bloodshed and disruption. Such hopes proved unfounded. The first major battle, at Edgehill on 23 October 1642, where Charles's forces confronted an army under the Earl of Essex, was a bloody stalemate which left Charles with a slight advantage but also left him unnerved at the prospect of another large-scale battle. The royalists pushed on towards London, and the capture of the capital might still have led to an early end to the conflict. Royalist troops under Charles's nephew, Prince Rupert, penetrated as far as Brentford, where they destroyed two parliamentary regiments. But further advance was blocked when the remnant of Essex's forces and the London-trained bands concentrated at Turnham Green, vastly outnumbering the royalists with 24,000 determined troops. Rupert retreated. The war was not going to be a short one.

By the end of 1642, therefore, England was embroiled in a civil war which nobody had envisaged in 1640 and which the majority of the population, even after Edgehill, did not want. The outbreak of this war, as our account here has implied, had little to do with a rising middle class or a transition from feudalism to capitalism. Maps of the areas under the control of the two sides at this stage of the war show a parliamentarian south and east ranged against a royalist north and west, and it has often been argued that this demonstrates that the economically advanced area of the country stood for parliament. It is difficult to refute this argument entirely, while it is undeniable that a number of port towns, and most northern industrial towns, notably Manchester, were parliamentarian. Yet the situation was more complicated than it might seem. All areas, even counties like Kent in the 'parliamentary' south-east, contained substantial elements opposed to the dominant party. One of the most solidly parliamentarian counties, Essex, owed its solidarity not to its advanced economy, but rather to the Earl of Warwick, later commander of the parliamentarian navy, who maintained control over his geographical powerbase as tightly as had any medieval overmighty subject. The fact that parliament sat at Westminster, while Charles was based variously at York, Nottingham and Oxford, was possibly as influential in the geographical division of the two sides as were any socioeconomic differences. At Edgehill an army officered by major landowners and led by a peer attempted to gain military victory as the means of enforcing a constitutional settlement on a monarch who had combined political ineptitude with a taste for a centralizing and innovatory governmental regime. This does not suggest a struggle on behalf of new social forces. Rather, it has more in keeping with those struggles between kings and barons which are the staple of medieval political history.

From English Civil War to English Revolution

The failure of Charles I to take London, or for parliament to defeat him in a decisive early battle, ensured what most people were anxious to avoid: a long war. For the bulk of the population, and many soldiers, the experience of that war was to be an essentially local one: a matter of sieges, of raid and counter-raid. Against this background the main lines of the great campaigns can be briefly sketched. In 1643 parliament suffered a number of military setbacks and at the nadir of its fortunes made a treaty with the Scots, gaining their military assistance in return for a promise that the English church would be remodelled on presbyterian lines. This policy paid off in July 1644 when an Anglo–Scottish army defeated a major royalist force at Marston Moor, ensuring the capture of York and the virtual control of the north. Jubilation over Marston Moor, however, was soon offset by Essex's disastrous West Country campaign, which ended with the surrender of his entire infantry force at Lostwithiel. This defeat crystallized growing dissatisfaction with Essex's generalship, and that of other noble commanders, among them the Earl of Manchester, general of parliament's Eastern Association army. Groupings in parliament desiring a more active prosecution of the war came to the fore, and formed the New Model Army, largely from Eastern Association units and what was left of Essex's troops. This was commanded by Sir Thomas Fairfax, the cavalry commander being a man who had distinguished himself at Marston Moor, Oliver Cromwell. The New Model, although neither as efficient nor as ideologically motivated as has been claimed, represented a marked improvement on parliament's earlier 'marching armies', and in June 1645 inflicted a decisive defeat on one of the main royalist armies at Naseby. This royalist defeat was followed a month later by another at Langport, and as the New Model and other parliamentary forces kept up the pressure the royalist war effort began to fail. By early 1646 the parliamentarian soldiers had little to do other than mop-up royalist garrisons.

The military history of the war, outlined all too briefly here, has been the subject of much historical writing. The war's impact on English society has yet to be fully investigated. Like so many wars, it was in most respects at best an inconvenience and at worst a disaster for those it affected. Traditionally minded Englishmen who, in 1640, had opposed what they saw as an increasingly centralizing and increasingly aggressive central government, now found themselves subjected to unimaginably tight governmental control. This was especially true in areas held by parliament, with their county committees and their attempts to associate counties which offended old notions of county localism. The need to win the war overrode traditionalism. Moderates who had been dismayed by the alleged tyranny of Laud and Strafford were even more dismayed by parliamentarian local government machines which they considered to be increasingly ruthless, arbitrary and subject to central control. Martial law, which Charles and Buckingham's policies had made such a target of criticism in the 1620s, was now widely resorted to, while the sequestration of royalists' lands constituted a major affront to the sanctity of property rights. Above all, taxation rose to previously unthinkable levels. Nationally, parliament's Weekly Assessment Ordinance of February 1643 envisaged raising every fortnight a sum equal to an old parliamentary subsidy. More locally, we find the treasurer of the Eastern Association in 1644 handling money equivalent to the whole of the prewar royal revenue, or taxpayers in Kent in 1646 laying out more every month in assessments than they had in any one year of ship money. Assessments, propositions (roughly equivalent to forced loans), excise and the costs of billeting troops at free quarter hit pockets hard.

The human costs of the war are harder to calculate. Perhaps 190,000 people died directly or indirectly as a result of the wars in England and Wales (many more died in Scotland and Ireland). Some 84,000 of these died in battle, an estimate which, if accurate, suggests a somewhat higher death rate against population than that suffered by England and Wales in the First World War. As with financial costs, perhaps, figures mean most in a local context. Twenty men went to the war from the Shropshire village of Myddle, for example, of whom 13 never came back and were presumed to have been killed. Petitions to quarter sessions in the 1640s and 1650s tell harrowing stories of men crippled or rendered chronically sick in parliament's service, and of the hardships of women who had been widowed by that cause, these being followed after 1660 by similar petitions from the royalist side. England may not have suffered the material devastation experienced in some parts of Europe during the Thirty Years War: but military casualties, the disease which came in the wake of any army of the period, the requisition of goods and horses, the destruction of crops, the depredations of troops billeted on, marching through or foraging in an area, the sheer intensification of the uncertainty of life that war brought with it: these added up to a formidable catalogue of human suffering.

Disgust at this suffering, combined with disquiet at high taxation and at the erosion of legality and of traditional methods of government, led to spontaneous action against the soldiers and the administrative machines that supported them. In 1645 groups known as clubmen emerged in the south and west, asserting local values against soldiers and tax-collectors alike. Clubmen associations seem to have been self-generating, usually arising after a series of confrontations between locals and plundering troops: the existence of clubmen in the western counties, for example, had much to do with the presence of notoriously undisciplined and rapacious soldiers in the area. Clubmen were essentially neutralist, although they were willing to join with troops from one of the contending parties when they wished to clear out especially unwelcome troops of the other. Clubmen caused military commanders on both sides some dismay but, in the long run, they stood little chance against disciplined troops, as the defeats inflicted on them by the New Model in the autumn of 1645 demonstrated. Even so, they did represent a widespread and genuine reaction to the war. By 1645 a large element in local society, from the gentry downwards, was heartily sick of high taxation, of county committees, of plundering soldiers, and of the feeling that traditional hierarchies, traditional political, religious and social values were being eroded.

Popular distaste at the impact of warfare was not the only emotion experienced as fighting petered out in 1646. There was also a genuine perplexity among the country's rulers as to what the next move should be. After winning the war, parliamentary leaders had now to negotiate the peace, and this still meant reaching a settlement with Charles I. But

Charles was not an easy man to bargain with, not least because he realized that there was a tremendous feeling in his favour among the war-weary nation. Most people, a handful of religious radicals and an even smaller number of political republicans apart, envisaged a settlement based on monarchy. Determining the exact nature of this settlement remained a complicated business. Something along the lines of the situation obtaining in the summer of 1641 seemed a possibility, and would probably have been broadly acceptable. But sinking the bitternesses engendered by three years of civil strife would not be easy, while religion still presented insoluble problems. Charles hankered after episcopacy, but the Scots, who continued to watch English affairs with interest, were anxious to see that implementation of presbyterianism which had been the price of their assistance in 1643. Among English parliamentarians two loose groupings, discernible from the early months of the war, now achieved greater definition. One, known as the Presbyterians, stood for social conservativism, a national state church (some of them were presbyterian in the religious sense) and an early settlement with the King. The other, the Independents, took a slightly more radical attitude towards social and religious matters, and was a little more anxious to gain real concessions and solid guarantees from Charles before any settlement. Against a background of war-weariness and ingrained pro-royalism, the various English groupings and the Scots settled down to negotiate with the King.

Early in 1647 their deliberations were interrupted by the emergence of a new element: the army. From 1646 it had been evident that the senior army officers, notably Fairfax, Cromwell, and Henry Ireton, regarded the forces under them as a political interest group entitled to have its opinions heard in any political negotiations. By the spring of 1647 their position was complicated by a wave of militancy among the soldiers of the New Model. Initially this concentrated on what were virtually 'trade union' concerns with pay and conditions: pay was seriously in arrears, troops were worried about suffering legal penalties for acts committed under orders during the war, concerned about provision for widows and orphans, and disgruntled at the prospect of being sent to fight in Ireland in reorganized units under unfamiliar officers. Regiments elected 'agitators' (i.e. agents or representatives) who met to co-ordinate rank-and-file demands. The initial discontent was given a broader context by contacts between the troops and a body of civilian radicals, the Levellers. Pay and conditions probably lay at the heart of most soldiers' discontents, but at least some of them were beginning to talk about their rights as freeborn Englishmen, and to argue that the New Model was more representative of the people of England than was parliament. The senior officers found themselves overtaken by their regiments, not least when the troops, led by George Joyce, a junior cavalry officer, kidnapped the King and took him into their custody. They reacted rapidly, re-establishing control in the summer of 1647. Army and civilian Levellers were deflected into constitutional debate in Putney church during the autumn, and pro-Leveller mutinies which broke out in the winter of 1647–48 were suppressed without too much difficulty. The outbreak of the Second Civil War the following spring took the troops' minds off politics.

The Leveller movement has been much studied: more so, perhaps, than its contemporary influence would justify. The Levellers were, essentially, a loose grouping whose main aim was to make the world safe for small property-owners. Despite their insistence on civil liberties and religious liberties, the Levellers limited political enfranchisement to adult male heads of household. Even so, the sentiments voiced at Putney, in army Leveller pamphlets, or in various drafts of the great Leveller constitution, *The Agreement of the People*, do demonstrate that something rather remarkable was happening in mid-seventeenth-century England. People outside the political nation had always had political opinions, however distasteful such a notion might have been to their betters. Now they were formulating these opinions, discussing them, publishing them, even planning to act on them. Not all soldiers were simply willing to go home tamely after fighting the great men's war for them. 'I would fain know,' asked Colonel Thomas Rainsborough during the Putney debates, 'what the soldier hath fought for all this while? He hath fought to enslave himself, to give power to men of riches, men of estates, to make him a perpetual slave.' Rainsborough at least was convinced that this was not good enough, and propounded a much wider view of human rights. 'Really I think,' he commented, 'that the poorest he that is in England hath a life to live, as the greatest he; and therefore truly Sir, I think it's clear, that every man that is to live under a government ought first by his own consent to put himself under that government.' Such attitudes were obviously unwelcome to civilian and military leaders alike, although Levellerism as an organized force was to be short-lived. The last flickerings of army Levellerism were put down early in 1649, and a number of mutinous soldier Levellers were court-martialled and shot. By that time the civilian movement was falling to pieces as lack of any concrete success meant that the initial impetus was lost.

The political situation had, in any case, moved on considerably. Early in 1648 renewed crisis loomed. There was still no settlement, taxation was still heavy, and troops were increasingly unpopular. Anti-parliamentarian and anti-military incidents began to occur late in 1647, and intensified in the early months of 1648.   Charles by now had won the support of the Scots who, ever hopeful of imposing a presbyterian settlement, agreed to invade England on his behalf. Widespread celebrations of the anniversary of the King's accession in March focused royalist feeling, and shortly afterwards full-scale revolts broke out. A number of strongholds in the north were seized for Charles, much of Wales rebelled and, most disturbingly of all, serious royalist revolts broke out in the old parliamentarian strongholds of Essex and Kent. The Second Civil War, essentially a series of unco-ordinated revolts against parliament, parliamentarian soldiers and parliamentary committees, had begun. Its duration was to be short. Parliament held London, and its experienced troops made short work of royalist rebels. Fairfax cleared Kent and, after a bitter siege at Colchester, Essex. Cromwell cleared Pembrokeshire and then moved north, where the royalists were being contained by a promising young commander, John Lambert. Cromwell inflicted a crushing defeat on the English royalists at Preston, and then mopped-up the half-trained Scottish forces in the north. Royalist garrisons at Carlisle and Berwick surrendered, and Cromwell entered Scotland without resistance. By the autumn, the Second Civil War had been won.

Yet the problem of finding a lasting constitutional settlement remained. Most people, including most parliamentarians, still wanted a negotiated settlement along traditional lines. The army leaders, convinced of Charles's wickedness after the further bloodshed of the Second Civil War, were aghast to find that the majority of the Commons were anxious to continue negotiations with the King. Parliament ignored a remonstrance stating the army officers' case, and on 5 December 1648 voted in favour of contin-ued negotiations with Charles. The army, which had already secured the King's person, acted quickly. On 6 December members attempting to enter the Commons found themselves confronted by troops led by Colonel Thomas Pride. The soldiers, aided by Lord Grey of Groby, who helped identify the unreliable MPs, excluded those who had voted in favour of negotiations. The members that remained – in effect the army's civilian supporters, most of them Independents – broke off negotiations with Charles. On 1 January 1649 the Commons declared that it was treason for the monarch to levy war on parliament and kingdom (the Lords had nothing to do with the business) and set out to try the King. After what his enemies at least regarded as due legal process, Charles was found guilty, and executed on 30 January. The institution of monarchy and the House of Lords were abolished in March. England was now a republic. The hopes, fears and aspirations of 1640 were a long way off.

Although power, in the last resort, rested with the army, rule now passed to those MPs who had not been excluded by Pride's Purge. These became known collectively, to contemporaries and later historians alike, as the Rump (i.e. leftover) Parliament. Some interpretations have portrayed the Rump as a bourgeois republican body, and the passing of a Navigation Act in 1651, and the entry into warfare against England's leading commercial rival, the Dutch Republic, have lent weight to the argument that commercial considerations played a major role in its policies. Detailed research, notably that carried out by Professor Blair Worden has uncovered a more complex situation. Certainly the social composition of the Rump was in no way novel: its membership, although a little less representative of the top stratum of county society, still consisted mainly of solid gentry. Its policies, too, were not as innovatory as some have claimed: the Navigation Act, for example, was based on economic assumptions which went back to the fifteenth century. The Rump's biggest problem was that of achieving respectability and the support that came with it, doing which implying the avoidance, as far as possible, of innovation and radicalism. This proved to be the Rump's undoing, for the army, although purged of Levellers, wanted further reform: of the law, of tithes, above all in matters of religion. The troops had been kept busy, fighting the Irish in 1649, the Scots in 1650, and defeating an Anglo–Scottish invasion force led by the young Charles Stuart in 1651. In 1652 they returned as a factor in English politics. The army grandees were increasingly alienated by the Rump's failure over reform. Dissolving the institution seemed the only solution, and on 20 April 1653 the army intervened decisively, with Cromwell entering the Commons with troops at his back and clearing the Rump out. By now the standing army, an entity unknown in England in 1640, was the dominant force in politics.

The dissolution of the Rump was followed by one of the most bizarre experiments in English constitutional history: the setting up of that body known variously as the Nominated Assembly or the Barebone's Parliament. If the Rump represented the last vestiges of traditional parliamentary authority, the Nominated Assembly represented something self-consciously new. Selected in the main by army officers and their civilian associates, many of its members felt that its main task was to accomplish that work of reformation which the Rump had so conspicuously left undone. The sweeping away of the old regime was thought by enthusiasts to have cleared the way for the achievement of something better, even, by some religious radicals, of the first steps towards rule by the saints. In the event it did little, mainly because even this body contained a sizeable group of gentry moderates. The members of Barebone's Parliament were caricatured as low-born tradesmen (Praise-God Barebone, from whom it took its nickname, was a London leather-seller), but four-fifths of them were in fact gentry of one sort or another, and about one-third would not have been out of place in any seventeenth-century parliament. The Assembly divided gradually between moderates and zealots, and after five months or so it was obvious that it was failing. On 12 December 1653, while the religious enthusiasts were at a prayer meeting, the moderate group voted to resign their power. The moderates went to Whitehall and relinquished power to Cromwell who agreed to accept this evident manifestation of the will of God. Once more troops were sent to the Commons, in this case to clear the House of the radical members.

It is probable that John Lambert was responsible for sending these troops in, and it is certain that he played a major role in drafting the constitutional plan that followed – the Instrument of Government. Power still rested essentially in the army, but Lambert's settlement was designed to promote both stability and at least a decent appearance of civilian participation. To many (probably including Cromwell) the Instrument

represented something like a return to the old principles of mixed monarchy. The most important element was the oligarchic Council of State, but
Cromwell, as Lord Protector, obviously enjoyed a quasi-monarchical role
while the House of Commons was reintroduced in an approximation of
its traditional form and for roughly its traditional purposes. Protector and
Council, it was true, had the right to raise taxation to support the army,
the navy and a civilian administration which alone cost £200,000
annually. Yet there was a general hope among the Instrument's supporters that its more familiar elements would encourage a return to stability
and, ultimately, would encourage acceptance among the political nation
and the population as a whole. Moderates might dislike the Instrument
and royalists hate it. But, as even they came to realize, it represented the
end of the days of bloodshed, of levelling notions, even of religious radicalism as a serious political force. As long as Oliver Cromwell lived, England
would enjoy a viable political system.

As we have seen, a conservative revolt by traditionally minded
landowners in 1640 led to the execution of their monarch, to the establishment of a republic, to the setting up of a government designed by
religious radicals, and then to something which, despite its apparent return
to traditional forms, owed its existence to a new force in English politics:
a standing army. The axiom that people make history, but that they
seldom make the history they expect to make, was brutally demonstrated
in the England of the 1640s. Whether or not all this added up to a social
revolution is debatable. Certainly, as Charles I on his way to the scaffold
would have agreed, there was a political revolution, but the accompanying social revolution was only partial. The abolition of the House of Lords
was a major blow to the peerage, and there is every indication that they
exercised little political or social power in the 1650s. The upper stratum
of the gentry, who had predominated in the Elizabethan and early Stuart
House of Commons, was largely eased out of central power. The seats of
the Rump, of Barebone's Parliament, indeed of the parliaments of the
Protectorate, were all filled with gentry, but these gentry were not drawn
so regularly from the upper ranks of their class. The emergence of the
army as a political force accentuated this process. The New Model did
not offer a real career open to the talents, yet the politically active
grandees, John Lambert, Thomas Harrison, Charles Fleetwood and John
Desborough would not, under pre-1640 circumstances, have exercised
decisive power in the state. In November 1648 the Commons were purged
by a colonel who had been a drayman in civilian life, while in 1653 the
head of state was an East-Anglian gentleman who had been obscure
enough before the wars. Even so, it is difficult to accept that these developments were the outcome of long-term social and economic change. The
arrival of such men in the political arena was essentially the product of
political conflict rather than the cause of it. After 1660 they were to disappear from that arena as quickly as they had entered it in the 1640s.

The reality of change, together with reminders of its limitations, is also obvious when local developments are considered. There were immense variations, but the main lines are clear. Every change of regime at the centre was accompanied by changes in local government personnel, with resultant erosion of the control of traditional élites. In the counties the old ruling gentry and peerage families were in large measure excluded. In some, like Essex, which had supported parliament and enjoyed an ample supply of gentry families, the process was not dramatic: many of the new justices and militia officers were drawn from established families, although perhaps from a junior branch, and a number continued in service after 1660. In others, like royalist Westmorland, the end of the war brought a thorough purge of the local administration, and the lack of suitable gentry meant that the new regime had to recruit its officials from outside the traditional circles. In many towns, too, the ruling oligarchies were replaced by what had previously been political outgroups whose members, although indisputably men of property, were drawn from a slightly lower level than the old élites. Everywhere the need for local governors with dedication to the central regime and with the correct religious ideas cut through traditional hierarchies. The end product was not full-blown social revolution, however. The new administrators were still usually drawn from propertied groups and, faced with the realities of local government, they seem to have conducted aspects of their work such as law enforcement and poor relief along traditional and familiar lines. Even so, the experience of change on a local level outraged many gentry. On the Isle of Wight, the royalist Sir John Oglander complained, 'in our unnatural wars ... most of the ancient gentry were either extinct or undone', and their power passed to 'a thing here called a committee, which over-ruled deputy lieutenants and also justices of the peace'. Oglander was dismayed by the social composition of this body, which included a pedlar, an apothecary, a baker and two farmers. More soberly, a declaration from Dorset at the height of the Second Civil War referred to 'the boundless lusts and unlimited power of beggarly and broken committees, consisting generally of the tail of the gentry, men of ruinous fortune and despicable estates', and called for government by 'men of visible estates and of unquestioned repute, well beloved by us'. The Interregnum might only have witnessed a partial and short-lived social revolution, but memories of it were to haunt the political nation for generations.

Further disquiet attended the emergence of the common people on to the political scene, through both the traditional medium of popular disturbance and riot, and in the novel ones of popular politics and low-born preachers. The Levellers were only the largest and most coherent of a number of radical groups which emerged after the wars. On 1 April 1649 a small group of agricultural labourers and poor artisans led by Gerrard Winstanley, a failed cloth-merchant from Wigan, tried to erect the basis for agrarian communism on St George's Hill in Surrey. Other groups of Diggers, as these idealists became known, were set up, but all faded after about a year, defeated by adverse climatic conditions and local hostility. By that time several even less coherent groupings had arisen from the chaos of plebeian theological speculation which the war had unleashed. Ranters, Seekers, Baptists, Fifth-Monarchy Men, all of them were eager to set up the rule of Jesus Christ in England, all of them convinced that this rule would see the shattering of traditional social and political hierarchies. People of property and of less enthusiastic religious tastes shuddered. The political nation was to remember the Interregnum not only as a time when local gentry power was subverted, but also as one when the lower orders threatened to get out of hand. 'O the tyrannical misery that the gentlemen of England did endure,' wrote Oglander with typical hyperbole, 'they could call nothing their own and lived in slavery and submission to the base multitude. O tempora, O mores.'

Many members of traditional élites were convinced that they were living through something very like a social revolution, and memories of the 'days of shaking' were to play an important part in shaping political attitudes well into the eighteenth century. English landowners had rebelled against their monarch before. But they had not experienced the trial and execution of their monarch in the name of the people of England, nor seen members of the lower orders developing something like a prefiguration of mass politics. Whatever the continuities of English history, it was obvious that something important was happening, and that it would be difficult to reassemble all that had come apart back into its original form. Many observers at the time feared that this might be the case. Yet ironically, even as political instability was at its most chaotic, as people spoke of days of shaking, worked to set up Christ's kingdom, executed a king, or tried to run a local administration on behalf of a new regime, a profound easing of pressure was taking place at the most fundamental level of society. The outbreak of civil warfare had coincided with a sharp discontinuity in that population growth which, although invisible to most contemporaries, had been one of the most important phenomena in English society for over a century. This discontinuity, recorded in the prosaic pages of the parish register rather than in the political manifesto, was to produce effects more far-reaching than alterations of regime at Westminster. In its demographic rhythms, as in its politics, England was changing from a dynamic and unstable situation to an inherently stable one: the days of shaking were reaching their end.

Notes

1 E.J. Hobsbawm, 'The general crisis of the seventeenth century', in Trevor Aston (ed.) *Crisis in Europe 1560–1660* (1965), p. 53.
2 Christopher Hill (ed.) *The English Revolution of 1640: Three Essays* (1940), p. 1.

3 Christopher Haigh, 'Introduction', in Christopher Haigh (ed.) *The Reign of Elizabeth I* (1984), pp. 2–3.

4 Roy Strong, *The Cult of Elizabeth: Elizabethan Portraiture and Pageantry* (1977), p. 15.

5 C.H. Wilson, *Queen Elizabeth and the Revolt of the Netherlands* (1970), p. 36

6 Conrad Russell, *Parliaments and English Politics 1621–1629* (Oxford, 1979), p. 1.

7 *Ibid.*

PART

I

FAMILY, COMMUNITY AND NATION

1

Population

The size and structure of the population is a fundamental of any society. Unfortunately, studying preindustrial populations is unusually fraught with difficulties. In England's case, a national census was not introduced until 1801. Odd statesmen in earlier periods might have expressed the desire to know the number of the country's subjects, but few of them did very much to acquire accurate information. Until very recently, therefore, the size of the population of England before 1801 has been either a source of conjecture, or has been simply ignored by historians. Over the last three decades, however, this situation has been ameliorated by the emergence of a new discipline: historical demography. Demography is the quantitative study of human populations, and historical demography is essentially the study of human populations in the past. Historical demographers collect evidence about the growth or decline of populations over time, of fertility, mortality, nuptiality, and the size and structure of families. The discipline is a highly technical one, and involves working through massive amounts of intrinsically tedious material: no branch of historical investigation demonstrates better the premise that research is nine-tenths tedium, and none owes more to the computer. Nevertheless, despite its technicalities and the sophistication of many of the statistical techniques it involves, English historical demography for the early modern period has now reached the level of development which permits the discussion of a working outline of overall demographic trends.

But the importance of historical demography goes far beyond the simple study of populations. It explores a number of related problems concerning married life and sexual behaviour. In the period with which this book deals, the more austere Christian moralists held that the sexual act was only licit if it took place between husband and wife. Intercourse outside marriage was an offence punishable before the courts (notably the ecclesiastical courts) throughout most of the period. Within marriage, according to the moralists, procreation was one of the main aims of sexual relations, and hence any attempts at contraception were sinful. Demographic history helps probe the reality of sexual behaviour which underlay this strict moral line. Moreover, the work of historical demographers, as well as illustrating long-term trends, also illuminates short-term fluctuations in the life experience of people in the past, notably those resulting from the impact of harvest-failure or disease. Life, especially for the poor, could be very precarious in the preindustrial world: the researches of historical demographers help illuminate this premise. There were yet wider implications arising from population movements: they could be reactions to, or even determinants of, long-term economic trends, especially price movements. In general, therefore, understanding patterns of population change and population structure is the most logical first step towards a wider understanding of early modern English society.

Population: the basic patterns

In 1538, as part of his *Injunctions*, Thomas Cromwell ordered that each of England's parish priests should keep a register noting the baptisms, burials and marriages occurring within their respective parishes. That the architect of the Henrician Reformation thought it necessary that such information should be gathered is an interesting example of the growing intrusiveness of the state, and it is instructive that many contemporaries thought that the introduction of parish registration would somehow be connected with increased taxation. In the face of such fears, Cromwell declared that the registers had been introduced 'for the avoiding of sundry strifes, processes and contentions rising upon age, lineal descents, title of inheritance, legitimation of bastardy, and for the knowledge whether any person is our subject or no'. He also referred, less reassuringly, to 'sundry other causes' for the keeping of parish registers, although he cannot have anticipated the uses to which they have recently been put. The registers have long been familiar to amateur historians or to genealogists following the details of an individual family. But a major breakthrough in the use of the registers came in the 1960s when English historians, following the lead of their French colleagues, realized that parish registers could be used to furnish details of collective fluctuations in births, deaths and marriages. Using parish registers for this purpose is, as might be imagined, accompanied by a number of complications. Few parishes enjoy an unbroken run of registers from 1538 until 1801. The usefulness of those that do survive is dependent upon the efficiency of the generations of clergymen charged with keeping them, and on the composition of the congregations to which they ministered. Religious nonconformists, the irreligious, and marginal elements within the parish were all unlikely to have their births, deaths and marriages recorded. Moreover, the registers record ecclesiastical ceremonies rather than actual events. Such information as they provide is often of a very basic nature, and they rarely provide details of such matters of interest as the cause of death or the social status of persons getting married. Even so, they not only constitute a unique source for studying population in the past, but also survive in bulk from an earlier period in England than in most continental states. Whatever the drawbacks of registers as an historical source, it is no accident that historical demographers should refer to the period 1538–1801 as 'the parish register era'.

We are fortunate that in the early 1960s what was then the Social Science Research Council set up the Cambridge Group for the History of Population and Social Structure, thus ensuring that a firm institutional base existed for the study of population history and related matters. The members of the Group, aided by amateur local population historians, set about examining parish registers. The first fruits of their labours have been described in a massive work by E.A. Wrigley and R.S. Schofield, *The Population History of England 1541–1871: A Reconstruction*, published in 1981, whose contents provide much of the basis for what follows here. As the authors stress, their work is in many respects a 'reconstruction'. Their findings are based on only 404 of England's 10,000 or so parishes, and even this small sample becomes smaller the further back in time they pursue their investigations. Their major technique is 'back projection'. This is a vastly complex operation, involving sophisticated statistical and computer techniques whose details, fortunately, need not detain us. Briefly, back projection involves reversing methods used to forecast future population trends from existing ones, and projecting these existing trends (or, to be accurate, those existing in 1871) backwards through time, using the evidence of the sample of 404 parishes as some sort of control. Wrigley and Schofield have evidently staked a great deal on one methodology, but their handling of statistical techniques is reassuring, as is the tendency for their projections to fit fairly closely with nineteenth-century census evidence and with figures for the eighteenth century compiled by John Rickman and published in 1801.

The basic trends are set out in Figure 1.1. This shows a rising population in the late sixteenth and early seventeenth centuries, a fairly static situation between the mid-seventeenth century and the 1730s, and a marked upward trend after that date as the population increase connected with the take-off into the Industrial Revolution began. The first half of this pattern, the steady growth up to about 1650, was probably the continuation of a long-term trend. Interpretations of late medieval demographic history vary, but there is a general consensus that for most of the fifteenth century, the population was either stagnant or declining. It began to rise towards the end of that century, perhaps because certain forms of disease had become less virulent, perhaps because the relatively favourable economic conditions of the period encouraged earlier marriages, and hence more children, among the people at large. By the late sixteenth century

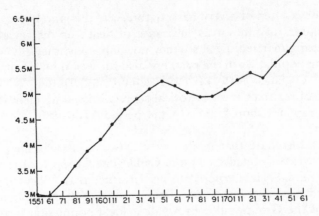

Figure 1.1 Estimated size of the population of England, 1551–1761. *Source*: E.A. Wrigley and R.S. Schofield, *The Population History of England 1541–1871: A Reconstruction* (London, 1981). Table A3.3 pp. 531–4.

the population of England was increasing at a rate which, although modest by modern Third World standards, was substantial enough. In the period 1560–89 the rate of increase was about 1 per cent annually, while life expectancy at birth for those born in the quinquennium centred on 1581 was 41.68 years, a higher expectancy of life than any known before the late nineteenth century. Against the general trend of demographic buoyancy must be set a number of setbacks: the disastrous late 1550s, when famine-induced disease and virulent influenza combined to kill perhaps one-tenth of the population, and the impact of a run of bad harvests in the late 1590s. Overall, however, England, in common with Europe as a whole, experienced steady population growth in the sixteenth and early seventeenth centuries.

This growth slackened around the middle of the seventeenth century, and a slight population decline probably set in subsequently. Population peaked at five and a quarter million in 1651, but then fell below the five million mark, expanding again (a marked setback in the late 1720s notwithstanding) after 1711, and more strongly after 1730. Explaining the post-1650 stagnation is difficult. Disease must have played a part. The bubonic plague, after its final fling of 1665–67, virtually disappeared from England, but its place was taken by virulent strains of other illnesses, notably smallpox and typhus. Average life expectancy at birth was low, falling into the low thirties for much of the period 1656–1701, and dropping to 28.47 years for those born in the quinquennium centred on 1681. Demographic studies of the peerage, which show a similar trend among that privileged group, suggest that disease was largely to blame. Another adverse factor was emigration to the American and West Indian colonies. Estimates vary, but maybe 300,000 people, many of them young males, left England in the second half of the seventeenth century to cross the Atlantic, a tendency which slackened after 1700 when Black slaves were thought to be a more attractive economic prospect than White servants shipped over for a limited period of service. More importantly, an unusually high proportion of the population, perhaps as many as 25 per cent, never married. The late seventeenth century was a difficult period for the farming and smallholding strata, and many people were unable to establish themselves sufficiently well materially to be able to contemplate marriage. In consequence, far fewer children were born. This suggests that the crucial factor in determining population growth in preindustrial England was not fertility or mortality but nuptiality. In short, it was the willingness or the ability of people to marry, and the age at which they did so, which determined the level of population growth.

Proof of this assertion depends upon a deeper knowledge of past demographic behaviour than that which can be gleaned simply from aggregates of baptisms, burials and marriages. This knowledge is provided by family reconstitution, which involves working through parish registers and drawing together all references to the individual families which lived in the settlement being studied. Under ideal circumstances, a family can be 'reconstituted' in the sense that the husband and wife can be identified, the dates of birth (and, all too often, death) of their children noted, and the subsequent marriage of these offspring noted in turn. The major problem with the technique is that ideal circumstances rarely obtained. Parishes usually experienced a high rate of population turnover, and the suspicion lingers that those families which the historical demographer can reconstitute were probably atypical. Once again, however, we must accept that a possibly defective technique furnishes better results than would be available in its absence.

One of the major discoveries attendant on family reconstitution was the finding that, contrary to a very persistent myth, the inhabitants of early modern England tended to marry fairly late in life. On the evidence of an early sample of 12 parishes, the mean age of first marriage for men was 28 years in the period 1600–49, 27.8 in 1650–99, and 26.4 in 1700–59. For women, the mean age of first marriage in the same three half-centuries was 26, 26.5 and 26.2 years respectively. This late age of first marriage seems to have been characteristic of much of preindustrial Europe, and is a major differentiation between the European experience and that of the modern Third World. The most important consequence of this late marriage pattern was that it acted as a means of limiting population increase: women were denied the possibility of bearing children for well over one-third of their fertile period. As we have suggested, the great disincentive to early marriage was an economic one: people were unwilling to join in wedlock before they had an adequate material base. The demographic implications if acquiring this material base became easier, and the age of marriage consequently fell, were massive.

The experience of the Leicestershire village of Shepshed illuminates the point. By the middle of the eighteenth century, the village was populated mainly by framework-knitters. The industry was booming, and hence the poor enjoyed and could expect some economic security, and were able to marry younger. In 1700–49 the mean age of first marriage in Shepshed was 28.5 years for men and 27.4 years for women, but these fell to 24 and 24.1 years respectively in the period 1750–1824. As a consequence, the annual net rate of reproduction rose from 1.12 in the first period to 1.74 in the second: or, to put it in more comprehensible terms, the population was capable of doubling itself every 40 years in the second period, as opposed to every 200 years in the first. Well might Arthur Young comment in 1770 that 'it is employment which creates population: marriages are early and numerous in proportion to the amount of employment'.

Late marriage meant fewer births and a slow rate of population growth. Moreover, a high proportion of those births that did occur were followed by the early death of the child in question. In rough terms, perhaps 15 per cent of children would die within a year of being born, while a further 10 per cent would die before their tenth birthday. Those reaching maturity could, on average, look forward to a relatively prolonged existence: men and women who achieved the age of 30 could expect to live roughly as long again. Children surviving the dangers of their early years lived in families which consisted, on average, of two adults and two or three children. Another myth decisively exploded by historical demography is that of the preindustrial extended family. Over 70 per cent of households consisted purely of parents and their offspring, perhaps with the addition of servants. Not much more than 10 per cent would contain relatives of the married couple, and only half of these would contain family members from three generations. Moreover, only about 4 per cent of households would contain more than one family. The basic assumption was that a married couple would live independent of all relatives other than their own children.

Another fundamental of early modern population structure was that children, despite high infant mortality, constituted a much higher proportion of the population than they do in a modern advanced country. Whereas the populations of modern industrial states are increasingly ageing, those of the early modern world were overwhelmingly young. On Wrigley and Schofield's calculations, around 1695 22.20 per cent of the population of England was aged less than nine years, and a further 17.46 per cent was between 10 and 19. Even in the demographically stagnant circumstances of the late seventeenth century, some 40 per cent of the population was aged less than 20 years. In periods of demographic buoyancy, like the late sixteenth century or the mid-eighteenth, the proportion may well have been more than half. As ever, a simple demographic fact masks a range of wider problems. Most importantly, did this peculiar age structure create a set of attitudes to various age groups different from that obtaining in the twentieth century? Wrigley and Schofield's estimates suggest that only 9 or 10 per cent of the population in the 1690s was aged over 60, which made elderly people a much rarer phenomenon than they are at present. How this would affect attitudes towards the aged, and the feelings of adults towards the mass of children and adolescents who formed such a large proportion of the society in which they lived, remains problematic.

A further peculiarity of early modern population structure arose from adult mortality. As we have seen, individuals reaching their thirtieth year could, on average, expect to survive into their late fifties. Nevertheless, this comforting average hides the fact that a higher proportion of adults than at present could expect to die in their prime, and that the end product of this would be a high number of broken marriages. Death, in effect, offered the same threat to marriage in statistical terms as does divorce in modern Britain. The average duration of a first marriage was between 17 and 20 years. Yet people were generally willing to give the institution a second try. In the seventeenth century about one-quarter of all people marrying had been married at least once before: a statistic which raises a number of intriguing questions about family life. Then, as now, many men and women must have experienced step-parenthood, and many children were forced to adjust to the remarriage of their mother or father. What impact this had on the nature of the family is, once again, problematic; it may be over-pessimistic to ponder on the durability of the wicked step-parent as a figure in folklore.

Despite the uncertainty of many of the conclusions which are to be drawn from the findings of historical demographers, it is clear that a number of the salient characteristics of the growth and structure of the early modern English population do emerge. It should be emphasized that over much of this section we have, perforce, been discussing averages, and that here, as elsewhere, averages can conceal wide variations. Even so, the broad lines are distinct enough. The population rose from three to just over five million between 1550 and 1650, stagnated and then fell slightly over the next 70 years, and then began to rise again, probably exceeding six million by 1760. These changes were mirrored, as might be expected, by changes in the fertility rate. This was high, with a gross annual reproduction rate of 2.8 in the mid-sixteenth century, fell to its nadir (a rate of 1.9) in the 30 years after 1650, and returned to its mid-sixteenth-century level by 1760. Mortality, while experiencing those violent short-term fluctuations which will be discussed in the third section of this chapter, also followed a long-term pattern which fitted the overall pattern of growth. Life-expectancy was at its highest between c.1565 and c.1585, and then fell throughout the seventeenth century to reach a low in its third quarter. After 1730 there was a fairly steady improvement, building up gradually towards the dynamic situation which obtained in the late eighteenth century. But the most important factor affecting long-term demographic trends was not fertility or mortality, but nuptiality: population growth or stagnation was determined above all by the average age of first marriage, and by the proportion of the population marrying, factors which were in turn affected by economic considerations. The historical demographers have, therefore, performed an invaluable service in mapping-out the framework within which debate on a number of other issues might take place. We shall turn to the most relevant of these immediately: the extent to which the births counted or calculated by historical demographers were under the control of those persons whose marriages they also count or calculate, and how far these marriages can themselves be fitted into a wider context of sexual behaviour.

Sexual conduct: an overview

Our discussion of birth rates, family size, the age structure of the population, and of fertility have all rested upon a basic assumption: that the population of the period was innocent of the practice of any sort of contraceptive technique. Early modern England furnishes surprisingly little evidence of contraception of any type. Contraception, it will be remembered, was considered sinful by contemporary moralists, while medical thinking on the subject was not very advanced. The sheath contraceptive was thought of primarily as a prophylactic against venereal disease, and it is in this guise, described as a 'condum', that it appears in the first English medical treatise to note its existence, published in 1717. Sophisticates and prostitutes doubtless knew of other forms of contraception, notably spermicides, pessaries and douches: but it seems likely that the bulk of the population did not. There may have been some folkloric forms of contraception, probably of very uncertain efficiency, but little evidence survives of these, and there is little evidence of recourse to that most obvious of contraceptive techniques, *coitus interruptus*. Historical demographers have occasionally found patterns of fertility in preindustrial England which suggest employment of this practice, but these have been isolated and dubious. Direct mention of *coitus interruptus* in contemporary records is rare. G.R. Quaife, in his study of sexual behaviour in Somerset between 1601 and 1660, cites only one explicit reference. A woman dissatisfied with the frequency and quality of her husband's fulfilment of his marital duties complained that he had 'carnally coupled with her of late years but once a quarter and then what seed should be sown in the right ground he spent about the outward part of her body'. Given the essentially private nature of contraception and other sexual practices (the records similarly contain little mention of oral or heterosexual anal intercourse, for example) it is perhaps dangerous to accept absence of evidence as evidence of absence. Nevertheless, it seems that contraception among the populace at large was little understood and infrequently practised.

Further support of this contention is provided by the frequency of bridal pregnancy, perhaps the most useful quantifiable index of extramarital sexual activity available to us from the parish-register era. A bride who gives birth to her first child within eight and a half months of marriage can usually be assumed to have been pregnant on her wedding day, and detailed investigation of individual parishes suggests that a high proportion of brides were in that condition. Such investigations show wide variations: in Clayworth, Nottinghamshire, 13 per cent of brides married between 1650 and 1750 were pregnant when they married; in Colyton, Devon, roughly half were over the period 1538–1799. Nationally, about one-fifth of brides in the sixteenth and seventeenth centuries, and perhaps one-third in the eighteenth, were pregnant on their wedding day. Obviously, there was little premium among the people at large on premarital chastity, and such reservations as there might have been about premarital intercourse were evidently waning as the eighteenth century progressed. Yet it is likely that these high levels of bridal pregnancy were not the outcome of promiscuity, and even less of some sort of primitive fertility test: rather, they resulted from sexual relations between what would these days be classified as 'engaged couples'. There was a widespread feeling that the promise of marriage, or the more formal marriage contract, constituted the point at which intercourse might begin. Certainly Puritan writers of handbooks on marriage railed against this attitude, and many mothers of illegitimate children insisted to the justices examining their case that sexual relations had only taken place after promise of marriage. The same was probably true of most cases of bridal pregnancy, with the important difference that the man involved was rather better at keeping his promises.

The proportion of illegitimate births was low, although any certainty in this matter is once more undermined by substantial problems of evidence. A number of factors militated against the registration of illegitimate births, the most likely of them being that the unmarried mother would become a runaway and thus slip through the net of registration. Nevertheless, illegitimacy rates have been calculated, and some sort of pattern does emerge, notably from the evidence of a sample of 98 parishes where illegitimate births were, apparently, regularly recorded. These births reached their peak around 1600, when they constituted about 4.5 per cent of all births, and then fell to their apparent nadir (almost certainly the result of under-recording) in the 1650s, when they constituted 0.5 per cent. Illegitimate births formed between 1.5 and 2 per cent of all births until about 1720, when they started to rise, regaining their 1600 level by 1760. These figures need to be treated with extreme caution: even so, it is noteworthy that the rise, fall and subsequent resurgence of illegitimate births followed the same pattern as overall fertility. There was a rise in the sixteenth century, a period of relative stagnation between 1660 and 1720, and a fairly rapid rise thereafter. Illegitimacy, it seems, kept pace with more general changes in fertility.

Rather more concrete evidence can be gained about the unmarried mother. Findings from the two counties so far studied in depth, Somerset and Essex, agree that mothers of illegitimate children were very often maidservants, a fair number of whom had suffered sexual exploitation by their masters or members of his family. Most unmarried mothers, on the evidence of their depositions to justices, were unfortunates who had been seduced or forced into sexual intercourse, or who had been given an unfulfilled promise of marriage. Peter Laslett has postulated the existence of a 'bastardy-prone sub-culture' of women who repeatedly bore illegitimate children. But these were untypical. Nevertheless, the wider problems of popular attitudes to illegitimacy, and the eventual fates of unmarried mothers and their children, await further research.

Although there are few references to contraception, there is considerable evidence that pregnant women, and especially unmarried mothers, might attempt to induce an abortion. Quaife's work on Somerset indicates that about one-fifth of men attempting to conceal the pregnancy of their partners suggested abortion as a solution to the woman in question, while scattered references show that the practice was fairly widespread. Most often, the method used involved some sort of powder or herbal infusion. In 1560 a defamation case in Yorkshire involved an allegation that a woman 'for fear she had been with childe did drynke white lavender and reeve'. In 1600 Alice Bradley, questioned by the Colchester authorities, told how the father of her illegitimate child came to her shortly after the pregnancy was discovered, and offered her a powder, 'willing her to take so much of ytt into a posset and so to drynk yt', which she claimed she refused to do. A century later Ann Foxall, a pregnant woman imprisoned in Warwickshire, on pretence of sickness 'attempted to take physic which may tend to the destruction of the child', and it was ordered that she should be taken before a justice of the peace 'to the end that especial care may be taken for prevention of so heinous a sin as infant murder which (as is feared) hath been intended'. Such cases surface regularly in legal records, and suggest that abortion was widely resorted to and that abortifacients were well known: it is impossible, however, to calculate how often unwanted pregnancies were terminated in this fashion.

Closely related to abortion was infanticide. The killing of newborn children, previously treated as a form of simple murder, was made a separate offence in 1624, the intent of the relevant legislation being to control the sexual behaviour of women rather than to protect young infants. The law was not popular with the legal profession, and by the mid-eighteenth century it was being enforced in a very haphazard fashion. Even so, it remained on the statute book until its repeal in 1803, and women were executed under its provisions up to that date. Prosecutions brought under this statute indicate that infanticide in England, in contrast to some ancient or primitive societies, was not prompted by any need to limit the population. The normal infanticidal mother was unmarried (infanticide within marriage was immensely difficult to detect), her motives in killing the child a mixture of shame and panic. In most cases the pregnant woman, usually young, often a servant, would conceal the pregnancy until the last moment, and deliver the child on her own. These circumstances, even if the child were not killed deliberately, were unlikely to be propitious for its survival.

Unfortunately, as with abortion, it is impossible to determine the incidence of infanticide. Thomas Coram, a principal promoter of the London foundling hospital opened in 1741, was reputed to have become committed to this philanthropic project because of the frequent spectacle of the bodies of newborn children flung on to London's dunghills. But such corpses were rarely noted in provincial coroners' records, and the incidence of court prosecutions for infanticide was not remarkably high. Eighty-three such cases were tried before the Essex assizes (whose records are slightly imperfect) between 1620 and 1680, and 31 women were hanged for the offence. Yet it is probable that only a very small proportion of child-murders were prosecuted. One Essex girl told how, on the birth of her first illegitimate child, her objections to killing it ('she was not so hard hearted') were brushed aside by a maidservant, who declared 'tush, it was not the first that she had maid awaie'. As so often, we are left pondering the significance of an isolated statement.

So far we have concentrated on relations within marriage or other stable relationships: there were, however, other outlets for sexual activity, particularly for men. The most obvious of these was prostitution, a subject which has so far attracted little scholarly attention, but whose history is potentially fascinating. The topic is beset by difficulties, not least of these being sources: far too often, opinions about prostitution in this period have been based on literary sources or upper-class diaries, while prostitution's legally ambivalent status has hindered its study through criminal court archives. These latter do reveal something of prostitution, and can be especially useful in describing the phenomenon in its non-metropolitan setting. Thus Quaife's researches in Somerset suggest that in rural areas there existed a number of small-time (and often part-time) prostitutes, but they were few in number and their services were not much resorted to. Prostitution in provincial towns has so far been little studied, although it is impossible that sea ports and, by 1760, such fashionable towns as Bath, should not have experienced organized prostitution. At present, the overwhelming bulk of our information comes from the London area, where popular literature suggests that brothels and organized prostitution were well established by the mid-sixteenth century (indeed, the last licensed brothels of medieval England, the Southwark stews, had only been abolished in 1546). Little is known, however, about either the structure of this prostitution, recruitment into it, or its connections with organized crime in London.

In the capital, as elsewhere, study of legal records helps take us beyond the literary anecdote, although it is evident that early modern legal systems, like their modern equivalents, had considerable difficulties in dealing with prostitution. For what it is worth, we know that an average of 500 prostitutes a year were committed to the houses of correction of Middlesex (a county encompassing a large built-up area on London's peripheries) and Westminster in the decades around 1700, but these committals tell the historian little about the structure or organization of prostitution.

These matters have, however, been afforded a preliminary investigation for the Elizabethan period, when the records of Bridewell confirm the impression given by contemporary popular literature. The authorities of Bridewell, understandably, tended to target brothels rather than casual street prostitutes, so the impression of organization may be overdrawn. Even so, these Elizabethan prosecutions demonstrate the existence of a well-founded network of brothels, many of them located in the poor, and badly regulated, parishes immediately outside the city walls, some three-quarters of them owned by women. There were also male pimps who played an important part in helping the brothels meet demand by providing links between prostitutes and brothel-keepers. Some indication of the extent, and potential profits, of commercial sex in Elizabethan London may be gained from Mistress Blunt, who kept six bawdy houses which she rented out at £1 a week each, while the most notorious pimp of the period, Henry Boyer, doubtlessly did well financially while supplying prostitutes to nine bawdy houses. What individual prostitutes charged remains uncertain, and in any case, then as now, such payments were open to negotiation. Obviously, women working in the more up-market and better-established brothels did best, even if they had to pay rent and give a proportion of what they earned to the brothel-keeper, although few could have equalled the £10 (roughly a year's wages for a labourer) earned by Thomasine Breame for an afternoon's work with a sailor. At the other end of the spectrum came such lower-class whores as Elizabeth Compe, 'a verie lewd queane', who informed the Bridewell authorities that she would be 'naughtie with anyone for iid'. Thus although further research is needed, it is evident that prostitution was an established part of at least London life by 1550, and that commercial sex was available, if only on an informal basis, over the country as a whole. Yet it remains unclear how far, either in the capital or nationally, prostitution regularly provided a sexual outlet for men. Fear of damnation after death and fear of the pox before it must have acted as powerful deterrents for many.

Not everybody chooses to express their sexuality through liaisons with members of the opposite sex, yet, at least before the late seventeenth century, homosexuality is an even shadier subject than prostitution.

Lesbianism is hardly mentioned in either contemporary records or contemporary comment. Male homosexuality attracted more attention, almost invariably of a hostile nature, and male homosexual intercourse (sodomy or buggery in contemporary parlance) was established as felony without benefit of clergy in 1563, an earlier statute of Henry VIII against this practice having lapsed. This legislation made secrecy in such matters highly desirable but, even allowing for this, concrete evidence of male homosexuality before the Restoration is difficult to come by. The reputations of Sir Francis Bacon, Christopher Marlowe, and the court of James I suggest that homosexuality was known among the élite and in the artistic world, and in 1631 the trial of the Earl of Castlehaven and various of his servants exposed an underworld of deviant sexuality to a fascinated public. Yet there is very little evidence of homosexuality among the population at large. Exactly one of the 1965 cases known to have been tried at the Essex assizes in the 60 years after 1620 was for sodomy, and even this was thrown out of court. The current values of society probably swamped individual sexuality, and individuals probably therefore felt little pressure to define their sexual proclivities. The emphasis of the modern gay movement on consciousness-raising is suggestive on this point: many people can have been only dimly aware that homosexuality existed as a sexual option. Certainly, before about 1700 there is little sign that contemporaries thought of homosexuality as a 'problem'. References to it are universally hostile, but they were generally very unspecific, lumping sodomy together with vice as a whole.

Yet by 1760 something like a male homosexual sub-culture existed in London, and was subjected to occasional attacks by the authorities. Thus in 1726 a number of raids were made on homosexual brothels or houses of resort in the capital, known at the time as 'molly houses'. An investigator told how in one such house he found 'one a-fiddling and eight more a-dancing country dances ... then they sat in one another's laps, talked bawdy, and practised a great many indecencies'. By this time a clearly defined homosexual stereotype had entered popular consciousness. In 1743 a case was tried at the Surrey assizes, as a result of which two men, James Hunt and Thomas Collins, were hanged for committing sodomy in Southwark. A waterman described how he went to watch the accused after being told by a woman that 'she suspected by the behaviour of the two men who had gone up Pepper Alley that they were mollies', and that when he overheard them 'they talked in a very ludicrous manner, and he was very well assured, that they were sodomites'. By the middle of the eighteenth century male homosexuality was becoming better defined both by those practising it, and by society at large. The persecution of homosexuals was also beginning. James Hunt, in the trial noted above, sought to defend himself by claiming that the chief witness against him and Collins was 'one of those who goes about and threatens to swear sodomy against people if they don't give him money'.

Animals formed another potential outlet for sexuality. Moralists deplored bestiality, popular literature reported monstrous births resulting from the coupling of human kind with brute creation, and sexual liaisons between humans and animals was made a capital felony in 1533, a status retained, with one brief interval, until 1861. Despite the horror with which it was regarded by legal and religious writers, bestiality was rarely prosecuted. Such court records as do survive sometimes provide graphic details. In 1731, for example, Ann Thelewell of Crosby, Lancashire, described how she saw Thomas Lucking lead a white mare into a yard, and then went on to

> set and place peices of wood under & behind the said mare and then stood upon the said peices of wood and did then loose down his breeches and put ye tail of the said mare aside ... and did then & there see him commit & act buggery with the said mare.

Yet bestiality, as we have noted, was rarely brought to trial. In Essex only nine indictments were brought against the offence between 1620 and 1680, and only three of the men accused were convicted. Contemporary moralists expressed their concern over this 'crime against nature', yet there is little in local court records to suggest that it was a frequent practice.

As has been suggested over the foregoing paragraphs, it is difficult to reach any firm conclusions about the sexual behaviour of our early modern ancestors, either inside or outside of marriage. All too often, argument must be made from a record which is silent, or which provides mere scraps of evidence. Arguing from statistics in many respects is either impossible or otiose. Basing conclusions on demographic patterns involves dependence on what may not always be correct inferences. Court records, although here as elsewhere potentially the most useful source of qualitative evidence about contemporary attitudes and behaviour, tell us little about the real levels of what contemporaries thought of as illicit or deviant sexual conduct. Above all, the sexual practices of the period have so far attracted little attention from serious historians.

Nevertheless, a few interim conclusions can be formulated. Even if standards of sexual morality would not have satisfied Puritan preachers, most people observed a rough and ready code in such matters. Bridal pregnancy was common, but promiscuity probably was not. Illegitimacy rates were low, although they were higher in England than in some Catholic states of the period. Organized prostitution was rare, at least outside the capital, and homosexuality was little heard of before the late seventeenth century. As discussion of contraception suggests, this was a society many of whose members were strangely innocent in sexual matters. Sexuality was little discussed other than in general terms, and most people were probably happy enough to accept contemporary definitions of what proper standards of sexual conduct were, even if they occasionally transgressed them.

Crises of mortality

Despite the emphasis placed on nuptiality as the most important factor affecting demographic growth, it remains true that mortality was generally high in the early modern period, and that there were episodes of unusually heavy mortality occasioned by disease or famine. Britain currently enjoys a low death rate: 11 or 12 people out of every 1000 of the population die annually. In early modern England a 'normal' death rate was about 30 per 1000 annually. Moreover, the death rate is at present static, whereas in the early modern period it could be extremely volatile, rising to three or four times its normal level under exceptional circumstances. The exceptional circumstances arose from harvest failure or from unusually virulent disease. In any underdeveloped agricultural system the failure of the main crop can easily push large sections of the population under the subsistence line or leave them terribly exposed to the diseases which follow malnutrition. Such well-documented case studies as the Irish famine of 1845–48 or famine in prerevolutionary China demonstrate this premise when the main crop was potatoes or rice. Much the same might happen when the grain harvest failed in preindustrial Europe. Disease is a less straightforward subject. Study of pestilence in the past has to be conducted in the face of contemporary description and diagnosis, while it is uncertain how valuable the findings of (for example) research into the bubonic plague in India in the 1890s or Manchuria in the 1920s might be in interpreting the progress of that disease in Stuart England. Explaining the behaviour of human beings gives historians enough trouble: explaining that of bacteria, rats, lice and fleas is even more problematic. Nevertheless, our discussion of population trends must take account of the contribution which pestilence, as well as famine, made to the 'crises of mortality' of the early modern period.

Any analysis of famine should logically begin with a consideration of what people actually ate. Existing research suggests that what the early modern English consumed adds up to a fair approximation of a modern dietician's nightmare. The rich ate well in terms of bulk, but their diet was very unbalanced. They enjoyed a high intake of protein, but ate few vegetables (thought by contemporary medical theory to engender melancholy and flatulence), little fruit, and little of what were known at the time as 'white meats' – milk, whey, butter, eggs and cheese. Thus many of the well-to-do ran the risk of deficiencies of vitamins A, C and D. The diet of the lower orders is more difficult to reconstruct. The food supplied to the inmates of the house of correction at Bury, Suffolk, in 1588 might be taken as some sort of indicator of what was thought of as basic subsistence. Two main meals a day were provided, each consisting of eight ounces of rye bread, a pint of porridge (probably a thick stew based on cereals or legumes), a pint of beer and four ounces of meat on flesh days, the meat being replaced by one-third of a pound of cheese or 'one good herring' on fish days. If this was an accurate reflection of what the poor ate, it seems that in good times they consumed a diet which was monotonous, which was deficient in vitamin C, but which at least provided the calorific intake needed by a manual worker. But it should be remembered that the poor were not a homogeneous mass. In-dwelling servants on large farms might enjoy a high daily intake of calories and what was, by the standards of the time, a reasonably balanced diet. The unskilled wage-labourer, on the other hand, was in a much more precarious position, and in years of dearth he and his family might well go hungry

The advent of dearth was normally the result of bad weather. A run of wet and cold summers had a disastrous cumulative effect on grain production over isolated periods, while over much of the second half of the seventeenth century Europe as a whole was suffering from a prolonged period of adverse climatic conditions which have been dubbed 'The Little Ice Age'. A wide range of evidence agrees that between 1645 and 1715 Europe experienced continuous bad weather, while there were also less prolonged climatic crises in the 1590s and 1620s. In the 'Little Ice Age' mean summer temperatures dropped by about one degree centigrade. Such a drop may seem small: yet the consequences of a change of even this magnitude could be serious. A fall of one degree centigrade in a north European summer means that the growing season for cereals is reduced by three or four weeks, and that the maximum altitude at which cereals can be cultivated drops by 500 feet. In the seventeenth century, when agricultural techniques were relatively primitive and large amounts of marginal land were under cultivation, such changes could have marked effects on the grain harvest. This in turn brought about serious difficulties for a population largely dependent on cereals as their basic foodstuff.

Famine was therefore triggered by bad weather which destroyed part of the grain crop. The absence of reasonably priced alternative foodstuffs meant that the demand for grain continued to increase despite high prices, and that any purchases of meat, fish, cheese or vegetables would be eschewed in favour of the ever more expensive grain. Speculation would worsen the situation (and provoke riots) as merchants held their stocks in hopes of yet higher prices. As the cost of the staple foodstuff rose, perhaps to several times its normal level, employment opportunities fell. Fewer agricultural workers were needed to gather the meagre harvest, while the diminishing proportion of the poor's income which was disposable on anything else than bread meant that artisans and craftsmen would lose employment as demand for manufactured goods fell. The poor might turn to purchasing inferior grain, from wheat to rye in southern England, for example. But this meant that even if the harvest of these inferior grains had not suffered as much as that of the favoured cereal, their prices would rise in response to increased demand. In years of really bad harvest people starved, while many others died after contracting diseases induced by eating inferior, unsuitable or rotten food. In particular dysentery, especially in that virulent form described graphically by contemporaries as the 'bloody flux', was likely to strike already enfeebled systems. More generally, hunger weakened resistance to disease among the poor, and heavy mortality might be caused by ailments which would not have been dangerous in normal times. Thus a Yorkshire doctor noted in the midst of dearth in 1727–28, when various ailments, notably suffocative angina, caused severe mortality, that

> Many of the little towns and villages were almost stripped of their poor people. ... I observed that very few of the richer people, who used a more generous way of living, and were not exposed to the inclemencies of the weather, were seized with any of these diseases at this time.

Cold and hunger reduced resistance to disease, but the process was socially selective.

In times of dearth, even in the eighteenth century, life for the lower orders could be hard and uncertain: yet by that time few people, even after the worst of harvests, would literally starve to death. Dearth created heavy mortality in the 1550s and 1720s, caused serious problems in the late 1590s, the 1620s, the period 1648–52, and the 1690s, and was responsible for widespread misery in many other years. But it was disease, either induced or encouraged by famine, rather than sheer starvation, which killed people. Although it would be otiose to claim that nobody in England died of hunger after that date, it appears that the bad harvests of 1623–25 were the last to occasion numerous deaths from starvation. Even in these years deaths were concentrated in the peripheral north west, and seem to have occurred most frequently among the more marginal members of society. The parish register of Greystoke, Cumberland, an unusually detailed source, records the deaths of a number of such people in 1623: 'a poor hunger-starved beggar child'; 'a poor hunger-starved beggar boy'; 'James Irwin, a poor beggar stripling born upon the borders of England ... died ... in great misery'; Thomas Bell, who 'died for very want of food and maintenance to live'.

After this famine more than isolated cases of starvation were unknown, even in the less agriculturally advanced areas of the country. Increasingly, English agriculture was able to provide just enough food for the population even in bad years, a contention which is supported by the experience of the 1690s. Then, just as had happened a century before, there was a run of bad harvests. In England, these provoked rioting and hardship, and sent the theft-rate up: they did not provoke mortality crises like those which killed a quarter of the population in some parts of France, Scandinavia and Scotland at the same time. Life for the poor in late seventeenth- and eighteenth-century England was not idyllic. In times of bad harvest most of them went hungry, many contracted fatal or crippling disease through malnutrition or eating contaminated food, and a few, especially the very young, the very old, and the vagrants on the margins of society may have starved. But the massive crises of subsistence which had afflicted England in the past, and which were still so menacing in Europe, had ended.

Disease, on the other hand, continued to kill, and people were largely helpless before it. The variety of potentially fatal diseases was impressive. There was diphtheria, a winter disease which mainly attacked children under five and which could, on occasion, kill up to 40 per cent of those it infected; dysentery which, as we have seen, so often followed famine; influenza, commonly described as 'the sweat' in the sixteenth century, which could also at its most virulent cause a case-fatality rate of 40 per cent; measles, again a child's disease, which all too frequently led to pneumonia; scarlet fever, another child's disease, although with a low fatality rate; smallpox, again most prevalent among children, with a case-fatality rate of up to 30 per cent; typhoid, an autumn disease which affected all age groups, with a case-fatality level of 15–20 per cent; typhus, spread mainly by lice, a disease of the winter and spring which attacked all age groups, sometimes killing half of those it infected; whooping cough, fatal mainly among young children; and syphilis, epidemic in Europe from the 1490s, although probably less virulent and less likely to be fatal by 1600.

These were the big killers, but there also existed a host of lesser diseases. In 1729, with hunger still weakening resistance, a doctor recorded the presence of 'chincough, rheumatisms, inflammations and a general scabbiness. All low grounds sore afflicted with obstinate quartans and tertians [i.e. malaria]. At Plymouth rheumatisms, arthritis, suffocating coughs, fatal to the asthmatic and consumptive. In May inflammatory fevers and chicken-pox; in June erysipelas and small-pox; in July a putrid fever, itch and scabbiness; in November a universal catarrh'. Sickness, always inconvenient, often fatal, was omnipresent in the early modern period.

By far the most dreaded disease was the plague. This is a disease of rodents, notably the black rat, *rattus rattus*, which is spread to humans by fleas. There are three main types of plague: bubonic, pneumonic, and septicaemic. The bubonic is the most common. On the first or second day of infection the victim develops a bubo or swelling of the lymphatic glands in the groin, armpit or neck. This is followed by coma, inflammation of the kidneys, and heart failure, with death (which usually comes in about five days of the first appearance of the bubos) occurring in 60–85 per cent of cases. Pneumonic plague is an extremely infectious disease passed from infected persons via droplets in the air produced when they cough, speak, or simply breathe. It affects the lungs, and almost invariably results in death. Septicaemic plague is, fortunately, very rare. It involves blood poisoning throughout the system, and can kill a healthy human being within 24 hours. Observers were particularly struck by three aspects of the plague: its suddenness, its high fatality rate, and the impossibility of doing anything to cure it. The only safe remedy was flight, and this was, generally speaking, available only to the rich. The poor stayed and died.

The history of the plague in England is a lengthy and contentious one. The disease was retreating by 1550, but it fought a number of stubborn rearguard actions. It was increasingly a disease of the towns, although it is typical of the plague's arbitrary nature that one of its better-known late visitations should have been in the remote Derbyshire village of Eyam. Most towns, and many villages, suffered at least one serious plague outbreak in our period: but the disease reaped most grimly, in terms of the absolute number of fatalities, in London. The Great Plague of 1665, which killed 70,000–100,000 Londoners, was only the last of a series of visitations which afflicted the capital. In 1563 London suffered a very high proportional loss from the plague for our period, when 20,000 people, perhaps one-sixth of the capital's population, were killed. There were moderate outbreaks in 1578 and 1582, with 6000 and 7000 fatalities respectively, and a more serious outbreak in 1593, which carried off 18,000 in the inner parishes alone. In 1603 the plague greeted the accession of James I by killing 30,000 of the inhabitants of his new capital, while in 1625, the year of Charles I's accession, another visitation caused 40–50,000 deaths there.

The progress of this 1625 outbreak illustrates both the suddenness with which the plague struck and its seasonality. In the four weeks ending 27 January there were only two reported plague deaths, in the next four weeks 12, in the next five weeks 23. Thereafter, fatalities rose as the arrival of warmer weather created optimum conditions for the plague to spread, until in the four weeks ending 25 August 16,455 deaths, or 84.74 per cent of those listed in the London Bills of Mortality, were attributed to plague. Some idea of the demographic impact of outbreaks of this type can be gauged from the fact that the parishes covered by the Bills of Mortality recorded only 6642 baptisms, as opposed to 53,871 deaths, between early January and mid-December 1625.

The behaviour of the plague was completely unpredictable: it is, for example, recorded as having caused only four deaths in London in 1664, the year before the Great Plague. Nothing in its history, however, would have been so difficult to predict, or has proved so hard to explain, as its disappearance from England. It continued to afflict townships throughout 1666 and 1667, sometimes causing heavy mortality, but after that date it seems to have left England until a few cases were reported early in the twentieth century. There is no entirely convincing explanation for this. The old school-book explanation which attributed the ending of the plague to the cleansing effects of the Great Fire of London is clearly untenable: many places outside the capital suffered from the plague in the two years after 1665, while many of London's outparishes, which were usually heavily afflicted by the plague, were untouched by the Great Fire. Another explanation revolves around the replacement of *rattus rattus* by the brown rat, *rattus norvegicus*, whose habits and relative inhospitability to fleas make it a less likely source of infection. Unfortunately, this explanation fails because the brown rat did not appear in large numbers in England until well into the eighteenth century.

The alleged connection between the end of the plague and better housing and sanitation also seems unconvincing. The living conditions of the poor did not improve so dramatically after 1665 as to make their residences inhospitable to rats, while it is noteworthy that Eyam, which suffered such heavy mortality in 1666, was a village of those stone cottages with slate roofs and stone floors which should have been so inhospitable to plague rats. The attractive theory that the existing strain of the bacillus responsible for the plague simply lost most of its virulence after 1665–67 has now been discredited, and emphasis placed upon more effective quarantine measures on the continent, which prevented the spread of the disease after 1700. Certainly the end of the plague in early modern England (the last fatalities seem to have been at Rotherhithe just across the Thames from the City of London in 1671) cannot be attributed to any human efforts.

In 1798 the Reverend Thomas Malthus published the first of his celebrated, if much misunderstood, works on population. It is ironic that he was one of the first generation of English men and women to be living under a new demographic regime which was vastly different from the one he described, a regime in which the 'positive checks' of famine and disease were no longer inhibiting population expansion. By 1798 England was moving towards those processes of mass urbanization and industrialization which were to permit the country to support a population many times greater than that obtaining in the middle of the eighteenth century. Yet even by then a corner had been turned. When the harvest was bad or trade depressed, many went hungry and famine-induced disease took its toll: yet the old crises of mortality had now gone. Similarly, although fatal disease was universal, after 1671 English communities were free of that most psychologically and demographically devastating of pestilences, the bubonic plague. Life was still uncertain, above all for the poor, yet the human condition was noticeably more secure than it had been in 1550.

That we are able to make such statements, and to trace the processes by which this situation came about, owes much to those scholars who have laboured to reconstruct patterns of demographic change, of mortality and of the incidence of disease. Yet it must be reiterated that the patterns they have found are, in many respects, averages: averages that are sometimes derived from massive, even national, aggregates. One of the jibes levelled against historical demographers, in particular by practitioners of more traditional forms of history, is that their search for statistical trends makes them lose sight of the individual. These strictures receive no support from the present author but, as some of the foregoing discussion of sexual behaviour has already shown, the type of aggregative analysis which is, quite properly, the initial concern of historical demographers leaves a number of questions unanswered, however successfully it resolves others. When looking at family behaviour, or the quality of married and family life, the quantitative work carried out by the demographers, however indispensable it might be, is essentially a first step. It is to the next step, attempting to gain qualitative insights into such matters, that we shall now turn.

2

Family life

The essentially quantified work carried out by historical demographers has added a great deal to our understanding of the marital and sexual life of our early modern ancestors. A number of other important matters remain: the forces that shaped the family, that led men and women to marry, to form households; the attitudes which husbands and wives had about each other and about the children they raised; and the processes by which material resources and moral values were passed from generation to generation. Moreover, there is the basic point that families develop, whereas some of the sources relevant to historical demography (notably parish listings) tend to freeze families or households at a given point. They tell us little about how the fortunes of families were affected as children moved out, as economic resources altered, or as the married couple at the centre of the family aged. Studying these broader, qualitative, issues raises a number of problems, however. Evidence about emotions is often difficult to come by, and is likely to be far easier to find among those social groups who kept diaries or wrote letters. The standard historical technique of supporting argument by citing examples is also unusually risky. In the early modern period, as now, some husbands and wives were more loving than others, some parent–child relationships were closer than others. In many ways, given this type of variable, and also those variables likely to arise between different social strata, writing the history of the family would seem to be a daunting exercise. Nevertheless, the historian must generalize.

Certainly, considerable amounts of relevant evidence survive. Among this mass of material a number of main categories can be discerned. First, there are the essentially personal materials, such as letters, diaries and autobiographies. Second comes that body of material which was generated by the family's concerns with property: wills, marriage contracts, apprenticeship indentures. Third there is the documentation, much of it unexplored, produced by litigation over family or marital matters. Fourth come the archives generated by the administrative and correctional procedures of local and central government bodies, such as court records or poor-law documents. Last, there are those administrative records which the previous chapter has already made familiar: parish registers, parish listings and tax records. Using these records involves a variety of difficulties. The first of the two categories listed above are heavily biased towards the propertied classes. These were obviously more likely to have left records about the transference of property, and were also the most likely to have had the leisure and education which were useful, although not essential, prerequisites for keeping detailed diaries. Moreover, much of this evidence, notably the diaries and correspondence upon which so much of the assessment of the quality of family life must depend, both survives in greater bulk and becomes more elaborate as time goes on. We must, therefore, when confronting 'new' attitudes be especially alert to the possibility that we might simply be finding better documented examples of what were, in fact, very old ones.

A substantial corpus of printed materials can be added to this documentary evidence. Much of the imaginative literature of the period touched on family matters, although given the limited utility of élite literature in telling us anything useful about the real life of the bulk of the population, very little use will be made of it in this book. Similar problems arise when dealing with the popular literature of the period. Numerous chapbooks, ballads, joke-books and proverb books refer to marriage. Unfortunately, this material carries its own problems of interpretation: much of it is didactic in its nature, and there is the difficulty of decoding the real attitudes which lie behind, or are even inverted in, a humorous or satirical work. Another printed source is the conduct book. From about the middle of the sixteenth century a number of writers, many of them clergymen, felt moved to write works on the proper nature of family relationships. These books are more useful in telling us about the expectations which a section of opinion held about such matters than contemporary reality: nevertheless, they do provide a fairly clear idea of what these expectations were. Together with the other printed sources we have noted, these conduct books add yet another body of source material upon which the history of the early modern English family might be based.

The early modern family: the debate

Historians of England have made varied use of this promising corpus of material. The starting point for any detailed discussion of the early modern English family is still a large and much acclaimed book first published in 1977, Lawrence Stone's *The Family, Sex and Marriage in England 1500–1800*. In this work, which attracted considerable attention both inside and outside academic circles, Stone set out to trace a number of changes in family and sexual behaviour over his period. The most important of these was a shift away from a situation where human relations were based on distance, deference and patriarchy to one in which they were constructed around 'affective individualism'. This shift, according to Stone, was the most important mental transition to have taken place in the early modern period and, indeed, in the last thousand years. Stone postulates three ideal family types. The first of these, the predominant one in 1500, he characterizes as 'the open lineage family'. Its features were its permeability to outside influences, the sense of loyalty which its members felt to a wide network of ancestors and living kin, and the way in which the interests of the individual were subordinated to those of the family group. Relations within the nuclear family were therefore not very intimate, and feelings between husbands and wives and parents and children were unlikely to have been much closer than those between neighbours. Family life for members of the open lineage family was characteristically open-ended, low-keyed, unemotional and authoritarian.

The second family type identified by Stone was the patriarchal nuclear family, which flourished between 1550 and 1700. This type emerged with the Reformation, and predominated between 1580 and 1640, after which date it fought a rearguard action against newer family types (it is worth noting that Stone envisages some chronological overlapping between his categories of family). Under this family form loyalties to kin, patron and local community declined, but were replaced by strengthened loyalties to the nation state or the monarch, or to a sect or church. This form was still characterized by a low level of affect among its members. Life was still risky, so the members of the patriarchal nuclear family made few emotional demands on each other, and the family remained a low-keyed institution. In general, Stone claims, the sixteenth and seventeenth centuries were a period when most individuals found it difficult to establish close emotional ties to others, where children were neglected or brutally treated, and in which adults regarded each other with suspicion and hostility. But after about 1640, or perhaps 1660, Stone argues, there arose a third family form, the 'closed domesticated nuclear family', which was to arrive as the dominant family type in the eighteenth century. This heralded an easier relationship between husbands and wives, and between parents and children, while this form of family also permitted the recognition of children as separate entities. Beneath all this, there lurked the growth of 'individualism'. People felt themselves more able to demand the right of privacy, the right of self-expression, and the right to the free exercise of their will. There was a greater interest in introspection and in the recognition of the individual personality. The overall outcome was that the interests of the individual were placed before those of kin, family, society, perhaps even the state. Moreover, these changes were, initially, more typical of the middling strata of society, identified by Stone as the great pacesetters. Unlike their betters, they were not preoccupied with pleasure or politics. Unlike their inferiors, they were not so concerned with sheer survival as to be excluded from the relative luxury of warm and caring family sentiment.

Stone's book, as we have noted, enjoyed a wider impact than that normally experienced by the work of an academic historian, and also received considerable favourable comment when it first appeared. But even those who reviewed the work favourably were anxious to point out some areas of weakness, while a few reviewers were devastatingly critical. It is the opinions of this latter group which have come to predominate: as Ralph Houlbrooke, author of the best synthesis yet written on the early modern English family has noted, 'hardly any aspect of Stone's enterprise has escaped severe criticism'.[1] This criticism, in fact, illuminates some of the wider problems inherent in writing on the subject of the early modern family. First, as we have noted, source material is biased towards the rich, and the historian wishing to correct this bias has to exercise considerable imagination and seek evidence in some unfamiliar quarters. Second, again as we have noted, changes in the bulk or quality of source material do not necessarily imply real changes in attitudes. Most seriously, the historian should not go into the subject with too rigid a model of what is expected to happen, and then ignore or distort evidence which contradicts that model.

Stone, like others, accepted a Whig interpretation of family history, one which made the 'modern family' the hero of his story. Certainly, he accepted unquestioningly the familiar model of the change from feudalism to capitalism, of the transformation of a traditional, group-based, kinship-dominated society into the modern capitalist system. Stone sees this process as involving (among other things): the throwing-off of the restraints imposed by the village, congregation, estate or family; the rise of the individual; the concomitant emergence of notions of absolute rights to private property; the rise of privacy itself as a desirable entity; and the arrival of affective family feelings based on 'modern' sentiments. Even if we do not accept Alan Macfarlane's extreme position on fundamental continuities in family and sexual matters between 1300 and the present day, it is clear that his objections to any easy acceptance of this very familiar model of social development are justified. The old model of the emergence of capitalism and of a rising middle class provides a framework within which it is all too easy to see the family making the transition from being a group-based, brutal and unfeeling institution towards its modern individualized and affective form.

Although we shall be exploring some of the more contentious areas of English family history in this chapter, it is worth reminding ourselves that there are several areas of considerable agreement in this subject. Most importantly, the old sociological myth that in the preindustrial or 'traditional' world the extended family was the norm has long been exploded. The relationship between the nuclear family and the wider kin is a problem which demands further research, not least because the household formed around the nuclear family was in many ways the point at which the kin groups connected by marriage shared and redistributed their resources. But, despite circumstances which might modify the general rule, the nuclear family was the normal residential arrangement, and occupied a central position in both the actual life and emotional expectations of most people. Complications arise, however, from the practice, common to most households above those of the labouring poor, of keeping servants. Even craftsmen or farmers of a middling rank would have a servant or two living in their household, and contemporary parlance and contemporary practice agreed in regarding these servants as members of the family. Their status varied between different strata. Among peers and gentry, servants might graduate to being trusted retainers. Among middling groups, they were often recruited from the kin of the husband or wife, a spell as a servant being regarded as a useful educational experience for a young relative. Among the yeomanry and artisanate, servants included everything from skilled and trusted workers to migrant workers of either sex, many of them indistinguishable from vagrants. These latter were often hired on a very temporary basis, and their employment was often terminated abruptly if they were caught stealing from their employer or, in the case of young women, if they became pregnant. Conduct books, the letters of the rich, and the court records of the period all suggest that domestic servants caused a number of problems. Nevertheless, most historians have agreed that they were an inescapable, and perhaps distinctive, feature of the early modern English household.

Another phenomenon of the period was the emergence of a distinctive household ideology. This has, indeed, been identified as one of the most far-reaching consequences of the English Reformation. The powers of the head of household, it has been claimed, were bolstered by the Protestant insistence on his duty to indoctrinate his family with piety and morality through the medium of daily prayers and Bible readings. Certainly the conduct books written by clergy fostered this ideology. But the most recent student of these conduct books, Kathleen Davies, has found little in them which demonstrates a serious break with pre-existing attitudes. The mutual respect and love between partners upon which Puritan writers insisted can be traced in pre-Reformation thinking. Their views on the ends of marriage, the ordering of the household, and their advice on how to attain the ideal form of domestic existence probably did little more than mirror current practices in the households of the middling sort. The advice they offered was conventional and highly generalized, eschewing detailed or difficult problems. The Puritans were, perhaps, unusual in their forthright rejection of the double standard in sexual morality and their denial of the lawfulness of wife-beating. Generally, however, the conduct books seem to be a prime example of how existing attitudes were made to seem novel through being discussed extensively in print. The upsurge of interest in the family by Protestant clergymen can be attributed to one basic fact: after the Reformation, the clergy were allowed to marry. Whatever other changes occurred in the early modern English family, the arrival of one new family type is irrefutable: the legitimate family of clergymen.

Although most of our discussion will focus upon affective relationships within the family, it should be stressed that this is only one of a variety of approaches to the history of family life. The demographic approach has been discussed: a third centres on the economic aspects of the family, on the problem of the household's material resources. This approach concentrates on property holding, property utilization and property transmission, as well as on employment, the family budget and working practices. Inheritance patterns and related matters have been the subject of considerable research by continental scholars. These have sharpened our awareness of the need to study the strategies by which families, and especially peasant families, maintained an optimum standard of living, both for themselves and for their descendants. For the yeoman farmer and the husbandman working the land, and for the artisan involved in domestic industry, almost all production was domestically organized, and intended for domestic consumption or for a known local market. This has long been familiar in general terms, although so far its implications have been little studied in their detailed local context. Such research as has been completed shows how family strategies operated and how they fitted in with what the wider kinship networks outside the household in question both needed and had to offer. One of the criticisms which might be levelled against those concentrating on the history of affective relationships is that they risk losing sight of the way in which certain aspects of sexual and marital experiences and expectations were interconnected with and affected by the way in which people won their living.

Such considerations underline the general suspicion that the history of the family is a very complex business. It is unusually prone to being obviated by the application of an inappropriate model. Even if this is avoided, allowance has to be made for a number of approaches, none of them mutually exclusive, which the historian of the family can legitimately follow. There are also the problems inherent in mastering a large and variegated body of source material. Nevertheless, the existing debate on affective relationships within the family suggests that we would be justified in concentrating on two particularly crucial areas: the relationship between husband and wife; and the relationship between parents and children. These are not the only two legitimate areas of interest, but it does seem, especially given the insistence on the importance of the nuclear family in our period, that it is there that the most important clues to the nature of family life are likely to be found.

Husbands and wives

A basic assumption put forward by Stone and others is that marriage before about 1660, or perhaps 1700, was likely to be undertaken for economic rather than emotional reasons. Among the élite, it has often been argued, the prevalence of arranged marriages demonstrates that marriage was essentially a property transaction aimed at furthering dynastic interests. Evidence dealing with a much broader social spectrum suggests that romantic attachment, if rarely entirely absent, was not the sole criterion upon which a mate was selected. The advancement of the person contemplating marriage, or of their family, the idea of parity in age and economic circumstances, and the character of the proposed spouse were all taken into consideration. Many authorities were extremely sceptical about the suitability of romantic love as a sound basis for marriage, and some saw it merely as a disruptive and irrational emotion. Such attitudes have provided considerable ammunition for those arguing that expectations of emotional fulfilment in marriage were low. Conversely, there is considerable evidence that passionate attachment, something like the romantic love with which we are currently so familiar, was regarded as normal, even desirable, by couples contemplating marriage in the sixteenth and seventeenth centuries. Evidence given in matrimonial causes before the church courts shows that the ideal of romantic love was familiar to all social groups by 1500, while ballads from the reign of Elizabeth show how deeply the concept was embedded in popular culture. The notion that romantic love was an invention of the mid-eighteenth century, whether a symptom of 'modernization' or not, seems totally wrong-headed.

Studying the reasons why people married is to some extent complicated by contemporary uncertainty as to what a valid marriage was. Getting married in early modern England is probably best interpreted as a long transitional process, begun by private agreement initially formalized by a contract, and endorsed by a public rite. Obviously the church was anxious to regulate this process, especially the public rite at its conclusion. The church's definition of what constituted a valid marriage had been formulated in the twelfth century, and this remained standard until Lord Hardwicke's Act of 1753. Assuming that no fundamental impediment (consanguinity, affinity, or pre-contract) existed, the fundamental principle was that marriage was an indissoluble bond created by the consent of the two parties involved and by solemnization in church. To the legal and popular mind, the contract by which the couple accepted each other formally was the essence of a valid marriage. The church was anxious that this contract should be made in a formal and public service, in the presence of witnesses and a priest. Even so, an indeterminable number of unions, especially among the lower orders, took place without any formal church ceremony. Clandestine marriages (many of them the result of a desire by the couple involved to evade constraints on freedom of choice) were also a continual problem.

Perhaps the most marked difference between married life in the early modern period and the present day was that legally dissolving an unsatisfactory marriage was, for most of the population, almost impossible. Today, over one-third of British marriages end in divorce, but in early modern England divorce in the modern sense was virtually unknown. Whereas most Protestant churches in the sixteenth century had included more liberal provisions for divorce among their religious reforms, the post-Reformation Church of England retained the traditional Roman Catholic position on the subject: namely, that a validly contracted or celebrated marriage could be ended only by the death of one of the spouses. The church did offer the chance of terminating a marriage by annulment, which depended on a demonstratinon that the marriage in question was invalid because of certain pre-existing conditions (notably that one of the married parties was already married when the marriage took place), or to defects in the form of marriage. Annulment should not be confused with divorce: it declared that a marriage had never existed, not that an unsatisfactory but legally valid marriage should be dissolved. For those locked in such unsatisfactory marriages who were unable to provide grounds for annulment (and the English did at least have Henry VIII's example to follow here) the best that the ecclesiastical law could offer was separation *a mensa et thoro* (from bed and board). This did at least allow heavily antagonistic spouses to live apart from each other, but it did not end their marriage: they were not allowed to remarry for as long as their original partner was alive, and were also legally expected to remain sexually inactive, thus maintaining marital fidelity even while living apart. In any case, it appears that neither annulments nor separations *a mensa et thoro* were frequent.

England's unique adherence among Protestant states to Catholic teaching on divorce led to some adverse comment among Elizabethan and early Stuart clerical writers seeking further reformation in the English Church, and it is perhaps significant that the Puritans in New England included provision for divorce in their legislative programme in the 1620s. The suspension of the church courts in the 1640s and 1650s allowed the debate over divorce to flourish anew (most famously through the writings of John Milton), while a common law action to permit legal separation was developed, although it too was little used while certain elements of the type of legal action involved remained legally uncertain. For the very rich, a new way of dissolving unsatisfactory marriages came with the development of Divorce by Act of Parliament. This depended upon actual or fictitious adultery by the wife, and was a cumbersome process, involving a common law action for 'criminal conversation' against the wife's accomplice in adultery, the awarding of separation on grounds of adultery by the church courts, and a dissolution of the existing marriage which allowed the right to remarry. From the outset, Divorce by Act of Parliament was the preserve of the very rich: the first three such Acts terminated the marriages of Lord Roos in 1670, the Earl of Macclesfield in 1698, and the Duke of Norfolk in 1700. Moreover, as these cases suggest, divorces of this kind were very uncommon. There had only been 16 such Acts by 1750, although from that date onwards they became more frequent, if still restricted to the wealthy. A wide variety of court records attest to the existence of unhappy, abusive or violent marriages, but for most of the population dissolving such unions legally was impossible. At the bottom of society, many marriages were simply terminated by the desertion of one of the spouses, or by mutual separation sometimes formalized by the ritual of wife-selling. The latter typically involved a husband accepting his wife's leaving him for another man in return for a token sum of money.

Logic suggests that this non-availability of divorce was especially serious for those joined in an arranged marriage. Some detailed research supports the familiar assertion that such unions were likely to prove emotionally unsatisfactory. The Verney family, an upper-gentry clan from Buckinghamshire, have been used as a case study. Their seventeenth-century family archives support the contention that there was a connection between marriages arranged for dynastic or financial reasons and a later family life which was patriarchal, authoritarian, and placed a low priority on physical or psychological gratification. Such family feeling as existed among the seventeenth-century Verneys evidently reflected little in the way of love or affection. Work on other gentry families, however, demonstrates a different situation. Love might be an important factor in the process of getting married, and the ensuing unions experienced mutual confidence and affection between spouses and, so far as elusive emotions can be traced in the historical record, real devotion. Although it is doubtless possible to find spectacular examples to the contrary, parents, however anxious they might have been to further their dynastic interests, did not usually drag a genuinely unwilling child to the altar. If nothing else, they were deterred by the probable consequences of forcing a child into a potentially unsuccessful union: a marriage that failed might engender enormous tensions among the wider kin, and would also be unlikely to achieve the aim of producing an heir. The resistance of the children in question should not be taken for granted. What they expected from marriage was often perfectly compatible with the interests of parents, kin and society as a whole. The love that might develop within an arranged marriage was not unconnected with the need for honour, status and security. Some arranged marriages worked well. In 1613 Henry, Earl of Huntingdon, commented that 'I myself was married when a child and could not have chosen so well myself nor been so happy in any woman I know', although it is indicative of attitudes at even this social level that he added 'but because one proves well it must not beget a conclusion'. Arranged marriage, like so many other aspects of family life of the period, is a rather more complicated phenomenon than might appear at first sight.

Among groups lower in the social scale, where dynastic interests were less predominant, freer attitudes to mate-selection might well have obtained. Phineas Pett, son of a Deptford shipwright, recorded how in the late 1580s he took 'such a liking' to his future wife that he 'determined resolutely (by God's help) either to match with her or never to marry again'. He eventually did wed her in May 1591 despite 'all my own kindred being much against my matching with her'. The marriage of his own son was arranged with that combination of approval from parents and affection between the future spouses which the conduct books recommended. When the matter was agreed, Pett noted that 'in the afternoon we had private conferences together and concluded the match and contracted the parties with free consent on both sides'. Miranda Chaytor's work on Ryton, County Durham, has revealed how courtship took place at the other end of the country at about the same time. Thomas Soley, a farmer from Cleveland, pursued an unsuccessful courtship of Agnes, the daughter of a widow named Margaret Smith. Soley opened negotiations through his friend Percival Gibson, a kinsman of the widow, describing himself as 'suitor to the widow Margaret Smith for the goodwill of her daughter'. He and Gibson visited the Smith residence, 'where they was well taken withall and welcome'. They discovered that the daughter whom Gibson originally had in mind for his friend was already married, but the widow, hearing that Soley had a good farm, suggested Agnes as a suitable alternative. She was, however, already 'in talk' about marriage with an 'aged widow man', and Gibson and Soley were told to return on Midsummer's Eve. They did so, and Soley and the girl were left alone in the house for the evening by the widow, she 'giving him the goodwill of Agnes as freely as God gave her to her'. Agnes 'liked not so well' the widower, but she insisted on the validity of the pledge she had given him: although Soley offered her a pair of gloves, she refused to take them, thus rejecting the tokens of intent which were so important in plebeian courtship. Despite the role played by her mother and her kinsman in the courtship, it was obviously accepted that Agnes was free to marry whom she pleased. The ballads of the period also portray a world in which individuals, although willing to seek the advice of 'friends' about their marriage plans, and pleased if they could get their approval, were expected to make their own choice of marriage partner.

One impediment to freedom of choice of marriage partner were the prohibitions upon marrying kin imposed by the church. The marital problems of Henry VIII had complicated matters, and the resultant general uncertainty was only partly assuaged by the 'Table of Affinity and Kindred' promulgated early in Elizabeth's reign. The doubts which remained about the prohibited degrees, even in the best circles, are demonstrated by the comments of Sir John Bramston, one of the leading gentry in Restoration Essex. Bramston recorded how a woman had married a member of his family who was her 'cousen german'. 'This mariage trubled me extreamely,' wrote Sir John,

not only because I knew my brother had very manie children to provide for, had little which he could part with, and, haveinge bred his son to a profession, had hopes of a better portion than I could give; but in truth my concernment was cheifly in the neereness in blood; it beinge but one degree from incest (brother and sister); yet tyme, and the perswasion of friends, prevailed with me to forgive that which was past remedie. I found too that the prohibition of the church had varied as to degrees, and was rather politicall, then for any prohibition of the Leviticall Law.

Among the lower orders, marriage within the prohibited degrees was probably not much worried about. In Elizabeth's reign Edward Ward, a Durham husbandman, married his uncle's widow. His wife justified the match before the ecclesiastical court by claiming that 'all the lordship and parich of Gainford' knew about it, 'and yet never found fault with the marriadg ... but rather thinks good of her, bicause she was his own uncle wyf'. Popular attitudes in this respect were evidently fairly relaxed, and represented yet another area in which the post-Reformation church had a long way to go in inculcating proper Christian standards among the people at large.

Once married, relations between spouses were not necessarily unloving. Husbands and wives may have been distant among the peerage, although even here the evidence is ambiguous. Among the next group down the social scale, the upper gentry, there is every indication that relations between the spouses were normally close, with frequent and spontaneous statements of affection and considerable emotional gratification. Consider Thomas Knyvett, member of a solid Norfolk family. Knyvett, born in 1596, married Katharine, the daughter of Sir Thomas Burgh, fifth Baron Burgh of Gainsborough, in 1620. During much of the subsequent decade Knyvett was away from home attending to legal business in London, and his letters to his wife display a touching and real affection. He habitually referred to her as 'Sweet Harte' or 'my deere Harte', and in letter after letter expressed his love for her. In October 1621 he wrote of 'the assured testimonies of my affection to you', signing himself 'thy loving husband who loves thee more than his owne life'. In November 1621 he began a letter by declaring 'Sweet harte I am forst yet to send the shaddowe of my selfe, the true affection of a substance that loves you above the world', and went on to assure his wife that he would 'rather be with you than in any place under heaven'. In April 1623 he told how 'I received thy kinde letter, and returne thee as true love and affection as can lodge in the hart of mortallitye'. A month later, he assured her that 'I have no more to say, but my everlasting love rest with thee, and that love makes me but halfe my selfe till I be with thee.' These sentiments were not merely the expression of the first joys of wedlock. In 1644, Knyvett, now aged nearly 50, still addressed his wife in loving terms. 'Sweete harte,' he wrote in one of his final letters, '... I cannot let any opportunity slippe that may expresse my love to thee.' Thomas Knyvett makes a very poor advertisement for a world where affect was low between spouses and where interpersonal relations in general were likely to be cool.

In discussing marital relations among the non-gentry middling sort, the next group down the social scale, it is interesting to turn to a different source providing a different perspective: the conduct books of the period. In 1622, at about the same time as Knyvett was penning the first of his affectionate letters to his wife, William Gouge, a London clergyman, published *Of Domesticall Duties: Eight Treatises*. In this, one of the longest of the conduct books, Gouge set out his ideas on the proper roles of the various members of the household, including husband and wife. His views, based wherever possible on scripture, were complex, although his starting point was a fairly straightforward assertion of patriarchal authority. The husband was the head of the household. The wife's first duty was obedience, an obedience based not merely on logical acceptance, but on her deep belief in the naturalness of her subordination to her husband. But this was no simple recipe for patriarchal tyranny: ultimate power rested with the husband, but it was to be rarely invoked. Gouge held that the normal relationship between spouses should be loving and based on shared responsibility. Conjugal love was to be expressed within the bounds of Puritan ideas on what was seemly: the wife was not to address her husband as 'sweet, sweeting, sweet-heart, love, joy, deare', and much less as 'ducke, chicke, pigsnie'. But a marriage without love was anathema to Gouge. 'If there be not love predominant in the husband,' he wrote, 'there is like to be little peace betwixt man or wife.' While attacking 'a fond conceit, that husband and wife be equal', Gouge insisted that the wife's position was 'the neerest to equality that may be: a place of common equity in many respects, wherein man and wife are after a sort even fellowes, and partners'. Gouge had reached the common-sense conclusion that although husbandly authority had to exist, to stand on that authority on every occasion was, in the long run, a pretty certain means of destroying respect.

More personal documentation confirms the impression given by the conduct books that marriage among the middling sort was companionate and loving. Ralph Josselin, the Essex clergyman and diarist, recorded a great deal about his married life. His marriage, for love, to Jane Constable began in 1640, and was to last for another 43 years. The marriage was not without its disappointments and, in its last decade, its strains, yet on balance it seems to have been an outstanding emotional success. Josselin frequently noted feelings of affection for his wife, and numerous expressions of tenderness between the two of them. These were especially noticeable when Josselin was away from home, on family business in London, for example, or when serving as an army chaplain in the Civil War. In 1651 he preached a funeral sermon on the wife of his patron, and one suspects that it was more than mere rhetoric which led him to refer to 'my dear wife ... her delightful imbraces; her counsel, spiritual discourses, furtherance, encouragement in the ways of God ... an helpe to ease me of the burthern and trouble of household-affaires, whose countenance welcomed me home with joy'.

Another social stratum, another source. Just as conduct books tell us about the expectations of married life among the middling sort, so the popular literature of the period might be expected to throw light on the expectations of the lower orders. In fact, this literature provides a somewhat ambivalent impression. Ballads, for example, are full of stories of shrewish and scolding wives, and of advice to bachelors to be careful in their selection of a mate, or even to avoid marriage altogether. The problem (as with a cognate source, the joke-book) is to ascertain how much the effectiveness of this essentially humorous material depended upon its blatant inversion of contemporary ideals. Ballads about unhappy marriages owed their impact to widely diffused and widely accepted notions of what a happy marriage was like. When ballads depict normal marital situations, the image they present, a lack of scriptural reference apart, would not have outraged William Gouge. The husband, ultimately, was the decision-maker, but the normal relationship between husband and wife should be loving and companionate. One ballad, written in the 1620s or 1630s, portrayed a poor man and his wife contemplating a hard year ahead of them (there were several such years for the poor in the two decades in question). The couple agreed that the problem of economic survival was to be overcome by their mutual efforts, and that these efforts were to be based on their mutual love and affection. Their hope was 'to pass this hard year ... without any strife'. If the popular literature of the period is any reflection of the actual conduct of the lower orders, we are again led to conclude that marriage was caring, companionate, and in many ways 'modern'.

Moving beyond this popular literature to find more direct evidence about the marital life of the masses is difficult. Lack of evidence makes their attitudes more obscure than those of their social superiors. Moreover, it seems logical that the institution of marriage should be especially vulnerable among the lower orders. With the best will in the world, a labourer and his wife must have found it difficult to keep the family going through times of bad harvest or economic depression, and it is no accident that the 1604 Bigamy Act was concerned with discouraging separations and remarriage among the lower orders. Conversely, scattered evidence which comes our way is not always suggestive of brutality. In 1573, for example, rumours reached Thomas Simpson, a Yorkshire farmer, that his wife was committing adultery with the local vicar. Before his neighbours, he asked her 'tell me trueth therein, wherein if thou shall declare truth I wilbe no worse unto thee then I have bene, and if thow will not declare a truth I will not beare so well with thee'. Even when faced with what many contemporaries would have regarded as the ultimate provocation, at least one member of the lower orders seems to have maintained humane relations with his wife. Other evidence supports the view that family life among the lower orders was nowhere near as uncaring as has sometimes been suggested. The wills of rural smallholders and artisans, for example, furnish innumerable examples of the dying husband taking great pains to provide for the future widow, and, in so far as the form of the document permitted it, expressing his concern for her in fond language. Even reports of marital homicide among the poor regarded such crimes as unnatural aberrations rather than as symptoms of a familiar brutishness.

The simple fact is that marriage in this period worked. Its purposes were seen by the church, and probably most contemporaries, as threefold: the procreation and bringing up of children; the satisfaction of sexual desires; and the formation of a lifelong, indissoluble partnership involving the mutual support of husband and wife. Then as now, the institution had its economic overtones: the mutual support was fulfilled partly by the property and skills which each party brought to the marriage. But this support, upon which contemporary writers placed such emphasis, was not just material. The assumption was that husband and wife should bring emotional support, indeed love, to each other, and that marriage should be a companionate and loving relationship. Something of the flavour of the expectations of the period was conveyed in 1659 when a County Durham man, Edward Newby, who combined farming six acres with being a pit overman, made his will. He declared 'that what estate he had, he together with his wife Jane had got it by their industry and therefore he gave and bequeathed all his whole estate to his loveing wife, to be at her disposall, and that if it were more, his said wife deserved it well'.

The husband was always considered to be the natural head of household, and to that extent marriage was a patriarchal institution. But this patriarchy did not constitute a harsh, tyrannical rule. Husbands were to assert their authority as sparingly as possible, and the assumption was that in a good, working marriage the friction which might provoke assertions of husbandly authority would be kept to a minimum. The writers of conduct books remembered that fundamental premise that so many historians have lost sight of: married couples had to live under the same roof, and this was a great incentive towards developing affection, co-operation, and mutual give-and-take. Above all, marriage was something which people seem to have found it difficult to do without: as far as can be seen, people of either sex were keen to get married, economic circumstances permitting, and the institution, not least when compared to the dismal prospect of staying single, was evidently thought to offer real personal advantages.

Parents and children

There is a large body of opinion holding that relations between parent and child, like those between spouses, were distant and unloving. One basis for this assumption is the high infant mortality of the period. Stone, for example, is insistent that this mortality made it foolish to invest too much emotional capital into anything as ephemeral as a child, and is equally insistent that this led to very cool parent–child relationships, in which obedience was commonly enforced with brutality. These tendencies were complicated by Puritanism, which, it has been argued, acted as a further disincentive to warmth between parent and child. Belief in immortality of the soul would lessen grief when a child died, while Puritanism might introduce new emphasis on curbing the will of the infant, both by harsh beating and overwhelming psychological pressures. Another view of early modern childhood was propounded by Philippe Aries, author of an influential book on the history of childhood. According to Aries, there was no developed concept of the child until well into the seventeenth century: children were regarded as little more than miniature adults, scant attention being paid to their separate emotional and psychological needs. Such views suggest that there was a vast gulf between modern assumptions on child-rearing and those of earlier generations.

Further complications were caused by step-parenthood, and by the custom of sending children out into service or apprenticeship. As we have seen, many marriages were terminated at an early stage by the death of one of the partners, and persons marrying for the second or third time might well find themselves in complex households, containing step-children or foster-children as well as any offspring of the existing union. It is perhaps significant that the writers of conduct books were pessimistic about step-parent/step-child relationships, seeing them as inherently difficult, and urging the need for love and respect on both sides. Interestingly, William Gouge at least thought that problems were as likely to arise from the child's inability to accept the new situation as the step-parent's. Analogous to step-children, in some respects at least, were the large numbers of children who would normally have left home by mid-adolescence. Among the rich, it was quite common to send boys to boarding school by the age of 10, while among all classes it was usual to place children of either sex into service or into an apprenticeship by the age of 15 or thereabouts. Children in service or apprentices would often be placed in the houses of relatives or friends of their parents, and there was frequently genuine care by parents over the child's welfare and progress in the new environment. Nevertheless, this practice, which may well have been unique to England in its frequency, does raise a number of questions about parental attitudes towards adolescent children.

Generally, however, writers on familial matters throughout our period regarded the tie between parent and child as one of the closest of human bonds. Parental love, so the author of conduct book after conduct book wrote, was an emotion of great breadth and depth. Maternal love was sometimes thought of as being stronger, especially when young children were under discussion, but it was otherwise expected that both parents would be equally loving towards their children. William Gouge wrote of 'that authoritie and affection which is mixed together in parents', and although he believed that parental authority was absolute, he was also insistent that parents should possess, and demonstrate, affection. This affection, like that between husband and wife, was to be clothed in godly decorum. But even allowing for this, Gouge's views on bringing up children were not so far removed from what many parents would regard as a common-sense approach. For the godly parent, child-rearing involved wholesome discipline and instruction in right religion, but the overriding concern was for the welfare of the child. Even the correction of children, a subject which has so obsessed historians (as Linda Pollock has commented, for some writers the history of childhood has simply been equated with the history of child abuse), was not to be brutal, and there is little idea of trying to break the spirit of the child. Gouge urged that correction should be accompanied by prayer, should be 'given in love', should suit the circumstances of the child's offence and their personality, and should never be done while the parent was in a temper. Above all, 'correction by word must go before correction by the rod'. Gouge advised parents to pursue a golden mean, eschewing both 'too much lenitie' and 'too much severitie' in bringing up their children.

Obviously, in reality the practice of parents would veer in either direction away from this mean. It is also probable that practices would vary between different social groups. At the top of society, considerations of lineage and dynasty might well have laid a greater stress on the notion, common in the conduct books, that having children was a good idea because it continued the human race. The heir to a great line who failed to engender children was at worst woefully negligent, at best the victim of bad fortune. The heirs that were produced, however, were perhaps more likely than the offspring of other social strata to be expected to conduct themselves with extreme formality before their parents: John Aubrey remembered how in his youth, before the Civil Wars, 'gentlemen of 30 and 40 years old were to stand like fools bareheaded before their parents'. Daughters were expected to show equal deference. Indeed, given the contemporary view that they were members of the inferior sex, and the reality of their more dependent status, girls were more likely to be subjected to parental pressures and parental discipline. There is some suggestion of a softening of attitude among the peerage after the middle of the seventeenth century, but it seems probable that throughout our period a number of factors would have conspired to inhibit the development of a close relationship between parent and child at this social level. These factors might include the involvement of the aristocratic parent in country society or national politics, the greater dependence on servants and tutors in bringing up the children of the élite, and the custom of sending aristocratic youths to boarding school, to the universities, or on the grand tour. Conversely, there is considerable evidence relating to the

upper reaches of society showing that the impression of parental domination given by such commentators as Aubrey was overdrawn.

Certainly, there was a firmly entrenched notion that peerage and upper-
gentry parents had a duty to bring up their children to the best of their
abilities. Grace Mildmay, whose life spanned the reigns of Elizabeth I and
James I, thought that 'parents have much to answer for before God, who
neglect their duty in bringing up their children, or prefer any care, labour
or delight in the world before their natural and necessary imployment'. A
little earlier a Somerset gentleman, Thomas Phelips, declared roundly that
'who is not careful for his family ys accompted worse than a heathen'.
Peerage and gentry parents saw it as part of their duty to discipline their
children, to instil a sense of obedience in them, and to encourage an
awareness of responsibility towards the lineage in them. None of this
would necessarily impede the growth of affection of something very like
the modern type. In July 1623 the Duchess of Buckingham, married to
what was probably the most powerful subject in the realm, sent her
husband a touching description of their infant daughter's behaviour in
response to his request for 'perticulers of our pretty Mall'. She told how
the girl had performed all sorts of childish antics, and declared 'I wood
you were but here to see her, for you wood take much delight in her now
shee is so full of pretye play and tricks'. Another member of the landed
orders who probably did not regard his main duty as a parent as crushing his offspring's will was Thomas Knyvett, whose loving letters to his
wife we have already noted. His correspondence was full of enquiries
about the health and progress of his children, notably his first child, a
daughter to whom he referred habitually as 'littel Pudd'.

Evidence from other social groups is equally unsuggestive of widespread
brutality towards children. Ralph Josselin, whose warm relationship with
his wife has been discussed above, enjoyed, or at least aimed at, a close
relationship with his children, seven of whom survived infancy. Even his
wayward son John, whose conduct caused his father so much grief, was
treated as far as possible with tact and understanding: Josselin constantly
made allowances for him, and hoped for his future amendment and a
general family reconciliation. Josselin's material investment in his children
matched his emotional commitment: his average annual income was £160,
and for a 42-year period he spent one-third of this on the rearing, education and marriage of his children. Henry Newcome was another clergyman who took his parental responsibilities seriously. Writing late in the
seventeenth century, he expressed the hope that 'I do not fall into reproach
for not providing for my family (for this is my constant fear lest I die and
leave nothing for my wife and children)'. These responsibilities included
disciplining his offspring, but the idea that this was a brutal or inhumane
process rapidly dissolves. Newcome recorded how 'I discharged my duty
of correction to my poor child [aged 12], prayed with him after, entreating the Lord that it might be the last correction ... that he should need.'

Expressions of grief at the loss of children were common. Early in the seventeenth century Phineas Pett noted that 'it pleased God to take from me my dear beloved son Richard, who died with me at Woolwich ... a great affliction unto me, being a very hopeful young man'.

Yet more evidence of the closeness of the bond between parent and child emerges from expressions of grief at the loss of parents, or from their children's remembrance of them. Such evidence can be found for all social strata. In May 1616 Lady Anne Clifford described her mother's death as 'the greatest and most lamentable cross that could have befallen me', and as late as November in the following year could note in her diary that 'I wept extremely to remember my dear and blessed mother'. Phineas Pett recorded in 1589 that 'it pleased God to call to his mercy my reverend loving father', and in 1597 that 'my dear and loving mother deceased at Weston in Suffolk'. Oliver Heywood, the West Riding nonconformist minister, gave what was probably a typical impression of the receiving end of Puritan childcare when he remembered that his mother was 'severe and sharp' against sin, and especially 'such sin as she saw us inclined to'. Yet he also remembered her with love, noting that she was 'very indulgent to us'. The children of Henry Newcome remembered him as a 'loving and faithful father to his children', and as a 'reverend and dear father ... whose authority we revered, and whose indulgent care over us was one of our greatest supports'. Similar attitudes, if less likely to enter the written record, probably obtained at the bottom of the social scale. It was Newcome, indeed, who in 1659 recorded the burial of a dyer, at which 'the cries of the children ... moved most that were present'.

It would therefore seem overly pessimistic to argue that the bad living conditions of the poor simply encouraged brutality towards children, or to assume that because the lower orders left so few easily accessible details of their emotional feelings that they had none. Scattered but persuasive evidence suggests that such notions are misconceived. Among the yeomanry there is considerable evidence of affection and care towards children. One early seventeenth-century commentator claimed that for the yeoman 'the bringing up and marriage of his eldest son is an ambition which afflicts him so soon as the boy is born, and the hope to see his son superior, or placed above him, drives him to dote upon the boy in his cradle'. One son of yeoman stock, Adam Martindale, recorded how his father, far from treating him with brutality, on one occasion intervened on his behalf with his schoolmaster, and told him to stop beating the youth.

People further down the social scale remembered their parents with affection. Roger Lowe, the Lancashire apprentice, visited his parents' grave with his sister in 1665, 'and stayed a while, and both wept'. Other sources allow us to infer that the poor or people of small property were caring about their children. The popular literature of the period took it for granted that caring for children was part of normal family life, even among the very poor. Smallholders usually did everything possible to provide for all their children when devising their wills. Perhaps most telling of all, it seems that everybody who was able to bear the costs involved greeted the arrival of a new child with a christening celebration. In general, there is little indication that sub-gentry groups were brutal or exploitative to their children, and considerable evidence to the contrary. For an isolated scrap of this evidence, let us turn to a letter written at some point in the 1720s by the steward of an estate in County Durham to the landlord, William Cotesworth, then resident in London. Along with more official matters, the steward told his employer how Harry Potts, one of the estate workers, had 'gott a son of which he's very fond ... he got it in his armes the morning it was born, which was yesterday, and said "Honny thou's my darlin and shall want for nothing as long as I am able to work for thee"'.

The overwhelming impression, then, is that parents of all social strata were concerned with the welfare of their children, loved them and, within the limitations of their material circumstances and cultural horizons, did their best for them. Children had to be socialized, and thus, in a broad sense, disciplined, but they were also welcomed. Ideas on the proper bringing up of children may have differed from those currently fashionable in modern Britain, but the basic aim of the early modern parent was clearly to bring up their children to the best of their abilities. Allegations that children were treated brutally in the past arise largely from selection or distortion of evidence, and from a failure to come to grips with past practices in their own terms. The involvement of young children in agricultural work or domestic industry illustrates this last point. This has often been portrayed as 'exploitative', and thus as a sign that poor parents regarded their children simply as an economic resource. Conversely, in a society where the range of employment choices was restricted and poor relief limited, teaching a child a few basic skills must have represented good sense to parents in the lower orders.

Even the emphasis which was placed on disciplining children has been made too much of by recent historians. Obviously parents, in early modern England as now, wanted their children to be disciplined: this makes being a parent easier and also, in the long run, is beneficial both to the child and to the adult it will eventually grow into. Yet this does not mean that parents were merely concerned to break the child's will. Evidence from all social groups suggests that most parents, although wanting obedient children, recognized and respected the fact that children had minds, wills and personalities of their own. Above all, there is little evidence of any marked collective change in child-rearing practices: if there were any innovations in the way in which children were treated, they arose from individual parents, rather than from any 'surge in sentiment' or 'rise of affective individualism'.

Our investigation of family life has concluded that relationships within the early modern family were more loving, caring and 'modern' than a number of recent historians have claimed. There is little evidence of that brutality in family life upon which Stone placed so much emphasis, and which led Edward Shorter to describe the early modern period as the 'Bad Old Days' of European family history.[2] Allowance has to be made for the unpredictable variety of family life, and for the fact that we are dealing with a world where life was more uncertain than it is at present, where healthcare was limited, hygiene little known, and poverty more immediate. Even allowing for all this, we are left with the impression that family life was warm and caring, and was expected to be so, with mutual love and respect between husband and wife, and between parent and child. That so many historians, some of them of considerable reputation, have thought otherwise is difficult to account for. In a broad sense, it is difficult not to accept the problems sketched by Macfarlane in his critique of Stone: the developmental model of English economic and social history has bedevilled much thinking on the early modern family. Historians have entered the field of family history with too firmly set notions of what ought to have happened.

In concentrating on affective relationships we have, perhaps, neglected a number of other issues. Perhaps the most pressing of these is the connection between the nuclear family and wider kinship networks. As we have argued, the extended family was not especially powerful in early modern England, and thus the ties between the nuclear family and the wider circle of relatives was probably weak. Nevertheless, the nature of such ties as did exist is a problem in urgent need of further research. Such contacts as there were may well have been more marked at the top of society, and were, among all social groups, likely to be heightened on certain specified occasions. Funerals, weddings and christenings were occasions on which the wider kin came together, while more generally people seem to have gone to their relatives when they wanted advice rather than material aid. The more detailed diaries of the period record contacts with the wider kin network, and some clues to the more general expectations of how individuals should behave towards their kin. Phineas Pett, for example, despite the harsh experiences of his own childhood after his father's early death, and the unhelpful attitude of his elder brother, regarded helping kin as normal. He recorded how, shortly after his marriage, he found himself responsible for another of his brothers and two of his sisters, 'and having little means but my hands to bring in anything, yet I refused not to do the duty of a brother to the utmost of my power'. He also noted how, after the death of his spouse in 1627, 'my only sister then living, Mary Cooper, departed this life the fifth of March for very griefe at the loss of my dear wife'. The extended family may not have been a characteristic feature of preindustrial England, yet it is obvious that affectionate feelings and a sense of family could extend far beyond the nuclear household.

All of which serves to remind us that the family is an institution which exists in relation to a number of others. Any historical study involves the

analysis of a defined subject, and thus an attempt to separate the phenomenon under consideration (in this case 'the family') from others: however
desirable it might be to approach history as a seamless web, confronting
the past in such a way makes it difficult to write history and almost impossible to read it. Yet it is clear that, despite the fact that the nuclear family
was in many ways the most important institution with which the mass of
England's population came into contact in our period, it was connected
with other phenomena, with other components of a total way of life. The
family in early modern England, it might be argued, is best studied in the
context of other connected institutions, of which service, friendship and
neighbourhood were the most important. Our next step, therefore, must
be to move outside the world of the nuclear family towards the wider
milieu of the local community within which people lived their daily lives.

Notes

1 Ralph A. Houlbrooke, *The English Family 1450–1700* (1984), p. 14.
2 Edward Shorter, *The Making of the Modern Family* (1976), p. 3.

|3|

Towns and villages

Most observers in early modern England who turned their mind to the subject would have regarded the family as the basic unit of social and political organization. All of them, however, would have been aware that people also lived in larger, more complex units. Beyond the nuclear family and the home there lay larger units of organization, arguably playing a larger role in shaping and controlling an individual's life in this period than they do today. Human beings, not least the early modern English, are bad at living in isolation: indeed, it is the consequent tendency for them to come together in groups which makes social history possible. Yet such groups are not merely statistical agglomerations. The human tendency towards gregariousness also involves the development of human relations, of human interaction, of interpersonal behaviour. The intensity of these phenomena, among other things, owes much to the size of the unit under consideration. In our period this could vary enormously: small villages or isolated hamlets with as little as 100 inhabitants, or London, with a population of well over half a million by the middle of the eighteenth century. Yet it is in these settlements, however varied, that people were born, met their future spouses, got married, had children, learnt trades, interacted with their fellow human beings, and eventually died. The local context is now seen as a vital one for historical study, and research on a local level has become a major growth area among historians.

Such research has proved to be of unusual significance for the early modern period. First, it permits the gaining of a fairly intimate knowledge of the attitudes, preoccupations and way of life of people quite near the bottom of the social scale. Second, it allows detailed study, and hence a detailed critique, of some of the preconceptions and received wisdom which still affect so much thinking about the preindustrial world. The nineteenth century experienced the dislocation attendant upon mass urbanization, mass industrialization and rapid demographic growth. Many thinkers experiencing these processes, not least among them the founding fathers of modern sociology, were convinced that they were living through changes which constituted a comprehensive break with the past. A new world of industry, capitalism, social mobility and social dislocation was being created, a world which was contrasted with the pre-existing 'traditional' world of stability and repose. An investigation of the towns and villages of preindustrial England, however, unearths a more complex and rather less reassuring picture.

Urban development

Despite its later claims to being a major urbanized nation, England in 1550 was not noted for the magnificence of its towns, and urban life was much less developed than in such favoured regions as the Southern Low Countries, Northern Italy, or parts of Germany. In 1588 the political theorist Giovanni Botero commented that in England, London excepted, 'although the country do abound in plenty of all good things, yet there is not a city in it that deserves to be called great'. Some of the centres regarded as towns by contemporaries and modern historians were very small indeed, and historians still suffer from some confusion about what exactly constituted a town in this period. A number of recognizably urban centres existed in 1550: York, Bristol, Exeter, Norwich and Newcastle. At the other end of the scale were five or six hundred settlements with a population of only a few hundred, differentiated from villages only in having a market or some specialist economic or administrative function. In this respect, as in others, size may not be the only thing which matters, yet it is clear that larger units than these must be involved before we can talk meaningfully of towns. It is, therefore, tempting to follow one of our leading exponents of urban history, P.J. Corfield, in concentrating on centres with a population of 2500 or more. By the mid-eighteenth century there were some 104 of these, containing between them about 22.6 per cent of England's population. Comparisons with the Tudor period are difficult because of deficiencies of data, but it is evident that the proportion of the population living in towns had at least doubled between the late sixteenth century and 1750. Urban life was becoming an increasingly common experience.

The early modern town was not defined merely by the size of its population: it possessed a number of other peculiar characteristics. It had a specialist economic function. Towns contained concentrations of industry (although few were 'industrial' in the full sense), specialist traders and producers, were markets and ports, and were also great units of consumption. Towns constituted not only large, but also uniquely concentrated centres of population: even if a town's inhabitants numbered only a few thousand, their proximity to each other was unusual for the period. Towns possessed (or in the case of emergent centres were developing) a sophisticated political structure. The new industrial centres of the eighteenth century might have only loose élites (indeed, the lack of a traditional ruling oligarchy has sometimes been seen as crucial to their growth), but the older urban centres had established governmental structures and a defined political and social hierarchy. The élites in such centres celebrated their dominant position in the urban polity through the pomp and circumstance of civic ritual and, towards 1760 at least, through municipal building projects and other collective schemes for improvement. The town also had an impact on its hinterland which went beyond the purely economic. Towns provided services: doctors, lawyers, educational institutions and the most advanced religious facilities were to be found in them, as, by the eighteenth century, were military garrisons and naval establishments. Moreover, from about 1700 at least, towns provided leisure facilities for all social strata, most notably the gentry and professionals of the area.

Above all, the early modern town acted as a magnet for immigrants, and hence provided a paradigm for mobility in a world which was normally anxious to think of itself as static. An observer at the end of our period noted that in the rapidly expanding industrial town of Birmingham more than half of the workers were not natives: 'many of them are foreigners, but the greatest part belong to the parishes of the neighbouring country'. Towns could not sustain their population, let alone increase it, without a constant influx of immigrants, whether from their immediate hinterland, or from further afield. The parish registers of many towns show that burials normally exceeded baptisms. Towns were centres of disease, as well as of more desirable things. They experienced, as we have seen when discussing the plague, mass epidemics, while they also experienced diseases which waged a steady war of attrition against urban populations. Some of these were directly connected with local environmental or industrial conditions: thus at Sheffield in the 1760s there was endemic mortality from a pulmonary complaint known locally as 'grinder's lung'.

Reconstructing patterns of migration is difficult, not least because urban immigrants were often drawn from the poorest, and hence least well documented, sections of society. There were also marked regional and chronological variations, and differences dictated by the size and function of the town in question. Nevertheless, a number of detailed studies of migration into towns have been completed. One of the earliest of these was Peter Clark's work on migration into a sample of Kentish towns over the period 1580–1640. At Canterbury, to take an extreme example, only 9.6 per cent of Clark's sample had been born in the city and had never moved outside it. Forty-one per cent had arrived there from other settlements in Kent, and 28.5 per cent of its inhabitants came from outside the county. Later work on a widespread sample of towns reveals that high mobility was still present around 1700. At that date, perhaps one-half to two-thirds of an average town's residents would be immigrants moving an average of 25 miles if male, a little less if female, to reach their new home. Typically, urban populations contained a disproportionately high number of women. Urban centres offered country girls and older women numerous employment opportunities as domestic servants, and consequently in some towns women exceeded men by a ratio of five to four. With either sex, however, the motives for migration to the town were varied. For richer, usually literate, migrants, often travelling slightly longer distances than the poor, the move to the town represented realistic prospects of betterment. Professionals and tradesmen anxious to expand their business, or gentlemen's sons apprenticed to rich merchants, were typical of this group. For the poor, migration was a more desperate process. Mostly they were lured by better employment prospects, but the baseline of their expectations was a low one: many of them were 'subsistence migrants', forced out of their home village by stark poverty and turning to the town in hopes of finding something to keep them going.

The economic fortunes of urban centres in fact varied enormously. In 1550 many of the older towns, notably Canterbury, Coventry, Gloucester, Shrewsbury and York, were undergoing severe problems. The early Tudor era was something of a crisis period for these and a number of other centres which had flourished in the Middle Ages. Some remained perdurable throughout our period, despite having a traditional economic base: Norwich, for example, or Colchester, both centres of textile manufacture. But by the end of the seventeenth century the new industrial centres of the midlands and the north were making their presence felt. Their most rapid growth, and their decisive contributions to English life, were to come after 1760: yet early eighteenth-century observers were well aware that England's urban centre of gravity was shifting. Newcastle-upon-Tyne, its wealth based on ever booming coal shipments to London, grew from around 16,000 inhabitants in the 1660s to 29,000 in the mid-eighteenth century. Leeds grew from 7000–8000 in 1700 to 28,000 in 1750, after which date it symbolized its local economic pre-eminence with the foundation of two cloth halls in 1755 and 1758. Over the same timespan Birmingham increased in size from 7000–8000 to 24,000. Manchester, that great 'storm city' of the Industrial Revolution, was still comparatively small in 1750, with a population of perhaps 9000, but it was already exercising a growing regional influence both through its own economic development and that of the belt of satellite towns which surrounded it.

It was not only the industrial centres which were growing in the early eighteenth century. Increased commercial activity meant that ports were also booming. Bristol increased in population from 12,000 to 20,000 during the seventeenth century, and by 1750 had reached perhaps 50,000. Liverpool numbered a mere 5000 in 1700, although even at that point it was experiencing rapid proportional growth: Defoe, visiting the town in 1705, thought that it had doubled in size since his previous visit of 1690, and its estimated population of 34,500 in 1773 suggests that this rapid rate of growth was maintained. There were some less familiar success stories. The most dramatic of these was the rise of Whitehaven, in Cumberland. Whitehaven owed its eighteenth-century expansion to the interest taken in it in the 1670s and 1680s by the Lowthers, a local coal-owning gentry family. The port benefited from a very active trade, notably in coal, with Ireland, and also became involved in the colonial tobacco trade, re-exporting this product to Europe. By 1758 Whitehaven's merchant shipping outwards had reached a prodigious tonnage, more than Bristol, Hull and Liverpool combined, and it was not until the very end of the eighteenth century that Liverpool outstripped it in this respect. Maritime development, however, did not just involve trade. The expansion of the Royal Navy witnessed the burgeoning of dockyard towns. Deptford and Woolwich, on the Kentish bank of the Thames, were already thriving centres in the sixteenth century, while by the late seventeenth century the most important dockyard was at Chatham, a town which, like Deptford, had a population of about 5000 in 1700. By that date the new dockyard town of Portsmouth was rising fast, while other royal dockyards at Falmouth, Plymouth, Sheerness and Harwich were making an impact in their immediate regions. In a certain sense, the larger dockyard towns were the nearest things to real industrial centres in the early eighteenth century. The presence of a naval dockyard gave a marked economic specialization to Deptford, Plymouth and Chatham, while in all three of these towns something like one-half of the male workforce found employment in or around the dockyards in the early eighteenth century.

The first half of the eighteenth century also witnessed the arrival of a very different type of urban centre, the spas, those 'holiday camps for the magnates of the kingdom'.[1] Drinking spa water probably first became fashionable around 1600, perhaps in imitation of German or Netherlandish habits. By the end of the seventeenth century there were about a dozen spa towns of any significance, the chief of these being Epsom Wells, Tunbridge Wells, Buxton, Scarborough (where sea-bathing was first established as a fashionable pastime in the 1730s), and, of course, Bath. As early as 1698 a French visitor to Bath commented that 'thousands go thither to pass away a few weeks, without heeding the baths or the waters, but only to divert themselves with good company', and over the next half century the town rapidly expanded its facilities to accommodate such visitors. Its first playhouse was built in 1705, the first pump room in 1706, the first assembly room in 1708, the first ballroom in 1721, and the second assembly room in 1728. By that date the architect–developer John Wood had begun his earliest project, the building of the Queen's Square (completed in 1735), designed to educate polite society to promenade 'in decency and order'. Such qualities were further encouraged by the presence of Beau Nash, Master of Ceremonies in Bath from 1705 to 1761. In 1742 Nash, apparently half-humorously, promulgated his 'Eleven

Rules of Conduct', copies of which were posted in places of resort. These were to form the basis of the behaviour of people of fashion in this most fashionable of spa towns.

But the spas were only the most obvious examples of a more general tendency for towns to develop as regional capitals, combining their functions as administrative centres and the locations of various services with a new role of arenas of conspicuous consumption. It was this tendency, above all, which allowed many of the older urban centres to revive their fortunes. York, for example, had by 1650 become virtually deindustrialized with the demise of its textile industry. Yet from about this date it emerged as a county capital in a new sense. In 1736 its historian Francis Drake noted that 'what has been, and is, the chief support of the city at present, is the resort to and residence of several country gentlemen and their families in it'. He remarked on the reasons why they came: 'the great variety of provisions, with which our markets abound, makes it very easy to furnish out an elegant table at a moderate rate'; the city's educational facilities, especially for girls; 'the diversions which have been of late years set on foot, and are now busily carried on every winter in the city', among them the Monday night assembly for cards and dancing, the Friday night 'musick assembly', and the stage plays acted regularly by 'the best strollers in the kingdom'. To these were added the social gatherings which attended the biennial assizes, and the 'horse-racing, balls, assemblies, &c' of the summer. Drake thought that 'the politeness of the gentlemen, the richness of the dress, and the remarkable beauty of the ladies' at York could not be equalled anywhere in Europe, but similar sights were to be seen in a number of other provincial towns: Beverley, Bury St Edmunds, Lichfield, Preston, Shrewsbury and, above all, Norwich. In this last city, whose population increased from perhaps 13,000 to 30,000 over the seventeenth century, all of the attributes of a provincial capital were added to the firm economic base provided by a durable textile industry.

The arrival of the town as a leisure centre for the local élite is almost certainly connected with a slackening of those social tensions which seemed to be so marked to many observers in the century before 1660. Over this century, one of the most persistent features of urban life was worry over what to do about the poor. Hearth-tax returns from the 1660s and 1670s, with their details of exemptions from payment on grounds of poverty, give some statistical impression of the extent of urban deprivation. In Colchester, 52 per cent of households were exempted, in Norwich 62 per cent, in the small Essex weaving town of Bocking a staggering 81 per cent. But by the 1660s the urban poor, like their rural counterparts, had become in large measure institutionalized. Their standard mode of self-expression, the riot, was common enough, but it was rarely really threatening or of long duration, and by the late seventeenth century operated in a context of general social stability. By that time the demarcation between areas where the rich and poor lived was becoming increasingly strong. Social zoning was not as complete as it is today, and the rich were not fully insulated from the life of the poor. Nevertheless, there was already a tendency towards a rough dichotomy between rich and poor urban areas. The poor, especially the newly arrived migrant poor, clustered in suburbs outside the city walls or in areas on the edge of the town: Sandgate at Newcastle, St Sidwell's in Exeter, St Giles' at Norwich, where 41 per cent of the population were listed as being poor in one Elizabethan survey. Conversely, the rich inhabited fashionable areas near the city centre: in parishes around the cathedral at Norwich, where the same survey revealed that only 7 or 8 per cent of the inhabitants were in poverty, in the 'upper town' at Lincoln, or in favoured parishes near the middle of York. Towns were still too small for such divisions to be entirely meaningful, but the divergence between rich and poor areas added to the worries of urban government.

One method by which those controlling that government sought to both publicize and confirm the social hierarchy was through the medium of public civic ritual. The Reformation had dealt a body blow to those already declining medieval celebrations of civic solidarity, the old Corpus Christi plays and processions. The medieval ideal of the inward-looking civic commonwealth with its local culture and local pride uniting social groups within the town was waning. Its place was being taken by the oligarchic rule of urban patriciates, acting more or less in tune with the demands of central government. The traditional notions of the 'unity, concord and amity' of the civic body were replaced by something like modern notions of class. But from the late seventeenth century it is possible to trace a revival of interest in civic ritual. To some extent this revival was connected with a desire to amuse or incorporate the lower orders, while some of the newly invented customs, such as the Godiva procession inaugurated at Coventry in 1678, were clearly connected with the new role of towns as leisure centres. Yet the most persistent theme, implicit or explicit, of this revived ceremonial was a glorification of the civic élite. In Norwich, to take a well-documented example, a grandiose mayoral inauguration ceremony was introduced in the late seventeenth century, probably in direct emulation of the Lord Mayor's Show in London. There was an elaborate procession, which by the early eighteenth century was enlivened by such spectacles as a massive model dragon, and a feast. In the 1690s Celia Fiennes noted that when the mayor was chosen, the citizens 'new wash and plaster their houses', while the neighbours of the incoming mayor were 'very exact' in beautifying their houses and in 'hanging up flags the colour of their companies, and dress up pageants, and there are plays and all sorts of shows that day'. Despite popular participation, it is difficult not to interpret such ceremonies as displays of social ascendancy by an increasingly self-confident urban élite. This mood was also conveyed by the construction of special mansions for the mayor, as at Newcastle in 1691 or York in 1724–30.

Perhaps the most elusive problem presented by the early modern town, however, is the degree to which life there constituted something qualitatively distinct. The town was considered as something apart by many contemporaries. In the late sixteenth century the legend of Dick Whittington became popular, suggesting that the capital at least was seen as a symbol of upward social mobility, while Elizabethan ballads with countrymen being duped by the faster-witted townsman point to a growing cultural awareness of the dichotomy between urban and rural life. By the middle of the eighteenth century many observers were elaborating on this theme. Thus William Hutton, on his first visit to Birmingham in 1741, professed himself to be 'surprised at the place but more at the people. They were a species I had never seen. They possessed a vivacity I never beheld. I had been among dreamers, but now I saw men awake'. Yet despite such comments, it is difficult to imagine that either the size or the nature of the early modern town were really sufficiently unique to persuade dwellers or visitors that they were being confronted by a completely different way of life. Norwich, if we may take the second largest English city of the time, had 30,000 inhabitants in 1693, of whom 90.5 per cent lived within the city walls, Norwich having the largest walled area of any provincial town. Even so, there were fields and grazing lands within the walls which, together with the flower gardens of the more prosperous artisans, gave even England's second largest city an essentially rural ethos. Thomas Fuller described Norwich as 'either a city in an orchard or an orchard in a city, so equally are houses and trees blended in it, so that the pleasures of the country and the populousness of the city meet here together'. The nature of interpersonal relations within towns in this period is a subject which awaits intensive work but it seems likely that in many urban centres face-to-face contacts were still the norm, and there is little sign of that anonymity which is so often advanced as an attribute of urban life. Only the nation's capital constituted a large enough urban mass for people to lose themselves in.

London: the growth of a metropolis

In 1550 London was the largest city in England and the only English town worthy of note by European standards. Its growth over the next two centuries was phenomenal. In 1550 its population stood at some 120,000. By 1600 it had risen to 200,000, by 1650 to 375,000, by 1700 to 490,000, by 1750 to 675,000, at which point London overtook Constantinople as Europe's largest city. The rise was not self-sustaining. London, like other early modern cities, suffered heavy mortality, with burials regularly outstripping baptisms in its parish registers. The population increase was caused by immigration: by the mid-eighteenth century, observers concurred that only one-third or one-quarter of the capital's population were London born. Some of the newcomers were foreign. There were already 5650 known alien residents by 1583, and large waves of immigrants arrived subsequently, Huguenots after 1685 and Irish and Ashkenazic Jews in the early eighteenth century. Generally, though, immigrants came from every corner of England, 8000 of them a year on average in the later seventeenth century. Despite the regular high mortality, and the terrible periodic epidemics typified by the Great Plague of 1665, the inhabitants of the capital grew ever more numerous. By 1750 nearly one in eight of England's population lived there.

The increase in population was matched by a growth in London's geographical extent. The sixteenth-century population increase was largely confined within the city walls, but after that date most of the new arrivals to London were housed in its suburbs. In the seventeenth century the population of the City of London proper remained stable, and may even have fallen, but the areas to the east of the city, to the north, between the Cities of London and Westminster, and south of the Thames around Southwark, all grew rapidly. In 1560 73 per cent of London's population lived in the City, a proportion which had fallen to 24 per cent in 1680. By that date, 32 per cent lived in the eastern suburbs, while the northern suburbs, those to the west, and those south of the river could each claim about 14 per cent. Some of the suburban parishes increased their populations rapidly: Stepney, for example, experienced a thirteen-fold expansion in the two centuries before 1795. In 1550 London was still essentially a medieval city, concentrated in, or immediately around, its walls. By 1760 it was a massive metropolitan centre. A map drawn in 1708, after the great seventeenth-century development, shows a continuous built-up area to the north of the Thames from Westminster in the west to Limehouse in the east. The spread northwards was already sending tentacles of building up the roads towards Islington and Hoxton, while on the south bank building was continuous from Southwark to Rotherhithe, and the riverside towns of Deptford and Greenwich were being sucked into the capital's orbit.

As might be imagined, the social topography of an area of this size was very varied. The more fashionable parts of the City itself were favoured as places of residence by the traditional merchant élite, and City parishes show that polarity between rich and poor areas which we have noted in provincial towns. The later seventeenth century saw the arrival of an important new development: the rise of the West End. After the Great Fire of 1666 the existing trend for civil servants, courtiers, and peers and gentry resident in the capital to move to large mansions to the west of the City became more marked. The way had been pointed by that early experiment in town planning, the development of Covent Garden by the Earl of Bedford and Inigo Jones. After the Civil War people of honour and quality began to settle in large numbers in Mayfair and St James's, and by the early eighteenth century there existed a firm differentiation between the mercantile City and the fashionable West End. At the same time the poorer suburbs, notably Southwark and what was to become the East End, grew in size and acquired a distinctly proletarian flavour. Attempts to check the growth of London were continual before 1660, evidence, among other things, of the constant anxiety which the growth of the suburbs caused the city fathers. By that date their control over the sprawling areas around the City was in many ways tenuous.

Life for the poor newcomer to these areas could be hard. Then, as now, London acted as a magnet for the rootless and the workless. The streets may have been paved with less desirable substances than gold, but wages were high (in some trades maybe twice as high as in some parts of the country) and employment prospects were more numerous and more varied. Even so, the constant influx of new immigrants meant that competition for cheap accommodation and unskilled jobs was high. Finding somewhere to live was a major problem for new arrivals. Many lived for a few pence weekly in common lodging-houses, outbuildings, or sheds set in out-of-the-way courts. London possessed its solid core of artisans: Spitalfields weavers, Southwark tanners, or the serious-minded heads of household whose dismay at immorality around Tower Hamlets led to the formation of the Societies for The Reformation of Manners in the 1690s. But it also possessed its underclass of criminals and prostitutes. The degradation and criminal proclivities of London's population, especially under the impact of the mass consumption of gin from the 1720s, have been exaggerated, both by respectable contemporaries and popular historians. Yet it is no accident that the early eighteenth century experienced not only commercial development, but also the rise of England's first great criminal entrepreneur, Jonathan Wild, the 'Thief Taker General'. Wild's career, which ended on the gallows in 1725, would have been impossible outside of a context of widespread corruption and widespread organized crime. Arguably, it would also have been impossible outside of a context of burgeoning metropolitan development.

The capital was not only attractive to the poor or potentially criminal immigrant. One of the remarkable qualities of London was that it was the city in which a number of nationally important institutions were concentrated. It was, obviously, uniquely large. It was also the place where uniquely large merchant fortunes were to be made, where the land market was centred, and where substantial amounts of credit could be raised. That great magnet for people of fashion, the royal court, was located there, as were the centres of legal activity, the superior courts of common law and equity. The Inns of Court and other educational institutions meant that the sons and, after 1650, the daughters of the wealthy were educated there. And London was, uniquely, the national focal point for the arts, for literature, and for taste and fashion. The sons of the gentry and of the patricians of provincial towns were apprenticed to wealthy London merchants. The parents of these youths flooded into the capital in search of patronage, fortunate marriages, or the latest designs in clothes or furniture, or to see the latest play or launch the latest law suit. By the early seventeenth century, despite repeated royal proclamations urging the gentry to return to the countryside, something like the London season had emerged. The Duchess of Newcastle remembered how her sisters had spent their time in the capital during the reign of Charles I:

> Their customs were in the winter time to go sometimes to plays or to ride in their coaches about the streets to see the concourse and recourse of people, and in the springtime to visit Hyde Park and the like places, and sometimes would have music and a cup in barges upon the water.

Such a routine, albeit with greater elaborations, would not have been out of place in the eighteenth century: by that date London had become a very large centre of leisure and taste for the rich.

The presence of the royal court, of educational and legal facilities, of places of entertainment and, above all, of the London season, meant that the capital's economy was heavily dependent upon the leisure and service industries. There were endless openings for domestic servants and for innumerable others, from sedan-chair operators to brothel-keepers, whose living depended upon the disposable income of the rich. But London's economic functions, despite some contemporary comment, were by no means purely parasitic. Its importance to the nation's trade could hardly be overstated. England's economic transition from semi-colonial status on the peripheries of Europe to world commercial power was essentially a London-based phenomenon. London dominated the cloth trade as it emerged from the wreck of the Antwerp entrepôt late in the sixteenth century, London merchants benefited massively from the first boom in American trade of 1620–40, and then benefited even more massively from the real take-off of overseas trade which came after 1660. The metropolis was also a centre of industrial production. The clothing trades were the most important, employing perhaps 20 per cent of the capital's male workforce around 1700. Leather workers, metal workers and building workers were also numerous, especially in the suburbs. There guild regulations and other controls were weak, and in consequence many artisans set up among the sprawling courts and tenements. Taking the seventeenth century as a whole, nearly three-quarters of the male workforce in the suburbs were involved in manufacturing, and their products were sold nationally. Others founded large enterprises to service the growing needs of London's population: one of the most typical, and most enduring, of these enterprises was the brewing firm over which Samuel Whitbread had established complete control by 1761.

Another vital facet of London's economic importance was its role as a consumer of goods produced in the provinces. The needs of the metropolis had, by 1760, forced something like a national market on England. The consequences of this process, the complaints of some contemporaries again notwithstanding, were mainly beneficial.

Regional economies were stimulated by London's demand. 'There is not an acre of land in the country, be it never so distant,' remarked Sir George Davenant in 1695, 'that is not to some degree bettered by the growth, trade and riches of that city.' Statistics underline such claims. In 1579 the capital imported 17,380 quarters of grain, mainly from Kent. In 1638 the total had risen to 95,714 quarters, with Essex and East Anglia added to the supplying areas. By 1750 London imported 1,275,700 quarters drawn from a more or less national market. By that date Londoners consumed annually 101,000 beeves, 702,000 muttons, and 180,000 hogs, cattle in particular being sent down from as far away as the Lake District and fattened in East Anglia or the outskirts of the capital before being slaughtered and consumed there. Coal imports were also massive, and coal owners and shippers alike in the north-east benefited from the ever-expanding metropolitan market. John Evelyn might complain of the 'hellish and dismall cloud of sea-coale' that hung over the capital, but it symbolized the integration of Newcastle and Sunderland, of Tyneside and County Durham, into the national economy. London also stimulated agricultural production in the Home Counties. Numerous market gardens grew up around the capital, aiding both the spread of capitalist farming and the diversification of the region's agriculture. Some of London's businessmen offered contracts for agricultural produce, among them Samuel Whitbread the brewer, who bought Hertfordshire grain and Kentish hops. Fruiterers established, and then leased, orchards, while butchers became graziers. Increasingly, traditional, personal forms of marketing in the capital were replaced by a process whereby small-scale producers, often distant from London, were joined to the consumer through middlemen. Thus the growth of the capital played a vital part in the rise of the entrepreneurial spirit.

The image of a socially mobile, fluid, and in large measure cosmopolitan London does raise the question of how far any sense of 'community', or indeed any sense of corporate identity, was present in the capital. This question has at least been posited for the Elizabethan period by Ian Archer, author of one of a number of excellent recent studies of the metropolis in our period. Archer stresses that, whatever the experience in individual neighbourhoods in the capital, London's government in the sixteenth century was unrelentingly oligarchic. The executive government of the City was invested in the Court of Aldermen, one for each of the City's wards, who held office for life. The Aldermen controlled the overall administration of the city, while the senior aldermen and the recorder (London's senior legal official) sat as justices of the peace and tried the capital's criminals. The Court of Aldermen filled gaps in its ranks as they arose by recruiting nominees from the wards, whom they had powers to reject, while the tradition that aldermen should come from one of

London's 12 great livery companies was normally respected (in the Elizabethan period most aldermen were also members of the Merchant Adventurers Company). These selection processes, and the realities of the expenses which holding civic office brought to an individual, meant that membership of London's aldermanic élite was the preserve of the wealthy. Responsibility for approving civic legislation and local taxation resided in the common council, whose membership numbered 212. These tended to serve for lengthy periods (an average of eight years in one sample ward), came from the more wealthy artisanal or tradesmen householders, and again tended to be drawn from the 12 great livery companies. Common councillors were formally elected by freedmen at the wardmote, but were frequently nominees of the sitting aldermen. The liverymen, some 10 per cent of London's householders in the reign of Elizabeth, had the right to vote for the Lord Mayor, for the City's sheriffs, and for members of parliament. This system was virtually unchallenged in the late sixteenth century: potential constitutional or factional problems had been ironed out in the late middle ages (the fourteenth century had been an especially contentious period in London politics), and even the potential for religious dispute in Elizabethan England did not disrupt the unity of purpose of the civic élite (this was to change in the seventeenth century).

Beneath these oligarchic governmental structures, most Londoners, certainly the adult male ones, lived in an interlocking network of institutional 'communities' formed by the parish, the ward and the livery companies. This network might at times produce a conflict of loyalties, not least because membership of a livery company implied involvement in a community of interests which was not as obviously geographical as was membership of a parish. But these institutions did have a useful function in channelling grievances among the capital's artisans which might otherwise have led them into direct confrontation with the capital's governors.

Obviously, in London as elsewhere, a sense of community should not be assumed on the grounds of the mere existence of institutions of communal organization, but in London such institutions were of prime importance and their functioning provides important clues as to what 'community' might have meant in the metropolis. This was especially true because in London, as in rural parishes, such governmental concerns as the levying of troops, the collection of many taxes and the enforcement of social regulations depended upon the co-operation of unpaid local amateur officials: in many respects, London's wards and parishes were self-regulating entities. One of the major developments of the sixteenth century was the emergence of the parish vestry as the key institution in London government, and by 1638 more than half of London's 109 vestries were select: in effect, the oligarchic central government of the capital was being replicated in its component parts. What this meant varied from parish to parish: obviously, a select vestry (like the very notion of community) meant different things in one of London's tiny inner-city parishes of 80 households from what it meant in, for example, St Olave's Southwark, where the vestrymen governed 1800 households. In general, however, the tendency was for vestrymen to be selected from the richer householders, many of whom would have previously served as constables or as other parish officers.

In many respects, the poor were only institutionally integrated into London society as recipients of charity. Yet there is ample evidence that many Londoners, the poor among them, appealed on appropriate occasions to a rhetoric of neighbourhood and community: defamation suits from London, for example, demonstrate a concern for honour and reputation as strong as that found in the 'face-to-face' rural settlement, and hence throw doubts on the supposed anonymity of the metropolis. And, as might be expected, the city authorities faced by potential unrest or dissidence were prone to deploy a language of communal solidarity and shared interests in their efforts to pacify the citizenry. That they were, in the Elizabethan period at least, normally succesful in this is perhaps evidence that this perception of civic solidarity was in some respects shared by the ruled, many of whom, as we have seen, were in any case integrated into parish-government structures.

Whatever the situation in Elizabeth's reign, by the mid-eighteenth century (and, indeed, for some time before) people were convinced that London was somehow unique. The experience of living in one of the largest agglomerations of human beings in Europe was thought by many to be qualitatively different from living in smaller units. Certainly the metropolis presented unique difficulties of control. The old élite of aldermen and common councillors, traditional in their views, oligarchic in their ethos, their supremacy symbolized annually in the Lord Mayor's Show, were in large measure unable to exert their influence over the massive expansion which took place outside the walls of the city. From the time of Defoe onwards calls were made for a body to co-ordinate the government of the metropolitan area. The middle of the eighteenth century saw the first steps towards the new municipal world of paving schemes and lighting projects, but anything very effective in such developments lay some way in the future. London remained in its government, its economic structure and in much else still essentially a preindustrial town. Even in 1760 open countryside lay only a little over an hour's walk from St Paul's, while in all but the most select areas the sights, sounds and above all smells of the capital were essentially rural. It is to this rural world, the mosaic of villages in which three-quarters of England's population still lived in 1760, that we now turn.

The village community

Over the last two decades a number of studies have been published dealing with the histories of specific rural communities. Their intent has been not merely to follow any narrow local or antiquarian line of approach, but rather to illustrate the macrocosm of national history through the microcosm of the individual village, and to explore more closely the social context in which that mass of human beings who so often receive little more than a passing mention in the history books lived out their lives. Writing such studies has been facilitated not only by changing attitudes among historians as to what the subject matter of their discipline might be, but also little less than a revolution in consciousness of the potential value of certain categories of local record. A number of these, notably parish registers, manorial records, wills and probate documents have been used not merely for genealogical research but also for the systematic reconstruction of community life. A growing number of settlements have been subjected to detailed research: Wigston Magna in Leicestershire, investigated in an important pioneering work by W.G. Hoskins; the contrasting Cambridgeshire communities of Chippenham, Orwell and Willingham; Myddle in Shropshire, where a remarkable history written around 1700 by one of the inhabitants, Richard Gough, formed an invaluable basis for further research; Terling in Essex; Knibworth Harcourt in Leicestershire, subject of a study ranging over the period 1280–1700; Earls Colne in Essex and Kirkby Lonsdale in Westmorland, investigated in a massive research project headed by Alan Macfarlane; and a number of other settlements, like Kelvedon Easterford in Essex or Keevil in Wiltshire, which have formed the basis of less-ambitious studies. The histories of these and other villages have permitted the construction of much more detailed impressions of what life in the preindustrial community was like.

One point which emerges readily from such histories is that the preindustrial village was not the static community of historical and sociological received wisdom. Early investigation of two midland villages, Clayworth in Nottinghamshire and Cogenhoe in Northamptonshire, demonstrated this. Through the unusual medium of contemporary parish listings, few of which survive, it was established that of 180 individuals living at Cogenhoe in 1628, 94, or 52 per cent, had arrived since 1618. At Clayworth, there was a turnover of population of 61.8 per cent in the 12 years between 1676 and 1688. This situation was not new in the seventeenth century: at Knibworth Harcourt, the maximum period of population turnover seems to have been the early fifteenth century. Similarly, although there were variations between regions, or even neighbouring parishes, the pattern was a national one. In Kirkby Lonsdale preliminary work suggests that hardly any farms were owned by the same family over the period 1642–1800, while at Earls Colne of 274 pieces of property listed in a rental for two manors in 1677 only 23 had been held by the same family in 1589. The idea that the preindustrial village possessed a stable population, and that preindustrial society was characterized by low geographical mobility must, therefore, be discarded. The average rate of turnover was not volatile (some 5 per cent annually in Clayworth and

Cogenhoe) and most new arrivals were probably immigrants from other villages in the area. Nevertheless, it is clear that the population of rural England was a mobile one. The early modern village may have been a face-to-face society, but the faces were constantly changing.

Another factor undermining any preconceptions about the stability of the Tudor or Stuart village was the increased social stratification of the period. English peasant society had always been stratified, but during the sixteenth and seventeenth centuries steady population growth and the gradual impact of agrarian capitalism meant that village society became increasingly polarized. There was a stratum of comfortably-off yeoman farmers and master craftsmen on the one hand, and a much larger body of labouring poor on the other. The process affected some settlements earlier than others. In Myddle and Wigston Magna marked stratification was not visible until the early eighteenth century; in Terling and Chippenham it was complete by the early seventeenth; in Willingham, where the peculiarities of the fenland economy permitted the survival of smallholdings, it had little impact. Individual case histories illustrate the main lines of change in many parishes. At Chippenham, there were 66 tenants in 1544. Of these 31 held two or more acres (10 of them above 50), 14 held less than two acres, and 21 were landless. By 1712 this pattern had changed. Thirty-one tenants held no land, five held less than two acres, and the remaining land was held by 13 tenants, nine of them farming those large holdings of 50 acres or more which would allow a family to survive the worst of bad harvests.

At Terling, taxation records allow us to trace much the same pattern. The lay subsidy of 1524–25 shows that at that date Terling possessed nine gentry and large farmers worth over £10 a year, a middling group of yeomen and substantial craftsmen worth £2–£8 annually, a group of 18 husbandmen and lesser craftsmen worth £2 in goods, and 21 labourers and cottagers worth less than £2 in land or annual earnings. The hearth-tax returns of 1671 reveal a different pattern. Seventy-six men were taxed in 1524–25, 122 households in 1671. The proportion of rich villagers had dropped slightly, from 11.8 per cent to 8.2 per cent of those taxed, but more marked changes occurred among the middling groups and the poor. In the earlier period, the two middling groups had formed 60.5 per cent of taxpayers, and labourers and cottagers 27.6 per cent. By 1671 the two middling groups represented 31 per cent of those assessed, the labouring poor and those exempted from the tax on grounds of poverty 50.8 per cent. Even in Terling the polarization of village society was not absolute, yet the fact that it had progressed markedly since the early sixteenth century was undeniable.

This polarization, this more marked social stratification, had implications beyond the purely economic dimension of differing levels of wealth. Local government officials, such as constables, churchwardens and overseers of the poor, were drawn overwhelmingly from the upper strata of village society. In Terling, for example, yeomen and wealthy craftsmen provided over half of the churchwardens, overseers of the poor, sessions jurors and manorial jurors, with the labouring poor being effectively excluded from these offices. Second, and more contentiously, it has been argued that a religious and cultural divide came to reinforce this divergence in wealth and power. Keith Wrightson and David Levine have argued that in Terling the richer villagers were more likely to welcome Puritan ideas, were more likely to be literate, and came increasingly to identify with the values of their social superiors rather than with those of the village community. The divergence was not merely between the rich and the poor, but between the respectable and the rough. How far this 'Terling model' is of universal applicability has been questioned, and it does seem likely that the village was unusual both in the precocity of its social polarization and (thanks to the presence of an active Puritan minister) the godliness of its more substantial inhabitants. Nevertheless, the economic and cultural fissures opened up during the sixteenth and seventeenth centuries in so many villages make it unwise to discuss 'the village community' in any simplistic manner. Indeed, by 1750 it is more tenable to talk in terms of two cultures in the normal village, one of the prosperous farmers and one of the labouring poor.

Further complications in discussing life in the early modern village arise from another factor: the nature of contemporary interpersonal relationships. As we have noted, one of the central presuppositions of nineteenth-century sociology was that idyllic social relationships had existed in the countryside before the advent of the Industrial Revolution. This view, sometimes degenerating into some soggy notion of 'Merrie England', has become firmly embedded in popular thinking. More recently, some historians have propounded a much more pessimistic view of the nature of human relations in the early modern village. A particularly extreme position was taken by Lawrence Stone, whose discussion of human nature around 1600 offers a very gloomy portrait of human relationships. Stone found a 'lack of warmth and tolerance ... at the village level', and a social environment where 'interpersonal relations were at best cold and at worst hostile'. He concluded that 'the Elizabethan village was a place filled with malice and hatred, its only unifying bond being the occasional episode of mass hysteria which bound together the majority in order to harry and persecute the local witch'.[2] Thus even without the divisive effects of social stratification, in Stone's opinion relations between English villagers were far from idyllic. Places where the only unifying bonds are episodic outbreaks of hysteria against deviants are not very pleasant to live in.

As we shall argue, this extremely pessimistic view about human relations within the early modern village is an essentially inaccurate and oversimplified one. Even so, the study of such rare gems as Richard Gough's *History of Myddle*, or of the more common if also more prosaic records of local courts, does provide examples enough of tensions within village communities. Witchcraft accusations, which will be dealt with at length in a later chapter, were commonly the product of a breakdown of neighbourly relations between the witch and her accuser. Other, if less dramatic, products of personal tension also entered the legal record. Scolding, like witchcraft a predominantly female activity, pointed to the existence of disruptive individuals and disruptive behaviour within the community. Scolds presented before the Archdeacon of Durham in 1600, to take a typical sample, included Isabel Remission, 'a verrey idle scolde & a disquieter of her neighbours with malicious speeches'; Mary Taylor of Auckland, who 'by her evill & rayling temper misusethe & formethe dissension amonge hir neighbours'; and two women from Denton presented because they were 'uncharitable scoldes & disquiet their neighbours'. Here we have those agents of communal strife so central to Stone's argument. Yet, conversely, we also have evidence which leads to a more optimistic view of the early modern villager. After all, the prosecution of scolds, like that of witches, drunkards, slanderers or the sexually immoral, only makes sense in a context where a clearly defined view of proper standards of behaviour, and of proper human relationships, exists. This might, under certain circumstances, add up to a 'tyranny of local opinion'.[3] Conversely, even in that case, it negates the interpretation which would portray early modern villagers as mutually antagonistic atoms.

Such issues are relevant to the most dramatic manifestation of community intolerance of deviant behaviour, the English variants of that European-wide phenomenon, the *charivari*. In England, the *charivari*, known variously as the skimmington, as riding the stang, or simply as a riding, normally took the form of group action, most often by male villagers, against those who were held to have infringed community norms. Usually the norms in question were those involving wifely subordination: husbands who neglected their position of authority so thoroughly as to allow their wives to beat them were the persons most often satirized in a riding. The form of the ritual varied, but a number of basic elements were usually present. Two men, one of them dressed as a woman, acted out the domestic discord in question. They would be carried sitting on a pole (the 'stang') as they did so, supported by other men, parading outside the house of their victims, often accompanied by other villagers beating pots and pans and producing a cacophony known as 'rough music'. The riding could sometimes be a product of more complex issues than might be apparent in the mere mechanics of the ritual, while it was occasionally sanctioned by the local élite. Even so, it seems incontrovertible that its fundamental function was to express and enforce collective standards against those who were felt to have infringed them, while its participants came overwhelmingly from the lower orders, perhaps from the rough rather than the respectable elements in the village. The intensity of the emotions which a riding could engender (if we may be permitted to use an urban example) can be gauged from an incident at Leeds in 1667, when the husband being satirized fired a shotgun into the crowd outside his house and killed two people. The 'tyranny of local opinion' could, at times, be very real.

As the riding or skimmington suggests, the notions of reputation and honour were central to the relationship between the individual and the community. As well as the concept of capital as an economic category, students of the preindustrial world would do well to ponder on the existence of the symbolic capital enshrined in good name or reputation. Such a notion would have been seen as being of fundamental importance by the early modern villager: it is, for example, instructive that the word 'credit' was still being used not just in its economic sense, but also in the sense of reputation or standing. Privacy was an unfamiliar concept: people were always, in a certain sense, on show, and conduct was evaluated through neighbourly comment and gossip. The prevalence of defamation suits in local courts suggests that a touchiness about reputation had penetrated far down the social scale and the way in which breaches of what was thought to be proper conduct might be commented on through public satire suggests a world in which shaming was seen as a means of social control. Villagers made rude rhymes about their neighbour's failings, and put them up in public places. Thus in 1618 at Bremhill, Wiltshire, 11 people put together a 36-line poem about one of their neighbours. They posted copies at strategic points in the parish, invited people in to hear the verses sung in alehouses, distributed them in nearby villages and in the local market town, and even asked the minister to read them in church after evening prayer (he refused). Specific and unusual deviant acts might prompt specific and unusual community satires. At Westonbirt, Gloucester, villagers reacted in 1716 to rumours of homosexual acts between George Andrews, the lord of the manor's bailiff, and a youth from Gloucester, by enacting a 'groaning'. This took the form of a mock birth, the child being represented by 'a wad of straw made up and dressed with clothes in that form', a parody of the christening ceremony, and a mock christening feast which was attended by 100 people from Westonbirt and the adjacent parishes. This incident, which was unusually well documented, obviously has to be interpreted in part in the context of the relations between the lord of the manor and his tenants. Nevertheless, it does demonstrate how affronts to popular moral standards could provoke apposite acts of community satire.

Yet such acts, along with the mocking rhyme, the defamation suit, the skimmington, even the witchcraft accusation, were only comprehensible in a world in which ideas about proper behaviour were clearly defined and thought to be generalized enough to make attempts to uphold them desirable and viable. Perhaps the most useful summation of these ideas resides in the concept of neighbourliness. Connected as it was with the Christian idea of living in charity with one's fellows, the concept of neighbourliness provided a useful working model upon which the evaluation of interpersonal conduct, of the behaviour of one's fellow humans, could be based.

The concept is difficult to define with precision, although its main attributes were probably those set out by Keith Wrightson:[4] residential propinquity, obviously, but also a few other things; mutual recognition of reciprocal obligations; a level of consensus over proper behaviour between neighbours; and some idea of a neighbourly relationship being horizontal, of there being some rough equality between neighbour and neighbour which transcended any detailed differences in wealth or status. The smooth running of neighbourly relations was less likely to figure in the historical record than those occasions when such relations broke down. But we can see the concept in its reality on a general level in those parish feasts or Whitsun ales which survived the Reformation, in such glimpses as we have of villagers chatting and drinking together in the alehouse, or when documents show them working with or gossiping about each other. Neighbourly tensions existed, but they were not characteristic, nor were they seen as being part of the desirable order of things.

This last point is supported by evidence of reactions to the neighbours locked in conflict. Thus in the early 1560s, when the Yorkshire settlement of Kirkby Overblows was disrupted by a feud between two of its inhabitants, it was observed that other residents 'did grudge and were much offended at the malice and hatred and disagreement betwixt the parties'. Three decades later two Yorkshirewomen at odds in a defamation suit were urged by their neighbours to reconcile their differences, one of the would-be mediators declaring that 'I would to God that yow two were frendes, for this is not the beste meanes neighbours one to sue another'. Similarly, scraps of evidence from wills point to the presence of strong ideals of friendship and neighbourliness. Taking other Yorkshire examples, we find Ann Richardson, a widow from Wistow, leaving another widow in the parish a cow in 1658, 'for her care and paines taken about me in my sicknesse', or Matthew Newcome, a tailor from Ricall, leaving a woman 'three shillings in respect of her diligence and care she hath taken with mee and hath been ready to doe earants and run for mee here and there'.

Despite all the evidence of tensions, it is obvious that people did have a sense of mutual obligations, of neighbourliness and affection towards their fellow human beings, and a clearly defined notion of proper human conduct. The early modern village, sometimes hostile to deviants, often wary of strangers, increasingly riven by a growing economic and cultural rift between rich and poor, should not be romanticized. Yet its inhabitants were not locked in continual mutual antagonism. Many of them were well regarded by their neighbours, who evidently had a very precise idea of what constituted the good life. People setting the ideal were, perhaps, summed up by Thomas Hayward of Myddle. He was remembered by Richard Gough as 'a person well reputed in his country and of general acquaintance. Hee was just and faythfull in affirming or denying any matter of controversy, soe that less credit was given to some men's oathe than to his bare word'. Communities where such people set the moral and social tone obviously had more than hysteria against the local witch unifying them.

It is, therefore, possible at least to speculate about both long-term changes in the nature of community relationships and in the contemporary perceptions of such relationships. But throughout our period, it should be remembered, concepts of community, and those notions of neighbourliness which were so crucial to these concepts, were based upon the evaluation of individuals and, by extension, on some shared idea of what proper human conduct was, of what constituted a decent human being: we return to Thomas Hayward of Myddle, that 'well reputed' and 'just and faythfull' man. As we have argued, the early modern village or urban community was, to employ yet again that much used but still valuable term, a 'face-to-face' society where people were constantly on show, and where the 'symbolic capital' or 'credit' of an individual was of prime importance. In such a context, what sociologists have called the presentation of self in everyday life was a major concern: what people did, how they did it, and the language they and others used in justifying or discussing what was done were weighty matters. Historians are only just beginning to examine the problem of the history of the self, and how perceptions of the self and the presentation of the self interacted with a wider system of community values.

Gender will be crucial to any such examination. Gender has recently emerged as a major analytical tool among social and cultural historians, although theoretical positions on what gender is and how it might be employed by historians are in a constant state of flux, thus putting any short definition of the term at risk to charges of oversimplification. If we might risk such charges, it would seem that the main point is that whereas sex, broadly speaking, is biologically determined (that is, most human beings are, fairly clearly, male or female in biological terms), gender, as understood in recent hitory writing, is essentially culturally determined. Indeed, one of the major forces initiating the current interest in gender was the insistence during the 1970s of women's historians, and the women's movement in general, that many of the divisions of sex roles thought of as 'natural' were, in fact, social constructs rather than the outcome of biological differences between men and women. What is expected of or what is thought of as appropriate behaviour on the part of men and women, or boys and girls, can vary, sometimes enormously, between different societies, between different strata within societies, or over time. And, it should be stressed, gender incorporates both men and women, masculinity and femininity: 'gender' as an historical category or tool of analysis is not, despite the titles appearing on many a publisher's list or the content of many an undergraduate history course, a substitute for 'women'.

Thus in any historical context, not least in the early modern English village community, gender, shaped as it was by the power relationships between men and women, influenced belief systems, institutions, social roles, images of the male and the female, and masculine and feminine identities. Recent historical research has shown how gender operated at a number of levels: the psychic, the cognitive, the interpersonal and the institutional, and how the range of gender roles operated in a variety of different cultures and periods serving variously to maintain the social order in some or promote change in others. The lived experiences of men and women were in many respects differentiated by the reality of gender as a cultural force. Moreover, gender was not just what men or women did or what they experienced: it was how their actions or experiences acquired meaning through interaction with the scrutiny of other human beings, themselves accustomed, consciously or otherwise, to see their social world through a gendered sense of vision. Thus gender formed one of those symbolic systems through which human conduct can be evaluated, and accordingly should be regarded as a process, as something which had to be redefined, clarified and negotiated, rather than as a static entity. Gendered identity, it is becoming apparent as historians apply the concept of gender in their researches, was a fundamentally significant aspect of the presentation of the self and of the individual's everyday conduct in early modern England. Equally, contemporary concepts of gendered behaviour were of crucial importance when people gossiped about their neighbours or sought to evaluate their conduct.

Accordingly, sensitivity to the potential of gender as a tool of historical analysis allows us to deepen our understanding of those neighbourly perceptions of the individual which lay at the basis of community relations. Constructing such an understanding is, for the modern historian, dependent upon sometimes very isolated shards of evidence. There are, of course, prescriptive sources, in particular those conduct books which we have encountered when discussing marriage and the family (two institutions of which, as was implicit in our discussion, experience could be very gendered). But here as elsewhere, how far prescriptive literature mirrored reality, not least the reality of the existence of the lower orders, remains problematic. Certain categories of court records, not least those describing defamation cases brought before the church courts, frequently furnish evidence on what these lower orders regarded as desirable standards of human behaviour, while the language of insult in defamation cases frequently furnish all too vivid an impression of what was considered reprehensible conduct. Thus adult males were expected to live peaceably with their neighbours, to pay their debts, to fill local office to the best of their ability and, if heads of household, to provide for those living under their roof and keep them in order. Indeed, this idea of keeping order was probably central to concepts of masculinity in this context: a man worthy of his neighbours' respect was expected to be 'master' of himself, of a craft, and of a household and family. Conversely, witnesses frequently gave evidence of what they regarded as improper male behaviour. Thus

Thomas Baytes, a 20-year-old clothworker from Sowerby in Yorkshire, giving evidence in a church court defamation case in the 1590s, described two other witnesses in the case, near to whom he had resided for seven years, the 'persons of very smale credit or estimation, very forward of theire tongues & much geven to drincking and haunting in alehouses & such persons as often tymes wilbe droncke & for such persons this examinate for his owne parte doth thinke of them'.

For women, neighbourly evaluation of this sort tended to concentrate upon sexual honour. Evidence from church court defamation cases from both Yorkshire and London demonstrate that for women the most resented, and most frequently hurled, defamatory epithet was 'whore'. Whereas the court records show that men litigated against a wide range of insults (some involving sexual misconduct, but also allegations of being thieves, perjurors, usurers, or simply 'rogues' or 'knaves') the decent woman was thought to uphold her good reputation fundamentally through the maintenance of her sexual good name. Conversely, more detailed evidence sometimes shows those wider attributes of peaceable and harmonious behaviour which were thought to be so desirable in men also operating when female conduct was being discussed, evidence that we should not fall into the acceptance of any simplistic binary opposition when analysing perception of gender. Thus in 1606 the vicar of North Moreton in Berkshire, giving evidence to Star Chamber about the reputation of a woman who had been suspected as a witch, declared that she was 'accompted a scolde & an unquiet body amongest her neighbours & a great curser & swearer & such an one as the woemen of the towne where she dwelleth will not accept of her companye at churchinges, weddinges or at the labors of childe birthes of woemen'. This particular woman had obviously so offended her female co-parishioners that she was unwelcome at a whole range of specifically female activities, while the vicar also commented that she was so disliked by her neighbours that they refused to take communion with her. Conversely, John Jerral, a husbandman giving evidence in defence of a woman in another late sixteenth-century Yorkshire church court case, claimed that she was 'a verie honeste quiete woman, and one not troublesome or quarelous amongste her neighbours', and that she was somebody who was generally well thought of. Such sentiments were clearly adjusted to the rhetoric of a law case, and were in any case mediated by a court's clerical staff: yet they do reveal much of what the period considered to be desirable conduct within the context of the local community, and it is clear that the expected conduct was frequently gendered.

Examining the hierarchies of social stratification, kinship, reputation, gender and (to introduce another variable) age help make comprehensible what has been described as the 'politics of the parish' in early modern England. As was suggested in the preface to the first edition of this book, social history should not be history 'with the politics left out', but, it will be remembered, it was also suggested at that point that 'politics' is a term which is amenable to a number of definitions. Certainly, detailed study of any parish or similar community in this period, urban or rural, leads us to what are, if only on a micro-level, political issues. There is, of course, the politics of social hierarchy, perhaps most obviously operating as we observe village élites struggling to control their troublesome and disorderly poorer neighbours. Study of this phenomenon helps us to understand how England's nine or ten thousand parishes managed, in some respects at least, to coalesce into a single political entity. But there is also that fascinating, if to the participants frequently very intense, politics of personal reputation, of the constant testing of conduct by co-parishioners and neighbours against a known and acknowledged set of assumptions about proper human conduct and proper neighbourly relations. These assumptions were malleable, and could be adjusted to suit particular circumstances and particular individuals. But however such communal reactions to human behaviour might be open to mediation, negotiation or accommodation, it remains clear that what was commonly referred to as the 'graver' or 'better' sort of parishioners had a clear idea of what such conduct should be.

It is fitting that a chapter dealing with those social units which historians tend to describe as communities should end with a discussion of the quality of those human relationships which allow any possibility of a meaningful community to exist. More detailed studies need to be done before we can understand these relationships or the community fully. What is evident, however, is that historians need to refine the whole concept of 'community'. So far no universally satisfying definition of this term has been arrived at by sociologists, and their ability to write articles with titles like 'The Myth of Community Studies' ought to fill historians with a proper sense of caution. There is also more need for empirical research. Comparatively few villages have been studied in depth, and detailed village histories for a number of regions have yet to be completed. This need for more empirical research is even more marked when considering urban history. So far, perhaps because of considerations of scale, urban historians have had little to say about the more intimate workings of the early modern urban parish. Until research has been carried out on a microscopic level, it will be difficult to discuss the possibility of distinctively urban concepts of neighbourliness, of proper human conduct, or of reputation. Generally, population turnover was more rapid in urban than in rural parishes, but it has yet to be established whether this rapidity or, indeed, any other factors, produced a qualitatively different set of attitudes.

Further problems arise from the nature of the sources. Both urban historians and students of the rural community have to work mainly from institutional records, from corporation archives, from parish registers, or from manorial rolls. This is inevitable, but it entails the danger that the historian, basing research on the records of an institution, might come away with too strong an impression of that institution's internal coherence and the degree of control which it exercised over those living under its aegis. The fact that so much of what we know about everyday life in the early modern period is derived from manorial or parish records might easily seduce us into taking too exalted a view of the importance of the manor or the parish. These considerations connect with the problems of establishing change over time in urban or village society. Historians are currently apt to employ some notion of 'the break-up of the traditional village community' as an historical *deus ex machina* as convenient as that earlier catch-all concept, 'the rise of the middle classes': almost anything can be explained by it, and almost anything can be adduced as evidence of it. This is not to deny that fundamental changes did occur over the two centuries before 1760. Sharpened social stratification, even if we baulk at rewriting two centuries of English history from the perspective of Terling, did have its impact. Together with those cultural changes associated with it, this stratification might well have rendered the older style of communal values redundant. Certainly, something very much like this process occurred in towns. There, if we may trust historians of urban ritual, late medieval notions of the urban body politic were replaced by the new, and essentially class-based, assumptions of the urban patriciate.

Yet perhaps the greatest changes arose not merely in the social composition or dominant social assumptions of provincial towns or rural communities themselves, but rather in the relation of these inferior units of social or political organization to the macrocosm of the nation state. As we have noted, one of the chief motors of change in the assumptions of urban and village élites was the increasing identity their members felt between their own interests and those of an ever more assertive central government. Obviously, this process was slow, piecemeal, and subject to infinite local variations. But increased literacy, a more intrusive set of religious beliefs which came to equate being Protestant with being English, the increased dynamism of the market economy, perhaps even the rise of the parish as a unit of secular, and hence state, administration: all these combined to ease the local community, whether urban or rural, into the mainstream of national life. If the local community was changing, it was not just due to the logic of internal developments, but also to the impact of wider forces.

Notes

1 Peter Clark and Paul Slack, 'Introduction', in Peter Clark and Paul Slack (eds) *Crisis and Order in English Towns 1500–1700: Essays in Urban History* (1972), p. 31.

2 Lawrence Stone, *The Family, Sex and Marriage in England 1500–1800* (1977), pp. 98–9.
3 Keith Thomas, *Religion and the Decline of Magic* (1977; Harmondsworth, 1973), p. 526. It should be stressed that the context of Thomas's comment is the rather unusual one of witchcraft accusations.
4 Keith Wrightson, *English Society 1580–1680* (1982), pp. 51–7.

4

The national community and the problem of order

One of the most significant developments in the history of early modern Europe was the emergence of the state in something like a prototype of its modern form. We tend, perhaps oversimplistically, to think of government in Europe before about 1500 very much in terms of the monarch, his household, and his immediate circle of advisers and officials. By 1800 something much more like the modern state was in existence. But defining 'the state' is somewhat difficult. The common use historians make of the term fluctuates between two ideas. On the one hand, the state can mean a number of specific phenomena, such as professional police forces, defined territorial boundaries, or a formal judiciary. On the other hand, as in the expression 'nation state', it can mean simply a discrete political agglomeration. Our use of the term in this chapter will veer towards the first of these notions: 'the state' will be used as a convenient shorthand to cover what might be described more properly as the state apparatus or the machinery of state: the institutions, personnel and ideologies which at once constituted and supported the structures of authority. It is the growth of these structures which has led historians to interpret the years between the late fifteenth and mid-eighteenth centuries as witnessing the origins of the modern state or (to employ a concept which is currently enjoying something of a vogue among continental historians) 'state formation'. Over Europe as a whole, individual rulers increased the powers of their administrations in pace with a more general transformation which affected the whole of society, a transformation in which both the influence and the aspirations of central authority grew rapidly.

Although England escaped that triumph of monarchical power which we know as absolutism, there can be little doubt that the country experienced a growth in both the power and the assertiveness of central government. Our period begins with the closing stages of that process which G.R. Elton has christened 'The Tudor Revolution in Government'. Historians have spent some time arguing about just how revolutionary this process was, yet it remains clear that some important changes did take place. Thomas Cromwell's impact on the practices of the central administration may or may not have been as important as Professor Elton has claimed: what is certain, however, is that they did not constitute the whole story. The new style of government and the urgent need to enforce the Reformation demanded a greater control in the localities. The changes at the centre of the 1530s, in which Cromwell played such a vital part, were followed by two decades which experienced a more general thrust towards stronger and more intimate government. There was a greater concern to ensure religious conformity; a flurry of legislation against treason and felonies; more extensive powers, especially those relating to the pretrial examination of suspects, were granted to justices of the peace; and a national militia system was brought into being, a certain urgency being added to this last by the peasant revolts of 1549 and Sir Thomas Wyatt's rising of 1554. At the same time as these developments took place, contemporaries began to use the term 'the state' in something like its modern sense.

The earliest such use seems to have been by an apologist for Henry VIII's religious policy, Thomas Starkey, in 1538. By 1582 the Roman Catholic William Allen could refer to altering a question 'from controversie in religion to the cause of the prince and matter of state'. In 1618, Sir Walter Raleigh in his Maxims of State could describe the state as 'the frame or set order of a commonwealth, of the governers that rule the same'. Although most commentators preferred such familiar terms as 'realm', 'body politic', or 'commonwealth', it is evident that they were not only living under a form of government which had undergone some important changes, but were also beginning to discuss government in rather different ways from those which had previously been current.

It is clear that a great deal altered in the organs of central and local government over the remainder of the period covered by this book. By the middle of the eighteenth century, however imperfect or undeveloped the state apparatus might appear by modern standards, it is clear that symptoms of modernity were present. The administration was not as closely tied to the person of the monarch or the chief minister as it had been under Henry VIII and Thomas Cromwell, and was acquiring a bureaucratic ethos. There was a sense of greater control, a confidence in the system of government which had existed only in a much more precarious and uncertain form in the mid-Tudor period. Moreover, the significance of this development of the state went far beyond the central administration. We have only to look at France, where venal office-holding distorted social and economic structures, or Spain, where the state financial apparatus created similar distortions, to realize that the growth of the state had important implications for society at large. Yet the state did not only distort society: it integrated it, both in practical and ideological terms. In so far as people had a sense of national identity in the eighteenth century, it owed much to this integrating function of the governmental machine and its agents. Our view of early modern English society would be sadly incomplete without a further investigation of these themes.

The growth of the state

Perhaps the best starting point in attempting to understand the nature of the European state in this period is to regard it as a vast machine designed essentially to raise money and to finance warfare. Medieval monarchs had been expected to advance their personal prestige and dynastic interests through waging war, but the sixteenth and seventeenth centuries witnessed the transition, via the mercenary, from the feudal host to the standing army. Broadly speaking, in 1600 no European power had a proper standing army. By 1700 none was without one, and the need to man, feed, clothe, arm, officer and pay the armed services became an important socioeconomic factor.

England was a late starter in all this. The English military system, as far as home defence was concerned, depended on the militia over the first three-quarters of our period. The militia's one great advantage was that it was cheap. It was organized on a county basis, and it was essentially amateur: the county commander, the Lord Lieutenant, was normally a peer, officers were drawn from the local gentry, and the rank and file were men of small property. When troops were required for service abroad in the Tudor and early Stuart periods they were levied on an *ad hoc* basis. Prolonged periods of warfare might see quite substantial numbers of soldiers being raised. Elizabeth's campaigns in the Low Countries, France and Ireland involved the levying of perhaps 100,000 troops between 1585 and 1603, while the various Stuart expeditions of 1624–27 involved about 50,000. Levies were normally drawn from the bottom of society: the potential quality of recruits can be gauged from a hope expressed by the Privy Council in 1624 that the levy of that year would remove 'unnecessary persons that now want employment and live lewdly and unprofitably'. About 10 per cent of these levies would normally desert between impressment and reaching their embarkation port, and another 50 per cent might be found unfit for service when they arrived there. One of the commanders of the disastrous expedition to the Isle of Rhe, for example, informed the Privy Council that he was rejecting 120 of the 200 men sent to him from Hampshire, being 'such creatures as he was ashamed to describe them'. Those thought fit for service were packed off with practically no training in the hope, normally fulfilled, that they would not be returning.

The outbreak of the Civil Wars, therefore, found England very badly behind the rest of western Europe in military affairs, and king and parliament alike were to experience considerable difficulties in forging an effective fighting force. In the Interregnum, however, the country had its first experience of a standing army. It did not prove to be an enjoyable one. Not only were the troops associated with a widely unpopular regime: they were also extremely costly. In any given year in the 1650s the armed forces would cost roughly £2,500,000, with the remaining expenses of state coming to some £200,000. By the Restoration opinion was firmly in favour of vesting national defence in the militia, but it was obvious that some form of standing force was needed. Parliament grudgingly allowed Charles II a standing army, which eventually amounted to about 6000 men in England, with a further 3000 in Scotland and 7000 in Ireland. Fears that James II was intending to use the army as a tool for imposing popery and absolutism did little to enhance its popularity, but it experienced rapid expansion after the accession of William and Mary in 1688. Both the size and the expense of the army grew with William III's wars, and continued to do so in the eighteenth century. At the end of our period, during the Seven Years War (1756–63) there were as many as 200,000 men in the British army. The Royal Navy also expanded. There was one royal ship in 1513, 34 at the time of the Armada campaign (the other 163 English ships involved were privately owned), 40 by 1640, 85 by 1652, and by 1665 a total of 160 with a tonnage of 100,000 tons, carrying 5000 guns and manned by 25,000 sailors. Thereafter the number of ships remained static, although marked increases occurred in tonnage, gun-strength and the size of crews.

The effects of this expansion were mixed. Some were beneficial. As well as providing career opportunities for intending officers, the forces made business for armament manufacturers, food contractors, and all sorts of craftsmen and technicians, from naval architects designing ships to cloth-workers making uniforms. Conversely, the growth of the army and navy, like increased taxation or attempts at improved law enforcement, created a greater intrusiveness by the state into the life of the individual. The most dramatic manifestation of this came with recruitment. The naval press-gang is familiar enough, and was justified by a legal decision of 1743 on the grounds that a navy was necessary for national defence, and that the press was the only way by which crews could be found for ships. It is less well realized that basically similar means were used to recruit into the army. As we have seen, the Tudor and early Stuart levy was seen as a useful way of purging society of ne'er-do-wells, and for many of them the process was more or less one of conscription. Most armies of the Civil War period, of the late Stuart era, and of the eighteenth century were raised in much the same way. Marlborough's wars were fought by troops who, at best, had joined to avoid poverty, and who at worst had taken the queen's shilling while drunk, or had simply been kidnapped. They were supplemented, as they had been in the Elizabethan period, by the off-sweepings of the gaols. Paid 8d a day before stoppages for food and equipment, and subjected to a discipline which was at times brutal, the late Stuart and Hanoverian soldier did not even have the consolation of knowing that he was held in high public esteem. Troops were not popular, and the news that soldiers were going to pass through an area or, even worse, be billeted there, was usually greeted with dismay. Demobilization brought its own problems. Court records from coastal counties show that in the Elizabethan period many criminal vagrants were returning soldiers, while in the eighteenth century the end of every war brought an increase in theft as men were discharged from the army and navy and took to stealing.

The army and navy were also very expensive. Individual redcoats at 8d a day or individual able-seamen at £1 2s 0d a month might come cheap, but the cost of large numbers of them, and of their arms, uniforms, food and equipment, soon added up. Taxes rose accordingly. England was fortunate that the country was little involved in large-scale and continuous foreign warfare until well into the seventeenth century, and was thus spared from the distorting effects of heavy taxation and a sophisticated state financial apparatus which troubled a number of other states. English taxation at the beginning of our period was at a very formative phase. Despite Thomas Cromwell's reforms, themselves modelled largely on the practices of the Duchy of Lancaster, state finance was still not fully divorced from the private financial arrangements of the monarch. Government was still thought of in many ways as a form of property, and its problems were seen as being similar to those of estate management. In normal periods, the monarch was expected to get by without direct taxation. This, traditionally, was only voted by parliament under extraordinary circumstances, and took the form of a type of tax known as the subsidy. Essentially a tax on landed and other forms of wealth, the subsidy was a very unhandy medium by which the state might extract wealth from the subject. Assessment was done locally by local men, and the money value of the subsidy was falling, its real value even more so in the inflationary conditions of the late sixteenth century. Sir Francis Bacon was probably right in thinking that the Englishman was 'most master of his own valuation and the least bitten in purse of any in Europe'.

The heavy taxation of the Civil War period, described in our introductory chapter, changed all this. Direct taxation rose to unimagined levels, while parliament introduced the excise, an extremely unpopular form of indirect taxation. The restored monarchy, while happy to retain the excise, attempted, unsuccessfully, to return to prewar levels of taxation. The real change came with William III's wars and the War of the Spanish Succession. The nine years of warfare which followed William's accession cost nearly £4,500,000 each year, and it has been estimated that over the period 1689–1713 as a whole the annual cost of warfare would average between £5,000,000 and £7,000,000. By 1688 Gregory King estimated that per capita taxation in England, while behind that experienced by the Dutch, was roughly equivalent to the French level. The period after 1688 also saw the development of a state financial machine, of which the most noteworthy aspects were the founding of the Bank of England in 1694 and the floating of the national debt, which amounted to some £139,000,000 in 1763. Taxation, state expenditure, and financial institutions had all reached levels current in other European states. The need to finance warfare had given a tremendous boost to the apparatus of British capitalism.

By the early eighteenth century England was also acquiring something like a modern bureaucracy. There was a sizeable hierarchy of civil servants, organized in departments, carrying on the work of government, keeping written records, and providing that continuity of government personnel which is one of the hallmarks of the modern state. Arguably, the lay bureaucracy was essentially a product of the Reformation, and might well have owed much to Thomas Cromwell. Despite the personal elements which were to continue in royal government, the mid-sixteenth century saw the arrival of career bureaucrats who were able to keep things going despite the death of a monarch or, indeed, of Thomas Cromwell. The career of William Cecil, Lord Burghley, is just one of a series of bureaucratic success stories, although the survival of personal elements is demonstrated by his ability to pass his political empire on to his son Robert.

But despite these changes the English administration was still small. In the early seventeenth century, there was a central 'court' of about 1000 officers. The officials involved locally in the collection of crown land revenues, as escheators and feodaries, as muster masters, or as clerks of the peace, amounted to only a few hundred more. This should be compared with the 3000 to 4000 officials serving the French crown in the single province of Normandy during the 1630s, or the 60,000 people (almost certainly an overestimate) supposedly working for the Castilian exchequer at about the same date. Like the standing army and the taxation system, bureaucracy developed late in England, while royal officials never became as numerous as those of other major states. Gregory King estimated that there were some 10,000 office-holders in the late seventeenth century, a figure which had only increased to about 16,000 by 1760.

Despite the use of such terms as bureaucrat or civil servant, those staffing the state administration during this period were very unlike a modern civil service. Recruitment was through patronage, officials regarded themselves essentially as the owners of their offices and, except at the highest level, the office-holder might not be removable at the will of the ruler. None of this prevented individuals, or even departments, from achieving expertise and professionalism, but it does make it difficult to accept that these office-holders formed a bureaucracy in the modern sense.

The rewards of office could be great, even though they varied enormously. In the early eighteenth century the master of the ordnance might get £1500 a year, one of his clerks a mere £40. All of these salaries, however, would be supplemented by fees and gifts. Thus the office of Lord Treasurer, one of the plum posts, carried a fee of £366 in the early seventeenth century, but was reckoned to be worth £4000 in reality. On this level, whatever the overheads, the profits of office were clearly enormous. Generally these profits went to representatives of big, landed families. There was no class of big office-holders in England along the lines of the French *noblesse de robe*. Most of those in the upper reaches of the bureaucracy were landowners and gentlemen who through talent, luck or the natural order of things found themselves to be the monarch's servants. The fall of Cromwell in 1540 or of Lionel Cranfield in 1624 demonstrated the likely fate of low-born career bureaucrats who got above themselves.

All European monarchies, even those with a bureaucracy or system of office-holding more developed than the English, were largely dependent on the co-operation of wider elements in society, notably the aristocracy, for the implementation of their rule. England, with its small royal bureaucracy, is an extreme illustration of this dictum: one of the peculiarities of the English governmental system was the degree of its dependence upon the unpaid amateur. As we have seen, the standing army, that most substantial product of the processes of state formation, came late to England, and was treated with considerable suspicion after its introduction. The more popular militia, it will be recalled, was a force whose hierarchy of ranks corresponded to the social hierarchy, and which was essentially local in its character. Justices of the peace were recruited from leading gentry families. Sheriffs were also normally gentlemen, although by the late seventeenth century they came only infrequently from the county élite. Chief constables were normally lesser gentlemen, as were coroners, clerks of the peace, and the grand jurors who sometimes acted as a mouthpiece for county opinion at the assizes and quarter sessions. Parish constables were recruited from the more substantial members of the village community, yeomen, the richer craftsmen and the like. We must never forget that ruling England depended upon the goodwill and co-operation of a broad section of property-owners. The basic medieval ethos of 'self-government at the king's command' pervaded English local administration throughout the early modern period.

The system, it is true, had its weaknesses. Justices of the peace might obstruct royal commands, carry them out half-heartedly or ignore them altogether. Similarly, parish constables might worry more about the hostility of their neighbours than the sanctions which a distant authority might impose upon them for any negligence. Yet these imperfections were shared by the paid bureaucrats of the period: provincial and overseas subordinates often ignored or reshaped instructions from London. Neither were continental office-holders immune from sloth, inefficiency, or wanton disregard of instructions from their distant superiors. The willingness to serve in local office, as justice of the peace, constable, overseer of the poor, or even as a juror, was widespread in English society and, despite the problems which recalcitrant or negligent officials might cause, served as an important means of integrating something like the top 20 per cent of the male population into the state administrative machine. This had important consequences for what many observers agreed was the principal function of secular government: the maintenance of order. Most regimes in history which have felt the need to justify their existence have done so by recourse to the argument that if they did not exist, all sorts of chaos would ensue. This argument was familiar to the regimes of our period: for most of the time it met with a ready response from the political nation.

Order

It is almost impossible to overstate the concern which commentators in late Tudor and early Stuart England felt about the need to preserve order. Society experienced its fair share of trouble, upheaval and unrest in the period, and writers reacted with continual assertions that complete disruption and utter chaos were imminent. This conviction, current among government propagandists and in clerical and legal circles in the 1530s, later became widespread among the governing class as a whole. By the Elizabethan period it was commonly held that the unquestioning maintenance of the existing social hierarchy was the only antidote to complete social breakdown. This assumption was connected to fashionable ideas about the nature of the cosmos, with their emphasis on correspondences and systems of hierarchy. It also owed a great deal to Reformation theology, with its stress on man's innate sinfulness and rebelliousness. Not only the monarch, but the whole of the social order existed by divine right, so rebellion was not only contrary to earthly authority, but also to the Almighty. As the Homily on Obedience (1547) reminded God-fearing Englishmen and women, if 'right order' was absent,

> there reigneth all abuse, carnal liberty, enormity, sin and Babylonical confusion. Take away kings, princes, rulers, magistrates, judges, and such estates of God's order, no man shall ride or go by the highway untroubled, no man shall sleep in his own house or bed unkilled, no man shall keep his wife, children or possessions in quietness, all things shall be common; and there needs must follow all mischief and utter destruction both of souls, bodies, goods and commonwealths.

The Homily was an early, and succinctly comprehensive, statement of what was, by the end of Elizabeth's reign, a commonplace. In England, as in the rest of Europe, educated men and women, confronted by a world beset by dynastic, religious, economic and social disruption, yearned for order, wrote at length about its virtues, and thought strong government a likely means of attaining it.

At the beginning of our period most observers, on the strength of both contemporary realities and what they knew of the Wars of the Roses, would have concluded that the greatest threat to order was dynastic strife. Even at the time of Elizabeth's death, noted so well-informed an observer as Sir Francis Bacon, there was a general fear of 'confusions, interreigns, and perturbations of estate'. These, given that 'foreign competition should be added to domestical, and divisions for religion to matter of title to the crown', were thought 'likely far to exceed the ancient calamities of the civil wars between Lancaster and York'. In fact, James I's accession in 1603 passed off smoothly, as had all those of the sixteenth century. After 1553, there was little real danger of a disputed succession. Any problems which Mary Queen of Scots presented were contained while Elizabeth prevaricated over her execution. Monmouth's Rebellion of 1685, despite its evident appeal among ploughboys and artisans in the south-west, aroused but little enthusiasm in the political nation. Even the Jacobite episodes of 1715 and 1745, despite contemporary fears of widespread support, had more of the air of an intervention by a foreign power than anything else. The one dramatic change of monarch which did take place in our period, that of 1688 when William and Mary replaced James II, was engineered in the full knowledge that the overwhelming bulk of the political nation would support it.

Protection for the reigning monarch and the dynasty was sought through the treason laws and the penalties they inflicted. The basic thinking on treason obtaining in the sixteenth century had been laid down in a statute of 1352. Legislation of Edwards III's reign was obviously ill-suited to the new needs of the post-Reformation state, and the treason laws, although ultimately based on the 1352 legislation, were extended steadily throughout our period. A number of Acts made it treasonable to interfere with the succession to the throne as established from time to time by statute. It was also made treasonable to recognize the sovereignty of the Pope, or to perform other acts hostile to the new religious settlement. Perhaps the period of greatest innovation came in the wake of Henry VIII's Treason Act of 1534, which formalized the notion that treason could be committed through written or spoken words, as well as through overt actions. Between that date and 1760, extensions of the treason laws, apart from some statutes and legal decisions making certain forms of popular disturbance treasonable, consisted of elaborating the old ideas of compassing the monarch's death or levying war against the monarch as acts of treason. These laws were enforced. State trials, sometimes involving the great and famous, are familiar enough. Close examination of local court archives reveals the scattered prosecution of very obscure people for treasonable or seditious words or actions. Although such prosecutions took place at later dates, it is noteworthy that the Tudors seem to have been the most sensitive to expressions of sedition among their low-born subjects, and the most likely to punish such expressions with death. Thus we find such examples as Mary Cleere of Ingatestone in Essex, burnt at the stake in 1576 after declaring that Elizabeth was 'baseborn and not born to the crown, but that another lady was the right inheritor', or William Francis of the same county, executed in 1587 for claiming that Edward VI was still alive. Such evidence supports the contention that the Elizabethan regime thought itself to be resting on very uncertain foundations.

This insecurity was, in large measure, unjustified. If dynastic problems were to worry the Tudors and, indeed, cause occasional difficulties down to 1745, at least the old style of aristocratic feudal rebellion was on the way out. As we shall see in a later chapter, this was connected with wider shifts both in noble behaviour and in the way in which the nobility exercised power. Yet the last big revolt, that of the northern earls in 1569, was significant not only in demonstrating the redundancy of such rebellion as a means to a political end, but also the government's incapacity for doing anything very immediately effective to counter such threats. While a royal army came together slowly in the south, royal agents in the north found themselves more or less helpless against a rebel force estimated at 3800 foot and 1600 horse. But the rebellion failed, largely because of a lack of resolution on the part of its leaders, the Earls of Northumberland and Westmorland. The two noblemen had been more or less forced into revolt. They had been dabbling in plots against Elizabeth for some time, and now felt that they were so deeply implicated that overt rebellion offered the only way out. The Duke of Norfolk, whose plans to marry Mary Queen of Scots and depose Elizabeth were central to the plot, had already lost his nerve, confessed all and thrown himself upon the royal mercy. Another potential ally, the Duke of Cumberland, studiously avoided trouble at the time of the rising. The events of 1569 demonstrate the unreality of noble rebellion in the old style not merely in terms of military power, but also in psychological ones. What was lacking in the north in 1569 was not the men, but the aristocratic will-power. The propaganda of the Tudor monarchy, and the ideas of obligation and obedience which it emphasized, had obviously made an impact upon the thinking of the national élite.

If noble revolt was less threatening than it seemed so, despite the fears of the many-headed monster among the propertied and in official circles, was concerted mass action by the lower orders. The mid-sixteenth century witnessed the last of the old style peasant revolts to be seen in England, the risings of 1549. As with the Northern Rebellion 20 years later, the events of 1549 demonstrate both the strengths and the limitations of revolt. Their extent was impressive, as was the degree of organization locally. Under the direction of those richer villagers who were the natural leaders of rural communities, the rebels mounted military operations and put together a fairly effective civil administration. If nothing else, they showed how, in the mid-sixteenth century at least, the lower orders were perfectly capable of organizing their own affairs without the gentry. The rebels also demonstrated that the many-headed monster, the anarchic rebellious meaner sort so feared by officialdom, was much more careful of human life than were the forces of order and restraint. The government showed no compunction in using foreign mercenary troops to shoot down their rebellious subjects, or in reminding them of the virtues of obedience with numerous executions, many of them summary, after the revolt. Yet the rebels, like their aristocratic counterparts of 1569, seem to have lacked the will to win. Their political culture, although allowing them to organize effectively enough locally, did not allow them to push matters to a success-ful conclusion. Kett's rebels simply occupied one provincial capital, Norwich, while the western rebels got bogged down in besieging another one, Exeter. The risings of 1549, like those of 1381, are invaluable in providing insights into the political aspirations and capacity for mass polit-ical action of the lower orders. Yet ultimately they demonstrate the inabil-ity of those lower orders to gain lasting redress for their grievances.

If there were no mass popular uprisings in the two centuries after 1549, there was a continual undercurrent of a small-scale local rioting. After the mid-sixteenth century those natural heads of village society who had been the leaders of the 1549 rebellions were becoming increasingly attached to official ideas of order: indeed, government propaganda published in the wake of the rebellions of that year thought it worthwhile to point out to such men that their challenge to their superiors might well encourage their own servants to disobedience. The two centuries after 1549 saw the transi-tion from popular rebellion to rioting by the poor. If the rebels of 1549 were concerned with regional, even national, problems, by 1760 the riot was usually local in its scope and provoked by the high price of corn in the immediate area. Sometimes, of course, rioting could be much more extensive, as in the Western Rising of 1626–31, or in some of the widespread rioting which occurred in a few dearth years in the eighteenth century. Essentially, however, the riot was local and concerned with short-term aims. This is not to say that the riot tells us nothing about more general popular notions. Historians have now rejected the image of the mob as a wild animal, acting with uninformed and mechanical brutality when faced with high grain prices or some other grievance. The crowd possessed a 'moral economy', a set of fairly sophisticated ideas on how things ought to be, which informed what its members did and said when they rioted. Hence the English grain riot, at least by the eighteenth century, frequently took the form of what the French call a *taxation populaire*. In a period of high prices the poor, usually with women taking a leading role, would take over a grain market or commandeer wagons loaded with grain. But they would not merely steal it. Rather, they would sell it off at what they felt to be a fair price, and then return the takings, sometimes with the neatly folded grain sacks, to the grain merchants. Surprisingly often, riots show order in the midst of disorder.

If rebellion was becoming less of a problem by the end of the sixteenth century, the opposite is true of crime. Reconstructing patterns of crime in any historical period, given the difficulty of ascertaining how far crime entering the historical record reflects reality, is a hazardous business. These problems are compounded for Elizabethan and early Stuart England by a paucity of surviving records, at least for serious offences. Moreover, much of the printed evidence relating to crime is strongly biased to commenting on what was thought to be happening in London. At the end of our period the writings of the Fieldings and others provided a vivid portrayal of the crime problem in and around the capital, a portrayal strongly supported by Jonathan Wild's career in the 1720s. But it would seem that developments in London were atypical. In so far as a national pattern can be reconstructed, it appears that the prosecution of serious crime, felony, rose rapidly in the late sixteenth century, reaching a peak in some areas in the late 1590s, in others in the 1620s. The disruptions of the Civil Wars meant that courts ceased to sit in some areas, but when the judicial machine resumed normal operations in the late 1640s the levels of prosecution were much lower, and were to remain so well into the eighteenth century. The homicide rate fell markedly, from 7 per 100,000 of population to 2.8 in Essex between the late sixteenth and late seventeenth centuries, from 5 or 6 per 100,000 to 2.3 in Sussex between 1660 and the 1720s. More surprisingly, prosecutions of property offences also fell dramatically. At the Essex assizes, such prosecutions in the early eighteenth century stood at about one-tenth of their level in the bad years of the 1590s.

Roughly the same situation obtained with the Court of Great Sessions in Cheshire, although the peak there had come in the 1620s. Other felonies, such as rape and other sexual offences, arson and even (outside Essex) witchcraft were very rarely prosecuted. Overall, prosecutions for felony, with the important exception of London, show England experiencing a mounting crime problem between about 1570 and 1630, and then enjoying very low levels of indicted crime in the century after 1660. Execution for felony followed a similar pattern. In Cheshire, 166 felons were executed in the 1620s, compared with 10 in the first decade of the eighteenth century. In Devon, perhaps 250 felons were executed between 1600 and 1609, compared with about 30 between 1700 and 1709. Even in London, about 20 felons were executed annually in the mid-eighteenth century, as opposed to an estimated 150 a year in the Jacobean period. The available evidence about reactions to serious crime provides evidence of a society which was experiencing a shift towards a situation where there was less tension over controlling the criminal, where there was less of a sense of being under pressure.

Executions underwent changes other than statistical ones. Among Tudor governmental innovations was the set-piece execution. This was probably first introduced for high-born traitors, and was later extended to common felons. Public execution was no longer a prosaic demonstration that crime did not pay. It also emphasized the importance of the whole structure of earthly and divine authority which had been offended. The person being executed became the central actor in a theatre of punishment, and their willingness to play the allotted role tells us a great deal about the nature of authority in Tudor and Stuart England. The condemned was expected to show obedience, penitence and contrition on the gallows. They were also expected to make a speech, in which a full confession was usually made to the offence in question, and expressions were made of sorrow, of the hope that they would serve as a deterrent example to others, and that the monarch under whose laws death was being suffered would enjoy a long and prosperous reign. The speeches also customarily contained a long confession of youthful sin, which was seen as leading inevitably to the serious offence for which death was being suffered. The public execution, so often treated by historians simply as yet more proof of the brutality of past ages, was in fact a highly structured ritual in which the authority of the state was demonstrated, in a dramatic fashion, to the public at large.

Changes also took place, it seems, in attitudes to another aspect of death: suicide. Suicide was illegal, classified as a felony, the goods of the deceased being, in theory, forfeit to the Crown. It was also a flagrant breach of the Christian moral code, and was widely regarded by theological commentators and legal experts alike as one of the most serious acts which rebellious mankind could oppose to the natural order of things. Thus to Michael Dalton, author of a handbook for justices of the peace, suicide was 'an offence against God, against the king and against nature'. Calculating suicide rates, thanks to peculiar difficulties arising from under-reporting and from paucity of evidence, is not easy. Such calculations as have been made suggest a rate of about four to six suicides annually per 100,000 of population, or somewhere between one-third and one-half of the rate currently obtaining in Britain. This figure provides ammunition for those arguing that the early modern world was a less stressful and more idyllic place than the modern industrial state. Sociologists see suicide as an index of social dislocation, and it is generally felt to be a more serious problem in advanced, industrial nations. The possible gap between actual suicides and what would be recorded as such by an early modern coroner prevents us from being too confident over this matter, as does the contemporary age structure. Children formed a high proportion of the population, but children rarely commit suicide: the low overall rate conceals a somewhat higher adult rate. More concretely, attitudes to suicide seemed to have softened from the late seventeenth century onwards. From about 1660, coroners and their juries were increasingly willing to classify suicides as *non compos mentis*, of unsound mind, thus removing some of the stigma from the deceased and preventing the forfeiture of their goods. The forces behind this change were complex, but it is difficult not to accept that they were linked to the growth of a more relaxed attitude to personal conduct and morality: indeed, the most recent work on the subject has suggested that there was a 'secularization of suicide' in the eighteenth century. If this is the case, it provides yet more evidence of a shift to a world where concern over humanity's rebelliousness and wickedness and the collapse of the cosmos was less intensive.

If the act of self-killing was seen as a challenge to the natural and divine order, so too was that condition which, by 1760, a few commentators were beginning to see as connected to at least some suicides: mental illness. Madness is another of those phenomena which, although frequently simply regarded as an unchanging given by historians, is defined, regarded and treated differently in various societies. Consistently, however, mental illness has a significance which goes beyond the experience of the individual sufferer: it may be a solitary experience for those on whom it is inflicted, but it is possibly the most social of maladies in terms of its impact on other people. And, while mad people do not necessarily have anything against the society in which they live, madness can take the form of a challenge to the logic or pseudo-logic of that society, in which the mad constantly test the rationality and humanity of their fellow beings: the history of unreason does not exist in isolation from the history of reason. Indeed, from the Elizabethan period onward works of literature, not least those of Shakespeare, demonstrate that writers were familiar with this premise and were willing to develop it for dramatic purposes.

Dealing with the insane in everyday life, however, was something which involved hard practicalities. Insane rich landowners might have their interests looked after by the Court of Wards before that institution's abolition in 1640, and by Chancery after 1660, while the poor law envisaged offering financial assistance to those responsible for caring for the mentally ill poor. What is obvious is that, before the later seventeenth century, the odd incarceration in the local house of correction notwithstanding, the assumption was that the insane should be looked after by their families. From the Restoration period, however, the foundation of private asylums marked a new departure in the treatment of the insane, although it seems that it was overwhelmingly the better-off sufferers who would be placed within them. It is, perhaps, easy to caricature the care of the mentally ill in this period, yet it is clear that some of these institutions, ill-regulated and out to make a profit, were marked by an uncaring and brutalizing regime. By 1760, more humane attitudes based on the notion that the insane could be treated and cured were coming into place, presaging such later developments as the foundation of such enlightened institutions as the Retreat at York, founded by Quakers in the 1790s. The definitive history of madness has yet to be written, yet it is obvious that in the two centuries we cover attitudes towards it, and ideas on how to treat it, were steadily developing.

The same, if we may return to an earlier theme, was true of crime. Not all crimes were the capital offences we have already touched upon.

Arguably, one of the most interesting developments over the first half of our period was a greater sensitivity to petty crime, and the emergence of a notion of the criminal which in some ways was very close to the 'criminal class' of Victorian social debate. Throughout the sixteenth century the authorities became more convinced of the need to control the poor. Recent research has suggested that these were becoming more numerous, and contemporary opinion was certainly convinced that they were becoming more troublesome. The most familiar product of these fears was the vagrant stereotype created in the Elizabethan and Jacobean periods by both a string of statutes and a lively body of popular rogue literature. But the vagrant was simply the best publicized symptom of much wider processes in which the poor were identified as a problem, attempts were made to control them, and hence they found themselves increasingly likely to be prosecuted for infringements of an ever-widening legal code. The process is perhaps best illustrated at village level. At Terling in Essex, for example, surviving documentation provides details of 306 prosecutions of villagers at the assizes or quarter sessions between 1560 and 1699, and a further 395 at the ecclesiastical courts between 1570 and 1639. In both cases, not only was there a peak in prosecution at the beginning of the seventeenth century, but there was also a shift in the use made of the courts. These were no longer being used to settle disputes between villagers of roughly equal status, but rather as instruments for regulating the behaviour of the village poor. This situation was merely a local microcosm of a much wider criminalization of the poor, of which the most concrete result was the construction of a national system of houses of correction. Their prototype was the London Bridewell, set up in 1552, and by the 1630s houses of correction were to be found in every county. Their functions included the brief incarceration of petty offenders, much like the modern prison.

The history of law and order in early modern England does, therefore, suggest that a transition had taken place. If there was a threat to order, it no longer came from the 'feudal' problems of noble ambition or dynastic disputes. Rather, it came from the less dramatic, more insidious, and in many ways 'modern' poor criminal. Yet even crime seems to have been less of a problem and, outside London at least, was being thought of as less of a problem in the mid-eighteenth than in the mid-sixteenth century. The agents of popular disorder had become less threatening, too. The many-headed monster bent on destroying social hierarchy and private property had been replaced by isolated groups of rioters fixing the price of grain or demanding higher wages. The London mob itself, before the Gordon Riots of 1780 at any rate, was regarded as an inconvenience rather than a threat. England was almost certainly a more violent society in the early modern period than it is at present. Tempers were lost more easily by persons of all social classes, and there is a more general sense that somehow people's feelings were nearer the surface, and more likely to explode. Yet it was not an impossibly violent society. On an interpersonal level, the homicide rate was falling, and there is evidence of the impact of that 'civilizing process' with which Norbert Elias has familiarized us. On a national level, the threats to order presented by dynastic strife, noble rebellion, and mass unrest among the lower orders were at worst an episodic threat: the horrified reactions to the outbreak of warfare in 1642, and the attempts at neutralism, show just how abnormal the chaos unleashed by the wars was felt to be. By the eighteenth century English society was stable and, in large measure, orderly: one suspects that in the Elizabethan period, for all the concern voiced about disorder, much the same was true.

Yet in the Elizabethan and early Stuart periods, it must be reiterated, this concern was voiced frequently, and was by no means restricted to worry over those themes which are now so familiar to modern historians: political stability, large-scale rebellion, or crime and delinquency. Disquiet over perceived or imagined threats to order ran much wider and deeper: indeed, as we have noted, contemporary notions about the desirability of a harmonious universe provided a cosmic dimension to these worries. Historians, used to studying early modern England through the analysis of political hierarchies or the hierarchies of social structure, have recently come to ponder on how order was maintained, and how concern over disorder operated, in other early modern hierarchies. Here as elsewhere, to take the most important example, gender has been recognized as one of the key pathways to deepening our understanding of the operation of order in this period. Most contemporary observers, whether the (mainly male) authors of prescriptive literature or male and female witnesses stating their opinions on such matters as they gave evidence in court cases, regarded the subordination of women to men as axiomatic. The common view was that women, especially married women, should be modest in their behaviour and attire, submissive to the male authority figures placed over them, chaste, patient, docile, thrifty and wise.

Obviously this model, like other models of subordination and order, was constantly being challenged in real life: as we have seen when discussing that institution where questions of gender were at their most urgent, the family, the gap between the recommendations of prescriptive literature and lived experience must, at times, have been very wide. The problem for the modern observer is to ascertain how far challenges to the broader gender hierarchies were a constant, and how far they fluctuated over time. The question is still an open one, and considerable research is needed before it can be fully answered. There have, however, been suggestions that the period 1560–1640, when England was a much troubled society attempting to get to grips with the only dimly understood implications of severe demographic pressures and marked socioeconomic strains, saw something of a crisis in gender authority. Certainly literary complaints of female insubordination seem to have become especially shrill in that period, while the increase in local prosecutions of that typical offence of the troublesome woman, scolding, may have reflected some real problems to match the literary comments.

We must emphasize that the current state of research into these issues makes it difficult to be precise, and that the notion of a crisis of gender relations in the Elizabethan and early Stuart periods is still a speculative one. The period certainly produced a substantial corpus of ballad, chapbook and joke-book literature in which the insubordinate or scolding wife and the hen-pecked husband figured prominently. Yet neither of these stereotypes was new in 1560, while there are obvious problems in interpreting what are essentially humorous or satirical sources, although it is worth reflecting that what a society laughs about can hold some important clues to what it worries about. Current thinking suggests that most women, most of the time, were willing to accept the general notion of male supremacy, although this supremacy, again as we have noted in our discussion of marriage and the family, would constantly be challenged and modified in practice. What is clear, however, is that over the century before 1660 and, one suspects, in most cases over the century that followed it, the writers of normative literature regarded male domination and female subordination as two of the main foundations of a well-ordered society. The tendency to see the family or household as the arena where this gender hierarchy needed its most constant nurturing leads us back to the early modern axiom that the family was the basic unit of, and a mirror of, wider social and political hierarchies.

If gender relations and female subordination are now seen as fundamental to early modern concepts of order, so too is age hierarchy, another issue we have already met when considering the family in this period. Obviously, age hierarchies are present in any society, and hence have perhaps tended to have been neglected by historians as an unchanging given. But here as elsewhere, serious analysis suggests a more complex situation, in which every culture so far studied has manifested different views on the social meaning of age, even if the differences are frequently only ones of degree. The ideal in early modern England, on the evidence of the normative and prescriptive literature of the period, was that, other things being equal, just as female should be subordinate to male, so should youth be subordinate to age. Youth, indeed, was seen by many contemporary observers as a very problematic period, when the untamed impulses and general lack of maturity of young individuals rendered them a battleground between good and evil influences. The elderly, conversely, might be regarded as sources of wisdom and experience, as repositories of local knowledge or local custom: certainly in court cases involving disputes over local customs and rights, it was the elderly who were most often brought forward to give their opinions.

Yet old age could also be viewed more negatively: it was sometimes presented as an age of dotage, and for many of the elderly, especially the elderly poor, the reality of the experience of the closing years of life must have been marked by growing mental and physical weakness, worsening health, a gradual loss of faculties and increasing poverty. At the other end of the social hierarchy, however, it seems clear that contemporary practice suggests that men were not seen to be fitted to bear high governmental responsibility until they had reached middle age. Thus between 1542 and 1642 the median age of Privy Councillors varied between 51 and 61, the average age of newly appointed Speakers of the House of Commons in the seventeenth century was 50, newly appointed Secretaries of State in the same century were normally in their fifties and, to take a more local context, in the seventeenth century sheriffs and aldermen at Norwich averaged 46 and 48 respectively when elected.

As with gender hierarchies, the age hierarchy was frequently challenged, although once again these challenges rarely resulted in anything permanent or effective. Young people were constantly involved in acts of insubordination or petty rebellion against their elders, but all this was so unthreatening as to be incorporated into the proverbial wisdom of the period. There were some excesses, such as the apprentices' riots in London where brothels were regularly attacked on Shrove Tuesday (indeed, one suspects that the analysis of apprentice culture in London and in such major provincial centres as Newcastle and Bristol might prove a useful way of gaining knowledge of the wider youth culture of the period), but even here the threat to hierarchy was a passing one.

Indeed, contemporary comment on apprenticeship contains some important insights into attitudes to age. There was a general feeling that young men needed to be inculcated with maturity and self-discipline before setting up as independent tradesmen or heads of household, and this was used to justify the seven years of subordination from the mid- or late teens which apprenticeship normally involved. A memorandum on the Statute of Artificers of 1563, probably written about a decade later, commented that until a man reached the age of 24 he would commonly be 'wilde, without judgement, & not of sufficyent experience to governe himselfe'. Much the same point was made in a discussion of apprenticeship nearly 80 years later by the Digger Winstanley, when the radical declared that a man should be 'of age, and of rational carraige, before he be a governor of a family'. It was an axiom of Renaissance humanism and one which, as far as can be seen, was widely shared in early modern England, that human beings should learn to control themselves before they attempted to govern others. Once individuals moved beyond self-control into the wider webs of authority it became evident that they were enmeshed in a system of interlocking hierarchies, marked most obviously by considerations of social position, age and gender. As William Gouge put it in his widely read *Domesticall Duties*, 'Yea, God hath so disposed every one's severall place, as there is not anyone but in some respect under another'. Ultimately, order rested upon the widespread willingness of most people, for most of the time, to accept their 'severall place'.

Towards a national consciousness

As our discussion of the problem of order has implied, the English were a people to whom obeying a national authority came relatively easily. But this was just one, if far from the least important, of a number of factors which were encouraging national integration over the early modern period. Certainly, England was a likelier prospect for such integration than were a number of the big continental monarchies. Privileged enclaves, like the Duchy of Lancaster, the Palatinates of Chester and Durham, or the Cinque Ports existed, and were capable of defending their rights. But they were much less powerful than many of their continental equivalents. England had nothing like that intense political fragmentation, that diversity of provincial representative institutions, regional privilege and urban rights which, for example, gave absolutism in France its peculiar flavour, or which proved such an impediment to Habsburg power in the sixteenth-century Low Countries. The country had no land frontiers with comparable powers. Wales was integrated into the English administrative system by Henry VIII, and after 1603 Scotland, isolated episodes apart, ceased to be a threat. By the eighteenth century, there was little sustained feeling of vulnerability or national crisis: wars were not only usually successful, but were also fought at a safe distance. England was more united linguistically than areas like the pre-Revolt Low Countries, the Habsburg Iberian possessions, or even France, where as late as the 1870s maybe half of the population spoke French as a second language at best. After the expiry of Cornish in the seventeenth century, people living in England spoke the same language. An agricultural labourer from the south-west might have difficulty in understanding his counterpart from Norfolk or Northumberland, but they were divided by accent or dialect rather than by language as such.

This potential for national unity should not obscure the presence of a number of smaller political units. There were 9000 rural parishes, over a hundred reasonable-sized towns and several hundred small urban centres. More importantly, there were 40 counties. Over the last two decades historians of early modern England have come increasingly to interpret developments in the period from a county viewpoint, and have argued that the century before the Civil Wars witnessed the rise of the county community. One of the earliest and most energetic proponents of this view, Professor A.E. Everitt, has traced a number of elements in this process. There was a growth in county administration, centred on the quarter sessions. The local gentry in counties as geographically distant as Kent and Yorkshire grew more wealthy, owning three-quarters of the land. The gentry also showed a marked tendency to marry within the county, with resulting proliferation and strengthening of kinship links locally: Mary Honywood, dying in Kent at the age of 93 in 1620, left 397 relatives in the county to mourn her. There was a growing interest in county history and local custom. William Lambarde's *Perambulation of Kent* (1576) was the first of a number of county histories produced by antiquarian-minded gentlemen or clergy, while a little later we find the Yorkshireman Sir William Fairfax demonstrating his pride in both his home area and his class by decorating the great chamber of residence with a frieze depicting 370 coats of arms of Yorkshire gentry. As well as gentry ascendancy, county towns added to the sense of local identity as they developed into regional capitals. All of this has led Professor Everitt to claim that, rather than being a unified entity, 'in some respects the England of 1640 resembled a union of partially independent county-states'.[1]

The work on the county community has proved very fruitful, not least in demonstrating that political activity was not merely limited to what happened at Westminster. Yet the concept of the 'county community' has a number of limitations, and it is possible to overstate the importance of localism and especially gentry localism. Setting aside the suspicion that the very grouping of so many documents in county record offices on a county basis might seduce the unwary into overestimating the importance of the county, a number of positive objections come to mind. First, although counties existed as unified administrative units, many were very economically varied. Second, even county administration was not invariably unified. Sussex, for example, was administered in two halves, while Lincolnshire was, by the late seventeenth century, divided into eight subunits, each with its own quarter sessions and group of attendant justices. After the Book of Orders of 1631 all counties were administered through the divisional system, and justices' notebooks of the subsequent period reveal that the focus of the normal working JP's activities was the division rather than the county. It seems, in fact, to have been very unusual for all justices to have gathered together at one meeting. When the justice did attend the assizes or quarter sessions he was reminded, as he was in many of his everyday duties, that whatever his localized allegiances he was part of a national system, and that England was a centralized polity governed by a common law. Changes in gentry taste towards the end of the seventeenth century dealt a further blow to localism. Although some county towns became important regional capitals, London was thought of as the pace-setter in taste and fashion by most gentry interested in such matters. Moreover, by this date the richer and more influential gentry were tending to marry outside their counties. The local county community may have triumphed in a certain sense, if we can trust the widely held notion that after 1660 the landed orders were left to run their shires with minimal interference from Westminster. Paradoxically, however, these same landed orders were becoming increasingly enmeshed in a metropolitan culture.

The law constituted another important integrating factor. One of the peculiarities of medieval England was the early supremacy of the king's law, a truly common law which ran in the village court leet in the same way as it ran in the Courts of Common Pleas and King's Bench at Westminster. After 1688 the common law was identified with the constitution. The law was generally regarded as one of the subject's main bulwarks against arbitrary government, and the concept of the rule of law became fundamental to popular political ideology. But the law performed much wider functions. It was essentially something in which people participated, part of the broad culture of the nation. Legal affairs, legal remedies and legal rights were constant preoccupations for people with any property at all, and for such people contact with the law through deeds, bonds and contracts could be frequent. The law was an important means of conflict resolution, and disputes over land, debt or reputation were settled through it. More notoriously, litigation was one of the phenomena of the age. The upsurge of litigation which can be traced back into the fifteenth century continued apace through the sixteenth and early seventeenth. The courts at Westminster, local ecclesiastical tribunals, and the assizes and quarter sessions in the counties all enjoyed an increase in business. The law was not simply an expression of class power: it was something which people used or were involved in, whether as debtors, witnesses, litigants, defendants or jurors. As such, it continued to be an important socializing force, inculcating both more law-abiding behaviour and a sense of national identity. As its name suggests, the law was common to all English men and (albeit with many provisos) women.

Religion was, on one level at least, less successful as a unifying force. The Tudor ideal of religious conformity had proved unattainable. Mary was unable to crush Protestantism, Elizabeth was unable to eliminate popery, and, after the Restoration, both the government and society at large had to come to terms with a plurality in religion. More generally, no regime had been able to bring more than partial spiritual illumination to the dark corners of the land. Puritan propagandists in the late sixteenth century, the post-Reformation nonconformist Oliver Heywood, and John Wesley in the mid-eighteenth century were all equally adamant that formal religion had barely touched large areas of the country and broad strata of the population. Nevertheless, the Church of England, as established by Queen Elizabeth of blessed memory, did provide an emotional focal point for many Englishmen. After 1588, and the triumph over the Armada, most people came to regard being Protestant as part of being English. This feeling, kept alive by the Gunpowder Plot, by tales of Spanish atrocities in the Low Countries, and by later accounts of Louis XIV's *dragonnades*, was firmly entrenched throughout the seventeenth and eighteenth centuries. By 1760 popery was equated with the black bread, wooden shoes and absolutist tyranny which were thought to characterize French life. More reflectively, religion provided a medium for philosophical discourse which even people of different Christian faiths could use. If nothing else, the King James Bible, probably the first book which most of the literate would read, was a vital part of national culture.

As we saw in the last chapter and have mentioned briefly in this one, London was a powerful force for national integration, economically, culturally and politically. One of the less obvious ways in which it centralized, however, was in its role as the clearing-house for one of the most avidly sought-after commodities of the period: news. Those claiming that English men or women had only a limited culture, its horizons more or less fixed by the county boundary, should ponder on the evident taste for a knowledge of wider matters. Newsletters, mainly describing foreign affairs, began to circulate at the time of the Thirty Years War. During the Civil Wars events in Britain were reported by numerous 'Intelligencers'. By the late seventeenth century newspapers proper were appearing, obviously in response to a widespread demand for news. An advocate of the freedom of the press wrote that he would be 'glad, especially when at a distance from London (and I suppose other country gentlemen may be of the same mind) to divert myself with some other newspaper besides the *Gazette*'. Within half a century, such country gentlemen might read one of four London daily papers, or one of the 35 newspapers being published in the provinces. The newspaper, at this date concerned mainly with passing on London news, was an important force in expanding local horizons and in bringing a sense of a national dimension to an increasingly literate population.

This increasing literacy was one of the most important outcomes of the educational developments of the period. Among the gentry, as will be described in a later chapter, attendance at Oxford, Cambridge, or the Inns of Court was becoming increasingly common in the century before the Civil Wars. Many Oxford and Cambridge colleges had strong regional biases, and it is possible that even a gentleman with some experience of higher education might return to his home shire having made only limited contacts with wider society. Even so, it is difficult to deny that this growth of higher education before 1642 helped to foster a common language of intellectual discourse and something like a national culture among the gentry. Many of them after leaving university continued to read books, kept in touch with their old tutors, and watched the progress of their younger relatives through university or one of the Inns of Court with interest. The grammar schools also helped foster some sort of national educational culture. There were many foundations of grammar schools in our period, the motive behind most of them being not only educational but also religious. Arguably they spread what was to become for many, including non-gentry, a widely shared culture, based largely on the Latin classics. Boys in Northumberland, East Anglia and Devon all had the shared experience of an adolescence spent learning Latin grammar.

The growth of a political culture provided another integrating factor. In the late sixteenth century, as we have seen, local élites were being brought into the national political system through those 'points of contact' to which Professor Elton refers: the court, the Privy Council and parliament. Interest in political issues was, however, spreading beyond the élite. The troubles of the 1620s seem to have created something like an informed electorate, while public opinion was a vital factor in the elections of 1640. In the early eighteenth century, about 300,000 men, or 5.5 per cent of the population, could vote (a higher proportion, incidentally, than after the 1832 Reform Act). By that date, despite tales of votes being bought for money or beer, many voters had a degree of political awareness, even if the most celebrated medium through which this awareness was expressed was the election riot. Thus we find Jonathan Swift writing from Leicestershire at election time in 1707 that 'there is not a chambermaid, prentice or schoolboy in the whole town but what is warmly engaged in one side or the other'. The decision to support, or even vote, Whig or Tory must have been determined by local circumstances, local personalities and local pressures: but it was a decision which was taken as part of a national context of which the decision-maker cannot have been ignorant.

By the mid-eighteenth century, therefore, a number of forces, many of which had been building slowly over the last 200 years, had combined to make England a coherent national state. Measuring the degree of this coherence, and attempting to compare it with that obtaining at other periods is, perhaps, impossible. It would have to rest on isolated anecdotes and isolated opinions. There was nothing as developed as that nationalism which has so characterized the twentieth century, a nationalism which was essentially the product of the nineteenth. Perhaps the greatest proof of this can be found in that acid test of how far people were willing to fight, and perhaps die, for their country. Recruiting for Marlborough's wars began by tricking yokels into taking the queen's shilling, and moved rapidly towards offering condemned felons military service as an alternative to being hanged. This contrasts strongly with the situation in 1914, when Kitchener's call for men produced a million volunteers in a few weeks. This would have been unthinkable in 1760, and even more so two centuries earlier. Yet it is clear that a sense of national identity was developing, and that by the eighteenth century this might already take the form of an ugly chauvinism similar to that with which more modern periods have familiarized us. When the influx of Dutch advisers and military experts which followed the accession of William and Mary provoked an outburst of such chauvinism, Defoe felt moved to satire:

The Pict and Painted Briton, treach'rous Scot,
By hunger, theft and rapine hither brought,
Norwegian pirates, buccanneering Danes,
Whose red-haired offspring everywhere remains.
Who, joined with Norman–French, combines the breed
From whence your True Born Englishmen proceed.

Measuring feelings of national identity, or levels of national integration, might be impossible: but the views lampooned by Defoe demonstrate that a gut-reaction sense of Englishness, if nothing else, existed, and could become a serious political force on occasion. They also remind us that, despite Nurse Cavell, patriotism can sometimes be far too much.

It also remains undeniable that the state played an important part in such integration as did take place. Under the early Tudors, the English monarchy was already English in the sense that a common law, language, system of government and body of customs which were recognizably English existed within the realm. Yet, in the period of state formation, such forces for unity were not enough. Thus it is possible, from the Reformation onwards, to trace the impingement of the state on the localities in a number of ways: through the law, through attempts at enforcing religious uniformity, through taxation, through military or naval conscription. Less dramatic, although of at least equal importance in the long run, was the gradual moulding of a sense of national identity both through official channels, those 'points of contact' between central authority and local society, and through less formal means: education, even newspaper reading. The end product of these processes was the development of a sense of national identity which was higher than anything which had existed previously. In 1550, localism was the dominant force in English society. Many people, despite the administrative achievements of the early Tudors and their ministers, still felt that their primary loyalty was either to their locality or to some great local patron. By 1760, despite the persistence of localism, a shift had occurred towards a sense of national consciousness: English society was a far more self-aware entity in 1760 than it had been two centuries earlier.

At the end of our period a sense of national identity was overlaying loyalties felt to other, lesser, focuses of allegiance. These focuses were varied and, on a day-to-day basis, were probably stronger, more immediate, than national ones. Among them were the region, the county, the town or parish, the family, a religious sect or a patronage network. Loyalty, or at least a sense of solidarity, existed towards all of these, as well as towards the wider notion of being English. Society as a whole, in the early modern period as now, comprehended a number of inferior units. A major problem emerges from this: how are we to regard one of the more important categories of inferior unit, those subdivisions of status, wealth and power into which society was divided? The crucial issue is the extent to which modern categorization by class is appropriate to early modern English society and, if it is not appropriate, what system of categorization should be used in its place.

The problem is an urgent one for those wishing to understand how society as a whole functioned. If we accept a class model, we also accept the implication that early modern England experienced class consciousness and class conflict. The most common alternative to a class model is one which sees society as a hierarchy, in which human beings thought of themselves as existing in an ordering of ranks stretching from the highest to the lowest. In this model, society was marked not by a consciousness of rival interests between classes, but rather by a deference to authority and an acceptance of what was regarded as a God-given social order. In class society, social divisions and their political consequences have been characterized as horizontal. In the alternative model, they are conceived of as vertical: loyalty would be to a trade, a parish, a region, a sect or a patronage network rather than to a class.

Certainly the language of class was virtually unknown before the late eighteenth century, and was not commonly employed until the early nineteenth. The fact that the word was not used does not mean that the thing did not exist, and the terminology which was employed does demonstrate that all strata of society had a clear notion of social divisions. Writers of analyses of the English social order were keen to enumerate different social groups. Some, like professionals, were difficult to fit in, while there was usually a lack of precision (probably arising from a lack of interest) when it came to describing non-élite groups. Yet there remained a clear notion that the handiest way of analysing society was through more or less horizontal gradations. Members of non-élite groups also seemed to have recognized that society was based on divisions of this type. The terminology used by participants in early seventeenth-century fenland riots included 'rich men', 'great men', 'a man of quality', 'sufficient men', 'the better sort', 'able persons of good estates', 'the meaner sort', 'the ruder sort', 'poor labouring men', and 'the common sort'. There was, however, no single equivalent to the modern term 'class', and rich and poor alike were inconsistent in their language of social analysis. Thus the naturalized Swiss Guy Miège, author of an account of English society in the early eighteenth century, began by writing about 'orders and degrees', but went on to employ a terminology of 'sorts': the 'middle sort', the 'common sort' and the 'meaner sort'.

The historian is also hampered by the lack of a fully articulated and watertight modern definition of 'class'. Marx himself, to whom we owe our appreciation of the central importance of class, left us no neat definition of it. The recent observation that anyone wishing to understand Marx's ideas on class and class consciousness 'must familiarize himself with the whole corpus of Marx's writing'[2] suggests that historians eager to clarify the matter will be kept out of mischief for some time. It is, perhaps, the modern insistence that class consciousness, if it has a meaningful existence, must be national, enshrined in class-based institutions, and articulate and focused, which has been the greatest barrier against an acceptance of a class-based model for early modern society. Only the landed élite could really aspire to anything like this: indeed, it has been argued that England was a 'one-class society', the class in question being the landed orders, the peers and the gentry. The opinions expressed by the lower orders about their betters during periods of popular disturbance clearly cast doubts on this notion. The poor, if lacking a fully developed class consciousness, had a sense of solidarity and a perception of their interests.

The most obvious solution, if it will not be rejected as too crude a compromise, is that in some ways early modern England was a class society, in others it was not. Even to the Marxist, the transitional status of the period, located as it was between the feudal and capitalist forms of society, would also logically make it a transitional period in terms of class formation. This in turn suggests that it should not be analysed, and that its inhabitants should not be categorized, in terms of class. Conversely, the evidence that exists of tensions and conflicts between various strata suggests that the hierarchical model, in which members of every social group accepted their position and deferred to their betters, is similarly lacking in full applicability. One highly placed observer commented in 1536 that in normal times 'all men' were 'almost at war with them that be rich', early evidence that at least one individual might have found a class-based model of early modern society comprehensible. As Keith Wrightson has pointed out, deference might be a response to the imperatives of a given situation, and 'did not necessarily involve, as is so often assumed, a full and unconditional subscription to a moral order which endorsed and legitimized the social and material subordination of the inferior'.[3] The two forms of social consciousness coexisted, to be brought to the surface on appropriate occasions. They were not mutually exclusive, but could survive together both as determinants of social relations, and in the mind of the individual. It is this dualism which explains the peculiar way in which 'paternalist' authority expressed itself in this period.

The whole problem is still, in many ways, an open one, and will continue to exercise historians for some time. The technicalities of scholarly debate should not, however, obscure the fundamental importance of the issue. The expression 'English society' implies (if we may take 1650 as our chronological reference point) about 5,000,000 individuals living together not as a mere agglomeration of atoms but as something rather more cohesive and positive. For 'society' to function on any level there must be rules, people must know how to behave, how to interact. If they are to do so, they must have some broader view of the social, of the ordering and analysis of that mass of human beings among whom they find themselves. Few of them between 1550 and 1760 saw that mass in modern class terms. Yet understanding how they did see their society remains one of the most valid aims of the social historian. So also is the related objective of analysing that society. My own suspicion is that neither the class model, nor the deference-hierarchy one is fully applicable. This does, however, make it difficult to write a book about early modern society, at least if we take terminological exactitude to its extreme. It is an especially urgent problem here, as we turn to a section dealing with the fortunes of different socioeconomic groups.

Although I would contend that something like modern class conscious-ness can be found in the period, I have avoided the use of the word 'class', except as a loose descriptive phrase, innocent of its full theoretical conno-tations. Likewise, my tendency to describe non-élite groups as 'the lower orders' does not mean that I think early modern England was a 'society of orders', as opposed to a class society. Generally, as I hope the next section demonstrates, I have tended to use contemporary phraseology whenever possible when examining the complexities of the social struc-ture: 'gentry', 'yeomanry', 'the labouring poor' and so on. When this is not possible, I have tried to use a non-controversial modern term: 'profes-sional', or 'aristocrat'. This might be seen as a retreat from pure intellec-tual rigour: writing comprehensible English does, however, sometimes involve compromise.

Notes

1 Alan Everitt, *The Local Community and the Great Rebellion* (Historical Association Pamphlets, General Series, 70) (1969), p. 8.
2 R.S. Neale, *Class in English History 1680–1850* (Oxford, 1981), p. 46.
3 Keith Wrightson, 'The Social Order of Early Modern England: Three Approaches', in Lloyd Bonfield, Richard M. Smith and Keith Wrightson (eds), *The World we have Gained: Histories of Population and Social Structure* (Oxford, 1986), p. 194.

PART

II

THE SOCIAL HIERARCHY AND SOCIAL CHANGE

|5|

The economy: an overview

In the three chapters which follow this we shall be examining the fortunes of the various strata of which society was composed. Our objective in this chapter is to provide a brief introduction to the economic history of the period. There are two main reasons for doing this. First, economic activities and economic development constitute an important avenue towards understanding how societies function. Second, ever since Marx, historians and others have been obliged to address the possibility of a connection between economic change and the fluctuating fortunes of various social groups. The problem of this connection is especially urgent for the early modern period. This, we must remind ourselves, has been interpreted by Marxist and liberal historians alike as one which experienced the fundamental shift from a feudal to a capitalist society, with a concomitant rise of the middle class. The issue is even more acute when studying the history of England, a country which is generally agreed to have possessed the most advanced economy in Europe by 1760.[1]

But with the economy more than most topics, any attempt to generalize or synthesize runs up against the obstacles presented by a near infinity of local, sometimes even parochial, varieties of experience. Agriculture, commerce and industry were all composed of a number of different sectors, and any general description of these broad categories of economic activity has to take into account interactions and shifts in importance between these various sectors. Second, we are confronted once more by the difficulty of having to discuss issues which, ultimately, need quantifiable data which is only rarely available from a prestatistical age. There are practically no series of figures for national agricultural or industrial production. A few contemporary estimates survive, while modern historians have made calculations, many of them necessarily approximate in their nature. Figures for the overseas import, export and re-export trades exist in series from 1696, although even these are beset by problems, some of them indicated by an estimate of 1733 that goods smuggled into the

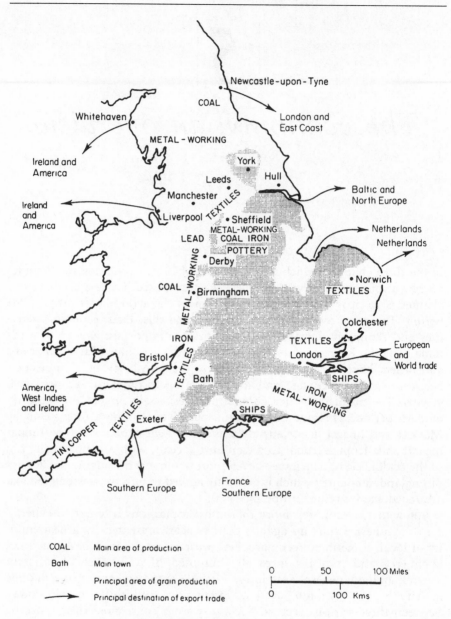

Map 5.1 The English economy *c.* 1700.

country represented one-third of the value of official imports. Any discussion of the economic trends of this period must therefore be couched in cautious tones, not least where national developments are involved.

An important interpretative problem remains. If, as we have argued, the writing of the political history of the period before 1642 has been distorted by the knowledge that a civil war broke out in 1642, so the economic history of the century (and in some ways the two centuries) before 1760 has been distorted by the tradition that a bundle of economic changes known as the Industrial Revolution began at that date. As with the Civil War, the Industrial Revolution has encouraged a search for long-term causes, for origins, for signs of modernity, for developments pointing the way forwards. Few historians now take seriously earlier suggestions that there was an 'Industrial Revolution' in the Tudor period, or that the economic history of England from 1550 should be interpreted as a steady evolution towards industrial take-off. Even so, it is difficult to study the early modern English economy without searching, even unconsciously, for the seeds of what has generally been regarded as a remarkable set of economic changes. But if we are to produce a more rounded picture, showing the obstacles as well as the advances, we must avoid searching merely for origins. It would not have been easy to predict the coming of an industrial revolution in 1760, and it has recently been suggested that the very concept of the 'Industrial Revolution' as defined in the textbooks and in popular historical folklore is an extremely questionable one. Initially, however, let us turn to that sector of the economy which was, throughout our period, the biggest single employer: agriculture.

Agriculture

Despite the burgeoning of commerce and industry, and the burgeoning of debate over such matters, the state of the agricultural base was the most important factor in the early modern English economy: proof of this point can be found in the fact that, well into the nineteenth century, the condition of the grain harvest was the most significant variable in the economic year. Unfortunately, discussion of agriculture is hampered by regional variations. Joan Thirsk traced 10 farming regions in Tudor and early Stuart England, Eric Kerridge found 40. Most agrarian historians agree that there was a broad division marked by a line running from the Tees in the north-east to Weymouth in the south-west. East of that line was the lowland zone, an area of mixed or arable farming. The highland zone, in which the major agricultural pursuit was the raising of sheep and cattle, lay to its west. Each of these zones, however, was itself full of variations. Among pastoral farmers there was a divergence between those who raised animals and those who fattened them, and between the different types of animals raised. The lowland zone included downlands, woods and brecklands, where corn was grown and sheep raised, the clay vales where corn and stock were combined in a number of variations, and the marshland areas where corn was grown and stock fattened for the market. The variety of local economic experiences was nowhere more evident than in agriculture.

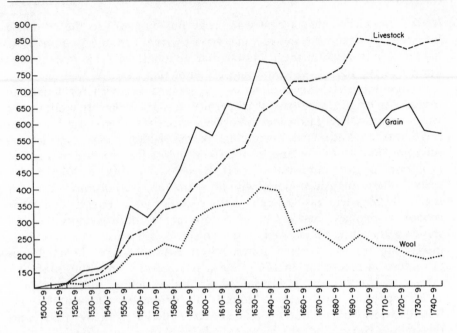

Figure 5.1 Prices of agricultural produce, 1500–1749. *Source*: Joan Thirsk (ed.) *The Agrarian History of England and Wales* (Cambridge: in progress, 1967–   ). Vol. IV, Table I, pp. 815–21; Table II, pp. 822–8; Table V, pp. 839–45. Vol. V, ii, Table I, pp. 828–31; Table IV, pp. 840–2; Table XI, p. 855. *Index*: 1450–99 = 100. (Figures for 1640–1749 recalculated.)

One way of generalizing from this complexity is to examine the long-term trends in the prices of a number of agricultural products. These are national estimates, once more subject to modification by local circumstances. Nevertheless, they do permit the delineation of broad patterns. Figure 5.1 shows fluctuations in the prices of three main groupings of agricultural products: grain (wheat, barley, oats and rye); livestock (sheep, cattle, pigs, horses, poultry and rabbits); and wool. What emerges from Figure 5.1 is a marked change in the behaviour of these prices around 1650. In the century and a half before that date agricultural prices had risen gradually. The factors affecting this rise have been much debated, but there is now a general consensus that the inflation of this period came mainly from the demand side, and was the outcome of a rising population: it was for this reason that the price of grain, the basic foodstuff, rose more rapidly than anything else. Livestock prices rose slightly less rapidly, while wool prices trailed badly: people had to eat before they clothed themselves, and prices reacted accordingly. After 1650, things changed. There were periods of bad harvest (notably in 1661, in the 1690s, in the late 1720s, and around 1740) which caused short-term increases in the price of grain, but the general trend was for grain prices to remain static, and then decline. The inflationary effects of an ever-increasing population were removed when demographic growth ended. Wool prices did not recover, evidence perhaps that supply was outstripping demand in this later period. Conversely, the greater disposable income among many groups created a demand for meat, and a consequent rise in the value of livestock. The prices of agricultural produce, like so much else, demonstrate the degree to which the mid-seventeenth century marked an important historical discontinuity.

For the 10 or so generations living through the period covered by Figure 5.1 this discontinuity was of more immediate consequence. As the figure demonstrates, a middle-aged man or woman of 1550 would have seen the price of grain triple over a lifetime, while by 1650 it was to more than double again, and stand at nearly eight times its mid-fifteenth-century level. This rate of inflation was slow by late twentieth-century standards, but it was serious enough for those dependent upon buying grain or bread in the market. Real wages failed to keep up with inflation, many people found their standard of living being gradually depressed, and in periods of bad harvest there was severe malnutrition and death from famine-induced disease or, more rarely, starvation. For those whose holdings made them immune from the effects of even the worst harvests (estimates on this point vary, but in an arable area with a three-crop rotation 50 acres, as we saw in a previous chapter, would be the safety line) the consequences of rising grain prices would be very different. Small peasants might be proletarianized and middling land-holders badly squeezed, but the big yeoman farmer would enjoy ample opportunities to profit from high grain prices and enlarge his holding as his poorer neighbours broke economically and sold up. It was in this century before 1650 that yeomen were able to have big farmhouses built and to send their sons to university. It was also during that century that a number of innovations were introduced which increased productivity in the grain-growing areas. The late sixteenth century saw the introduction of what was known variously as ley farming, alternative husbandry, or up-and-down husbandry. This involved varying land use between a period of growing crops and another of grazing animals, with consequent benefits for the soil. Around 1650 there came the floating of water meadows and the introduction of clover and other new grasses as animal feed, which meant that there were more animals, more manure, and hence more grain. The introduction of the turnip as animal feed reinforced this development.

The gradual spread of these innovations, together with the traditional expedient of bringing more land under cultivation, meant that grain production was adequate for national needs by the last third of the seventeenth century. By that time, however, arable farmers were under pressure. Ample supplies of grain were being grown, yet the expansion of the home market had ended. Foreign markets offered an outlet, and from the 1670s

England was a regular exporter of grain. The other solution open to the arable farmer faced by falling grain prices was diversification. In the period before 1650 the yeoman farmer could make a profit, the odd year of glut apart, simply by growing grain. In the century after that date, especially in lowland England, the arable farmer had to be more enterprising to succeed. It was this period which witnessed an ever-growing complexity in English agriculture. National population was not expanding, but the proportion of it living in towns, notably London, was. Marginal improvements in living standards meant that many people, notably the growing stratum of moderately wealthy town-dwellers, could afford better and more varied diets. Thus farmers within striking distance of London or other large centres rented their land for fattening livestock, some of it, in London's case at least, driven down from the far corners of the country. Others became dairy farmers, producing milk, butter and cheese for the urban market. Many small farmers gave up trying to scratch a living from grain, and turned to commercial market-gardening: this offered possible returns of £20 to £30 per acre annually, compared with the £1 or so offered by grain production. The practical advances of the century after 1650 were mirrored by a flourishing of theoretical works on agriculture. There had been a number of earlier writers on the subject, notably the Elizabethan Thomas Tusser, but it was Sir Richard Weston's *Discourse of the Husbandrie used in Brabant and Flanders* of 1650 which set the trend for serious publication on farming, as well as acknowledging where many of the new techniques came from.

These agrarian developments affected more than crop prices and marketing: they also influenced rents for agricultural land and tenurial arrangements. English land tenures were massively complex. Briefly, however, they fell into three main categories. The first was freehold, which offered solid rights amounting almost to absolute ownership. The second was leasehold, which normally gave defined rights over a piece of land for a stated period of time in return for rent. The third was copyhold. The exact conditions of copyhold tenure were dictated by local manorial custom, but they usually involved the payment of traditional or nominal rents or services which were economically unattractive to the late sixteenth century landlord. The tradition that copyhold was destroyed and transformed into leasehold by grasping landlords in the late Tudor and Stuart periods has been exploded, but it remains clear that a variety of factors were working for the gradual replacement of copyhold by leasehold tenancies. The conditions of these could be more easily adjusted by landlords to take advantage of prevailing economic circumstances. In the early sixteenth century perhaps two-thirds of land-holders were copyhold tenants. By the late seventeenth century the proportion had dropped to one-third, many of them small farmers. Connected to this change in tenurial arrangements was another of the main themes of the agrarian history of the period: the disappearance of the small land-holder. As with the alleged attack on copyhold, the rapidity and completeness of this process has been exaggerated: in 1760 there were still many small farmers in England, not least those living in the highland zone whose fortunes had been improved by rising livestock prices. Nevertheless, over much of the lowland zone primogeniture and the logic of two centuries of increasingly commercial arable farming meant that English rural society was moving towards its distinctive tripartite division: landlord, prosperous tenant farmer, and agricultural labourer.

Enclosure was another element in these agrarian changes. In the early sixteenth century enclosure, and especially enclosure involving the conversion of arable land into sheep pasture, was identified as a major social evil, a cause of depopulation and pauperism in the countryside. Moreover, up to about 1650 enclosure was a regular cause of rural rioting. But, the strictures of moralists and the attentions of mobs notwithstanding, enclosure was neither sudden nor widespread enough to be disruptive in our period.

Enclosure for conversion to pasture became less attractive as grain prices outstripped those for wool, and after 1550 enclosure was primarily a means of obtaining more efficient arable farming. Although the traditional open fields with their scattered strips of holdings were more responsive to change than has sometimes been claimed, the compact holdings which enclosure offered were obviously more amenable to improved management and increased productivity. In some areas, therefore, the progress of enclosure could be represented as a symbol of the clash between the new demands of capitalist agriculture and the old ethic of the peasant family farm, although denials that a real peasant consciousness ever existed in England complicate the point. Further complications arise from the tendency for enclosure to be initiated not by landlords, but rather by the tenants of a manor or, more accurately, by powerful groups among those tenants. This could have serious consequences for those poorer tenants or squatters whose rights, especially rights to common, were being curtailed. The sporadic rioting against enclosure precludes our taking too idyllic a view of the process, while nothing said here in any way denies the misery caused by rapid and large-scale enclosure in the late eighteenth century. Enclosure increased steadily over the seventeenth century, but it was essentially localized and piecemeal. Even so, the proportion of the country's land area under enclosure rose from some 50 per cent in 1600 to 75 per cent in 1760. Down to near that date low grain prices meant that enclosure was gradual, not an urgent priority for landlords. After 1750 the situation was to change radically.

In general, the history of agriculture in early modern England was one of steady progress. The more sceptical historian might harbour doubts about the claims which have been made (notably by Eric Kerridge) for an 'Agricultural Revolution' in the seventeenth century. Such improvements as were made were often merely local initiatives, and were rarely technologically revolutionary in themselves. Nevertheless, these constant small-scale improvements added up to a considerable total advance, and real gains were made. Grain yields per acre increased by 30 per cent between 1450 and 1650, and perhaps by as much again over the next 100 years. As we have noted, by the late seventeenth century England was an exporter of grain, a position which it continued to enjoy in the following century: in 1750, the record year, 1,500,000 quarters of grain, or 10 per cent of national production, were exported. Similarly, there is scattered but persuasive evidence that the quality of livestock improved. Concern over livestock feeding, the nature of fodder, and the quality of pasture, virtually unknown in 1550, became commonplace in agronomist writings after 1650. Such animals as the cow weighing 1741 lbs which amazed the townsfolk of New Market, Shropshire, in 1749, were clearly exceptional: yet the figures which are available suggest that the average weight of cattle and sheep had increased over the two centuries before that date. The size of herds remained buoyant: it was thought that there were 13,000,000 sheep in England in 1741, an estimate which, if accurate, indicates that they outnumbered the country's human inhabitants by two to one.

English agriculture, therefore, made marked advances between 1550 and 1760. By the latter date, even in bad years, the nation's population could more or less be fed from the nation's agricultural production. There were other signs of advance. Agriculture in England was, by contemporary standards, very capitalistic. Obviously, many small farmers were still imperfectly integrated into the market economy or capitalist relations. Others, however, were fully involved in commercial agriculture. To the ambitious farmer or improving landlord capital and credit were of prime importance: enclosing or floating a water meadow was an expensive business, while setting up as a sheep or cattle farmer might involve the outlay of £80 to £100 and the acquisition of at least 50 acres of good pasture. Less easily quantified are the attitudes to those changes and innovations which the rise of commercial agriculture entailed. Agricultural writers were prone to decry the conservativism of farmers: Walter Blith, writing in the mid-seventeenth century, was insistent that 'your mouldy old leavened husbandmen, who themselves and their forefathers have been accustomed to such a course of husbandry as they will practice, and no other' were a major obstacle to progress, and this was still a persistent theme of Arthur Young's works more than a century later. Yet the study of the diffusion of new crops and techniques (notably Joan Thirsk's work on seventeenth-century tobacco cultivation in England) reveals a widespread eye for the main chance and a willingness to innovate if the risks involved were not too high. The writer who claimed in 1757 that 'every day produces new inventions and improvements in agriculture' was obviously overstating his case: but it is difficult to leave an analysis of mid-eighteenth-century English agriculture without having formed an impression of a dynamic and, by the standards of the day, technologically and organizationally advanced agrarian sector.

Commerce

If progress in agriculture, however impressive in sum by 1760, was essentially slow and piecemeal, progress in trade, and especially in overseas trade after 1660, was rapid and decisive. As far as overseas commerce was concerned, England in 1550 was very backward, enjoying a semi-colonial status on the fringes of Europe. The country's major export, amounting to 80 per cent of the total, was woollen cloth, much of which was sent abroad undyed and unfinished. Other exports were primary products or raw materials: tin, lead and leather. Export of these commodities was overwhelmingly controlled by foreign merchants based at Antwerp. By 1760 all this had changed. The Dutch commercial ascendancy of the seventeenth century, so galling to the English, had been broken. England was now the entrepôt of the world, exporting manufactured goods to her colonies, exporting finished cloth and other manufactures to Europe, and re-exporting large quantities of colonial goods there. Merchant capital constituted an increasingly sizeable proportion of national wealth, while merchants themselves were patently becoming more prosperous. Colonial (and hence commercial) policy was now one of the major factors affecting diplomacy and warfare: the concern shown for the acquisition of colonies in the peace treaties of 1713, 1748 and 1763 is ample proof of this point. English trade in 1550 was essentially limited to the North Sea and the Atlantic coast of Europe. By 1760 it was global in its extent.

This growth was a seventeenth-century phenomenon. The decline of Antwerp as an entrepôt and its eclipse after the rebellious Dutch closed the Scheldt in 1585 left English merchants seeking a new access to markets and to the wider financial connections they so sadly lacked. The Tudor voyages of discovery, so celebrated in earlier generations of textbooks, added little to national wealth. Some advance came after 1600, with the opening of the far east by the East India Company and the first quickening of trade with the American colonies. Even so, in 1640 woollen cloth exported to Europe still accounted for 80 per cent of English exports. The pace of long-distance commerce accelerated in the period 1640–60, and then advanced massively over the next 30 years. By the later seventeenth century, as D.W. Jones has reminded us, the London merchant community included not just those working the long-established trades with Europe, but also those

> who had employed their resources in taking Newfoundland cod to the tables of the Catholic south, Sicilian grain to Italy, New England victuals to the Caribbean, slaves from Benin to the West Indian islands and to the tobacco plantations of Virginia and Maryland, and in exchanging Bengali and Gujerati piece-goods, together with those of the Coromandel coast – sometimes against each other, and sometimes in conjunction with cargoes of silver – in exchange for

the cotton of the Gujerat, the sugar of Bengal, the rubies and sapphires of Pegu, the tin of Siam and the Malay peninsula, and the gold of China and Arakan.[2]

Behind the lyricism of this passage there lies a basic fact: by 1700 England stood at the centre of a world market.

There were various elements in this new situation. Cloth was still the major English manufactured export, but now the heavy broadcloth exported to northern Europe in the Tudor period had been supplanted by the lighter products of the new draperies. These were exported to Spain and to the Mediterranean and had, by 1700, largely defeated Spanish, Italian and Dutch competition. The most important development of the later seventeenth century, however, was the expansion of extra-European trade and, in particular, of the re-export of colonial goods. Between 1640 and 1700 exports of English products, mainly textiles, rose from an estimated £2,500,000–£3,000,000 to £4,500,000. Over the same period re-exports rose from less than £100,000 to some £2,000,000. Sugar and calico were major elements in this re-export trade, but around 1700 the most important commodity was tobacco. In 1619 Virginia and Maryland sent 20,000 lbs of tobacco to England, where it was a luxury, costing £1–£2 per lb. By 1700, 22,000,000 lbs of tobacco was exported from these two colonies to England, where it sold to all classes at 1s per lb. At that time, two-thirds of tobacco coming into England was re-exported to European markets.

Another aspect of this burgeoning long-distance commerce was the growth of the slave trade. As far as English merchants were concerned, slaving really developed after the 1660 Navigation Act and the formation of the Royal Africa Company in 1672. The Company was extremely successful, exchanging calicoes and assorted manufactured goods for slaves on the West African coast, and shipping perhaps 5000 people a year to the sugar plantations of the West Indies. After 1700 Bristol and Liverpool merchants joined their London counterparts in this profitable but obnoxious trade. The growth of all these areas of commerce was aided by the development of the English merchant fleet, which grew from perhaps 100,000 tons around 1610 to 200,000 tons in 1660 and 340,000 tons in 1686. It was this which made the seventeenth-century Navigation Acts, with their insistence that trade between England and her colonies should be carried in English ships, and that all major imports from the continent should be carried in vessels either from England or from the country of origin of the product in question, so important. Similar legislation had been passed in 1485, 1489, 1532, 1540 and 1558. The novelty was that now there was enough English shipping to make the legislation effective.

The boom in trade may have levelled off after the commencement of warfare in 1689, although the most recent research has suggested that this trend may have been less marked than was previously thought. Certainly

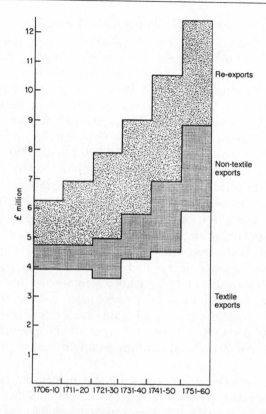

Figure 5.2 Average annual value of English exports (excluding specie) and re-exports, 1706–1760. *Source*: A.H. John. Aspects of Economic Growth in the First Half of the Eighteenth Century, *Economica*, 28 (1961), p. 178.

a number of European states adopted protectionist policies, and in some areas the products of indigenous textile industries may have competed successfully with English cloth exports. But any downturn which may have occurred was certainly reversed in the 1730s. After that decade, trade recovered because of a new stimulus: the market provided by the population of the American colonies. Between 1700 and 1776 the population of British America increased ten-fold, reaching perhaps three million by the later date. This rising population constituted an ever-expanding market for English manufactured goods, particularly small brass and iron wares: nails, including six- or ten-inch spikes, were sent out by the million to a region that built its houses of wood, as were axes, ploughshares and other agricultural implements, cutlery and pewter goods, firearms, buckets and buttons. Exports and re-exports in the first half of the eighteenth century, as Figure 5.2 demonstrates, therefore underwent some important changes. In 1700, non-textile exports constituted 17 per cent of total exports, but in the 1760s they constituted 33 per cent. Increasingly, these went to North America. Moreover, as Figure 5.2 shows clearly, re-exports continued to be a major, and by 1760 an expanding, aspect of English overseas trade. The efficiency and potential of this commerce was illustrated by the 'triangular trade' which developed from slaving. Exports of re-exports went from Britain to West Africa, slaves were taken from there to the West Indies, and the slave ships then returned to Britain laden with colonial goods. During the period 1680–1780 the slave population of the British West Indies rose from 60,000–70,000 to 400,000, with an equal number in what were, by that date, the rebellious American colonies.

This emergence of England as the world's entrepôt, described by some historians as a 'commercial revolution', was obviously of central importance. Many contemporaries certainly thought so, and from about 1650 foreign trade became a staple topic of economic debate. The merchant community grew both in wealth and in self-awareness: the nervous, unselfconfident, almost apologetic tone of Tudor and early Stuart merchant propagandists was replaced by a ready acceptance of the significance of overseas commerce. Moreover, as we have noted, trade, overseas commerce and colonial expansion became major concerns of statesmen, while merchant pressure, for example that of the powerful West India lobby in 1739, could be an important factor in pushing the nation into war.

Government involvement in the economy before the late seventeenth century was normally conservative in its intent and (as the disastrous Cockayne project of 1613–17 demonstrated) could be damaging in its outcome. Even so, there was a growing feeling that the mercantile interest deserved support and protection from government. But this did not amount to the 'mercantilism' of older textbooks. Most of the policies advocated and followed were essentially traditional, as is demonstrated by those most familiar symbols of English mercantilism, the Navigation Acts. Similarly, government innovations in the management of the economy, notably the tariffs of the very late seventeenth century, were developed not as a consequence of long-term planning or deep-seated economic philosophy, but were essentially short-term fiscal expedients designed to raise money to finance warfare. Once very basic guidelines were left behind, early modern governments were as unlikely to follow coherent and far-sighted policies in overseas trade as they were in anything else.

The importance of overseas trade, and the claims for the coming of a 'commercial revolution', should not obscure the importance of internal trade. Foreign commerce was more likely to create great wealth for individual entrepreneurs, and to provide striking success stories in which the rewards of ambition and enterprise could be celebrated. In total, however, internal trade was much more important. Reconstructing exact figures is impossible, not least because many domestic transactions were still based on barter. Nevertheless, estimates by such commentators as

Gregory King in 1688 and Arthur Young in 1770 suggest that the value of cash transactions on the national market rose from about two to about three and a half times the value of goods sold abroad. These estimates were little more than approximations, yet they do indicate that internal commerce was increasing more rapidly than foreign trade, and that the problems of transporting, distributing and marketing goods for home consumption were of central economic significance. Indeed, the very penetration of colonial goods into the country at large would have been impossible without a highly sophisticated domestic commercial system: without such a system, tobacco would not have been as widely enjoyed as it was by 1700, and tea, coffee and calico would not have become familiar consumables over the half century which followed that date.

Transport was a vital factor in this internal commerce. The old image of early modern roads as being unimaginably bad must now be rejected as a caricature: yet the comments of contemporary travellers and occasional coroners' inquests on unfortunates who were killed when horses stumbled or carts overturned on bad roads, or who were drowned in ruts or deep potholes in the highway, do demonstrate some of the problems attendant on road travel. Legislation of 1555, making each parish responsible for the upkeep of roads within its boundaries, proved unenforceable. The best answer available was the turnpike trust, by which the upkeep of roads was financed by tolls levied on the traffic passing over them. The first Turnpike Act was passed in 1663, and they became common after 1700. But turnpikes were only local solutions, and were fiercely opposed by riot and other means during the years 1730–50. Water transport provided an alternative to roads. The age of the canal had not yet dawned, but there was considerable interest in extending and improving the network of navigable rivers, and in many respects transport by internal waterways was already cheaper, quicker and more reliable than by road.

Coastal transport was also very important. The fleet of vessels which carried coal from the north-east to London increased from 78,000 tons in 1702 to 125,000 tons in 1773, and other coastal shipping more than doubled over the same period, reaching 90,000 tons by the latter date. In the early eighteenth century England enjoyed a transport system which encompassed internal waterways, coastal shipping, stage coaches, carriers, even a national postal service of sorts. Some indication of the growth of this system (and, by implication, of the growth of internal trade) can be gauged from private Acts of Parliament dealing with the improvement of river navigation, improving harbour installations, and establishing turnpike trusts. There were 50 such Acts in the period 1660–89, 59 between 1690 and 1719, and 130 between 1720 and 1749. The transport of goods and individual travel, even in the mid-eighteenth century, were obviously more risky and slower affairs than they are today: yet by that time, something like a relatively efficient national transport network existed, and played a vital role in economic life.

Developments in local retailing help illustrate this point. That most traditional forum for the sale of consumer goods, the fair, was still important. In 1746 it was estimated that there were 3200 fairs in England and Wales, and scattered evidence shows that almost anything could be bought at them. Nicholas Blundell, an early eighteenth-century Lancashire gentleman, recorded buying 'muslin, ribbon, gloves etc.' for his wife, shoes, 'iron skewers for ye kitchin', powder and starch, three gross of corks, 'sugar horns', flowers, roots and cord, as well as 'pack cloth for ye goods' on one visit to Chester fair, and on other occasions bought 'toyes for ye children' there. Traditional markets also continued to flourish, with an estimated 874 market towns in England and Wales in 1690, and 637 in 1720. These familiar retailing agencies were supplemented by two others. The first were the petty chapmen: itinerant pedlars who brought a wide range of small wares, pins, ribbons, buckles, books, clothing materials and the like to the countryside and the small town. Such people had always existed, but it seems probable that they grew in numbers from the 1670s, and government licensing reveals the presence of 2559 of them, some 400 with pack-animals, in the 1690s.

By then the shop in something very like its modern form had also emerged. The provincial shop, selling a host of small wares, notably non-perishable goods, was one of the most important factors in the formation of a national economic system. Shops, particularly in the provinces, were more in the nature of general stores than specialized enterprises, but they represented important pointers towards modern retailing. In 1726, for example, Defoe noted how shopkeepers were beginning to display their goods, 'a modern custom ... and wholly unknown to our ancestors'. By the middle of the eighteenth century England was moving towards having an integrated national economy. Throughout our period England was free of serious internal customs barriers, and by 1760 the United Kingdom and its colonies constituted the largest free-trade area in the world. What is striking is that there was no lack of goods and commodities to trade in. Some of these, as we have seen, were brought in from the colonies or from other distant markets. Others, conversely, were the products of native industry: it is to this that we turn next.

Industry

The common practice of using the term 'preindustrial' when describing society and the economy in early modern England has tended to obscure the extent to which the country was industrialized. We have merely to turn to so familiar a source as Defoe's *Tour through the Whole Island of Great Britain* to confirm this, at least as far as the early eighteenth century is concerned. Defoe found what he described as 'manufactures' almost wherever he went in England, and was insistent that their presence added to local or regional prosperity. He found widespread textile manufacture: serges in Devon, stuff-weaving in Norfolk, bay-weaving in Essex, 'fine Spanish and medley clothing and drugget making' in Wiltshire, 'white clothing' in Gloucestershire and Worcestershire, kersies (a type of coarse narrow cloth) in West Yorkshire. There was also metal work around Coventry and Birmingham, and more generally in Warwickshire and Staffordshire; iron-working in Yorkshire and Lancashire; coal-mining over much of the midlands and the north; mining of iron in Yorkshire, and of copper and tin in Cornwall. England was certainly 'prefactory' when Defoe wrote, but to call it 'preindustrial', however useful that evocative term might be, does seem a little illogical. Popular conceptions of the Industrial Revolution, with their emphasis on heavy industry and large units of production, have tended to miss this point. Industry was widespread in England a long time before the Industrial Revolution. But it was organized in distinctive ways, and was essentially handicraft industry, concerned predominantly with the production of textiles and of small manufactured articles.

When Defoe wrote, England was becoming known for the variety and quality of its manufactures, and in many industries had taken a leading technological and organizational position. This was far from the case in 1550. As with commerce, England's industrial standing was very inferior at that date. The only industry of note was textiles, in particular the production of that heavy broadcloth which was distributed to northern Europe via Antwerp. But this broadcloth had to be finished in the Low Countries before it could meet European standards, and the English industry was generally unable to compete with the best European manufactures in the production of high-grade cloth. The technological lead in a number of other industries, notably glass-making and paper-making, was held by Italians, while Germans had the technical advantage in the metallurgical and mining industries. There was little in the mid-Tudor period to signpost England's future role as part of the 'first industrial nation'.

In 1550, and throughout our period, a large amount of industrial production was carried out in the household under the control of a skilled artisan aided by apprentices, journeymen and the members of his family. The leather industry, brewing, baking, tailoring, cobbling and the building trades were all characteristically organized around units of this type, and this organizational form was especially important in towns. In the late Middle Ages urban craft industries were organized through guilds: bodies which attempted to protect a skilled workforce and which aimed to ensure the maintenance of proper standards in both craft-training and finished products. The guilds, well suited to the relatively static conditions of the fifteenth century, were eroded by the impact of the population increases of the sixteenth and early seventeenth: the skilled urban workers upon whom the guild system depended were undercut by cheap rural labour. Even so, the skilled artisan and his household remained the basic unit of production in many industries. Such artisans, especially in the countryside, often demonstrated another peculiarity of the early modern economy: its dual nature. Many craftsmen would combine their 'industrial' trade with agricultural pursuits, either raising crops or, more commonly, animal husbandry. Thus a large proportion of the 'industrial' workforce would also be involved, if only for domestic consumption, in agricultural production.

By the mid-sixteenth century the independent craftsman was being increasingly supplanted by workers organized on the domestic or putting-out system. By that date population increase had created a pool of cheap labour as economically depressed peasant families sought the means to earn a few extra pence a week. In industries where the techniques of production were accessible to the poor rural household, where tools and equipment were cheap, where close supervision of the workforce was not essential, and which involved the working-up of materials of small value, the putting-out system developed. Characteristically (and there were many variations) a merchant or other entrepreneur, connected to a wider network of credit and finance than would be accessible to the individual craftsman, provided materials which would be worked-up into a finished product and then returned for marketing. Conditions for the workforce under this system varied enormously. Some workers in the putting-out system were proletarianized, dependent on wages they and their families earned to get them through the week. Others were able to enjoy a semi-independent status and still devote time to agriculture. Two industries in particular depended on putting-out. The first of these was the textile industry, in which women and children in the rural and poor urban family, as well as the head of household, would be involved in the various stages of processing wool into cloth. The second was that constituted by a group of the metal-working trades, notably nail-making, in which strips of iron would be supplied to outworkers for working-up into a finished product.

Even in 1760 the proportion of the industrial workforce employed in large-scale enterprises was very low. Most often such enterprises existed for straightforward technological reasons than for any considerations of economic efficiency: as D.C. Coleman has pointed out, it is difficult to operate a blast furnace or build a ship in a cottage. Mining of necessity similarly involved concentrated groups of workers. Such concentrated units of production as did appear, like the slitting mills for the metal industry which arrived in the 1620s, or the 200 paper mills which existed in England by 1714, were usually fairly small-scale enterprises. But by that latter date larger industrial units had arrived on the scene, while the precursors of the modern factory were not far distant. In 1700 the largest concentrations of industrial workers were gathered not in those institutions with which historians of the Industrial Revolution have familiarized us, but rather in royal dockyards. It is therefore no accident that one of the biggest industrial enterprises, that founded by Ambrose Crowley on

Tyneside in the 1680s, owed much of its expansion to contracts for the Royal Navy. It was not until 1724 that the first modern factory proper, John Lombe's silk mill at Derby, was in operation. It depended on machinery driven by water power, it employed 300 women and children who kept the mill going in two shifts through a 24-hour day, and it undercut the price of Italian imports by 30 per cent. It also failed in the next decade, but was followed by others like it. However falteringly, the first steps towards factory production were being made: yet it was far from clear in 1760 that this mode of production was going to develop very far.

Attempting to analyse industrial production in terms of three main methods of organizing the workforce must not obscure the sheer diversity of industrial organization in the early modern period. Sometimes this was even evident within narrow regions. In the Weald of Kent, for example, textile production based on the putting-out system coexisted with an iron industry organized on centralized units employing water-powered blast furnaces. Equally, it was evident when looking at individual industries: thus silk production involved not only John Lombe's pioneer factory, but also those epitomies of craft artisans, London's Spitalfields silk weavers. Nowhere is this diversity more clearly demonstrated than in that most important industry of all: textile production. As we have seen, in 1550 the main product of this industry, which was just coming to the end of a 50–year boom, was heavy broadcloth destined for export to northern Europe. Smaller amounts of Yorkshire kersies were exported to the Baltic, while some West Country cloth went to France and the Iberian peninsula via Southampton. From the late sixteenth century, particularly in East Anglia, traditional methods of production and products were supplanted by the new draperies. By the end of the next century, textile production, although to be found to a limited extent over most of the country, was mainly concentrated in three areas: the West Country and East Anglia, where production was mainly through putting-out; and the West Riding of Yorkshire, where producers were characteristically independent artisans who might combine weaving with farming. From that date further complications were added to the textile trades as the production of textiles based on wool was supplemented by silk-weaving, linen production and cotton manufacture.

Tracing trends in other industries is more difficult. The mining of coal, a commodity seen as vital to England's later industrialization, was increasing, but hardly decisively. British production as a whole went up from 210,000 tons annually in the 1550s to 2,982,000 tons in the 1680s. This was clearly a dramatic proportionate rise, but it came from a low baseline and was not maintained. Production had barely doubled from 1680s levels by the 1770s, when it reached 6,000,000 tons annually, still rather less than a ton per head of population. Coal was used in brewing, salt-boiling and glass-making, and experiments with coke early in the eighteenth century demonstrated its potential for steel production. Its main role in our period, however, was as a cheap source of fuel for the poor, rather than as a key to industrial take-off. Much coal mining was on a small scale, with shallow or open-cast pits being worked by 50 men or less. Metal-mining and working were hardly going through a dynamic phase.

Lead production in the reign of Charles I stood at about 12,000 tons annually, and was to rise only sluggishly over the next century. About 26,000 tons of pig-iron were produced annually between 1625 and 1635, a figure that had probably only increased to 30,000–33,000 tons by 1750. Indeed, in the early eighteenth century the English iron industry was relatively static, organized in scattered units which in some cases were only worked intermittently, and producing a low-grade product which was generally inferior to imported Swedish bar-iron. Abraham Darby's celebrated experiments with coke at that time might have pointed the way forward, but they had little immediate effect: in 1760 there were only 17 coke-fired furnaces in England, and charcoal was able to meet most of the sluggish iron and steel industry's modest needs. Those traditional industries so often ignored in accounts of the Industrial Revolution were probably more significant and in a healthier condition. The leather trades, for example, would probably repay close investigation as exemplars of early modern industrial production: certainly the estimate that there were 3000 leather-workers in Southwark in 1619 suggests a formidable degree of concentration. Generally, there is little sign that those heavy industries which were later to figure so prominently in the Industrial Revolution were of any great significance in 1760. English manufactures were increasing in volume and diversity, but their production was organized overwhelmingly through artisans or the putting-out system, and what was produced was normally small consumer goods. It is significant that Adam Smith took a Birmingham pin-manufactory as his model of the division of labour.

Although the recent trend among historians has been to emphasize the slow and piecemeal nature of industrial development in early modern England, convincing claims have been made that there was one region where a substantial shift had taken place by 1760: the Tyneside mining area. Keith Wrightson and David Levine's work on Whickham, a township on the Durham bank of the Tyne, has demonstrated this process in microcosm, while study of the area more generally has made it clear that the developments they trace were not limited to one parish.[3] Certainly, whatever the figures for the development of the coal industry nationally, the speed with which coal production on Tyneside increased from the 1570s is striking.

Let us take one index: the record of coastal shipments of coal, most of it bound for London, noted in the port books of Newcastle-upon-Tyne. These show that between Michaelmas 1563 and Michaelmas 1564 some 32,951 tons of coal were shipped from Newcastle, a total that had risen to 162,552 tons between Michaelmas 1597 and Michaelmas 1598.

Between Christmas 1633 and Christmas 1634 a total of 452,625 tons was shipped, this total rising to 616,016 tons in the twelve months following Christmas 1684, while, to take another index, by 1703 about 600 ships were involved in taking coals from Newcastle. These totals may be contrasted with Lancashire, whose coal pits were producing between 1000 and 1500 tons annually in the seventeenth century. The impact upon local society of the processes which underlay these production figures was massive. Thus Whickham, a parish which in the 1570s had been a mainly agricultural community with a few industrial interests, was transformed by the 1660s into a township four-fifths of whose population, if we can trust inferences which can be made from taxation records, was made up of the labouring poor employed in mining. Whickham and the Tyneside area as a whole experienced the arrival of a form of industrial production which prefigured those later developments which traditional historiography has described as the Industrial Revolution: an industrial production which was large-scale, centralized, involved a heavy investment of capital, which was dependent upon the presence of a concentrated body of wage labourers, and whose shifting dynamics dictated technological innovations, notably the development of drainage techniques which allowed pits to be sunk deeper and nearer to the river, and wooden wagonways which permitted horse-drawn wagons of coal to be shifted more easily from the pits to the riverside. By 1736, indeed, Henry Bourne, an early historian of Newcastle, could claim that Tyneside's wagonways 'could vie with some of the great works of the Roman Empire'.

Such regional exceptions aside, however, the suspicion lingers that the imminent onset of an Industrial Revolution was not very evident in 1760. It should be remembered that the Industrial Revolution of the school textbooks does rather tend to diminish in stature when subjected to close analysis. Even as late as 1851 most people in employment in Britain worked in non-mechanized sectors. Such major changes as did occur were limited to a few geographical areas: south Lancashire, the Black Country, the east midlands, parts of the West Riding, Tyneside. Even in some of these areas change was quantitative rather than qualitative: the Sheffield and Birmingham metal-working trades, for example, were still largely organized on the basis of small workshops well into the nineteenth century. The 'other' industrial revolution, powered by tools, small machines and human muscle rather than the steam engine, and involving women and children domestic workers as much as male artisans and factory operatives, was also equally important at that date.

Continuities are easy to find: but the origins of mass industrialization remain elusive. It is a commonplace that there was some connection between these origins and the earlier rise of commercial farming and of overseas trade, but it is difficult to pin down the exact links. Students of capital formation have, in fact, found that there was surprisingly little of it around in the late eighteenth century, when it might cost

£30,000–£40,000 to found a textile factory. Calculations suggest that 6 per cent of national income was invested annually in 1688 and 7 per cent in 1760, which does not indicate great advances in capital formation. Similarly, there was little certainty of any connection between the old industrial areas and the new ones. The theory of proto-industrialization, which provides a useful analysis of the putting-out system, founders on this point. In some areas, notably the West Riding, the old domestic system did pave the way for the factories: in others, notably the West Country and East Anglia, it patently did not. Above all, there is little to suggest that factories would have seemed the most obvious way of increasing production to the majority of contemporaries: they would probably have chosen a more effective use of the putting-out system. There was little in English industry in the middle of the eighteenth century which signposted the Industrial Revolution of traditional historiography.

Searching for the origins of the Industrial Revolution in the first half of the eighteenth century is not, therefore, the most profitable of occupations. Indeed, the whole concept of the Industrial Revolution seems open to question, or at least in need of more stringent definition. If it is equated with factory production it obviously had not progressed very far by the end of the eighteenth century. By that time people living within a 10–mile radius of Manchester, or in the Halifax area, were obviously experiencing something rather new. Workers elsewhere, even if living in a region experiencing a higher level of industrial activity, might not have been aware of any qualitative change. Arguably, this was not to arrive until the middle of the nineteenth century, when half the population found itself living in towns, when the old dual economy had withered away, and when the railways had revolutionized transport. All this was far distant and totally unforeseeable in 1760. The Industrial Revolution, if the term is not to be discarded as redundant, came much later, and was a much more gradual process, than has generally been imagined. This argument can be supported by a telling statistic from 1800. In that year, England possessed 1200 steam engines with a combined horse power of 20,000. Their contribution to the nation's energy resources was dwarfed by the 1,287,000 actual horses existing in England at that point.

Even if we remain cautious about the origins and progress of the Industrial Revolution, it is still incumbent upon us to assess such changes in the economy as did occur. Perhaps the most striking of these was the rise of financial expertise and financial institutions in England. In 1550 English overseas trade was largely in the hands of Antwerp finance houses, and no English commercial enterprises could rival the resources or expertise of the big Italian or south German banking houses. English financial institutions, although developing gradually, really arrived in the 1690s, largely as a result of the need to finance William III's wars. The founding of the national debt and the Bank of England in the 1690s, and of government stocks, annuities and lotteries, set the basis for a fully fledged financial system. This system developed rapidly in the early eighteenth century: the South Sea Bubble crisis of 1720 is evidence of the arrival of a new world of financial speculation and financial sophistication. Puzzlingly, however, while banking, speculation, and the mechanisms of credit grew in sophistication, the currency itself remained in a poor condition. The debasement of the coinage by mid-Tudor regimes is familiar enough, but over most of the two following centuries English coin was inferior, and much of the currency in circulation was clipped, cut in pieces, or foreign. Silver coin had less face value than its intrinsic worth, and hence was either heavily clipped or melted down and exported as bullion. Many gold coins, especially those newly minted and of full weight, suffered the same fate, while by the eighteenth century much of the copper coinage was hardly worth regarding as currency. English capitalism advanced in a period when metal coin, the basic circulating medium, was of very poor quality.

Whatever its quality, money in particular, and the spread of commercial economic relations in general, were major forces for national integration. The emphasis on locally or regionally based economic studies should not obscure the gradual evolution of a national economic system. The point was illustrated neatly by Defoe (admittedly an active propagandist of commerce) in his *Complete English Tradesman* of 1726. Defoe imagined a suit of clothes which might be worn by 'the poorest countryman' or 'any servant in ordinary apparel'. The coat of this imaginary suit was made of Yorkshire cloth and lined with shaloon from Berkshire, the waistcoat was of Norwich calimanco, the breeches of drugget from Devizes in Wiltshire. The suit was complemented by yarn stockings from Westmorland, shoes from Northampton, garters from Manchester, leather gloves from Somerset, a felt hat from Leicester, a shirt 'of home made linen from Lancashire or Scotland', and held together by buttons from Macclesfield, 'or if they are metal, they come from Birmingham or Warwickshire'. Defoe (who carried out a similar exercise involving the clothing of a tradesman's wife and the furnishings of a tradesman's house) drew the obvious conclusion: the 'making up of one ordinary suit of clothes' involved 'in some part, almost all of the manufacturing counties of England'. He also claimed that 'all these manufactures must be found in all the remotest towns and counties of England, be it where you will'. Diaries, account books, details of local markets and the inventories of chapmen and shopkeepers support Defoe's assertions.

Readers of the works of Defoe and of other tracts from the early eighteenth century will be aware of the complexity of the choice of consumer goods then available, and of the existence of what was in many ways an advanced economy, of a society with a high level of material culture. Housing was improving in quality, so that by 1760 even many of the poor lived in dwellings which were designed to stay up for more than one generation. The rich and comfortably off were able to furnish their rather more spacious residences with a wide range of goods, some home-produced, others brought in English ships from far and exotic corners of the world. Such people were also able to indulge their taste for sartorial fashion. Throughout our period, those well enough off to be able to do so took an interest in their clothes, and moralists and preachers decried excess in apparel along with other moral failings. By the eighteenth century fashion was constantly changing and closely observed: newspapers regularly carried reports of new clothes, and the latest modes from France were eagerly studied. Moreover, if contemporary comment is to be trusted, even the lower orders were dressing well, perhaps better than most of their continental counterparts: fashion was ceasing to be the prerogative of the rich.

The backward economy of 1550 had, by the eighteenth century, burgeoned into what might plausibly be described as the first modern consumer society. This was crucial to the later industrial take-off: a society in which the material standards and expectations of the bulk of the population are static, in which people are content with what they have, is unlikely to engender economic change. Once more we must reflect that even small increases in real wealth, and the willingness to spend such increases on non-essential manufactured goods and better food, would have a considerable total impact on industrial and agricultural production. Economic history must never lose sight of the basic truism that human beings are consumers as well as producers. Although most economic histories of the eighteenth century are dominated by steam engines, factories, and coal and iron production, small and even frivolous manufactured goods were of great significance both to industrial production and to material culture. In a sense, John Spilsbury's invention of the jigsaw puzzle in the 1760s tells us rather more about the nature of the English economy than does the invention of the spinning jenny or of Compton's mule.

It is also evident that the lower orders, even the labouring poor, were beginning to share in this consumer society. The comments of contemporaries, both English and foreign, were insistent on this point. Sometimes such observations had a patriotic tinge: it was, after all, the eighteenth century which constructed the archetypal Englishman as the robust, beer-swilling and roast beef-eating John Bull. Thus Josiah Tucker, around the end of our period, claimed that 'were an inventory to be taken of the household goods and furniture of a peasant, or mechanic in France and of a peasant and mechanic in England, the latter would be found on average to exceed the former by at least three to one'. More commonly, observers complained that the lower orders' desire to consume and dress as well as their betters was symptomatic of an undesirable social emulation which would eventually obliterate all hierarchy. Such complaints, which can be found in the Middle Ages, seem to have become especially pointed in the eighteenth century, and systematic modern research has lent at least some substance to them. Work on real wage-rates has shown a modest, but perhaps significant, rise in the wealth of wage-earners in the late seventeenth and early eighteenth centuries. Other research, following Josiah Tucker's advice to look at the inventories of peasants and mechanics, has revealed that after about 1700 members of both these groups were beginning to enjoy what such Elizabethan writers as William Harrison had regarded as luxuries newly appearing in yeoman households: linen sheets, window curtains, cutlery, iron and brass ware, all sorts of household goods. Even the rioting of 1758–59 over high grain prices could be interpreted as a sign of rising expectations among the labouring poor.

By 1760 England was moving towards a set of economic relationships and economic attitudes which were recognizably 'modern'. When we find Dr Johnson declaring in 1759 that 'the art of advertising is now so near perfection that it is not easy to propose any improvement' we are forced to admit, however much we may regret that the statement did not prove accurate, that we are confronted by an essentially 'modern' comment. This creates a number of problems. Above all, it casts doubt upon the validity of using the English economic experience as a model for developing Third World countries. Comparisons between early modern England and underdeveloped modern economies can provide some stimulating insights, but at least by the eighteenth century the levels of material culture and commercial complexity were higher in England than those obtaining among a modern Third World peasantry.

A second problem is that of ascertaining the degree of change in economic attitudes over the two centuries after 1550. England in 1760, we have argued, was characterized by an economic life which was complex, capitalistic, commercial, market-oriented, geared increasingly to consumerism, in many ways 'modern' in its basic assumptions. It remains unclear how far this produced new social attitudes, or how far the rising material culture and the increasing commercial complexity of the early eighteenth century merely interacted with existing attitudes, reinforcing them or diffusing them more widely. Arguably, England in 1550, although manifestly less-developed than in 1760, was populated by people who in many ways possessed 'modern' attitudes in economic matters, especially that individualism which is held to be a product of 'modernization' or of the growth of capitalist economic relationships. Economic mentalities and institutions (notably the law relating to property) were intrinsically amenable to capitalism, even if population growth and the impact of a world market had yet to activate them. But above all, economic change had not, by 1760, produced sufficient social change to create new notions of class conflict or new political aspirations. English society was far from static. Yet most people, even members of the ever more prosperous middling groups, were unwilling or unable to envisage social relations other than in terms of what was essentially a traditional view of social hierarchies.

Notes

1 For details of economic regions *c.* 1700, see map 5.1 on p. 134.
2 D.W. Jones, 'The London Merchants and the Crisis of the 1690s', in Peter Clark and Paul Slack (eds), *Crisis and Order in English Towns 1500–1700: Essays in Urban History* (1972), p. 315.
3 David Levine and Keith Wrightson, *The Making of an Industrial Society: Whickham, 1560–1765* (Oxford, 1991).

|6|

The landed orders

Throughout most of early modern Europe the dominant social group, both politically and economically, consisted of large landowners known most often as nobles to contemporaries, and as aristocrats to modern historians. Social theorists had long argued about the origins and nature of nobility, but by 1550 it was more or less accepted that it was a form of distinction bestowed, or simply acknowledged, by the ruler and recognized by society at large. Members of the nobility preferred land as a source of wealth, power and status: they despised manual work or commerce for, as an English writer put it in 1669, 'tradesmen in all ages and nations have been accounted ignoble'. Nobles (or at least leading noble families) were immensely rich, immensely powerful, socially exclusive, socially endogamous, and obsessed with the principles of honour and heredity. Above all, they felt themselves to be people of distinction, set apart, superior, and recognized as such by society. They were accordingly able to command attention from others in the form of respect, obedience, flattery and admiration, attention consequent not only upon their power and wealth, but also their distinctive qualities. Charting the fortunes of this group has been one of the major tasks to which historians of the period have applied themselves.

In England such endeavours have been complicated by unusual difficulties of definition. Over most of Europe, nobility was a status to which was attached numerous rights and privileges and, generally, a title. Thus membership of the nobility and the rights accompanying such membership were relatively clear. In England noble legal privileges were few, and the right to hold a title was restricted to a small group within the landed élite: the peerage. This has caused considerable confusion among historians, not least those who have attempted to maintain a clear distinction between the 'aristocracy' (normally equated with the peerage) and the gentry. Contemporaries would have found neither the terminology used in establishing this dichotomy, nor the dichotomy itself, particularly meaningful. 'Aristocracy', until the eighteenth century at least, usually meant a form of government rather than a social class, while 'aristocrat' in its modern sense was essentially created by the rhetoric of the French Revolution. Sixteenth- and seventeenth-century observers used 'nobility' (or the Latin *nobilitas*) to describe peers and gentry alike. They made a distinction between the *nobilitas major* (normally, as far as the lay nobility was concerned, the peerage, and such upper gentry as knights and esquires) and the *nobilitas minor* (the lesser gentry) but this distinction was essentially one of gradations *within* a class. In theory at least, peers, poor gentry, and the various strata which lay between them all shared a number of attributes: the most important of these was gentility.

Discussing gentility exercised a number of writers in the Renaissance, the printing press, here as elsewhere, assisting the proliferation of works dealing with a subject which had attracted attention in the Middle Ages. Ideally, gentility and nobility were qualities inherited from a very distant original. Sixteenth-century theorists were insistent on this, and those English gentry who fabricated genealogies going back to the Trojans or even to Adam evidently shared their views. But as so often, theories about society diverged from reality. The mere facts of demography ensured this: on average, a peerage or gentry family died out in the direct male line every three generations, and hence for the nobility to maintain its numbers newcomers had to be recruited. There were various pathways to this recruitment, and successful entrants usually needed both wealth and social graces. Yet, as social theorists admitted grudgingly, in the last analysis a gentleman was anybody who could get away with being accepted as such. Thomas Smith, writing in the 1560s, concluded that 'to be short, who can live idly and without manual labour, and will bear the port, charge, and countenance of a gentleman, he shall be called master ... and shall be taken for a gentleman'. A century and a half later Daniel Defoe, discussing that upward social mobility which allowed a man of merchant origins to enter the gentry, remarked how 'his eldest son, bred at the university, and thoroughly accomplished, is well received among the gentry in the country and upon the valuable fund of his true merit, as if he had been a gentleman by blood for a hundred generations before the conquest'. Gentility in England was defined by cultural, rather than economic or legal, criteria.

In this chapter, therefore, we shall examine the *nobilitas* as a whole, the poor or newly accepted gentleman as well as the most powerful peer of the realm. It has, however, proved impossible to break entirely from the confusion of modern usage: terminological exactitude has been sacrificed to the need to write clear English. Whenever possible, the term 'landed orders', meaning the peers and the various strata of the gentry, has been used, but the terms 'nobility', 'gentry', 'gentleman' and even 'aristocrat' have also been employed, at times perhaps a little imprecisely. We can at least derive comfort from the knowledge that this imprecision was shared by most early modern writers, as well as most modern historians. Our investigations will follow three broad, and at times interconnected, lines: first, the landed orders' wealth, how they acquired their income and how their economic fortunes fluctuated; second, their power, in both the political and social realms, and on both the local and the national levels; and third, their lifestyle, the values, mental attitudes, and types of behaviour which were thought to characterize them.

Wealth

One of the most persistent of historical myths is that surrounding the alleged fortunes of the upper reaches of the landed orders in Tudor and Stuart England in general and in the century before the Civil Wars in particular. The myth has two major components. The first is that the *nobilitas major* were firmly imbued with a precapitalist ethic which resulted either in a general economic incompetence or in an attachment to traditional notions which placed a greater emphasis on paternalism than on profit. They were, therefore, vulnerable to the hard-nosed bourgeoisie who were, according to this myth, rising steadily at the aristocracy's expense during the period. The second component is closely related to the first. The nobility were not only failing to maximize their profits: they were also squandering such wealth as they did possess or acquire, rather than investing it rationally. Economic historians are not, generally speaking, a body of people given to an extravagant lifestyle. Confronted by the Earl of Leicester, whose funeral in 1588 cost nearly £1000, or Lord Sydney, who spent £220 on his clothes for a Christmas masque in 1602, or the Elizabethan Earl of Southampton, who lost a wager of 1100 French crowns on a game of tennis, or eighteenth-century squires drinking a bottle of port or two after dinner, the average economic historian turns with a sigh of relief to the more rational activities recorded in the account books of London or provincial merchants. The old nobility, as frivolous as they were feudal, were obviously going to become casualties in an age which, on this interpretation, witnessed the transition from feudalism to capitalism, and its concomitant, the rise of a capitalist middle class.

This general notion was given a new twist and greater precision by an article published by R.H. Tawney in 1941. Tawney, writing from a neo-Marxist position, was anxious to demonstrate that the Civil War was essentially the product of new social forces. Unfortunately, given the weakness of the commercial bourgeoisie in England in 1642, he was forced to look further afield for these forces, and found them in the gentry. For Tawney, the gentry became a sort of bourgeoisie of convenience. The attributes hitherto thought characteristic of a rising middle class were now bestowed upon country squires, particularly those who had recently acquired that status via trade or the law. Given 'the ruin of famous families by personal extravagance and political ineptitude', and the fact that 'the whole structure and organization' of the estates of the old nobility were 'now obsolescent', with noble wealth 'cumbrous, conservative, difficult to divert from its traditional routine to new and speculative enterprises', the way was now obviously clear for economically efficient newcomers. 'It was agricultural capitalists,' wrote Tawney, 'who were making the pace, and to whom the future belonged', 'classes representing a more businesslike agriculture'.[1] Rarely had the triumph of a new social group over one whose economic and social attitudes were totally outdated been more forcefully asserted.

This triumph would have been a lot less obvious to many contemporaries. The *parvenu* gentleman may have farmed his estate efficiently, but this was not a rapid way to riches. Indeed, down on the Isle of Wight Sir John Oglander (admittedly a man much given to grumbling) complained in 1629 that 'It is impossible for a mere country gentleman ever to grow rich or to raise his house ... by only following the plough he may keep his word and be upright, but will never increase his fortune'. Among the 'vocations' which Oglander thought likely to lead to wealth was, interestingly enough, that of courtier. For, as Lawrence Stone has demonstrated in his masterly portrayal of aristocratic economic activity, those at court were uniquely well placed to grasp opportunities to improve their fortunes. Courtiers and their clients can be found investing in joint-stock companies, enjoying the fruits of monopolies, holding lucrative offices, making fortunate marriages, deriving profit from customs farms, revenue farms, and the collection of old debts to the Crown, from various trading privileges, and from the management of the lands of recusants and wards. Attendance at court was a costly business: a courtier peer might spend £91,000 a year there in the reign of James I, and it is these expenses which have led many historians to see the court simply as a place where the old nobility wasted its wealth. Doubtlessly much money was squandered and many fortunes were ruined there. Yet, as Stone's analysis had demonstrated, going to court is probably best interpreted, in its economic aspects, as a risky investment: if it paid off, the rewards were massive, especially in terms of that liquid wealth which landholders so often lacked. One of Tawney's *parvenu* gentry, farming his land as efficiently as he may have been, would have looked very enviously at the £4000 a year which the office of Lord Treasurer was estimated to be worth early in James I's reign.

Equally, detailed investigation reveals little evidence that the peerage lacked economic acumen. Direct involvement with trade was out of the question: this would lead to derogation, loss of noble status. But investment in a joint-stock company or in a privateering venture, even in the business of mining, was acceptable and, given the realities of such activities, well suited to the aristocratic taste for gambling. There is, moreover, ample evidence that the upper nobility were alert to the need for efficient estate management. There were some problems in adjusting to the sixteenth-century inflation, and the period 1580–1620 does seem to have been one of financial difficulties for the peerage as a group. But in the long run their income from rents had overtaken inflation by 1640, and the detailed estate surveys and greater professionalism among estate stewards of the early seventeenth century point to an increased managerial efficiency.

Similarly, peers and old-established gentry were aware of the possibilities offered by extracting the minerals which lay beneath the broad acres they owned. Thus in Yorkshire the coal- and iron-extracting industries were firmly under the control of peers and upper gentry, and by 1672 the lead mine and smelting plant in Swaledale in the North Riding were giving Lord Wharton and his partners an annual profit of £3200. Perhaps the most perfect example of the entrepreneurial spirit in the period of Tawney's rising gentry was provided not by some rural capitalist newcomer, but by a representative of one of the longest established noble houses in England, George Talbot, Earl of Shrewsbury during Elizabeth's reign. Shrewsbury was the largest demesne farmer of his day, owned a ship called the *Bark Talbot* which was sent on privateering expeditions, controlled three iron mines, was involved in lead-mining, coal-mining and glass production, dabbled in trading ventures, and owned extensive sheep flocks. Arguing from one example, however striking, is, as ever, dangerous: but the upper nobility of Tudor and early Stuart England give the impression not of economic ineptitude, but of being anxious to grasp any opportunity to make a profit and of being uniquely well placed to do so.

The gentry themselves were not a homogeneous group, and the fortunes of individual gentry families were widely divergent. Regional variations have to be taken into account, but detailed local studies have revealed a broad national pattern. One of the best of these studies, that by J.T. Cliffe on the pre-Civil War Yorkshire gentry, refutes any simplistic idea of a rising gentry. Cliffe found 679 gentry families in Yorkshire in 1642. Of these, 73 enjoyed a landed income of above £1000, 244 enjoyed between £250 and £1000, while 362 had an income of less than £250 a year, 238 of these less than £100. There were many variations, but the general drift of Cliffe's findings is that those families which were already well-established were doing better from economic developments in the century before the Civil Wars than were newcomers on small estates. Indeed, far from rising, 397 of the 963 gentry families extant in Yorkshire between 1558 and 1642 experienced financial difficulties, and 87 of this group had to sell all their land. Studies of other counties, even if sometimes presenting different overall conclusions, suggest that Tawney's portrayal of the pre-1642 gentry as a rising class was a gross oversimplification: some gentry rose, others fell, and a number stayed roughly where they were. It is difficult to trace an overall trend, while even those families who did succeed were not invariably the thrusting newcomers of the Tawney thesis. In 1642 the two richest gentry families in Yorkshire were the Ingrams of

Temple Newsam and the Saviles of Thornton. The Ingrams, true to Tawney's model, had founded their fortunes on merchant wealth and financial speculation in London, and held estates in Yorkshire worth £9000. Against this example of *parvenu* wealth, however, must be set the Saviles. They held lands worth £7000 a year, almost as much as the *arriviste* Ingrams, yet they were one of the most ancient gentry families in the county.

Even proponents of the notion that the peerage underwent a crisis in the years before 1642 would find it difficult to deny that they made a striking recovery in the century after 1660. Calculating the annual average income of peers can at best provide only a rough guide to their wealth, yet there is little doubt that it rose over our period. On Professor Stone's figures, a peer's landed wealth averaged £2200 in 1559. On the eve of the Civil Wars the figure had risen to £5000: a sum, Stone estimated, some five hundred times greater than the annual income of an unskilled labourer in full employment. This figure probably obtained over much of the seventeenth century, but rose over the eighteenth. In 1760 the peerage were obviously a group who were doing very well. People who could afford to have their houses built by Vanbrugh or the Adams brothers, the grounds around those houses landscaped by Capability Brown, the portraits which hung in those houses painted by Reynolds, and the furniture to put in those houses made by Chippendale or Sheraton make unconvincing victims of economic depression.

Income from land provided only a proportion of the wealth of the landed orders, and those at the top of the heap were well placed to profit from these divers sources of wealth. The early eighteenth century peerage were as eclectic in their pursuit of economic advancement as Elizabethan aristocratic entrepreneurs like Shrewsbury had been. They continued to exploit mineral deposits, invest in trade, enjoy the fruits of office, and make advantageous dynastic marriages. They were also now able to invest in government funds, obtain commissions in the army for their younger sons, and exploit urban, and especially London, building development. The rational running of their estates, although essential, was neither the only nor the most important way to real wealth. The Fox family, mere gentry who had progressed steadily since the Restoration through office-holding, really arrived when Henry Fox, the first Lord Holland, secured the Paymastership in 1757. On his death his fortune was sufficient to pay off his sons' debts of £200,000 and leave them a comfortable sum besides. The Russells, Earls, and later Dukes, of Bedford, were already worth £10,000 a year at the Restoration, but their fortunes increased rapidly when marriages in 1669 and 1695 brought them massive concentrations of property in Bloomsbury and estates in Essex and Surrey. John, first Earl of Ashburnham from 1730, translated the modest wealth his family had accumulated through managing their estates well, quarrying, and money-lending into a real fortune by marrying and outliving three wives, each of whom came with a dowry of about £10,000. Opportunities like this were simply not open to the mere gentleman, however assiduously he might manage his estates.

The re-establishment of the economic power of great landowners after 1660 was symbolized by the adoption of the strict settlement. This was a legal device under which the titular owner of an estate was in effect merely the life tenant, unable lawfully to alienate the estate for a period longer than his life, or to sell it outright until his eldest son came of age, and able to mortgage it only for set amounts and set purposes. The aim of the strict settlement was to prevent sales of land from the family estate, and thus to ensure the continuance of the estate and seat through restricting the rights of the heir. In the last resort, the strict settlement was an insurance against the ruin of family fortunes through spendthrift heirs, and it is indicative of its attractiveness that by the middle of the eighteenth century perhaps half the land in England was subject to this legal device. Nevertheless, as Professor Stone has argued, the strict settlement was not, in practice, very strict. 'Effective controls,' he writes, 'lay not in legal documents, but in states of mind'.[2] As soon as lawyers invented the strict settlement, other lawyers sought ways of modifying or circumventing it, and it was probably its resultant flexibility which made it so important. Even so, the strict settlement demonstrated a feeling among large landowners (and it was rarely resorted to by small ones) that it was both possible and desirable not only to consolidate the family estate but also to ensure that it continued beyond the next generation. The upper nobility now felt able and willing to contemplate long-term strategies for the continuity of their lines.

Conversely, for many of the gentry, and especially the lower gentry, the century after 1660 was one of economic uncertainty and financial stringency. The buoyant agrarian economy, the rising prices for agricultural produce and the rising rents for land which had formed the context within which the pre-Civil War gentry are supposed to have risen was replaced by a world in which prices and rents were relatively stable. To this lack of buoyancy was added, at least between 1690 and 1730, the pressures of the land tax and other fiscal demands. At the same time other aspects of expenditure, notably dowries for daughters, rose steadily. A few prospered even under these conditions, while a majority, perhaps, maintained their position. But a substantial minority were forced to sell up, and there is certainly considerable comment to suggest that in the late seventeenth and early eighteenth centuries small and middling gentry saw themselves as a depressed group. At the very least, the discrepancies in wealth between the various strata of the gentry which we have noted before the Civil Wars continued. At the end of our period Joseph Massie attempted to estimate the national income structure. On his calculations, England around 1760 contained 480 gentry families with an average annual income of between £2000 and £4000, and another 640 with about

£1000. Beneath these there came 2400 families with between £600 and £800 a year, with another 14,400 gentry families below them with between £200 and £400 annually. Keeping up gentility on £200 a year cannot have been easy: as Arthur Young commented at the time, many 'gentlemen of moderate estate' were on a level with 'my Lord's secretary, his gentleman, or his gentleman's mistress'.

This overview of the economic fortunes of the landed orders, whatever allowance we make for individual exceptions and regional variations, does seem to provide a general pattern. In the period before the Civil Wars there was an exceptionally fluid land market. This was the product of the Dissolution of the Monasteries, the sale of Crown lands to finance warfare in the 1540s, and the break-up of a number of large estates in the reign of Elizabeth. This fluidity, combined with rising agricultural prices, provided a context within which many gentry, established and newly arrived, were able to profit economically. The rise of gentry families and the fall of others can be traced fairly easily in the fourteenth and fifteenth centuries. But in the second half of the sixteenth peculiar circumstances made these familiar processes more volatile and, in some areas at least, a fair proportion of gentry fortunes changed markedly for the better. Between 1660 and 1730 low rents and prices, coupled with heavier taxation after 1690, made life more difficult for the gentry in general and for the lower gentry in particular. The peerage, taking the period as a whole, managed, some difficulties between 1580 and 1620 apart, to increase their rent rolls, and were more than able to offset the expenses attendant upon their way of life through access to high office, advantageous marriages, good investment opportunities and (mainly before 1642) all manner of hand-outs or favours from the Crown. The outcome of all this was that the upper reaches of the landed nobility were still in 1760, and for many years after that date, wealthier on average than any other social group, even the upper stratum of merchants. Gregory King's estimates of the 1680s, Joseph Massies's of 1759–60, and (if we may look ahead a little) Patrick Colquhoun's of 1801, all agreed that the wealth of peers and the richer gentry was higher than that of the most affluent merchants. There was, in 1760, precious little evidence of any loss of economic ascendancy among the upper reaches of the landed orders.

Power

In the traditional interpretation which we addressed in the previous section, a decline in noble power was regarded as an inevitable concomitant of their supposed economic failure. This view held that one of the major achievements of the early Tudors was the reimposition of control over a violent and fractious nobility who had demonstrated their innate brutality when they were allowed to get out of control during the Wars of the Roses. The curbing of the nobility, it was alleged, together with the supposed Tudor penchant for middle-class advisers, entailed a rapid downgrading of the power of the nobility. This was thought to be particularly true when that most dramatic manifestation of the overmighty nobility, their recourse to military force, was under discussion. The early Tudor period saw the erosion of the old-style 'bastard feudalism', with its bands of retainers and its defiance of the king's law. More intensive investigation, however, reveals that noble military power and bands of armed retainers lingered rather longer than has sometimes been thought. Under Elizabeth, such magnates as the Duke of Norfolk and the Earl of Leicester still had the capacity to mobilize private armies, while in 1599 we find the Earl of Pembroke assuring the Queen that in an emergency he could provide '300 horse and 500 foote at the leaste of my followers, armed at myne own costs and with myne owne store'. Nevertheless, the overall tendency was for forces of this type, and the attitude of mind which underlay them, to disappear gradually. Partly this was due to the influence of the monarchy and of central government, partly to a change in aristocratic lifestyle.

The military power of the aristocracy, measured in their ability or willingness to mobilize private armies, may have been in decline by 1600. But by that date it was obvious that they were exercising power in other ways, and that these alternatives were more than compensating for any military enfeeblement. In the late Middle Ages a nobleman's power was measured by his ability to control armed men. In the mid-eighteenth century, it lay in his ability to control pocket boroughs and patronage networks in the House of Commons. The political context in which power might be deployed was different, and the processes by which that difference emerged are important: but the people exercising power were essentially the same. In the years before his execution in 1521, the Duke of Buckingham, an immensely wealthy titled aristocrat, demonstrated his power by building the last privately constructed castle in England. In 1760, another immensely wealthy titled aristocrat, the Duke of Newcastle, demonstrated his power by his control of parliamentary connections. Between these two dates, peers and gentry can be found adjusting to the changing political world in which they found themselves in much the same way as they had adjusted to the changing economic conditions of the period: no opportunity for advancement was lost.

The number of seats in the House of Commons increased, 119 new borough seats being created between 1547 and 1584, the period of most rapid expansion. These seats were most often created at the behest of courtier peers, high officials and influential upper gentry, and those who filled the seats were overwhelmingly the gentlemen clients or relatives of the creators. In an era when religion became an issue, noblemen were able to exercise influence through their control of appointments to ecclesiastical livings. The Earl of Pembroke controlled 38 in 1575, the Earl of Dorset some 30 in 1625, the Puritan Earl of Warwick 24 in 1632. On a local level, the steady increase in the numbers of the justices of the peace and the creation of the militia meant that there were numerous niches in which the county gentry could demonstrate their status and exercise their power, again normally as the outcome of their attachment to some great man's patronage network. In Yorkshire in the years 1625–42 some 161 gentry, drawn from 136 of the 750 gentry families extant over those years, served as sheriff, justice of the peace or militia deputy lieutenant. As Dr Cliffe's analysis has demonstrated, these local offices were filled disproportionately by the upper gentry.

At the basis of aristocratic power lay the notion of patronage. Near the beginning of our period, a Yorkshire gentleman named Christopher Wandesford warned his son 'not to be too frequent an attender at court', but urged him 'yet to have some dependence there upon some person of honour and power, who may give countenance, will be needful'. At the end of our period the centre of politics had shifted from the court to parliament, but we find Lord Chesterfield offering his son much the same advice: 'in our parliamentary government, connections are absolutely necessary'. Abilities might help obtain success, but the patronage of a great man was vital. Conversely, great men recognized fully that one of the proofs of their power was their ability to attract clients and further the interests of the same. The client, whether an individual or an institution, might expect considerable advantages from the relationship: obtaining an office or some preferment, receiving a favour in a law-suit, having a petition to the monarch presented in a favourable light. Thus in the Elizabethan period 11 borough corporations, nine bishops, two deans and chapters, and both universities were clients of the Earl of Leicester, and paid for his protection either in fees for sinecure office or in annuities.

The client–patron relationship, as we have hinted, extended into the local sphere. In Yorkshire, for example, 22 of 31 deputy lieutenants appointed during Thomas Wentworth's period as Lord President of the Council of the North were friends or relatives of the great man. The old, easily visible bastard feudalism of the late Middle Ages may have gone, although it is likely that even this was dependent on a wider variety of patronage and clientage than the bands of armed retainers which were its most notorious feature. In its place came a system whereby physical force was increasingly redundant as a means to the end of maintaining the power of a nobleman. The acquisition and maintenance of such power, however, remained of paramount importance.

Even the decline of noble interest in things military can be overstated. As we have seen, magnates could still claim to have the ability to raise substantial armed forces late in Elizabeth's reign, and in the early stages of the Civil War both sides included units raised by noblemen commanders from their tenantry. Even as late as 1688 the old power of the upper nobility to raise armed men locally was vital. The ability of peers to take control of substantial areas was crucial to the success of William and

Mary's cause, and in some localities events suggested that little had changed in such matters since the fifteenth century. Thus in Norwich Henry Howard, the Duke of Norfolk, took control of the city with 300 armed men, and then went on to hold East Anglia for the Protestant Cause. More surprisingly, the county militia system, so often regarded as the means by which the Tudors supplanted the feudal host, could be harnessed by the would-be overmighty subject to further his ends. The ranks of the militia, after all, did correspond to the gradations of the social hierarchy. It was, accordingly, possible to incorporate a county's militia organization into an aristocratic political machine. Perhaps the most striking example of this is provided by Robert Rich, the Earl of Warwick. Not only did Warwick, from the 1620s, build up formidable connections with the East Anglian gentry and construct a Puritan power base in south-east Essex: he also gained control of the county's lord lieutenancy, and in 1642 marched the Essex militia against the royalist cause as effectively as any medieval overmighty subject had marched his retainers against his monarch. After about 1700 the old noble military ethic was being channelled into state service, and martially minded gentlemen were buying commissions in the standing army. Yet even here we are witnessing a redefinition of the aristocracy's role rather than a complete change: the *raison d'être* of the medieval knight was to fight, ideally in the service of his feudal overlord. With the emergence of a professional officer corps within the standing army there occurred yet another example of the nobility making advantageous adaptations to the new conditions in which they found themselves. Moreover, any account of declining military ambitions and abilities among the aristocracy must take into account the impossibility, Cromwell's ascendancy apart, of any large-scale military force not being headed by a nobleman.

As this last point suggests, the idea that somehow the early modern state was hostile to the 'old' nobility is sadly misconceived. To the nobility, the state apparatus was a source of endless opportunities for advancement and profit: as the state expanded, so did the opportunities. Renaissance theorists were insistent that, a few exceptional cases apart, high office within the state was by logic and the natural order of things the prerogative of the nobility. In 1531 Sir Thomas Elyot published *The Booke Named the Governour*, the first English work to explore the theme of the Renaissance gentleman. To Elyot, it was 'of good congruence that they, whiche be superiour in condition or honour, shulde have also preeminence in administration'. Developing the theme, he declared that

> the potter and the tynker, only perfect in theyr crafte, shall littell do in the ministration of justice. A ploughman or carter shall make but a feeble answere in an ambassadour. Also a wayver [weaver] or fuller shulde be an unmete captaine of an armie, or in any other office of governour.

From Elyot's day until the twentieth century these 'offices of governour' were the preserve of the nobility, broadly defined. In the early modern period, therefore, the relationship between the nobility and the state was not one of conflict, but rather one of perceived identity of interest. The landed orders, of whatever rank, normally had everything to gain from the existing system and little to gain from upsetting it. By the beginning of the seventeenth century there was every sign that even gentry from the traditionally independently minded border areas were anxious to be integrated into the national system. Thus in 1604 a petition from gentlemen in eastern Northumberland declared that they wished 'not only to be rydd of the bad men of the border', but also expressed their desire 'to be at libertye to use our landes to our most profytt and comodytie as in other partes of England beinge of the like case doe'. The landed orders, even in the most peripheral corners of the realm, now felt they had a stake in a political and economic *status quo* which operated ever more obviously in their interests.

Perhaps the most basic point is that central government needed the landed orders to run the local administration and preserve order locally on its behalf. In the middle of the seventeenth century, James Harrington declared that 'a monarchy divested of its nobility hath no refuge under heaven but an army', and the experience of the 1650s had proved to monarchy and nobility alike that the army was the less agreeable alternative. At its most dramatic, aristocratic administration might take the form of control of large blocks of territory. Although factionalism normally prevented complete hegemony, and on occasions might split local power networks, the degree of control which could be achieved at certain points was impressive. At the accession of Elizabeth I in 1558, for example, large areas were under the domination of various great dukes and earls: Bedford in the south-west, Pembroke in Wales and Wiltshire, Arundel in Sussex, Norfolk in East Anglia, Derby in the north-west, Huntingdon in the north midlands, Shrewsbury and Northumberland in the north-east. Such large territorial powerbases became less common as time progressed, but the Crown had always to work through or with local élites. Most obviously gentry supplied the justices of the peace upon whom local administration and law-enforcement depended, and the militia officers upon whom local defence depended.

What is manifest, however, is that the landed orders were only too willing to serve. This had much to do with those changing concepts of gentlemanly behaviour constructed during the Renaissance and refined by Christian Humanism and Puritanism. Gentlemen could turn to such classical texts as Cicero's *De Officiis* or to more recent works to reassure themselves that holding an office in the service of the state could be as honourable as serving it in a military capacity. Sometimes, there might be direct financial rewards: when Sir John Reresby became governor of York in 1682 he gained not only the satisfaction of serving his monarch but also a fee of £500 a year. Essentially, however, it was the thirst for prestige rather than desire for financial gain which drove the gentry to take local office. One commentator remarked sourly of those wishing to be justices of the peace in 1693 that 'if they can gain the title of right worshipful, and have their neighbours stand bareheaded to them, they have their design'.

Effective government in early modern England depended upon such men, and landed wealth was intimately entwined with both local and high politics. On occasion, factional strife between big landowners could impede or disrupt local government. In the early seventeenth century, for example, Somerset was disrupted by feuding between John, Lord Poulett and Sir Robert Phelips, while in Yorkshire factions gathered behind Sir John Savile and Sir Thomas Wentworth. These factional problems became especially difficult when those involved in them were local office-holders, so that gentry feuding would have direct and disruptive consequences for local government. Other, perhaps more predictable if less serious, disadvantages attended the dependence on the local gentry as justices. Despite some contemporary jibes, only a few JPs found themselves in trouble for direct corruption or perverting the course of justice, but there is ample, if scattered, evidence of justices using their position to help their own or their family's cause, or to disadvantage their enemies. That magistracy could be used as a vehicle for self-aggrandisement by its holders was a constant concern of both central government and contemporary commentators, yet it seems that most justices attempted for most of the time to maintain some semblance of impartiality and efficiency. And, if some justices can be found abusing their power, there is evidence that others took their responsibilities very seriously indeed. A number of them left manuscript collections of their 'charges' to jurymen: in effect, speeches in which the virtues of the English law and the English government were praised. Others kept elaborate notebooks detailing their administrative duties, while handwritten annotations in printed justices' handbooks provide yet further evidence of a serious-minded approach to the office. Few justices may have reached the ideal of the legally knowledgeable and completely conscientious magistrate dealing out impartial justice, but there is little doubt that the new ideals of public service through office-holding were being internalized.

There is, however, some suggestion that these ideals may have been losing their vitality among the top layers of county society by the mid-eighteenth century. More research needs to be done to tease out regional variations, but evidence from a sample of counties indicates that leading gentry were retreating from holding the office of justice of the peace from about 1700 onwards, and that justices, and more particularly active justices, tended to be drawn from the lesser gentry. The reasons for this trend have yet to be fully investigated, but it points to changing fashions in how gentility might be displayed and enjoyed. The upper gentry were, perhaps, now more interested in seeking prestige through sociability with their fellows at their great country houses, in enjoying the London season, or in involving themselves in party politics. Moreover, by the eighteenth century local administration and law-enforcement had been in large measure routinized, and held few attractions for the socially or politically ambitious gentleman.

Indeed, the new world of parliamentary politics which followed 1688 was one in which aristocratic faction and aristocratic influence continued to be of prime importance. In Yorkshire, and doubtless in many other counties, the political affiliations of nominees for the baronetcy became more important than ancient lineage, while in all areas periods of Whig or Tory ascendancy were accompanied by purges of the justices of the peace and other local officials. The interplay of faction, aristocratic and gentry influence, and party politics became most obvious at elections. As the costs of electioneering rose, it became all the more important for gentry supporters of political connections to mobilize voters. Thus in 1701 we find a Cheshire gentleman informing his steward which contestants he was supporting, and instructing him that 'I would have you take especial care all my interest [i.e. dependents or tenants] appears for 'em, letting me know the names of each particular person (if such there be) who doe not comply with this my reasonable desire. Pray bee very careful! and stirring herein.' We can imagine a medieval baron calling out his armed retainers in much the same tones.

Noble power was not maintained merely through threats: holding together an 'interest' also involved showing that paternal concern for one's locality to which deference was the reciprocal response. In the 1720s a foreign observer commented that the owners of large country estates 'are like little kings, according to the good they do and the extent of their bounty'. It was this need to do good and distribute 'bounty', this dependence upon maintaining local reputation through, at least occasionally, rejecting the cash ethic, which has so bewildered economic historians. To a broad body of gentlemanly opinion, being an oppressive landlord was not only immoral, but also likely to prove counterproductive when attempting to keep the respect, and hence the acquiescence to the *status quo*, of the masses. Noblemen were expected to behave in certain ways, one of which was to maintain a certain level of (in the modern sense) generosity. To fail to do so would be to attract popular hostility to the individual nobleman or gentleman and, by extension, to the whole concept of hereditary nobility or gentility. Peers and gentry alike can, accordingly, be found treating the lower orders well, and advising their fellows to follow their example. In a typical passage Henry Tempest, a Yorkshire gentleman, advised his son in 1648 to 'oppress not thy tenants, but let them live comfortable of thy land, as thou desires to live of their labours, that their soules may bless thee and that it may go well with thy seed after thee'. The hegemony of the landed orders depended upon much more subtle entities than brute force.

This hegemony had, in fact, been given a powerful boost by the Reformation and the consequent secularization of church lands. In the wake of the sale of former monastic and other ecclesiastical properties many gentry families acquired not only land but also the right to appoint the parish priest: a rough estimate suggests that the gentry controlled at least 1500 livings, about one-sixth of the total, by 1600. Although this did not put an end to conflict between parson and squire, it did mean that under ideal circumstances any preaching the local clergyman might do in support of earthly hierarchies would be of immediate benefit to the local gentleman. It was also from about the middle of the sixteenth century that England's parish churches began regularly to manifest two important features in their internal arrangements. The first was the construction of a special and usually prominent pew for the local squire and his family, in effect a remodelling of the church interior for the benefit of the local landowner. The second was the developing taste for ornate funeral monuments and tombs. Such monuments had existed in pre-Reformation days, but from the early Elizabethan period they became more lifelike and more elaborate, probably reaching their most lavish in the reign of James I. Visitors to English country churches can still find themselves confronted by funeral monuments which mark the generations of the local gentry families. Congregations in the past, gathered in church in the presence both of these monuments and the living representatives of the relevant gentry clan in their private pews were given a regular weekly reminder of the nature of social hierarchy.

The net product of all this was the continuation of overt aristocratic power in the localities. On occasion it could be very overt indeed. When, for example, the redoubtable Lady Ann Clifford, Countess of Dorset, Pembroke and Montgomery, travelled between her northern residencies in the middle of the seventeenth century, her journeys assumed something of the character of a royal progress. She went in a horse litter, followed by coaches carrying her ladies-in-waiting and her other female servants, then her manservants on horseback, then a train of baggage-wagons carrying her household equipment. Neighbouring gentry and others rode out to accompany her, sometimes to the number of 300. Such displays reflected the wider reality in which they took place. The ascendancy of the landed orders in the countryside was far from absolute: the correspondence of any eighteenth-century estate steward affords examples enough of undeferential tenants and defiant cottagers. Yet, in general, the gentry and peerage maintained their rule by exercising a flexible paternalism over country dwellers who, again in general, seem to have been willing enough to respond with a deference which was far from unquestioning but which was nevertheless very real. Occasionally, symbols of this paternalism/deference equation enter the historical record: the ox-roasting, the harvest supper, the treat given by the successful candidate after the election. But most often, the extent of the landed orders' hegemony must be inferred, as direct evidence is not forthcoming. Yet this should not surprise us: after all, power is at its most potent when it can operate silently.

Lifestyle

In 1660 there appeared the first edition of a much reprinted work, the anonymous *The Gentleman's Calling*. At the beginning of the book, the author established five qualities which, he felt, characterized the gentleman. Two of them, wealth and authority, we have already considered. There remain three others: 'an ingenious and refined education'; 'reputation and esteem'; and 'time', by which he meant leisure. It was these qualities which gave the gentleman his distinctiveness: society owed the gentleman deference not merely because he was rich and powerful, but also because he possessed certain inherited and acquired qualities which, as we noted at the start of this chapter, were felt to set him apart from the common run of humanity. Historians have spent considerable time analysing the wealth of the landed élite, yet it is probable that their essential nature could probably better be grasped through a social history of snobbery. The social theorists of the Renaissance were insistent that the nobility were, literally, a race apart (the modern notion that aristocrats are blue-blooded is a distant echo of this idea) and that they showed their apartness by living a distinctive lifestyle, by possessing a distinctive set of manners, by behaving and comporting themselves in a distinctive way. For the *parvenu*, acquiring these elusive qualities was as essential in the quest for social acceptability as was acquiring wealth. What is evident, however, is that despite the theorists' insistence on ancient lineage as being essential to gentility, these attributes could be acquired, by the son or grandson of a *parvenu* if not by the *parvenu* himself. We return to the basic premise that in England gentility was essentially something which was defined culturally.

Perhaps the most vital component of this cultural definition arose from that conspicuous consumption which has so often been written off as an irrational aberration by sober-minded economic historians. Despite their strictures, it remains clear that in the early modern period the ability to consume conspicuously was thought to be one of the distinctive attributes of a great man or woman. This ability could express itself in various ways: in the maintenance of the pomp that accompanied high office; in attendance at court; in keeping up traditional standards of hospitality in the country; and in frittering away wealth for pleasure. Evidence of all of these, not least the last, is easy to come by. Money might be spent on drink, banquets, gambling and mistresses: or, with an eye to more lasting conspicuousness, on houses, clothes, furnishings or works of art. Culturally, such spending was not irrational: it was one of the things which the rich and powerful were meant to do. Popular expectations in this respect were neatly summed up in 1651, when the Cheshire justice Henry Bradshaw heard it reported that somebody thought that 'a stranger would not think he was a man of that eminency in the county, he going so plain in apparel'. Nor was noble conspicuous consumption entirely lacking in economic rationality. Again, we must restate our suspicion that economic history, with its emphasis on human beings as producers, has rather tended to underestimate their importance as consumers. The presence of freespending nobles created a great deal of work for those in the service, luxury or building industries. That they defined a pattern of consumer behaviour for the middling sort gave them an even greater significance: the landed élite very much set the pace in the early stages of the development of consumerism.

Along with more concrete entities, the nobility avidly consumed those improved educational facilities which appeared in the sixteenth century, and thus helped to add further sophistication to the concept of the gentleman. In 1536 Sir Ralph Eure was able to refute charges of penning a treasonable letter by declaring that he was unable to write anything other than his signature. A generation or two later, such an excuse would have come much less convincingly from a knight. Education, especially the non-utilitarian classical education favoured by Renaissance thought, added a polish to the gentlemanly veneer, while the common idea that education helped curb those animal passions to which the vulgar were prone gave yet more weight to the notion that the educated gentleman was somehow a being apart. There was, moreover, an important practical consideration behind the noble thirst for knowledge. Once it became obvious that those serving the state needed to be educated, the education of noble youths was seen as a vital barrier against the penetration of well-schooled commoners into high office. Accordingly, in the second half of the sixteenth century being a gentleman came to involve acquiring a number of attributes. The gentleman had to know how to fight, and military service on behalf of the Queen or the Protestant Cause was an essentially honourable activity. But now the gentleman had also to be able to cap a Latin quip, turn a sonnet, understand a little theology, dance a galliard and display good table manners. Noblemen and women became cultured as never before. By the early seventeenth century the noble patron of the arts had emerged, a notable example being Thomas Howard, Earl of Arundel, owner of the first full-scale art collection in the country. After the Restoration noble patronage blossomed, with such peers as Montague, Exeter, Pembroke, Manchester, Shrewsbury, Strafford and Oxford taking a leading role. These men had a sound knowledge of literature, art, music and architecture, as well as at least a passing respect for genius. Accordingly, they treated artists and men of letters well, became their patrons, and surrounded themselves with works of art. High culture in the late seventeenth and eighteenth centuries was essentially aristocratic in its tone.

Inextricably linked with the more elaborate Renaissance notion of
gentility was the more elaborate Renaissance court. For the first three-
quarters of our period the court, despite its jungle morality and its capacity to induce spectacular failures, was regarded as the font of fashion and
the hub of politics. Making a good impression there, and acquiring the
right contacts, were therefore matters of some importance. Some young
hopefuls achieved effortless success, like Sir Christopher Hatton, who first
came to Elizabeth I's notice 'by the galliard', when she admired his
dancing at a masque at the Inns of Court. Others made a less fortunate
début. John Aubrey noted that when Edward de Vere, seventeenth Earl of
Oxford, was presented to the same monarch 'making of his low obeisance
to queen Elizabeth, happened to let a fart, at which he was so abashed
and ashamed that he went to travell, 7 yeares'. The Queen's bluff reply
when he returned ('My lord, I had forgott the fart') was scant recompense
for the ruining of the fortunes of one of England's oldest noble houses
which his travels had incurred: yet the story does demonstrate how
seriously making a good impression at court was taken. Clearly, the very
varied courts of Elizabeth I, James I and the two Charleses acted as a
magnet for the socially or politically ambitious, and accordingly played a
key role in aristocratic culture. By the early eighteenth century the court
was ceasing to be the key focal point for people of fashion, but many of
its functions in this respect were now taken over by the upper echelons
of smart London society. The smart salon now replaced the court,
although many of the older rules continued to apply.

Another institution whose rise helped offset the court's decline as a
centre of noble culture was that most durable monument to conspicuous
consumption, the country house. Naturally, the size of the dwellings of
the landed orders varied as much as their incomes, and the houses of many
of the lower gentry were scarcely distinguishable from those of the more
prosperous yeomen farmers. At the other end of the scale things were very
different. In the early seventeenth century Hatfield House had cost
£39,000 to build, and Audley End perhaps £80,000. A century later Castle
Howard cost the Earl of Carlisle £35,000 for the mansion, £24,000 for
landscaping the surrounding grounds, and £19,000 for the Mausoleum.
Even the building of a more modest seat was an expensive business, while
the additional burdens of furnishing, decorating and maintenance would
have to be added to these initial costs, as would any subsequent extension, improvement or rebuilding. But this expense was obviously thought
to have been worthwhile. The country house was essentially a vehicle for
displaying power and taste, and for the very great reputation might rest
as much upon the possession of a magnificent house as it might upon any
other gentlemanly attribute. The stately home served to impress client
gentry, relatives and tenants. Sir Henry Wotton in his *Elements of
Architecture*, published in 1622, described the country house as the
'theatre of hospitality' and, as we shall see, entertainment was still

regarded as a means of impressing social equals and social inferiors alike. More generally, foreign observers saw the taste for living in country houses as one of the peculiarities of the English nobility. Certainly, the importance of the country 'seat' loomed large in the collective consciousness of that group. Indeed, one historian has gone so far as to conclude that 'from some eighteenth-century memoirs one might suppose that England was a federation of country houses'.[3]

As the stately home's function of impressing people suggests, the concept of reputation was central to the gentleman's consciousness. Reputation was derived from honour, and it was honour which provided the gentleman both with a sense of his own worth and with a notion of the standards by which the rest of the world would be expected to judge him. Thus the gentleman felt himself to be continually on show, continually acting life out as if on a stage, continually establishing, re-establishing and living up to his reputation. 'Honour is not in his head who is honoured but in the hearts and opinions of other men,' wrote John Cleland in his *The Institution of a Young Nobleman* of 1607. Reputation and honour might easily be lost, and hence had to be jealously guarded. Honour was a subject much discussed among the nobility, and such phenomena as the numerous disputes and arguments which occurred over matters of precedence demonstrate how theorizing over this matter could be translated into practice. However inaccessible it might be to modern observers, the nobility's code of honour was something precious, at times almost sacred, to it. Above all, they felt it to be one of the main things which set them apart from other men. Honour, along with heredity, was one of the great preoccupations of the noble mind.

Perhaps the most dramatic offshoot of this preoccupation with honour was the emergence of duelling: indeed, the author of *The Gentleman's Calling* could state in 1660 that 'a man of honour is now understood onely to be one that can start and maintain a quarrel'. Despite contemporary claims for its antiquity, the duel of honour was essentially a product of the Renaissance, and entered England late in the sixteenth century. The duel has never been subjected to serious investigation by historians of England, and any suggestions about fluctuations in the appeal of this institution must therefore be very tentative. The practice, although never as common as in Louis XIII's France, was causing governmental concern in the reign of James I, while the biographies of a number of aristocrats attest to its renewed acceptability in the reign of Charles II. Duelling probably underwent something of a decline in the more staid era of the Hanoverians, but it persisted in England well into the nineteenth century. But whatever its incidence, it is obvious that duelling was regarded throughout as representing an aristocratic honour code which transcended both the laws of the land and the strictures of religion. More remarkably, it seems to have enjoyed a wide degree of acceptance from non-élite groups: when a duel had been properly fought, for example, juries normally refused to find the successful duellist or his seconds guilty of murder. Honourable men were necessary to the nation, it was argued, and duelling was a small inconvenience to suffer in return for this greater good of the maintenance of honour. Thus one observer wrote in 1723 that 'it is strange that the nation should grudge to see half a dozen men sacrific'd in a twelvemonth to obtain so valuable a blessing as the politeness of manners, the pleasures of conversation and the happiness of company in general'. The nobility preserved the ascendancy of its values, even while its members were killing each other.

If duelling was one of the peculiarities of the nobleman, so was the need to keep up hospitality. In 1698 a writer defined hospitality as 'a liberal entertainment of all sorts of men, at one's home, whether neighbours or strangers, with kindness, especially with meat, drink and lodgings', and described it as 'an excellent Christian practice'. A number of cultural influences ran together to encourage the landholder to maintain hospitality. As our 1698 author's description of it as a 'Christian practice' suggests, there were scriptural justifications for it. To these might be added, encouragingly in a period which laid such an emphasis on classical culture, the writings of the ancients, with Aristotle, Cicero and Seneca all providing later readers with analyses of hospitality. And, third, habits of hospitality were seen as being traditional to the English landowner. Interestingly, however, many observers, especially in the period c. 1580–1630, appeared to think that this tradition was a dying one, and expressions of regret at the discontinuation of this aspect of established custom were a consistent theme in the literature of social complaint of the age. As so often, the reality of the situation is more difficult to reconstruct than a contemporary literary critique. Doubtless the presence of a greater body of poor and the realities of an in some ways harsher economic climate made keeping open house for all comers an unattractive prospect, but hospitality was still widely regarded as one of the desirable and laudable qualities which a gentleman might possess.

But for most gentlemen and noble landowners, however deeply they might have accepted these broad religious and cultural dimensions, hospitality's main function was to offer the dual prospects of promoting social harmony and maintaining the great man's position in what was in many respects a deeply hierarchical society. Gentlemen, as we have noted, were expected to be generous: the two words have an identical etymological root. Tudor rustics might chortle over the proverbial saw that 'a great housekeeper is sure of nothing for his good cheese save a great turd at his gate', but the landed orders were alert both to their duties in providing hospitality and to the benefits which would accrue to them through discharging such duties. Sir Richard Cholmely remembered how before the Civil Wars he

> entertained strangers who came to dinner, which was ever fit to receive three or four besides my family, without any trouble;

whatever their fare was they were sure of a hearty welcome. Twice a week, a certain number of old people, widowed and indigent persons, were served at my gates with bread and good pottage made of beef, which I mention that those which succeed may follow the example.

Contemporary complaints that hospitality was in decline suggest that such examples were being followed increasingly infrequently. Nevertheless, enough evidence survives to indicate that the old notions of hospitality were being maintained by at least some of the landed orders well into the eighteenth century. Traditionalists were doubtless pleased to find such examples as the early eighteenth-century Warwickshire gentleman Sir William Broughton, who was esteemed in his locality as 'a generous neighbour, a hospitable entertainer of his friends at his table, and a constant reliever of thr poor at his gates'.

By that time, however, the upkeep of hospitality by the bigger landowners at least probably had more to do with managing local society than with traditional obligations of Christian duty. Thus we find Lord Hervey writing to the Prince of Wales in 1731, describing how in the country dinner of 'beef, venison, geese, turkeys, etc.', together with 'claret, strong beer and punch' would regularly be offered to 'a little snug party of thirty odd', consisting of 'lords spiritual and temporal, besides commoners, parsons and freeholders innumerable'. Hervey continued: 'in public, we drank loyal healths, talked of the times and cultivated popularity; in private we laid plans and cultivated the country'. All this was far removed from the old disinterested notion of hospitality, yet it evidently remained an essential part of aristocratic conduct and aristocratic control. The great man was expected to perform acts of generosity, and those who failed to do so might lose more in reputation and local standing than they gained in pounds, shillings and pence. The welfare of the poor might have become the responsibilty of the parish rather than that of the local landlord, but both they and their more prosperous neighbours still had expectations of their betters. Typically, Sir John Hotham, one of the richest squires in pre-Civil War Yorkshire, earned the disrespect of 'all sorts of people' on account of his 'very narrow living'.

At the end of our period, as at the beginning, the crucial test of the nobleman or noblewoman lay in their ability to stand out from the crowd, to demonstrate their distinctive and superior breeding through their distinctive and superior behaviour. Anybody who doubts this was true of the mid-eighteenth century can do no better than turn to the letters written by Philip Stanhope, Earl of Chesterfield, to his illegitimate son. The youth was travelling on the continent to improve his education, and the Earl was anxious that 'le petit Stanhope' should do well in the *beau monde*. Accordingly, his letters provide invaluable insights into what gentility entailed at the time. The old concern for deportment was still there: the lad was advised 'to observe what people of fashion [itself a very indicative phrase] do with their legs and arms, heads and bodies', so that he would reduce his own to 'certain decent laws of motion'. He was also instructed to 'wash your ears well every morning, and blow your nose into your handkerchief whenever you have occasion, but, by the way, without looking at it afterwards'. The insistence on a wide range of accomplishments ('your dancing master is at this time the man in all Europe of the greatest importance to you') was also there, although the noble attachment to the cult of the amateur meant that no accomplishment should be practised with too much skill. Thus education was a good thing, but 'deep learning is generally tainted with pedantry, or at least unadorned by manners'. Music was a pleasing accomplishment, and the person of fashion should go to concerts, but they should never perform before the general public themselves. Above all, the idea of being on show, of maintaining reputation through everyday behaviour, was of great importance: 'mankind, as I have often told you,' wrote Chesterfield, 'is more governed by appearances than realities.' It was this constant awareness of, and demonstration of, the niceties of 'good breeding', rather than any purely economic attributes, which marked out the gentleman or woman. Trade might bring derogation but, as Chesterfield told his son, 'there are some pleasures which degrade a gentleman as much as some trades could do'.

'Good breeding' was something which contemporary social theorists thought was at its best when inherited, but which reality dictated could be acquired. But behind the notion that in England a gentleman was somebody who behaved like, and was accepted as, one, there lies a fundamental problem: that of recruitment into this supposedly exclusive group. It has been long held that one of the distinguishing features of the English landed élite, in fact one of the crucial factors in its survival, was its relative elasticity, the fact that it was not a closed caste but rather an 'open élite'. Social graces mattered, but access to this élite rested, in the last resort, with wealth. 'Let her not be poor how generous [i.e. of gentle descent] soever,' Lord Burghley advised his son about the choice of a future wife, 'for a man can buy nothing in the market with gentility.' Nevertheless, access to the upper reaches of landed society was considerably less open than has sometimes been claimed. Few joined the peerage purely on the strength of non-landed wealth: sons or grandsons of eminent merchants might enter the charmed circle of the titled, but few families did so in one move. Even those recruited into the gentry were not, at least before 1700, so variegated a group as has often been claimed. Of Dr Cliffe's 679 Yorkshire gentry families extant in 1642, only 108 had their origins outside landed wealth: 35 had their origins in office-holding, 29 in the law, and 34 in trade.

Obviously, such trends are subject to immense regional variations, and detailed local studies provide some surprises. Thus newcomers among country-house owners in London-influenced Hertfordshire in fact fell in number in the second half of our period, from 36 per cent in 1659 to 22 per cent a century later. These and other figures support the growing suspicion that access to the landed élite was becoming more rather than less restricted as the early modern period progressed. In remote Northumberland newcomers among country-house owners fell from 13 per cent in 1699 to a mere 2 per cent in 1759, while throughout our period families founded on recent gentry wealth formed a very small proportion of upper gentry lines. Even so, the general impression is one of steady if, outside the metropolitan area at least, unspectacular recruitment of new families into the landed orders.

Marriage, as Lord Burghley's comments suggested, might serve as another connecting channel between the landed orders and those anxious to join them. Yet here as elsewhere, the situation was more complex than it might at first appear. Marriage between peers and commoners was very unusual: throughout our period, the children of peers married spouses who were normally the children of peers themselves or, if not, came from peerage families (Burghley's son, for the record, married into a well-established, if politically ill-advised, family from the *nobilitas major*). Between 1540 and 1659, 87 per cent of peers' wives were drawn from the peerage (old and new) or the upper gentry: even in the years 1630–59, only 4 per cent had merchants and 2 per cent lawyers for fathers. Similarly, the social origins of Professor Stone's owners of country houses were located firmly in the landed orders. In his three sample counties over the period 1550–1749 as a whole 60 per cent came from landed backgrounds, 10 per cent from trade, and another 10 per cent from office-holding or professional backgrounds: figures that were as true for the end of our period as for its beginning.

More fluidity existed at the base of gentry society, but among the peerage and upper gentry social endogamy was the norm. Social fluidity, in fact, seems to have been encouraged not by marriage into the élite but by the diffusion out of it due to the need for younger sons, even of quite established gentry families, to make their way in the world. As younger sons never ceased to complain, this was forced on them by primogeniture: while their elder brother inherited the estate, they had to earn their living. The problem was more acute for a poor gentry family than for a rich one, and may not have much affected the upper reaches of the peerage: even so, it did mean that many members of the landed élite had relatives in the professions or in trade. Numerous examples illustrate the point. A typical one was provided by the various fates attending the younger brothers of Sir George Sandes, a late Stuart landowner. One studied medicine at Leyden in the Dutch Republic, another took up soldiering in the Low Countries, two were apprenticed to merchants, and one to a London woollen draper. Younger sons may have looked enviously at the eldest brother enjoying the family estate, but at least they were preserving the fluidity of the English ruling class. Some, indeed, provided yet more evidence of its flexibility by succeeding as merchants, investing their wealth in the purchase of a landed estate, and founding a new gentry line themselves.

Social mobility into, and out of, the various strata of peers and gentry was, therefore, a fact of life, despite the insistence of traditionalists on the value of ancient lineage. That this was accepted, at least by the eighteenth century, is demonstrated by the Peerage Bill of 1719. This Bill, part of Stanhope's attempts to engineer a more manageable parliamentary system, aimed to restrict the royal prerogative to create new peers. In essence, the Bill was designed to prevent any numerical additions to the English peerage (the Scottish peerage was to be drastically remodelled) after the creation of six new peers. From that time, new peerages would only be created in order to replace old lines which failed. Serious constitutional issues were involved, and the Bill provoked an active pamphlet debate after it was first introduced in February 1719. It was finally thrown out of the Commons in the November of that year, by 269 votes to 177, not for any purely constitutional reason, but because Walpole was able to play on upper gentry dismay at the prospect of themselves or their descendants being denied access to the peerage. If the Bill was passed, Walpole warned, 'there will be no arriving at honour, but through the winding-sheet of an old decrepit lord, or the grave of an extinct family'. MPs shared such fears: 'For my part,' observed one, 'I never desired to be a lord, but I have a son, who may have that ambition.' The nobility of England, as recruitment into the upper gentry or peerage marriage patterns demonstrate, was far from being an open élite: yet, as such attitudes show, it was never, even in its upper reaches, a closed caste.

Notes

1 R.H. Tawney, 'The Rise of the Gentry, 1558–1640', *Economic History Review*, 9 (1941), pp. 5, 9.
2 Lawrence Stone and Jeanne C. Fawtier Stone, *An Open Elite? England 1540–1880* (Oxford, 1984), p. 76.
3 H.J. Habakkuk, 'England', in A. Goodwin (ed.), *The European Nobility in the Eighteenth Century: Case-Studies in the Nobilities of the Major European States in the Pre-Reform Era* (2nd edn, 1967), p. 4.

|7|

Non-landed élites

As we have implied at various points, one of the most deeply entrenched concepts in the general interpretation of the early modern period is that of a rising middle class. Marxist and liberal historians alike have been in broad agreement in accepting this element in their shared developmental model (it is no accident that 1848 saw the publication of both The *Communist Manifesto* and the first volume of Macaulay's *History of England*). By the early twentieth century the rising middle class was seen as possessing a crucial role as an agent of historical change in the sixteenth, seventeenth and eighteenth centuries. This view, perhaps most handily encapsulated in A.F. Pollard's *Factors in Modern History* of 1907, accredited numerous important phenomena to the bourgeoisie: the Renaissance, the Reformation, Europe's colonial expansion, the 'new monarchies', nationalism, the rise of the House of Commons and the English Civil War. The new middle class made money, shouldered aside the effete and obsolescent aristocracy, and sought and gained the ears of monarchs. States where these processes were thought to have reached full maturity, like England, prospered. The rest fell.

It is now many years since that master of historical iconoclasm, J.H. Hexter, published his paper on 'The myth of the middle class in Tudor England', which not only challenged simplistic thinking on that particular topic, but also implied a number of ways in which the idea of a rise of the bourgeoisie in the early modern era might be questioned. Other historians, Marxist and non-Marxist alike, have since rethought the nature of class composition and social change in the period. The old, straightforward notion of a 'rising middle class' is no longer tenable among professional historians, although it seems to survive in the broader historical consciousness. Yet historians must confront the incontrovertible fact that things did change, not least in England, between the mid-sixteenth and the mid-eighteenth centuries. By 1760 England was more commercialized than it had been in 1550, possessed a rich and mature trading section, and also had a lively and variegated élite which incorporated substantial non-landholding elements. If we are to deny any simplistic notion of a rising middle class, there is obviously an onus upon us to provide an alternative model, or at least an alternative explanation, of what happened.

Perhaps the initial problem is a definitional one. As Hexter made clear, one of the difficulties with earlier use of the term 'middle class' is that it is so elastic that it 'attains all the rigour of a rubber band'.[1] And, given that Hexter wrote many years ago, it is worth noting that a recent analysis of the London middle class still demonstrates the considerable problems of definition. When we read that the 'huge social and financial gulf between the rich Levant merchant and the small shopkeeper', did not really matter as they were members of the same social class because 'both men engaged in essentially the same type of activity. They were both turning over capital for profit',[2] we have a sense of being confronted by, if not quite a rubber band of a definition, at least one which manisfests a high level of elasticity. The definitional problem has been further complicated by the recent interest which social historians of early modern England have taken in the 'middling sort'. This group appears, on the strength of the writings of historians who have emphasized its importance, to have been at least as amorphous as the middle class of older historiography, but since its social and economic centre of gravity is generally presented as having been rather lower than that of the more familiar middle class we shall delay discussion of its members until the next chapter.

Taken in the original Marxist sense of 'bourgeois' (and this is not *the* original sense of the word) the 'new' groups who were allegedly coming into prominence in the early modern period should be easy enough to identify. They were those people who drew their wealth, and eventually their power, from trade, commerce and industry. Hexter convincingly demonstrated the problems attendant upon historians' inability to restrict their discussion of the middle class to such people. But a real difficulty remains: namely that any discussion of what (if only as a convenient short-hand) might be described as the middle class has to include not only those involved in commerce or industry, but also what we would today describe as members of the professions. This in turn raises the problem of what a profession is. Sociologists have clear ideas on this point, and although over-dependence on their notions might do a disservice to the historian, they are worth considering. Professionals, in current sociological theory, combine an almost personal relationship with their clients with a sense of public service (this latter point has attracted considerable comment from radical sociologists: they have claimed that the 'public service' aspects of modern professional activity usually involve a monopoly of the right to practise in the field). They also have a depth of knowledge, especially of theoretical knowledge: a professional is often a member of a 'learned profession', with qualifications gained after a period of training. A profession in the modern sense is also organized and institutionalized, often through a professional association, and thus constitutes not merely a vocation, but also a social group with its own hierarchy, its own type of commitment, perhaps even its own social life. This group existence, and concomitant group consciousness, leads members of a profession to claim a certain status. Sometimes this status is recognized by society as a whole.

Obviously professional groups are different from a commercial or industrial bourgeoisie, yet they, like such a bourgeoisie, obviously form part of the middle class. One section of this chapter will accordingly be devoted to the most numerous, most important, and certainly most studied professional group in early modern England: the clergy. Briefer attention will be given to the two other 'learned professions' of the period, the law and medicine, and to a newly emergent profession, that of the military or naval officer. Initially, however, we will focus our attention upon the bourgeoisie proper: rich people who derived their wealth from trade, commerce or industry.

Merchants and industrialists

In 1710 the Reverend George Plaxton noted that Henry Iveson, a merchant, had become mayor of Leeds. 'His father was an underclerk in the Post-Office,' the clergyman observed, 'and his grandfather a repairer of old tarbants and vests; however, this illustrious son has by his merits, industry and some other ways, arrived to the favour of great men; and is supposed to be worth 400 purses.' The career of these three generations of Ivesons, as encapsulated by Plaxton, demonstrates that type of upward social mobility beloved by historians who argue that a dynamic middle class was constantly rising to challenge old élites. These 'new' groups, it will be remembered, were supposed to have possessed a different ethic from the old aristocracy. Distinguished by a more austere lifestyle and a keener sense of the potentials for economic gain, the traders and manufacturers were predestined to sweep away the old landed nobility. But as we have seen, the old landed nobility were rather more economically aware and certainly longer-lived in their social ascendancy than historical tradition would have us believe. Close scrutiny of early modern merchants and manufacturers reveals that with them, too, all was not as simple as some views of the past have claimed.

The essential point is that, however things may have changed in the late eighteenth century, up to 1760 it was merchants rather than industrialists who were the prominent group. Whatever their future importance, industrialists had only a limited significance, not least among those urban élites where their influence might have been expected to be most marked. In older towns, such as Gloucester, the dominant groups among the ruling councillors and aldermen over the first half of our period were commonly drawn from the distributive trades or food-processing. In the second half, they were drawn from the distributive trades or professional groups. The textile, metallurgical, and leather industries boasted few men rich enough to aspire to high civic office. The situation was more varied in the expanding industrial centres of the north and midlands. Yet even there merchants might still form the dominant group, as at Leeds, or there might be no clear-cut distinction between merchanting and manufacturing, as at Halifax. Most manufacturers and industrialists worked on a very small scale, essentially providing for a local market. Typical of even their more prosperous members was Richard Price, a Worcestershire scythe-smith, who died in 1605. He was worth £186 19s 6d, including an anvil and tools worth £5, iron and steel worth £9, and 'scythes ready wrought', valued at £100. A century and a half later production in such centres as Birmingham and Sheffield was still essentially based on the master craftsman rather than the large-scale industrialist. In 1759–60 Joseph Massie, attempting a national analysis, estimated there were 2500 families of manufacturers worth £200 annually, 5000 worth £100 or more, 10,000 worth between £70 and £100, and 62,500 worth about £40. This contrasts sharply with his estimates of merchant wealth. To take the analysis no further, at the top of the merchant hierarchy Massie discerned 60 families worth £1000 or more a year. There were, doubtlessly, men making modest fortunes from textile production, from metal-working or from mining. In 1760 they were, in national terms, limited in importance and virtually innocent of any sense of separate class identity.

Throughout our period it was the merchant who was the dominant element in the money-making sectors of the middle classes. Merchants were rarely directly involved in manufacture: their main activities were as wholesale traders in home or export markets, as buyers and sellers of raw materials, of goods and of overseas imports. This was not the sum of their financial activities. As far back as we have records they invested in land: after 1700 they can be found investing in government securities, transport schemes, and (to a lesser extent) industry and manufacture, while by 1760 they were diverting their expertise into banking. As with the gentry, however, not all merchants were equal. Returning to Massie's estimates, we find that of England's 13,000 merchant families of 1760 some 10,000 were earning £200 a year. Local studies confirm the impression that most merchants were operating on a small scale. In Hull, for example, of 116 merchants involved in overseas trade in 1702, 94 made less than 10 shipments, and many only one or two. Nevertheless, as with manufacturing, the burgeoning of capitalism depended upon the regular influx of small-scale operators, contributing to economic progress through their sheer numbers rather than through high *per capita* income. Arguably, the capitalist ethic is best demonstrated by these small operators, individuals like William Stout of Lancaster, who set up shop there during the winter of 1687–8 on £130 capital.

As Stout's autobiography demonstrates, the lifestyle and outlook of these small traders was very different from that of the rich merchant. For the charmed circle at the top of the merchant hierarchy large amounts of money were to be made. In London, which offered the largest fortunes, merchant wealth could be dazzling. Some man were making substantial fortunes in the century before 1650, but it was in the period after the Restoration that merchant wealth really took off. The years 1667–93 saw the arrival of a number of business tycoons who left £100,000 or more at their deaths. It also saw the arrival of a solid body of men worth £10,000–£20,000, obviously in very comfortable financial circumstances by the standards of the time. But these successful merchants showed a tendency to retreat from active trade, or at least to diversify away from it. Quite simply, one of the fruits of their success was that they did not have to struggle as hard as a small-scale merchant on £200 a year, or William Stout on his £130 capital. By 1700 provincial merchants can be found administering customs, acting as receivers for Crown and ecclesiastical revenues, and collecting land and hearth taxes. Bourgeois thrift and business efficiency might have been vital in the early stages of a merchant's career, but the pathway to real wealth lay not so much in trade itself as in financial dealing, in manipulating money rather than buying or selling goods. Those at the top of the business community, in both the national and the local contexts, were differentiated from small merchants not only by the degree of their wealth, but also by the variety of sources from which it was created.

Moreover, the ethos of the upper merchants was one of oligarchy rather than free enterprise and social mobility. In London, to take the extreme case, holders of high civic office were recruited from an exclusive group. Members of the Court of Aldermen, for example, were elected for life, and the Court, which distributed a vast patronage in terms of office-holding, was virtually self-perpetuating. By the middle of the eighteenth century a city patriciate had emerged in London, and from that time permanent city dynasties came into being. The situation in most provincial towns, and especially the older established ones, was broadly similar. At York, oligarchy had long been entrenched, and throughout our period a fairly tight control was exercised over the city's affairs by its Privy Council. From the late sixteenth century the influx of wealthy newcomers into the city was slackening, and the York economy, like its civic government, came increasingly under the control of established families. The civic rulers were recruited from a narrow section of the city's trading and manufacturing interests, and from a limited number of interrelated families whose members had the leisure to hold civic office and the wealth to maintain civic office's dignity and defray its expenses. Other older urban centres show a number of variations, but the central theme of tight control through an established merchant oligarchy was common. Exeter in the century before 1640 possessed an oligarchy very like York's.

Norwich over the following hundred years experienced what has been described as a transition from oligarchy to plutocracy. Even in small towns, like Maidstone in Kent, the majority of freeholders were excluded from political power by the creation of an oligarchic common council. Generally, the urban élites of early modern England have the appearance not of bustling bourgeois agents of change, but rather, to quote Peter Clark, of 'conservative, introspective magisterial cliques'.[3]

The trend towards oligarchy can even be traced in some of the emergent centres of manufacture. In Sheffield, long famous for its metallurgical industries, a Company of Cutlers was set up in 1624. Yet the objective of this Company was not to encourage new enterprise, but rather to close the way to competition. The cutlers were also only too anxious to maintain good relations with local magnates. In 1680 Sir John Reresby recorded attending the annual cutlers' feast with his wife and family. 'The master and wardens,' he wrote, 'attended by an infinite crowd mett me at the entrance into the town with musique and hoboys.' 'An extraordinary dinner ... at the charge of the corporation of cutlers' followed, after which the local burgesses 'invited me and all my company to a treat of wine at a tavern'. The leading industrialists of Sheffield thus make a poor showing as a group anxious to challenge existing social hierarchies, and other industrial towns would probably show much the same pattern. At Newcastle, for example, a city booming as coal production increased in the seventeenth and eighteenth centuries, the power of the local élite, embodied in the Corporation and in the Hostmen Company, underwent no real challenges. The increasing importance of merchant dynasties in Hull demonstrated how ports also experienced the consolidation of oligarchy.

Lest these comments should be regarded as taking too pessimistic a view of the development of the middle class, it should be pointed out that a number of recent studies have taken a more positive line on the emergence of, to use Marxist terminology, a bourgeoisie in the eighteenth century. There were some decisive changes taking place among at least some urban élites, although it is clear that these changes were essentially working themselves out in local contexts rather than having any decisive impact on a national level. Evidence on this point is provided by one of the towns which were beginning to manifest the symptoms of the new, industrial, culture: Halifax in West Yorkshire. Study of economic and social developments within this town, an important textile-producing centre from the seventeenth century onwards, demonstrates an important shift which could be described as the transition from a middling sort to a middling class. The creation and acquisition of wealth lay at the basis of this process. Production of cloth did not really take off until about 1760, but by that date there was already a recognizable group of 50 or 60 important and wealthy merchants and manufacturers in Halifax, who were increasingly demarcated both from the workers they employed and the gentry of the area by the income they derived from the cloth trade and their entreprenurial and market-oriented attitude about how to augment that income. Some idea of the dimensions of their wealth is given by the partnership set up in 1760 by two Halifax merchants, Samuel Lees and John Edwards, which had an initial capital of £12,000.

But as historians are now fully aware, class is not just about economics: it is also about consciousness and culture, and in particular in this case a culture which went further than the culture of commerce upon which economic success was founded. It is evident that by the mid-eighteenth century Halifax's middle class possessed both these entities in good measure. That a coherent sense of a corporate self-identity – in effect a middle-class culture – existed among them is demonstrated by the numerous voluntary associations which they founded, associations involved in such diverse activities as building a canal or starting one of those circulating libraries which, by the mid-eighteenth century, were becoming one of the hallmarks of an urban community which was self-consciously establishing its own cultural identity. The presence of this sense of identity can perhaps best be demonstrated by two rather different cultural products which appeared just after our period: the reverend John Watson's *History and Antiquities of the Parish of Halifax in Yorkshire*, published in 1775, its publication mainly made possible by subscribers from the town's textile industry who were willing to spend a guinea on an advance copy; and that monument to local civic pride, Halifax's Piece Hall, again financed by public subscription, which enjoyed its gala opening on 1 January 1779. Clearly, in some of the developing industrial centres, that feeling of local middle-class consciousness which was to become so important a cultural force in Victorian England was already stirring in the second half of the eighteenth century.

Whatever was happening in the provinces, there were also, it has been argued, important developments in the formation (or, indeed, making) of the middle class in late seventeenth and early eighteenth century London. Peter Earle's study of the London middle class between 1660 and 1730 has attempted to demonstrate this point, although the difficulties of delineating this process and convincing the reader that it really happened are perhaps greater here than they are for a town like Halifax. The crucial problems are twofold: first, as we have already noted, there are the sheer problems of placing in one social category people of massively different wealth, a problem when analysing the middle class in any context, but one which is especially acute for early modern London; and, second, the fact that the London 'middle class', however defined, were rather numerous. Earle's study is based on a sample of 375 inventories taken after the deaths of members of this class, and hence represents little more than a fraction of the membership of that social group. Even so, a wide variety of the group's activities (marriage, running a business, raising capital, going bankrupt) can be studied, although what is perhaps most interesting for

our purposes is that Earle takes an essentially cultural model of class development, and sees that culture very largely in terms of artefacts and material goods. In his conclusion, he notes what he terms 'the vast number of
vaguely middle-class things' which either orginated in the period with
which he was concerned, or whose use or existence became more common
in it, among them

> clocks, laudanum, fire insurance, street-lighting, novels, newspapers,
> tea-drinking and the three piece suit ... eating too much sugar, statis-
> tics, economics, hobbies, clubs, the national debt, undertakers,
> accountants, workhouses and the Society for the Propagation of
> Christian Knowledge.[4]

These present a different set of criteria, and a different chronology, from
those interpretations which would see the rise of the middle class in terms
purely of economics or in terms of its members' willingness to challenge
pre-existant political hierarchies. How valuable an alternative method the
cultural approach to class formation and class consciousness will be still,
however, remains to be fully tested.

What is clear is that the commercial and industrial middle class,
especially in the form of the urban oligarchs of both London and the older
provincial cities, as yet offered no political or ideological threat to the
established noble or gentry élites. Indeed, with their belief in hierarchy and
their anxiety to maintain order they essentially shared the landed orders'
view of politics and society. They also, if we may restrict ourselves to the
very upper reaches of urban society, in many respects shared their lifestyle.
The merchant (or, perhaps more accurately, the merchant's father) might
have to show the bourgeois traits of thrift and diligence while he was
accumulating his wealth. But once he had arrived as a member of the local
urban élite, he was as eager as the traditionally minded nobleman to
demonstrate his wealth, status and social ascendancy through conspicuous consumption. As we have noted, one of the reasons (indeed justifications) for oligarchic rule in towns was that only the rich could afford the
time and expense involved in holding high civic office. The period was
one which placed a high value on display, spectacle, on pomp and circumstance; and those ambitious to enter the local urban élite, like those
ambitious to enter the 'county community' of the gentry, had to embrace
conspicuous consumption as part of their lifestyle.

More generally, by the early eighteenth century at least the taste and
culture of the upper stratum of rich merchants were in many respects
identical to those of the peers and gentry in the surrounding countryside.
The charges of philistinism and vulgarity which were levelled against
factory-owners in the Victorian era could not have been applied to
eighteenth-century urban oligarchs. The notions of a division between
north and south, between the gradgrindian industrial ethic and that of

cultured aristocrats, between a leisured rural upper class and a money-making urban one, were simply not present in the mid-eighteenth century. Merchants and their wives kept abreast with cultural developments, read the latest novels or London newspapers, had their portraits painted, and sometimes even patronized artists of national reputation: James Parmentier came from helping to decorate the Earl of Carlisle's palace, Castle Howard, to paint the mural on the staircase of the Leeds merchant John Atkinson, and the portraits of a number of his fellows. Urban oligarchs also participated in the burgeoning urban culture of the period, attending balls and public dinners, concerts, cock-fights, horse-races, lectures and the theatre. Their lifestyle was not that of the careful bourgeois of historical myth. 'Many merchants,' wrote a correspondent to the *Leeds Mercury* in 1740, 'divide the week between their pleasures and their business and what they gather with one they scatter with the other.' This correspondent, like many later historians, had thought that 'the merchant himself was but a mere ant ever solicitous for what he never had time to enjoy'. For him, as for the historian, closer examination of the bourgeoisie created a somewhat different impression.

The close affinity in culture and outlook between the urban oligarchs and the country gentry was reinforced by a number of contacts. Many of these were commercial. Merchants provided loans and mortgages to the gentry, joined them in business and industrial ventures, and took gentry sons into their firms as apprentices. By the mid-eighteenth century ever-growing merchant wealth meant that merchants were also joining the gentry in county government as sheriffs and militia officers. By that date marriage between the two sectors, for long a regular feature of country life, was becoming more common. Above all, successful merchants often left the counting house for the pleasures of a country life and the desirable status of country gentleman. An early Stuart apologist for the merchant, Thomas Mun, claimed that

> the memory of our richest merchants is suddenly extinguished; the son being left rich, scorneth the profession of his father, conceiving more honour to be a gentleman (although but in name), to consume his estate in dark ignorance and excess, than to follow the steps of his father as an industrious merchant.

Local research adds substance to this complaint. Thus in the eighteenth century such families as the Fentons, Ibbetsons, Kitchingtons, Milners, Prestons and Rookes all left Leeds to settle in country estates. Some of these families continued to be very successful. William Milner, nicknamed 'Alderman Million' locally, bought into the decaying Fairfax estate early in the eighteenth century. The family severed itself from trade in 1740, and by 1800 was making £12,000 annually (an average peer's income), mainly from rent rolls and investments in the Aire-Calder navigation. The capacity of the landed orders to absorb the upper stratum of the owners of mercantile wealth was remarkable. Their willingness to be absorbed in turn demonstrates how far removed England still was from being a land dominated by the bourgeoisie.

Portrait of a profession: the clergy

As we have suggested, any discussion of the 'middle class' has to include not just merchants and industrialists, but also professionals. In early modern England the most developed profession was the clergy. But the clergy were a pretty variegated lot. This was certainly true in 1550, when the massive differences between the incomes and the career prospects of the various members of the clergy create difficulties in regarding them as a unified profession. Before the Reformation, the lower non-monastic clergy could be divided into two broad groups. The educated, non-resident, beneficed clergy, who enjoyed a definite career structure and who included many individuals who might hope to enjoy high office in church and state formed one. The unlearned, resident parochial clergy, the vicars or assistant curates, their lack of education, low career prospects and low income relegating them to a clerical proletariat, formed the other. After the Reformation this dichotomy gradually became less marked, but there were still great differences between individual clergymen. The local clergy could now be divided into three main categories. At the bottom were the various types of curate. A curacy was usually regarded as a temporary post, held by a newly ordained priest for a few years before obtaining a benefice. For a poor man without patronage or exceptional abilities, however, holding a curacy, or going from one cure to another, might become a permanent situation. Next came vicars, incumbents in those parishes where the church was appropriated and the 'great tithes' of grain and hay passed to the appropriator, after 1558 most often a wealthy layman. Rectors, in contrast, enjoyed full rights to the relevant clerical dues and hence were, on average, the wealthiest of the parish clergy: in mid-sixteenth-century Lancashire, for example, they were three times better off than vicars.

The notion of an 'average' clerical living is in large measure a false one. The variations were enormous: neighbouring parishes differed massively in their value, and clerical incomes ranged from the £5 a year on which some curates contrived to struggle along, through to incomes comparable to those of the middling gentleman. There were, broadly speaking, three sources of income for a parish priest. The first was the tithe, in theory one-tenth of the agricultural produce of the parishioners. Obviously, the tithe would vary according to the size and fertility of the parish, and could also, given harvest fluctuations, vary from year to year. In some parishes tithes had been commuted and, after the price rise of the sixteenth century, might have a very low value. Second, there was the glebe: a tract of land which could be of any size or fertility, and which the incumbent could either farm himself or rent out (the parsonage itself might be rented out by a pluralist priest). Third came the fees paid to the incumbent at times of churching, baptism or burial. These were normally small, and included a number of traditional offerings which it might be thought not worth the bother of collecting. Some priests did well out of these sources of income, others did not. The position of these latter became even more precarious after the Reformation, when the arrival of clerical marriage meant that the poor clergyman might have to support a wife and children as well as himself. Detailed local studies of clerical incomes present a bewildering welter of figures, which do little to clarify the problem. Perhaps the most telling calculation came in 1736 when, as a result of an initiative encouraged earlier by the then deceased Queen Anne, central government set out to investigate the value of clerical livings with a view to augmenting them. It was found that 5600 of England's 11,000 livings fell below the official poverty line of £50 a year. Little wonder that, throughout our period, clerical poverty should be seen as one of the major problems confronting the church.

Some clergymen were clearly in dire financial straits: yet the official value of a living was not always an accurate guide to what could be made from it. Take, for example, the finances of Ralph Josselin, vicar of Earls Colne in Essex. In 1650 a parliamentary survey valued this living at £28, one of the poorest in the county. Yet the accounts noted in Josselin's diary reveal that the clergyman's income in the years of his incumbency, 1641–83, averaged five times that sum. The basic income was augmented by an annual gift of £20 from the living's patron, Mr Richard Harlackenden, this sum being doubled when Josselin considered leaving Earls Colne after the Restoration. For eight years he also taught school locally, an experience which he enjoyed immensely and which brought him £70 a year, while over the 1650s he received £150 or so from parliamentary augmentations. He also built up a sizeable bloc of land in the parish, which added another £70–£80 to his annual income. Josselin's accounts demonstrate the dangers of assuming that clergy were as badly off as the official value of their living might suggest. Some clergy were very poor. Others, like Josselin, were able to augment their livings with fees from school-teaching, gifts from their patron, or commercial farming; yet others enjoyed the fruits of pluralism or some form of extra-parochial preferment. Assessing the living standards of the clergy is therefore very difficult: perhaps the basic point must be that they were never so low as to prevent a regular influx of ordinands.

At the opposite end of the professional spectrum to the parish clergy sat the bishops. These, too, experienced considerable variations in wealth. At the end of our period a document drawn up for the young George III showed that while some sees enjoyed a high income (Durham with £6000 a year, for example, or Winchester with £5000), others were so poor as to be unattractive to able candidates. Bristol was the poorest, at £450, while Oxford was worth only £500. Most bishops, however, enjoyed an income and a way of life comparable to that of the upper gentry or peerage, not least with regard to conspicuous consumption. Bishops, like other great men, were expected to have crowds of retainers, fine clothes and fine dwellings, and were expected to distribute lavish hospitality when alive and endow sumptuous funerals when dead. The Elizabethan episcopate, aware that they were dealing with a monarch with strong opinions over such matters, were always anxious to maintain a port appropriate to their situation: Whitgift, when Archbishop of Canterbury, kept a retinue of 60 well-clad retainers. Two centuries later, bishops were still conscious of the demands of their status. 'It is taken notice of, you know, if things about me are not as they should be,' remarked Richard Hurd, Bishop of Worcester, and keeping them thus meant roughly what it had meant in Elizabeth's reign: keeping a good table, keeping the episcopal palace and outbuildings in good repair and good decorative order, providing accommodation for high-born travellers, and making lavish, if sometimes ritual, displays of charity. The old traditions of good-lordship lived on, generally underpinned by efficient estate management. The church was a great landowner and this, allied to the impact of the consumption patterns of a bishop and his retinue, could often have a decisive influence on economic affairs in the cathedral city and its hinterland.

Some bishops, then, lived extremely well. By 1760 a large proportion of them had also been born well. The Elizabethan episcopate, as analysed by Dr Heal, although containing some sons of the upper gentry, was composed largely of men of modest background. By the middle of the eighteenth century sons of the peerage, a group largely absent from the episcopate since the Reformation, were regularly appointed to sees. A correspondent to Bishop Hurd commented in 1752 that 'our grandees have at last found their way back into the church. I only wonder they have been so long about it.' Appointments to the upper levels of the clerical establishment bore this statement out. Such appointments were also, in the Hanoverian period, being affected by political considerations. 'No man can now be made a bishop for his learning and piety,' grumbled Dr Johnson a little after our period, 'his only chance for promotion is his being connected with somebody who has parliamentary interest.' Arguably, this was a myopic view: prelates had always advanced through the avenues of patronage, and these had been diverted, blocked or opened up as a result of politics. By Johnson's time politics were focused on parliament but in earlier periods other forms of political activity had operated with similar results. Even in the eighteenth century, moreover, the presence of an active and reliable prelate could be vital in preserving a regime. A good example is provided by Thomas Herring, Archbishop of York from 1743 to 1747. Herring was not only a staunch supporter of the Whig cause in normal times, doing what he could to influence elections: he also played a key role in preparing York against the possibility of a Jacobite attack in 1745, self-consciously modelling himself on medieval warrior-prelates as he did so. The power and influence of archbishops still went far beyond the merely ceremonial.

Mention of the preferment of bishops raises the more general questions of recruitment into the clerical profession and advancement within it. The most vital issue in both these matters was patronage. Most livings lay within the gift of the Crown, of great laymen, of the church itself, or of collegiate, guild or similar institutions. In Leicestershire in 1714, for example, the Crown controlled 16 per cent of livings, the parish clergy 10 per cent, and bishops, colleges and corporate bodies another 10 per cent. Peers controlled 22 per cent, knights and baronets 11 per cent, esquires 25 per cent, and mere gentry 4 per cent. Thus, in what was probably a not atypical county, the landed orders controlled nearly two-thirds of appointments to clerical livings. Becoming an incumbent, accordingly, entailed either being related to or attracting the attention of a person of influence. For the rich, in an age when favours were regularly done for kin, there was no real problem. For the low-born the main hope was to make the right contacts while at university, or reap the rewards of a few lean years of faithful service in a curacy. For such lowly entrants into the clergy, certainly in the eighteenth century, a life-long incumbency in a country parish was normally the best that could be hoped for. By 1700 any notion of the clergy as a profession open to the talents, perhaps a near reality in the century before 1642, had ended. In the Hanoverian period priests from non-gentry backgrounds had the most trouble finding livings, went into the poorest ones, and very rarely left them to go further up the system.

If clerical poverty was a constant problem, so were the clergy's educational standards. The unlearnedness of the clergy had attracted massive adverse comment on the eve of the Reformation, and concrete evidence can sometimes be found to support the criticisms of humanist scholars. A poor state of affairs was revealed when John Hooper, the recently appointed Bishop of Gloucester, examined his clergy in 1551. Of the 311 under scrutiny, 168 could not repeat the Ten Commandments, 39 were ignorant of where the Lord's Prayer came in the Bible, while 34 could not say who its author was. Such a situation was intolerable in an age which increasingly saw the presence of a learned clergy as the vital first step towards the existence of an effective one, while it also meant that Hooper lacked not just good parish priests but also a skilled middle management of educated senior clerics. One of the greatest achievements of the Elizabethan and early Stuart church was to transform the clergy into a graduate profession. There was the usual variety of local experiences, but the general tendency is undeniable. If we may return to the Leicestershire clergy, we find that in 1576 only 15 per cent had degrees. This figure rose to 31 per cent in 1585, 58 per cent in 1603, and 90 per cent in 1642, at which level it was roughly to stay over the remainder of our period. By the Civil Wars, therefore, the clergy of the Church of England were overwhelmingly graduates, many of them with higher degrees. But by the eighteenth century the costs of sending a boy to university were deterring many non-gentry families from so doing, or from letting him stay on for a further degree if they did. Thus there was increased pressure towards a more socially exclusive clergy, and against advancement for those plebeians who did enter the profession, most of whom would not have been able to go further than a Bachelor's degree.

Formal qualifications are not, as anybody who has been a university teacher will know, a necessary guarantee of professional ability. In the Civil Wars (especially during the mid-1640s) about a quarter of England's beneficed clergy were deprived of their livings. The charges against them, generally speaking, were centred mainly on their attachment to Laudian innovations and their lack of enthusiasm for the parliamentary war effort. They also included many complaints which suggest that a proportion of the overwhelmingly graduate clergy of mid-Stuart England were not doing their job particularly well. Some of these complaints had a timeless quality, and would not have been unfamiliar two centuries earlier. Priests were accused of drunkenness, sometimes while carrying out their priestly functions. Others were supposedly guilty of sexual immorality, although few of them had to endure anything like the unusually colourful allegations of sodomy brought against John Williams, vicar of a Sussex parish. Other complaints had a distinctly post-Reformation flavour. Clergymen were accused of being ineffective or unclear preachers, of allowing their parishioners to play football or other unlawful games on the sabbath, or of not devoting enough time to private study or the spiritual welfare of their households. Even after the Restoration complaints against the parish clergy suggest that a number of problems lingered on. Between 1662 and 1714 complaints were recorded against 213 Leicestershire clergy in the local ecclesiastical courts, a large proportion of the 950 or so who officiated in the county between those two dates. Nearly half of them, however, had simply let buildings get into decay. A mere 7 per cent were reported for neglecting their church duties, and serious moral lapses were apparently very rare indeed. A mild anti-clericalism persisted throughout the eighteenth century, but the glaring moral and educational deficiencies among the clergy which had traditionally fuelled such a sentiment had largely been eradicated.

By 1760 it was just possible to describe the clergy as a profession in something like the modern sense: there were recognized entry qualifications in the shape of university degrees, there was some sort of career structure, a sense of professional solidarity, and developed ideas on professional conduct. It remains unclear, however, how much difference all this made at the most important if elusive point: that of the contact between the parish priest and his flock. Many assertions have been made about the impact of the Reformation on the clergy, but little attention has been paid to how this worked itself out in the context of the clergyman's everyday working life. In many ways, one suspects, the higher educational and moral standards may have done much to distance the clergyman from his flock. Incumbents like the Kentish vicar who, in the 1540s, advised a sick parishioner to drink holy water might well have attracted the ridicule of educated humanists, but they were obviously performing a useful and reassuring function for their parishioners. The issue awaits further research, yet it seems that many clergymen, however learned, still regarded their pastoral functions as crucial. In the mid-seventeenth century Ralph Josselin recorded how he visited the sick, attempted to arbitrate local disputes, tried to persuade parishioners against suicide or unsuitable marriages, and defused an incipient witchcraft accusation. At the same time George Herbert wrote *A Priest to the Temple*, regarded in the late seventeenth century as the basic guide to an Anglican minister's professional duties. The clergyman, according to Herbert, had to set high standards: he should avoid drunkenness and tavern-haunting; he should keep his word, for 'neither will they believe him in the pulpit, whom they cannot trust in conversation'; his apparel had to be 'plain, but reverend, and clean, without spots, or dust, or smell'. He was also to be learned, with the Bible at the centre of his knowledge, although the ideal parson 'condescends even to the knowledge of tillage'. But he also, insisted Herbert, had to act as a lawyer, schoolteacher and doctor to his parishioners. Whatever the standards were upon which the upper clergy gained advancement, for most parishioners the evaluation of the clergyman probably depended on such matters over the whole of our period.

Other professions

In 1550 the only occupational group other than the clergy enjoying anything like professional standing were the lawyers. Even by that date law had been important in English society and, as we have seen, acted as an important social cement. After the constitutional struggles of the seventeenth century this function widened, and the common law was seen as being of crucial importance in the preservation of English liberties. The law was also something in which people participated, and something with which people of moderate property would come into contact. It was, moreover, the medium within which was conducted that most popular of contemporary pastimes: litigation. The full history of early modern litigation has yet to be written, but there is every indication that most courts experienced a massive rise in business from the late fifteenth century onwards. This meant that the services of lawyers were increasingly in demand, but in 1550 there existed only the basic elements of a legal profession proper. Skilled judges sat in the Westminster courts and rode

out on the assize circuits twice a year, yet legal practitioners included not
only these judges learned in the law, but also local men whose relationship to the law was analogous to that of a cunning man to medicine. The
next two centuries were to witness the rise of a legal profession from this
chaos, although the process was a slow one.

   The first lawyers to achieve professional consciousness and professional
status were barristers. In 1550 there already existed a rough division
between those who prepared the procedural aspects of a suit and those
who actually studied the law and pleaded in court. The barristers, representing this second category, grew steadily in importance in the century
before the Civil Wars, and emerged as a major force after them. Certainly
their numbers were increasing. There were 184 calls to the bar in the
1570s, 383 in the 1580s, and 515 in the 1630s. Calls peaked at 714 in
the 1660s, then seem to have fallen away, totalling 300 at most in the
1750s. This decline must be related to the increased cost of becoming a
barrister. In the early seventeenth century a would-be barrister could
manage on £40 a year, but by 1700 the annual expense was approaching
£200, which meant that a full legal training of seven or eight years might
easily cost £1500. Despite contemporary jibes that the legal profession
offered a unique avenue for upward social mobility, it apparently became,
like the clergy, more socially exclusive from the seventeenth century
onwards. Even before the Civil Wars, something like half of those called
to the bar came from the landed orders: by the mid-seventeenth century
the costs of a legal education were acting as an effective barrier to
plebeians wishing to become barristers. And, again like the clergy, high
legal office, acquired through a mixture of ability, family connections and
patronage, was open to an increasingly restricted circle.

   The legal practitioner which the ordinary man or woman was most
likely to come into contact with, however, was not the high-class barrister but rather the small-town attorney. These were far removed from the
men at the top of the legal hierarchy. Their function, the provision of basic
legal services, was essentially similar to that of the modern solicitor. Their
training lay not in attending an Inn of Court, but rather in the more practical medium of an apprenticeship. The attorney advised litigants involved
in or contemplating suits in the Westminster courts, looked after the legal
aspects of local commercial or land transactions, drew up conveyances,
contracts and bonds, and supervised local manorial courts.
Contemporaries were full of complaints about the numbers, low social
origins, and lack of skill of country attorneys, yet by the mid-eighteenth
century their status was beginning to rise. In 1739 affluent London attorneys formed a Society of Gentleman Practitioners in the Courts of Law
and Equity, and the Society did much to raise the professional standing
of the attorney in the years that followed. The later eighteenth century
saw the formation of local law societies (the first was founded at Bristol
in 1770) which took this process further.

As with lawyers, the two centuries after 1550 witnessed the rise to professional status of doctors. In the mid-sixteenth century the providers of medical services were as varied in status and education as were the men of law. It would be all too easy to approach the history of the medical profession through a series of horror stories. Medical knowledge was primitive, its theoretical basis only slowly escaping from the ancient but misleading teachings of Galen and Hippocrates, its practical aspects dominated by such harmful remedies as bleeding and the all too common recourse to purges and vomits. The poor could not afford what would come to be regarded as proper medical services, and had recourse to the local barber-surgeon or cunning man or woman. This latter group, with their sympathetic magic and herbal remedies, at least did little positive harm to their patients, and were evidently very popular. Richard Bernard, author of a tract against witchcraft published in 1627, was just one of many writers who wrote against cunning people: he recognized that the fact that 'physicke is very chargeable' was something which helped make them very attractive to the poor. The comprehensive scope of folk medicine probably added to the attraction: that great compendium of traditional plant medicine, the *Grete Herball* of 1526, prescribed remedies for ailments as varied as 'stench of the armholes' and 'swollen ballocks'. Barber-surgeons were regarded as more legitimate, and may have been quite skilled: in London, for example, they early acquired a reputation for curing venereal disease. Their local standing is perhaps best illustrated by 'Old Rosewell', who kept a barber-surgeon's shop in Bristol in the early eighteenth century. He was 'so celebrated that on a Sunday morning there were swarms of persons to be bled, for which each paid 6d to a shilling', and who would be sold a quart or two of ale after this treatment to fortify them on the way home.

Cunning people and barber-surgeons apart, there were perhaps 3000 medical practitioners in England by 1700. Traditionally these were divided into three groups: in ascending social order, the surgeons, the apothecaries and the physicians. In practice, the dividing lines between these categories was never absolute, and the continuous dissolution of such differences as did exist, with the gradual levelling out of the social ranking of the three groups, carried on over our period. The Royal College of Physicians attempted to maintain its monopoly in the London area, especially against the apothecaries, but in the provinces distinctions between the three branches were difficult to maintain. Thus by 1700 apothecaries and, to a growing extent, surgeons, were referred to by their clients as 'doctor'. The training these men received varied. Medicine as taught at the English universities was at a low ebb, and its preference for theory over practice can be gauged from contemporary reports that one seventeenth-century professor of medicine at Oxford could not stand the sight of blood. For many country apothecaries and surgeons, however, as for country attorneys, apprenticeship with an experienced local practitioner was probably a more effective professional education than that offered by formal institutions. Physicians and, increasingly, surgeons could also benefit from study abroad. In the late Elizabethan and Jacobean periods a few English medical practitioners studied at Padua, location of the most famous medical school of the time. Early in the eighteenth century some 360 of them were studying at Leyden under the great Hermann Boerhaave, while from 1726 the existence of an excellent medical school at Edinburgh meant that Scottish-trained doctors came to dominate English medicine.

In many respects people were helpless before disease and pain, and doctors, like lawyers, were satirized as people who used specialized knowledge to make money out of the misfortunes of others. This viewpoint could be supported by cases like that of James Younge, who late in the seventeenth century was able to make £120 in one year from treating venereal cases (his practice included Plymouth Naval Hospital), or charge up to £70 for treating a case of piles. We must retain a proper scepticism about the medical profession. We must also resist any 'Whig Interpretation' of medical history. Yet it remains clear that the training, social status, professionalism, and perhaps even ability to heal of medical practitioners was rising, and that by 1760 something like a 'medical profession' in the modern sense had emerged. Without doubt, there was money to be made from medicine. The biggest rewards, by the early eighteenth century, went to formally qualified London physicians. But surgeons and apothecaries also did well in the capital, and even in the provinces a skilled and well-connected physician might make £500 a year.

Improved formal education at Leyden, Edinburgh, or other centres like Rheims, might be supplemented by experience gained in the new teaching hospitals. In Queen Anne's reign England possessed only two hospitals in the modern sense. These were joined by the Westminster Hospital (1720), Guy's (1724), St George's (1733), the London Hospital (1740), and the Middlesex Hospital (1745), while by 1755 a further 12 major hospitals had been founded outside the capital. Medical practitioners, although comparatively few in *per capita* terms, were increasing in number. At Bristol, for example, there were in 1754 five resident physicians, 29 apothecaries, and 13 barber-surgeons. Medical provision was still woefully inadequate by modern standards, but it was probably infinitely better than it had been two centuries before. Moreover, the developments which had occurred since that earlier date had ensured that something like a professional consciousness was spreading among medical men.

Recent research on medicine and healing, especially that dealing with eighteenth-century developments, has, however, reinforced the sense that a formally qualified 'medical profession' in the modern sense had, by 1760, still not entirely etablished a monopoly on providing medical care. The older forms of folk medicine were still available to the poor, but it is now evident that there were a large number of providers of medical services, most of them described both by hostile contemporaries and later

writers as quacks, who found their clientele among the middling orders
or the better-off artisans and farmers. These men carried out such basic
surgical techniques as tooth-drawing or bone-setting as effectively as the
formally qualified, while they were also responsible for the provision of a
formidable range of patent medicines, some very cheaply priced, which we
know from the diaries and correspondence of the period were widely
consumed. Given early eighteenth-century England's claims to have been
a consumer society, it should come as no surpise that medical services and
medicines should be consumed as freely as anything else, that these should
be freely available commercially, that what were virtually medical entrepreneurs should rise, and that market-place medicine should become big
business. Medical services were still relatively under-regulated in Georgian
England. Moreover, recent research has stressed the importance of patients
in creating a demand for this wide range of medical treatment. It was
probably the rather low expectations of patients, indeed, which explains
one of the more surprising features of the history of medicine in our
period: the way in which people continued to go to doctors despite the
uncertainty of their being able to provide a cure. A certain realism must
have tempered any optimism that even the best qualified doctor or the
most trusted folk or patent remedy would really be of much help.

Lawyers and doctors, together with clergymen, have traditionally formed
the core of the 'learned professions', and by the mid-eighteenth century
were, however grudgingly, regarded as such. By that date men following
a number of other callings were joining them as professionals, although
these newcomers might not deserve or expect the appellation 'learned'.
The most clearly defined of these (schoolteachers and architects have also
been suggested as possible candidates) were the members of the officer
corps of the army and navy. Professional army officers, described by Swift
as 'a species of men quite different from any that were known before the
Revolution', were essentially a product of the late seventeenth century. A
few English officers had at earlier points acquired expertise while
campaigning in the Low Countries, Ireland, or during the Thirty Years
War. As the early stages of the Civil War demonstrated, this expertise was
not very widespread. But talent came to the fore as the struggle progressed,
and in the Interregnum England acquired not only its first standing army,
but also a politically active body of career officers. The experience of the
Interregnum made the whole idea of a professional standing army repugnant to the political nation. Yet the small force granted grudgingly to
Charles II was maintained, grew bigger under James II, and mushroomed
during the constant warfare of William III and Queen Anne's reigns. One
necessary consequence of this was the creation of a number of posts for
officers. At the height of the War of the Spanish Succession there were
3600 commissioned officers in the British army. This figure fell to about
2000 in the postwar peacetime establishment, but by 1749, during the

Seven Years War, it had risen again to 4000. The development of the standing army, therefore, created massive career opportunities.

In England, as in most European states, these opportunities were open overwhelmingly to the offspring of the lower nobility. Even Cromwell's officer corps was not so socially open as myth would have it, while Charles II's officers were a demonstrably socially exclusive group. Of 188 officers serving with standing regiments in England between 1661 and 1685 only 3 per cent were not the sons of peers, knights, baronets or gentlemen. As the army expanded, a commission was seen as an attractive opening for a younger son, and the money needed to purchase one (£400 for an ensigncy about 1750) compared favourably with the costs of getting a youth set up in another profession. The degree to which the officer corps was professional in the modern sense is, however, problematic. Little formal training seems to have been given, while promotion, like initial entry, was dependent on purchase. It could be an expensive business: to quote 1750 prices again, a lieutenant-colonelcy would cost some £3500. Examples of fraud and inefficiency abounded. George II, despite a series of orders, found it impossible to get a certain proportion of his officers ever to go near their regiments at all. The problems were highlighted in 1743, when the commander of the British forces in Germany, anxious to make an early start to the campaigning season, found a substantial number of his officers absent. Many of them were involved, as MPs or otherwise, in politics and, as their commander complained, claimed that 'their preferment depended on the interest of their friends at court', with whom close contact had to be maintained. Thus even at the end of our period the British army-officer corps was not fully professionalized. Yet (if we may set aside the suspicion that what is really needed is a history of NCOs) the fact that the units they commanded held together through such bloody slogging matches as Dettingen (1743) or Fontenoy (1745) does say a great deal about their abilities. The full development of professionalism and professional self-consciousness among army officers probably did not occur much before the early nineteenth century. But by 1760 the framework for this development was clearly in existence.

At that date something much more like a professional ethos, as was appropriate to a service where technical ability was as important an attribute in an officer as the willingness to die gallantly, existed in the Royal Navy. Again, the exploits of Elizabethan seadogs and the efficiency of Charles I's ship-money fleet notwithstanding, this was essentially a product of the late seventeenth century. Before about 1670 officers of the Royal Navy were not a professionally defined body: they were largely untrained for naval duties, had no clear career structure, and had only temporary tenure. From that date, a number of reforms by Charles II set a new tone. The institution in 1677 of a system of 'Volunteers per Order' ensured that young men of good family should get sea experience in the navy. The insistence on a strict examination for candidates for lieutenancy, as well as the demand for three (later raised to four, then six) years' sea service before being commissioned to that rank, did much to improve standards. Entry into the naval-officer corps was essentially restricted to sons of the gentry, but at least gaining a commission and subsequent promotion were not dependent purely on court connections or purchase. The needs of warfare helped professionalism develop further. In the 1690s the Admiralty gradually clarified the notion of a chain of command, attempting to reduce the element of caprice in promotion by adopting the principle of seniority. Service had its drawbacks. As in the army, peace brought retirement on half pay and an end to promotion prospects for many, while even in times of active service (setting aside the risk of death, disease or disablement) pay could be irregular and inadequate, and the windfalls which prize money provided very uncertain. Yet by 1760 the Royal Navy had attained a considerable degree of professionalism among its officers: this was to be a major foundation for its remarkable achievements in the late eighteenth and early nineteenth centuries.

By 1730, it has been estimated, there were some 55,000–60,000 men practising a profession, an increase of some 70 per cent over 1680. This development, together with the possibly less dramatic expansion of the mercantile and industrial sectors, ensured that the English élite was both larger and more varied in the mid-eighteenth century than it had been at any previous point. Yet it is difficult to accommodate this growth to any of those simplistic notions of a rising middle class to which we alluded at the beginning of this chapter. Above all, although élites were now larger, more variegated, and more wealthy, there is little evidence that access to their higher reaches was any more open than it had been in 1550. On the contrary, as we have seen with merchants, clergymen, lawyers, doctors and army officers, entry in general, and certainly entry to the upper levels, became increasingly restricted to men of wealth, birth and connections as the eighteenth century progressed. The celebrated interplay between merchants and gentry, so long thought of as an English peculiarity, became more restricted by the high premiums which a Hanoverian gentleman needed to get his son apprenticed into a really good business.

Correspondingly, the costs of a university education, of legal and medical training, and of a military commission all rose to such levels as to debar the sons of the poor. This increased restrictiveness can be traced in the emergence of merchant and professional dynasties. Long-established professions, like the clergy, and new ones, like army officers, both demonstrated this trend. There was, moreover, considerable intermarriage between various sectors of the non-landed élite, and with the gentry. By the mid-eighteenth century the landed orders and the members of other sectors of the English élite had, certainly below the very highest levels, fused into a vast interrelated mass. The ties of kinship constantly cut through the interests of individual sectors, and created a fusion of wealth and attitudes which makes it difficult to maintain a meaningful distinction between the aristocratic and the bourgeois.

Mention of kinship and marriage reminds us that this chapter, with its concentration on purely male activities, has allowed little mention of women. There were no women clergymen or lawyers and, the transvestite heroines of popular ballads notwithstanding, no women army or navy officers, while the advent of the male medical profession meant the downgrading of such female medical practitioners as midwives and village cunning women. The married woman might, although perhaps more frequently in smaller enterprises, play an important part in running a business. But the most important function of the middle-class woman was the management of the household. In 1631 Gervase Markham had made this point in the introductory comments in his *The English Housewife*. After noting that the 'offices and employments' of the husband, 'who is father and master of the family', were 'ever for the most part abroad', Markham continued:

> it is now that we descend in as orderly a method as we can to the office of our English housewife, who is the mother and mistress of the family, and hath her most general employments within the house; where from the general example of her virtues, and the most approved skill of her knowledges, those of her family may both learn to serve God, and sustain man in that godly and profitable sort which is required of every true Christian.

A later advice book for woman, *The Ladies' Calling*, was equally insistent on this point: 'Oeconomy and household management', declared its third edition of 1725, was 'the most proper feminine business'. Evidently, the male writers of conduct books in our period were envisaging a division of labour and responsibilities in the middle-class household which in some respects seems to have presaged the 'separate sheres' ideology of the Victorian period.

As ever, we are left wondering how far reality reflected the recommendations of the conduct-book writers, yet at the very least it is evident that the experience of the new polite culture which was emerging in mercantile and professional circles in the late seventeenth and early eighteenth centuries was essentially a gendered one. Quite apart from its more obvious economic and administrative aspects, household management carried special overtones to the élite woman in an era when conspicuous display meant so much. Social visiting was a favourite pastime among the rich and comfortably off, and the rites and exchanges which hospitality entailed gave an important role to the wife of the successful merchant or professional. It is no accident, if we may return to *The Ladies' Calling*, that the ability to cope with 'that round of formal visits among persons of quality' was seen as being crucial for the ladies, or would-be ladies, at whom the work was directed. Thus élite women, although largely denied any direct involvement in a career or business life, had an important function in the household, and also had an important role, in both county society and in provincial towns, in setting the social tone within which 'persons of quality' moved. As our discussion of the upper reaches of merchant society suggested, social tone is far from a trivial matter: it is of vital significance when attempting to understand wider aspects of group consciousness and group self-perception.

Intimately connected to these issues of élite sociability and élite consciousness, in whose construction wives and daughters played such a crucial role, was the impact of what have been described as 'urban gentry' or 'pseudo gentry' in provincial towns. These existed in small numbers in the late sixteenth century, but really grew in numbers and importance after 1660. To some extent, their arrival was one aspect of that general increase in the size and variety of the non-landed élite which we have noted. But by the eighteenth century, their presence was attributable to more specific factors. By that date investment in the stocks or in urban property provided a safe, passive use for wealth, which above all acted as an attractive alternative to putting money into land. The successful merchant or professional man wishing to enjoy an elegant lifestyle and to perpetuate the fortunes of his family was no longer obliged to join the rural gentry, although a number still opted to do so. For those who did not town life, as we have seen in an earlier chapter, was, by the early eighteenth century, providing an agreeable environment for persons of fashion. A provincial town, with well-developed leisure facilities and yet still inexpensive to live in, provided an appropriate habitat for professionals, merchants, visiting gentry and that new social phenomenon which appeared after the Treaty of Utrecht, the officer on half pay. These men and their families both enjoyed and contributed to a growing provincial urban culture.

But these groups had not as yet developed anything like a separate class consciousness, and certainly did not see their existence as offering any sort of challenge to the *status quo*. Hexter argued that the Tudor 'middle class' offered 'no threat to aristocracy or monarchy', because it had 'no ideology of class war or even of class rivalry'.[5] Much the same was true in the mid-eighteenth century: such successful merchants as Sir Henry Ibbetson of Leeds, with his leisured lifestyle, his knighthood, and his art collection makes an unlikely challenger of aristocratic hegemony. There was little evidence of bourgeois penetration in the central organ of government at that time: parliament. About 55 merchants sat in the House of Commons of the Long Parliament, a total which had increased to about 60 by 1754. Another 60 or so lawyers and perhaps 40 army or navy officers, neither of them groups notable for their criticism of the existing social or political order, could be added by the latter date. The non-landed élite was, by 1760, growing in numbers, wealth and influence. Yet it lacked either the economic base or the self-conscious ideology which would allow it to challenge the English *ancien régime*. That development came with a different century, another set of people, and a new framework for political and ideological debate and action.

Notes

1 J.H. Hexter, *Reappraisals in History* (1961), p. 74.
2 Peter Earle, *The Making of the English Middle Class: Business, Society and Family Life in London 1660–1730* (1989), p. 5.
3 Peter Clark, *English Provincial Society from the Reformation to the Revolution: Religion, Politics and Society in Kent, 1500–1640* (Hassocks, 1977), p. 141.
4 Earle, *The Making of the English Middle Class*, p. 336
5 J.H. Hexter, *Reappraisals in History*, p. 113.

8

The common people

In this chapter we shall study the bulk of the population, those people ranked beneath the gentry and their urban equivalents. Elsewhere in this book we examine the family and community life, the religion, the educational level and culture of such people. Here our main concern is with their material life, with their economic fortunes. Studying these matters is impeded by two major difficulties. The first is lack of evidence: broadly speaking, the further down the social scale the stratum being studied, the less evidence there is about its members. Second, despite the tendency of their social superiors to describe the common people or groups among them under some blanket term, it remains clear that they were variegated: the lower orders were not merely an undifferentiated and amorphous agglomeration.

A number of labels, at once varied and general, were applied to the common people. William Harrison, writing in the 1570s, referred comprehensively to 'yeomen, and artificers and labourers', while many of his contemporaries would have described such people simply as 'the commonalty'. Most highly placed observers showed a similar lack of precision when describing their social inferiors throughout our period. Certainly, there was no term corresponding to the modern 'working class'. 'Labouring poor', although frequently employed, described only one section of those with whom we are concerned here, as did 'manufacturing poor'. 'Artificer', widely used in the Tudor period to describe a craftsman or industrial worker, was less commonly employed in the eighteenth century, when such people were likely to be called 'manufacturers'. The difficulties are compounded by the vagueness of many occupational and status labels. 'Yeoman' and 'husbandman' were, as we shall see, loose descriptions which could include men enjoying vastly different levels of wealth, while even 'labourer' could encompass anything from a skilled farmworker with his own few acres of land, some livestock, and pasture rights, to a landless proletarian working for day wages. Cutting through this confusion is difficult but, at the risk of oversimplification, a threefold division will be followed here. First come those who might reasonably expect to live in modest comfort, and who might, in many cases, achieve a modest prosperity. Second there were those for whom work for a money wage or its equivalent was the main way of getting a living, and for whom life, although hard and often precarious, usually afforded at least some security. Third, there come those for whom life was a continual and often losing battle: the poor.

Yeomen, husbandmen and urban masters

As we have suggested, one element among the common people was a stratum (or perhaps more accurately a collection of strata) of people who, under normal circumstances, might expect to live in a state of at least modest comfort. This group has recently attracted considerable attention from social historians, some of whom have argued that they formed a distinct body in England's social hierarchy, most frequently described as the 'middling sort'. Having made this claim, the social historians in question have experienced considerable problems in defining how exactly this middling sort might be characterized (similar problems, we have noted, are to be encountered with that older form of social categorization, the middle class): the difficulties are illustrated by the fact that some definitions of the middling sort would seem to include 50 per cent of England's population. The most satisfactory way of defining the middling sort would appear to rest on notions of independent economic activity, a strong sense of household, and the likelihood that the male head of a middling-sort household might well expect to undergo the responsibilities of local office-holding at some stage in his life. As ever, finding watertight descriptions of a social category has proved difficult here and, until a more sophisticated definition has been developed by interested historians, it seems safest to use the term 'middling sort' as sparingly as possible. In this section, therefore, while being aware of the need to keep this broader social category in mind, it seems safest to procede by a discussion of three separate relevant social groupings whose definition is less problematic.

Most contemporaries, certainly before 1700, would have agreed that the yeomen were the most affluent and important non-élite social stratum. Defining membership of that stratum, however, presents some difficulties. The traditional definition of a yeoman, a man holding freehold lands worth 40s or more annually, was clearly inoperative by 1550: inflation had rendered the financial qualification nonsensical, while many men with leasehold or copyhold land were described as yeomen. Generally, the term implied a substantial farmer, able at the very least to support himself and his family from the produce of the land he farmed. Thus Sir Thomas Smith, writing shortly after 1550, after discussing the traditional definition of yeoman, declared that the word 'now signifieth among us a man well at ease and having honestlie to live, and yet not a gentleman'. By 1760, at which date the term was beginning to acquire a nostalgic ring, men who would previously have been described as yeomen were being called tenant farmers or simply farmers. More precise definition is made difficult by the massive variations in wealth experienced by yeomen. Edward Chamberlayne, in the 1669 edition of his *Angliae Notitia*, thought that 'very ordinary' yeoman incomes might be £40 or £50 annually, although £100–£200 was not rare, and that some Kentish yeomen (traditionally regarded as an unusually wealthy body) might be worth up to £1500. Detailed work on yeomen's probate inventories, listing the value and nature of their possessions at death, lends substance to these estimates. A run of inventories for the years 1638 to 1723 for the central Essex parishes of Writtle and Roxwell, show yeomen leaving goods and money worth between £19 4s 6d and £1873 14s. Yeoman wealth might very well have varied regionally, but information from other areas suggests that this sort of range would not have been unusual in the seventeenth century. Table 8.1, comparing inventories from Writtle and Roxwell with yeoman wealth from the Gloucester hinterland, illustrates this point. Despite regional variations, it is clear that yeomen were a social group whose members enjoyed massive variations of wealth, and that some of these members might become very prosperous indeed.

Table 8.1 Yeoman wealth in mid-Essex (1638–1723) and the Vale of Gloucester (*c.* 1600–1700).[1]

	Essex	Gloucestershire
£1000 +	1	1
£500–1000	2	11
£250–500	13	55
£100–250	17	138
Less than £100	15	157

This prosperity, although to some extent dependent upon individual luck, owed much to a hard-headed attitude towards getting and spending. Leaving statistical averages for ideal types, we find that most Tudor and early Stuart commentators saw frugality of living, an unostentatious but solid way of life, as the prime yeomanly virtue. Robert Reyce, analysing Suffolk society early in the seventeenth century, thought it was the yeoman's 'continual under living' which allowed him to 'grow with the wealth of the world'. Nathaniel Newbury, preaching in Kent in 1652 a sermon later published as *The Yeoman's Prerogative*, praised thrift, deplored waste and extravagance, and warned against squandering all by 'loose and luxurious courses'. The successful yeoman needed little such advice: despite the numerous acts of charity and occasional displays of wealth they made, they were above all rural capitalists. Thus Anthony Strong, a Sussex yeoman, was described as one who 'did not use to keepe mony lyinge idlely by him, but as soon as he had gathered together any some [i.e. sum] of value he eyther bought land therewith or put the same out to interest'. Thomas Byng, a Hertfordshire yeoman, was remembered by his son in 1592 as 'a man that always loved money well and disposed to great thrifte and was alwaies carefull to encrease that porcion that he had'. This businesslike attitude could easily degenerate into something nastier: at about the same time a Westmorland man was described as 'a yeoman that liveth by usurie ... and love of money and by gripinge of poore men by usurious contracts and bargains'.

The fortunes of the yeomanry, as far as it is possible to generalize, fluctuated much as did those of the gentry. In the century up to 1650 many yeomen profited from rising agricultural prices. As we have seen, one of the products of that century was a more marked stratification of village society, with a stratum of rich yeoman farmers dominating many parishes. The large-scale rebuilding of farmhouses attests to the increase in yeoman wealth during this period, as do the large number of yeomen's sons who went to university, entered the church, or rose into the lower ranks of the gentry. After 1650 came a century of stagnation in agricultural prices, compounded by war taxation after 1688, the demands of a more luxurious way of living, and the need to provide ever-larger dowries for daughters. Many yeomen, like many small gentry, found themselves under considerable economic pressure, and were eventually squeezed out of their holdings. Nevertheless, a number of yeomen managed to prosper even under these harsher conditions. There may have been little new building of farmhouses in the early eighteenth century, but inventories, even from such peripheral areas as Westmorland, show signs of rising living standards among yeomen and tenant farmers. Indeed, by the mid-eighteenth century a group which had once been praised for its frugality was being criticized for sliding into luxury. The failure of some Sussex farmers around 1740 was attributed not to the climatic problems or cattle murrain of the period, but rather to the 'general luxury of the women (who do nothing but drink tea) and the idleness of the men'. In 1760 John Mordant, author of *The Complete Steward*, could comment on 'all grasping farmers who can now lay in their port wine by the pipe, and send their daughters to boarding school, to make as genteel an appearance as those of their landlords'.

Such luxuries were beyond the reach of the next group down the hierarchy of rural society: the husbandmen. Again, precise definition is difficult. Usually, the husbandman was a small-to-middling farmer for whom life was a struggle, who was always vulnerable to economic disaster, but who could expect to get by in all but the very worst years. Reyce's comments on early Stuart Suffolk seem widely applicable: the husbandman 'though he thriveth ordinarily well, yet he laboureth much, and if the frowning years should not sometimes diminish his crop, hee would never care what hee offered for the hyre of hands'. In most country areas, certainly before the late seventeenth century, husbandmen were more numerous than yeomen: a Gloucestershire muster roll of 1608, for example, listed 927 yeomen and 3774 husbandmen. They were also less wealthy. Once again, we are confronted by men described as being in the same social class displaying substantial variations in wealth: some men described as husbandmen on testamentary or legal documents were as rich as small yeomen, others were barely distinguishable from the more prosperous labourers. Our sample of mid-Essex inventories, however, shows that the average husbandman was considerably worse off than the average yeoman. Thirteen inventories listing the goods of husbandmen survive within this sample, falling within the period 1637–84. These give an average wealth of some £44, while yeoman inventories for the same years give an average of £260. A larger sample of probate inventories for 14 counties over the period 1580–1700 has 1071 yeomen with an average wealth of £206, and 470 husbandmen with an average wealth of £76. These average figures should not obscure the fact that, even as early as the 1560s, some husbandmen were enjoying modest comfort.

It is difficult to discover very much about the way of life of these small and middling farmers. David Hey's work on the Shropshire village of Myddle, which includes the most detailed reconstruction of the fortunes of a sample of small farming families yet written, suggests that this stratum, unexpectedly perhaps, was more stable than their yeoman betters, with many families farming the same tenement from 1524 to 1700. Hey argues that whereas fortunes might be quickly made, and as quickly lost, among yeomen, the more limited economic opportunities and horizons of husbandmen meant that there was less scope for them to take risks, and hence less chance of their failing. Their material standards, relative to other groups, varied little over the generations. Farming carefully, working the smaller tenements that were unlikely to be attractive to speculators, and supported by a tight net of kinship relations, the husbandmen formed the most permanent element in Myddle. As we have noted, the agrarian changes of the period were working against these small farmers. But in areas which were still characterized by small farms, it seems that this sort of stability was the norm.

Analysis of middling and small urban masters is beset by problems similar to those encountered when studying their rural counterparts. Once again, we find the same descriptive label covering marked disparities of income. In late Stuart Gloucester, for example, there were tailors varying in wealth from £3 to £329, bakers from £19 to £747, and inn-holders from a low level to £529. Clearly, those in the upper reaches of urban craft production or retailing might be doing very well, sometimes as well as the rich yeoman farmers whose younger sons might be counted among their apprentices. Trying to analyse these groups more systematically is, however, difficult, and it is noticeable that it is a task which few urban historians have attempted. The best information so far available comes from taxation returns which, whatever their drawbacks as a source, do give at least some notion of the distribution of wealth and hence, by inference, of social structure. These suggest that English urban society was already markedly stratified in the early sixteenth century. Thus at Worcester, on the evidence of the 1525 subsidy returns, the 800 families listed fell into an upper class of 4 per cent, with 18 per cent independent traders, 13 per cent self-employed artisans, and 66 per cent employees. Later taxation records, notably those of the hearth tax of the Restoration period, can be used to demonstrate a similar pattern for other towns in later periods. The Worcester findings can be compared with those based on the 1662 hearth-tax returns for Lincoln. There some 48 per cent of households lived in small dwellings with one or two hearths, nearly 40 per cent in modest houses with between three and five hearths, 10 per cent in houses with between six and 10 hearths, and the top 2 per cent in houses with 10 hearths or more.

Taxation returns, like probate inventories, give only a static impression of wealth at a given point. Occasional survivals of material of a more personal nature give us insights into the outlook and experiences of those whose wealth is listed or assessed. One such is the autobiography of William Stout. Stout, born of yeoman stock in Lancashire in 1665, spent his adult life (he died in 1752) as a shopkeeper and wholesale trader in Lancaster. He became a very wealthy man – wealthier than the people with whom we are concerned here. But his account of his early life, and of the fortunes of his relatives and neighbours, provides a fascinating portrait of the shopocracy of a small town of the period. Their world was one in which diligence and sloth brought their appropriate rewards, but one which was complex and, in economic terms, sophisticated. Both geographic mobility and their involvement in the national economy meant that they did not lead isolated lives. Stout travelled occasionally to London, had trading interests which spread to New England, and took an interest in international affairs.

Even more remarkable was Nehemiah Wallington, a London Puritan artisan who lived between 1598 and 1658, and who throughout his adult life compiled a body of writings which probably originally ran to 50 volumes of perhaps 20,000 manuscript pages. These were mainly concerned with spiritual matters, or with the religious interpretation of political events, but they do contain occasional insights into the economic life of the small independent urban artisan. Wallington was a master craftsman, free of the Company of Turners. But wood-turning was not a prestigious or prosperous craft, and Wallington, who in any case was not a very good businessman, was locked in a constant struggle to make ends meet. In a good year in the 1640s he might have an income of £640, yet he never quite managed to escape from financial instability. The absence of any detailed accounts makes it difficult to penetrate the economy of Wallington's workshop, yet it is evident that he was plagued by unpredictable fluctuations in his daily takings and by a lack of cash reserves. He was continually in debt to a network of small creditors, while his situation was made even more difficult by the disruption of trade attendant on the Civil Wars. The difference between his life and that of William Stout demonstrates how varied the experiences of small urban producers and shopkeepers could be.

So far our discussion has concentrated mainly on men. This is because, generally speaking, women were excluded from the direction or control of economic enterprises. Yet it is obvious that the wife's contribution was vital to the economic fortunes of most yeomen, husbandmen and urban masters. The degree of wifely involvement, however, probably varied from couple to couple, and according to the exigencies of short-term circumstances. In times of crisis, or when a business or farm was being built up, the wife's involvement in economic activities was likely to be heavy. Otherwise, her role in the management of commercial, agricultural or industrial activity might be limited. There is every indication that, for many farmers and urban masters, a good wife was regarded as a blessing, and a mutual involvement in the running of the household and the economic enterprise could produce a deep affection based on a sense of shared labour and shared struggle. Generally, however, the wife's main responsibility was in the running of the household and in directing the less central aspects of the farm or workshop. There is little evidence of women setting up farms or commercial enterprises on their own, although many, like William Stout's mother, might continue to run a family enterprise after the death of their husband. Research into the economy of Oxford between 1500 and 1800, for example, has discovered that no married women can be found in the town trading in their own right, that only 22 widows ran their own businesses, and only 236 apprenticeships were made to women. There was evidently little place for the independent woman running her own enterprise in our period. At best, the independence granted by widowhood would allow this, although even here the high contemporary rate of remarriage suggests that it was an option which most women in the relevant social strata rejected.

Summing up the experience of the groups examined in this section is difficult. Perhaps the dominant impression, arising from both detailed research on sources dealing with their economic life and from reading such personal memoirs as survive, is of the uncertainty of their world. The fortunes of an unusually well-documented group of yeomen, those of Myddle, as described by their contemporary, Richard Gough, demonstrate this point: one of their number made a fortune from tanning, another died a lonely death from drink in an alehouse. It has been calculated that they faced a 50 per cent chance of failure, and that failure was as likely to result from personal shortcomings as from economic circumstances: in particular, a number of Myddle yeomen or their wives simply drank away their fortune. Urban producers and retailers faced much the same risks. Fire was, perhaps, more of a risk than for farmers, and in an age before insurance many a tradesman or craftsman faced ruin after an accidental blaze. More, perhaps, suffered by falling into one of the numerous crevasses offered by the contemporary system of debt and credit. Nehemiah Wallington, living in a state of constant indebtedness, was on occasion only saved from financial embarrassment by a fortuitous day of successful trading. William Stout, looking at the problem from the creditor's viewpoint, noted how he suffered 'as is too frequent with young tradesmen' from offering too much credit to customers in his first year in business. Evidently, though, as with the yeomen of Myddle, it was lack of diligence and an over-addiction to drink and good company which ruined tradesmen. Stout recorded how his time-expired apprentice, John Troughton, went steadily to the dogs, was imprisoned for debt, became bankrupt, and was finally lost when a ship whose company he had joined foundered *en route* for America. Another of his apprentices, John Robinson, 'served his time and then began to trade for himselfe, but was not so industrious or careful as he ought, fell to drinking and broke'. He then went off to London, married, spent his wife's portion, left her, and went to America. Even allowing for the contemporary taste for moralizing, Gough's and Stout's accounts of their acquaintances show how important the 'Puritan' virtues of following the calling and diligence were to people of small and middling property.

These, then, were some of the more human issues and more personal stories which lay behind the sometimes impersonal-seeming broad trends which are central to the economic history of early modern England: the rise of capitalist farming, the squeeze on the small landholder, the emergence of a more commercial and more diverse urban economy. Some small owners, through luck, diligence and an ability to exploit the opportunities which their increasingly complex economic environment offered, were able to advance themselves, sometimes considerably. Others broke; some stayed where they were. Many more detailed studies are needed before we can generalize about these varied experiences. What is striking, however, is the frequency with which factors other than purely economic ones affected the fortunes of these people of middling property. Lack of diligence was, as we have seen, a sure road to ruin. Yet, in the last resort, no amount of diligence or business acumen would stave off the consequences of a run of low grain prices, of a number of insolvent debtors, or of a workshop destroyed by fire. Moreover, as with the gentry, the vagaries of demography could cause considerable economic problems. As happened sometimes at Myddle, a husbandman with numerous offspring might have to labour for others until the children were old enough to contribute to the family economy or fend for themselves. William Stout doubtless owed much of his worldly success to the fact that he never married: unlike his brother Leonard, who was faced with bringing up three sons and five daughters. Life was, therefore, fraught with a number of difficulties even for those doing moderately well: for people lower down the social scale life was even more precarious.

Labouring folk and mechanic people

For most of the population, earning a living meant hard and at times unremitting physical labour. Work in the early modern period was tough, monotonous, dirty, at times brutalizing, and affected by the whims of the weather. Modern notions that work might be satisfying, fulfilling, or even interesting would have been laughable to the overwhelming majority of our Tudor, Stuart or Hanoverian forebears. In an age when such things were taken literally, the Bible itself gave the final word on work: it was part of the curse laid by God on Adam at the time of the Fall. Literate labourers and artisans found their lot neatly summarized in Genesis: 'in the sweat of thy face shalt thou eat bread, till thou return into the ground, for out of it wast thou taken'. Anybody arguing for the dignity of manual labour had to contend with contemporary aesthetic, educational, scientific and moral assumptions.

The reality of work was as different from the modern situation as were the assumptions about it. Today, people in employment normally work throughout the year for a set money wage, and that wage forms all of their income. Things were very different before the coming of the factories. First, work was seasonal. This was self-evident in agriculture, where there were the constant problems of finding enough hands to gather the harvest, and of finding enough work for people to do over the remainder of the year. Industrial production was also, to a considerable extent, affected by seasonal variations. The result was that underemployment was chronic. Many people could not work for a wage all the year round, and had to find ways of augmenting their income. Those with a small agricultural holding and rights to pasture animals obviously had a buffer against the vagaries of working for wages. Others turned to by-employments. Some 60 per cent of labourers named on a Gloucestershire listing of 1608 were exercising supplementary trades, while in Terling, Wrightson and Levine found men working as labourer and cowleech, labourer and fiddler, labourer, cooper and tinker, or labourer, tailor and shopkeeper. Further complications arise from the contemporary custom of substituting food and drink or other forms of payment in kind for part of the money wage. There were also perquisites, the industrial worker's equivalent of pasture rights: miners might get a coal allowance, weavers might keep the waste ends of a piece of cloth, workers in royal dockyards might keep the 'chips' or waste pieces of the wood they worked. All this helped to eke out meagre wages or provide a reserve against a spell of unemployment, but it makes it clear that many workers were not fully dependent on a money wage in the modern sense. Indeed, even in 1760, many people, especially those employed in running a family farm or a family workshop, were not 'employed' or 'wage earners' in anything like the twentienth-century usage. The presence of such people helps make comprehensible the contemporary view which equated wage labour with a loss of freedom: Winstanley the Digger (admittedly not an unbiased commentator) could observe that 'the poor that have no land are left still in the straits of beggary, and are shut out of all liveliehood but ... by working for others as masters over them'.

Working hours were generally long. In appropriate seasons, agricultural workers would labour for as long as there was daylight. Industrial workers were in much the same case. Nehemiah Wallington laboured in his calling from six in the morning until seven or nine at night. A Norwich clergy-man wrote in 1675 of 'a weaver whom I see before four of the clock in the morning and after 8, 9, 10 at night hard at work ... and all for a few shillings at the end of a week'. A poem of 1730, set in Yorkshire, showed farmer-weavers working from five in the morning until eight at night, while an investigation of 1747 found that 14-hour working days were not uncommon in many London trades.

In some of these trades, however, long hours might be ameliorated by a degree of control on the part of the worker over how long was worked at one stretch, or how quickly a piece of work was completed. This practice, another characteristic of prefactory work-rhythms, attracted considerable adverse comment from the mid-eighteenth century, as employers seeking a better-disciplined workforce were confronted with semi-independent artisans who were used to working by the piece or by the task rather than by the hour, and who might be accustomed to taking a weekly holiday of heavy drinking on 'Saint Monday', and compensating for it by working all-out over the four following days. Such a work pattern was clearly inappropriate to the new world of the factory and the division of labour: in the factory you clocked on and off, with the hands of the timepiece dictating the work-rhythm.

Working conditions might be very dangerous. Coroners' inquests, one of the great neglected sources of early modern social history, include numerous examples of what the late twentieth century would describe as industrial accidents. There were farmworkers killed by unskillfully handled pitchforks or by overturning carts, or through more bizarre misfortunes, like the Cheshire man drowned in 1657 while 'washeinge a certaine wedder sheep in a certaine pitt of water'. Metal workers might be impaled on red-hot bars of iron, miners killed by collapsing pits, quarrymen killed by falling rocks. The age was, moreover, as innocent of health precautions as it was of safety measures. It was axiomatic to Adam Smith that every trade had its peculiar illness or disability, while the first book on occupational sickness, Bernard Ramazzini's *De Morbis Artificum Diatriba* (1700: augmented English edition 1746) was insistent that the doctor investigating illness among the common people should ask what work they did. Some idea of the deformities inherent in different trades can be gained from the various titles given to industrial bursitis: bricklayer's or miner's elbow, weaver's bottom, housemaid's knee, hod carrier's shoulder and tailor's ankle. Working with chemicals or metals brought its own problems: lead-workers were normally poisoned after a few years' employment, while the proverbial madness of hatters was due to the paranoia attendant on poisoning caused by the mercury used in the making of felt hats. The heavy nature of much of the work of the period meant that ruptures were frequent, a situation which was to be acknowledged by the foundation of the National Truss Society in 1786. 'To be short lived and unhealthy,' concludes one historian of eighteenth-century labour conditions, 'was the normal lot of many workers.'[2]

Entry into this uncertain and unhealthy world of work began early in life. Nineteenth-century exposés of child labour in factories or the mines should not obscure the use made of children by both prefactory industry and agriculture: it was the separation of children from family production which was novel, and distasteful, in the early factories. By 1760 a few children were experiencing work in these new units of production: William Hutton, author of a history of Birmingham, remembered how, in 1730, he had begun work in a Derby silk-mill at the age of eight, so small that he had to stand on special pattens to make him tall enough to reach the machinery. This was new, but the experience of child labour was not. Children in country areas were taught the simpler agricultural tasks, such as bird-scaring, at a very early age. Elizabethan censuses of the poor, like that completed at Norwich in 1570, showed five- or six-year-olds contributing to the family income with their wages, and adolescents as chief breadwinners. Our 1675 observer of Norwich weavers recorded 'children from their infancy almost' involved in various of the simpler aspects of textile manufacture, while a generation later Defoe, looking at the West Riding textile industry, found 'hardly anything above a few years old, but its hands were sufficient to itself'. Early physical work was evidently the lot of most poor children.

It was also the usual experience for poor women. Women, as we have seen, were largely excluded from the management of economic enterprises. They were, however, an essential part of the workforce. Girls and young women were expected to play their part in working the family farm, as were farmers' wives. Many servants in husbandry were women, like the one on William Stout's father's farm, who was kept 'to do the hardest house service and harrow work, hay, and shear in harvest, so that the family and concerns was managed in good order as could be expected'. Women were also employed in industrial production, sometimes in rather unexpected places: thus a visitor to Birmingham in 1741, looking into blacksmiths' workshops, found 'one or more females, stripped of their upper garments, and not overcharged with the lower, wielding the hammer with all the grace of their sex'. Generally the eighteenth century was a period of downgrading of women workers. In agriculture, although women were invariably paid less than men for comparable tasks, it seems that the work they were expected to do, barring a few specialized or unusually heavy jobs, was before 1760 much the same as that done by male workers. In industry and manufacture, on the other hand, women usually performed the less responsible and less well paid work and were, by 1700, being pushed into trades considered as inferior, like millinery or mantua-making.

Recent rethinking of the subject has deepened our understanding of women's work and women's experience of work in the early modern period, although there is still some debate about the nature of long-term changes in the female work experience. Alice Clark's classic study argued that the shift from a household-based to a capitalist-, and especially factory-based, economy led to a downgrading of women workers and a lessening of women's work opportunities. Perhaps it can still be argued that things did get worse after 1760, but even before that date women industrial and rural workers were more likely to be economically marginalized than men, although there are some complications with this overall picture. It has been argued, indeed, that even women's work experience immediately before and during the Industrial Revolution was not one of an undifferentiated deterioration, but rather a more complex matter in which variations existed between regions and between trades. Additionally, the growth of economic specialization in both town and countryside, while constraining the work-employment opportunities of some women might enhance those of others. And, perhaps in all periods, women's work experience was connected to the female lifecycle: thus changes in industrial organization which might disadvantage the married woman working from within the household might broaden work opportunities for geographically mobile single women. A further set of complications is suggested by the lingering suspicion that our notion of female work, and our views on women's experience of work, might rest on an inherently flawed conceptual framework, given that there is still a tendency to define work in terms of the male experience of a social process.

Yet whatever these provisos, the current state of research and conceptualization suggests that over the early modern period the working conditions of women were, in general, deteriorating. Women working for wages, even in the late medieval period, had tended to be given what was regarded as inferior work, or paid less than men when they were performing comparable tasks. The fact that the population was relatively low in the fifteenth century, and therefore wage-earners were in a seller's market, may have made the position of female workers less unequal, but the

pressures of demographic expansion which began in the sixteenth century
were to challenge this. By the mid-eighteenth century a higher proportion
of the female population was working for wages and, in general, the
inequalities which have been noted for the late medieval period were even
more marked. For many, especially in London, drifting in and out of
prostitution was the remedy for poor and irregular wages. Even if they
did not resort to this desperate shift, it is evident that women were most
often found at the casual, menial end of the labour market.

For many, apprenticeship was a vital stage in the experience of work.
Indeed, that great statement of Tudor economic philosophy, the Statute
of Artificers of 1563, made it illegal to practise any craft without having
served an apprenticeship of seven years. Normally, apprentices were male:
perhaps only 10 per cent of those apprenticed by their parents, and 25–30
per cent of those pauper children apprenticed by the parish or by charitable organizations, were girls. Apprenticeship normally began at about
14 years of age, and had the effect not merely of teaching a craft (many
could be learnt in a few weeks) but also of keeping adolescents under
control. With some 40 per cent of the population under the age of 20,
apprenticeship obviously played a part not only in integrating young
people into the workforce, but also in maintaining a general discipline
over them. The apprentice was bound by a personal and legal document
to his master, usually with a premium being paid to the master by the
child's parents. There was normally no official cash remuneration for the
apprentice – bed and board were all that could be hoped for – while the
master enjoyed near-parental rights over the apprentice, including those
of physical chastisement.

The conditions under which apprentices lived varied enormously. Some
were very badly treated; others, with conscientious and godly masters like
William Stout, were well cared for and taught their trades thoroughly. In
some places a sort of apprentice culture grew up. This was certainly the
case in London, and scattered evidence from other towns suggests that
similar conditions obtained in the provinces. Nevertheless, the institution
of apprenticeship, although holding-up well in 1750, was to disintegrate
rapidly in the late eighteenth century. A new ethos of capitalist development and free trade was replacing the old ideas on economic practices,
while the declining economic position of journeymen made the comple-
tion of seven years' training seem increasingly irrelevant. But before that
time, most master-craftsmen and retailers would have an apprentice or
two around their shops, and apprenticeship was an experience shared by
a large number of adolescents.

For many people, especially young women, service in an employer's
household without formal apprenticeship constituted an important stage
in life. A surprisingly high proportion of adolescents and young adults, as
we noted in our discussion of the family, would enter service and be
regarded as a normal feature of the household. As with apprenticeship,

service normally began in the early teens, and was experienced by a very significant number of young people. Averaging out listings dealing with six preindustrial English settlements shows that of males, 35 per cent of the 15–19-year age group, 30 per cent of those aged 20–24, and 15 per cent of those aged 25–29 were in service. Of women, the respective proportions for these three age groups were 27 per cent, 40 per cent and, again, 15 per cent. Putting it rather differently, on the evidence of settlement papers it appears that between the late seventeenth and the early nineteenth centuries perhaps 81 per cent of the labouring population had been in service at some time in their lives. Some servants joined one of those retinues which great men were expected to keep: there were 81 on Lord Rockingham's establishment in 1767, from the chaplain, housekeeper and steward at one end to the maids and stable boys at the other. Upper servants in such households enjoyed considerable responsibility and drew correspondingly high wages. More commonly, however, servants were employed not to maintain and display a great man's way of life, but rather to help keep that peculiar mode of production, the household economy, going. As the Elizabethan William Harrison expressed it, these were 'not idle servants ... but such as get both their own and part of their master's living'.

There were various ways of getting a service. Sometimes the arrangements were casual: thus in 1647 Adam Eyre, retired from his captaincy in parliament's army and returning to yeoman farming in Yorkshire, asked a neighbour 'to let me have one of his daughters for a mayd, and he promised mee I should, but he could not spare one yet by reason of his wife's being ill'. More frequently servants hired themselves for a specific period, ideally for a year: indeed, one observer commented in 1755 that 'in general, the law never looks upon any person as a servant, who is hired for less than one whole year; otherwise they come under the definition of labourers'. This view was perhaps too inflexible: people can be found negotiating a service of a few months. Nevertheless, the term 'servant' normally denoted a person hired by the year (often being hired at a hiring fair), living in the employer's household, usually, in sub-gentry households at least, eating with the employer's family, and 'paid' overwhelmingly in board rather than cash. For the employer, servants represented a way of gaining extra labour in those medium-term periods when the family enterprise needed it: when it was expanding, or when the employer's children were too young to work or had left home. For the servant, it gave the opportunity over the years of adolescence and early adulthood to get a sum of money together which would form the economic basis for marriage. Like apprenticeship, this institution, so typical of the early modern world, was deteriorating rapidly around 1800. By the early nineteenth century nostalgic observers were to speak of household service, with its overtones of paternalist caring and patriarchal control, as part of a lost world of idyllic social relationships. After 1760, soaring grain prices made feeding servants a less viable proposition (payment in kind always made more sense in periods of static prices), the more affluent lifestyle of farmers and urban masters made them less willing to share their meal-tables with their servants, and population growth ensured the existence of a docile and cheap workforce. Household service in its old sense was one of the major casualties of the economic changes of the later eighteenth century.

As descriptions of getting a service remind us, migration, normally in search of work or better working and living conditions, was a common experience among the lower orders of early modern England, and a standard aspect of most people's experience of work: we return to the point made in an earlier chapter that, despite sociological myth, early modern England was a society which experienced a high degree of geographical mobility. The patterns we have noted earlier, particularly when discussing population movement into towns, were part of a broader social and cultural phenomenon whose main outlines have now been uncovered. Migration from the countryside to the town is familiar enough, but people moved around to gain a service, to enter an apprenticeship, to seek harvest work or, as we have suggested, simply to find work of any sort. Several samples of relevant materials for the late Elizabethan and early Stuart periods suggest that something like 80 per cent of the popula-tion moved at least once in their lifetime, and scattered autobiographical material suggests that more frequent moves were not unusual. In the later seventeenth and early eighteenth century the level of migration had fallen somewhat: better living conditions and a more effective poor relief system probably diluted the push factors which sent the poor on the road, while the settlement laws helped regulate those who did. Moreover, in this later period regional variations in migration become more marked, with a greater disposition to move in East Anglia, for example, than in the west of England. But throughout there was a tendency for the better off among the common people to move less frequently and less far than labourers or the poorer artisans, many of whom must have shaded off into the vagrant poor whom we shall encounter in the next section of this chapter.

If migration between places where work might be found was a common experience for the workforce in this period, the composition of that workforce was already being varied by immigration. The reactions of the native English to this fact varied. There had probably always been aliens resident in seaports in England, but the early modern period was to witness the influx of a variety of larger groups of settlers. Perhaps the first of these within our period were 'flemings', refugees from war and religious conflict in the southern Netherlands who settled mainly in eastern England in the later sixteenth century. These appear to have been generally accepted, if occasionally suffering from bouts of hostility when times were bad, and in towns like Colchester they might form a hard-working and largely self-regulating community. Probably much the same could be said of the Huguenots who settled in London, notably after the prosecution of French Protestants intensified after the Revocation of the Edict of Nantes in 1685, and who were especially associated with the silk industry in Spitalfields. Yet these immigrant workers were the occasional victims of English xenophobia, an experience suffered more frequently in the early and mid-eighteenth centuries by London's Irish immigrants. These were held to undercut the wages expected by the native workforce (the common fate of immigrants in any reasonably developed country) and hence were from time to time rioted against. The extent of these xenophobic manifestations, unwelcome though they were, should not, perhaps, be overstated.

Mention of immigration leads to a topic which has produced much interesting, if at times rather speculative, work in recent years: the history of Blacks in early modern England. There was certainly a Black presence in England during this period, although references before the eighteenth century are rather scattered: the Black trumpeter shown on a manuscript illustration of jousting held to celebrate the wedding of Henry VIII and Catherine of Aragon in 1511; the five African slaves brought by a merchant to London in 1554, who apparently adjusted well to English food and English customs, but who had rather more problems with the climate; 'Lucy Negro', the seemingly well-known Black prostitute who appeared at the Gray's Inn Christmas Revels in 1594; and, an interesting early example of what was to become a common theme, a Privy Council order of 1596 which declared that there were too many 'blackamoors' in England, and that no more should be admitted. Despite this order, a steady trickle of Blacks did enter the realm. By the later seventeenth century it was fashionable to have a Black servant or two, and this tendency continued into the eighteenth. Estimates of the numbers of Blacks vary widely, and probably reflect current opinion rather than objective fact. For what it is worth, it was claimed that there were 20,000 Blacks in London by 1764, and 40,000 by 1783, although a more sober estimate puts the figure for late eighteenth-century London as low as 5000.

The Black experience in England was varied. Some Black servants made their way up the servant hierarchy, became modestly well-off, married English women, raised families and integrated themselves fully into English life. Perhaps rather more were economically marginalized, and entered the historical record as casual workers, sailors, street entertainers, beggars or prostitutes. Many of them were, or had been, slaves: the legal standing of Black slavery in England was ambivalent until well into the eighteenth century, and even Lord Mansfield's celebrated judgement against the phenomenon in 1772 did not put an end to it immediately. By that date, however, it was evident that at least some Blacks were doing rather better than merely surviving in England: in 1764 a club for Black servants was noted at Fleet Street in London, whose members, 57 in number, met to wine, dine and dance.

The experience of work in early modern England, like the workforce itself, was thus a very varied one. Attempting to trace the general fortunes of the labouring poor and the lesser artisans over the period is accordingly difficult: any general statement has to be modified by regional variations, or local economic shifts which might make one group of workers prosper or decline contrary to an opposite general trend. Even the most obvious index of the workforce's fortunes – that of the value of real wages – is beset by difficulties. Many people were simply not wage-earners in the modern sense: apprentices, servants, family farmers, family artisans. Others might derive their wages partly in kind, or in truck payments, rather than cash. As ever, regional variations introduce further complications. Wages (like prices) were characteristically highest in London, and probably at their lowest in East Anglia. But despite all these problems, some sources suggest that the proportion of people wholly or largely dependent on wages might, in some areas at least, be high. In 1524 taxation returns showed 36–66 per cent of taxpayers being assessed on their wages in different parts of Devon, 23–41 per cent in Lincolnshire, up to 90 per cent in some urban parts of Leicestershire. Two centuries later the importance of wages is neatly demonstrated by the insistence among economic commentators (who, needless to say, were not dependent on wages) that they should be kept low. 'Every one but an idiot,' declared Adam Smith, 'knows that the lower classes must be kept poor or they will never be industrious,' while in 1739 Sir William Temple had opined that high wages would make the poor 'loose, debauched, insolent, idle and luxurious'. By 1760 the wage was obviously regarded as an important element in the economy: throughout our period, although there may have been few wage-earners in the modern sense, most working people would have been dependent on wages at some stage in their lives. Despite all the qualifications, a long-term index of real wage values therefore remains the handiest indicator to changing fortunes among the masses.

Part of one of the best known of these indexes, that constructed for building workers' wages in the south by E.H. Phelps Brown and Sheila V. Hopkins, forms the basis for Figure 8.1. This index sets money wages against the price of a 'basket' of consumer goods (mainly foodstuffs), and thus shows changes in the real purchasing power of these building workers. As Figure 8.1 demonstrates, the resultant impression is a gloomy one. The fifteenth century had been a period of modest prosperity for the wage-earner, but real wages fell rapidly in the early sixteenth century, then continued to decline steadily until the 1610s, when they stood at little more than one-third of their 1450–75 level. Population growth produced a glut on the labour market, and those trying to sell their labour suffered accordingly. The levelling-off of population growth after about 1640 eased the situation, and real wages doubled over the century 1630–1730, only to fall again when population increase after that date once more created

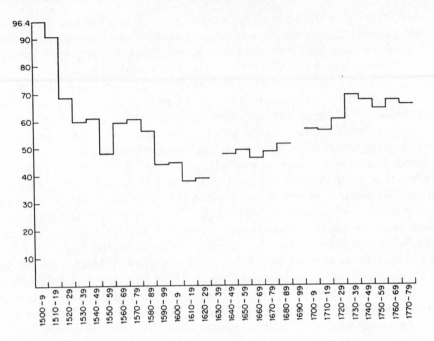

Figure 8.1 Value of real wages of building workers in southern England, 1500–1780. *Source*: E.H. Phelps Brown and Sheila V. Hopkins, 'Seven Centuries of Building Wages', in E.M. Carus-Wilson (ed.). *Essays in Economic History*, 2 vols. (London, 1962), volume 2, pp. 194–5. *Index*: 1451–75 = 100.

a pool of cheap labour. In broad terms, the century before the Civil Wars was one of hardship for the wage-earner, while that after 1660 was one of gradual improvement. But at any date within our period it is difficult to see how a labouring family survived economically.

Estimating the budget of such a family is difficult, not least because such a process normally assumes that the male head of household would work for six days a week and 52 weeks a year: an unlikely situation given the seasonal nature of most work and the endemic underemployment of the period. Some calculations, however, have been made, and demonstrate the hardness of the labourer's lot. At Terling, poor-law payments suggest that a pauper family of husband, wife and three children would cost £13 14s 0d to keep for a year in the late seventeenth century: £9 14s 0d on food, £2 on clothes, £1 on fuel, £1 on rent. An agricultural labourer, given contemporary local wage-rates, would earn £15 12s 0d annually, given the unlikely eventuality that he worked every available day of the year. The margin, even allowing for the wife and children's earnings, was a very narrow one. Other estimates have shown an even narrower margin, or left the historian making the calculation wondering how a poor family could get through the year.

Contemporary comment supports the drift of these calculations: many of those dependent on money wages, especially before the late seventeenth century, had trouble getting by. A preacher of 1622 declared that labourers 'are scarce able to put bread in their mouths at the week's end, and clothes on their backs at the year's end'. A petition on behalf of Essex textile-workers in 1631 claimed that 'there are not less within that county than 40 or 50 thousand who live by these manufactures, not being able to subsist unless they be continually set on work and weekly paid. And many of them cannot support themselves and their miserable families unless they receive their wages every night.' In 1675 it was stated that the average Norwich weaver 'cannot stay for his wages until the end of the year, but hath it from week to week; possibly they cannot stay so long, but must have it from day to day'. For such people and their dependents, survival rested on an 'economy of makeshifts'. The family would struggle along on the head-of-household's wages, on what the wife and children might earn, on the corn gathered through gleaning at harvest time, on the desperate shifts of petty borrowing or pawning. For some, the temptation to poach or steal became overwhelming: a rise in thefts always followed a bad harvest or a trade depression. Alternatively, props to survival were provided by that great institution of English life: poor relief.

The poor law

'The old poor law,' one recent historian has declared, 'provides the key to a social understanding of the eighteenth century.'[3] Certainly, by the early years of that century the range of support it offered was wide. A list drawn up at Headcorn in Kent in 1700, showing 13 households or individuals receiving regular relief, was fairly typical. It included the elderly: William Sholock, a widower aged 70, who had been receiving poor relief for 12 years; Mary Duke, a widow aged 75; Richard Norris, aged 76 and his wife of 61. It included those with large families: John Elger with his wife and five children, one of them Mary, a lame girl aged 13; Richard Baker, with his wife and four children; Mary Wood, a widow with three children. It included the permanently disabled: Elizabeth Richison, 'under-witted', who had received relief for 19 of her 58 years; Sarah Ripley, 'a dumb girle aged 19'; and John Kemp, a lame man of 37. The individual sums awarded to these Headcorn paupers might seem niggardly, rarely more than a few shillings a week: yet they obviously added to that margin of security which these individuals must have craved continually.

This outdoor relief for the long-term poor was accompanied by occasional relief given to people who were temporarily down on their luck, a category which naturally expanded when times were bad. Dearth or trade depression sent poor-relief expenditure soaring: William Stout noted that at Lancaster in 1730 'the last harvest being a dearth of corn, encreased the poor, soe that our poor tax was advanced from one hundred to two hundred pounds a year'. At Goudhurst, Kent, in 1744 the parish vestry awarded 'half a bushell of wheat per week' to Richard Doe, 'upon account of his broken legg ... till he can help himself', while John Farmer was allowed a bushel a week until he had recovered from his 'lame arm'. In 1740, a bad year, the vestry at Lenham in the same county helped one man pay his rent, bought another a new hedging bill, gave Daniel White 'ten shillings to buy him some new toolls', gave Goodman Chapman five shillings to get his tools out of pawn, and gave Goody Stedman two shifts, as well as awarding the usual doles of food and money. By that date the poor law even extended to spiritual matters, with the burials, marriages and religious instruction of the poor all being provided for by the parish rate. The poor law did not offer anything like total security, yet it evidently went a long way to providing some sort of safety net for those at the base of society.

By 1700 the poor law was one of the most important facts of everyday life. The amount paid annually in poor relief was, by contemporary standards, massive: between 1685 and 1701 the national yield from the poor rate rose from £665,000 to £900,000. The impact on a local level over the previous century had been striking. Richard Gough of Myddle noted in 1700 that he had 'heard my father say that the first year that he was married (which was about the year 1633) he paid only four pence to the poor, and now I pay almost twenty shillings per annum'. Remarkably, the more fortunate, in town and country alike, were willing to pay their poor rates. Naturally there were disputes, and a few individuals made problems over paying their contributions, or paid ungraciously. Yet poor relief, organized locally through the parish for the most part, was normally well administered and, to a limited extent, effective. From the mid-seventeenth century the poor rate became the most regular and familiar form of taxation in England, and the administration of the poor law and the related problem of settlement became the most consistent concern of parish and local government. The problem of poverty was, by the late seventeenth century, a major theme of national social debate. Schemes to aid the poor were mooted, ever-growing in their scope and complexity. The need to educate poor children gave rise to the charity-school movement, and the need to make the poor religious was an important motive force behind Anglican evangelicanism. More concrete measures followed a statute of 1723 which encouraged the building of workhouses: by 1777 some 132 of these, with provision for 5799 people, existed in Kent alone. By that time the poor law permeated numerous aspects of life: employment, the regulation of wages, the fixing of prices (especially grain prices), apprenticeship, marriage, settlement, and the treatment of the elderly.

The origins of all this lay in the sixteenth century. Traditionally, poverty had been dealt with by freerange begging and by the charity of better-off individuals and the church: both these phenomena, despite the introduction of systems of relief, were to continue throughout our period. The church, other corporations, and prosperous people from peers, gentry and rich merchants down to yeomen farmers all contributed alms or bequests to the poor. But as the economic and social problems attendant on population increase emerged in the early sixteenth century it became evident that new remedies were needed. These came from two sources. First, individual town governments, often motivated by a traditional sense of civic responsibility, began to experiment with measures for relieving and controlling the poor: stocks of corn were laid up in good years or brought from the Baltic in bad, beggars were licensed, work was provided and eventually, following London's example of 1547, consolidated systems of poor relief were set up. These were often underpinned, as in London's case, by a compulsory rate on better-off householders. At the same time a second, parallel, development was taking place: central government legislation was gradually erecting a national poor-law system. The first Act attempting to deal with the new problems came in 1531. There was further legislation in 1547, which included unenforceably harsh measures against vagrancy, but the next important legislation, very much connected with the economic attitudes which gave rise to the Statute of Artificers, did not come until 1563. This, among other things, paved the way for a system based on the parish and a compulsory poor rate. Further statutes of 1572 and 1576 clarified thinking on the issue by including as objects of official concern the able-bodied poor who wanted work but could not find it. This steady development of attitudes and measures was crystallized in the late 1590s, that period of bad harvests and widespread fears of social breakdown. In 1598 a near-comprehensive Act, confirmed and extended in 1601, was passed which formed the basis for poor-law policy until the late eighteenth century.

The basic premise behind this legislation, and behind most of the local initiatives, was that the poor could be divided into three groups. First, there were what Elizabethans described as the 'impotent' poor: those who were poor through being ill or disabled, or because they were too young or too old to earn their living. These, familiar enough in medieval thinking on the poor, were obviously deserving. Second came those who were willing to work but could find none, or whose families were so large or whose wages were so low that they needed assistance. These were, perhaps, less unequivocally deserving than the first category, but the realities of the sixteenth century rendered them familiar and acceptable. The third category, perhaps the one which agitated contemporaries most, were those who were fit and able enough to work, but who wilfully refused to do so. Tudor and early Stuart moralists directed a barrage of adverse comment against such people who, according to most commentators, achieved their most pernicious form in the vagrant.

Such commentators were anxious to impress upon their fellows the numbers of sturdy beggars, rogues and vagabonds on England's roads. It was claimed in 1569 that there were 13,000 rogues and masterless men in the country. In 1577 William Harrison put the figure of vagrants at 10,000, and a Jacobean ex-highwayman suggested 80,000. These figures were simply guesses, although the concern which lay behind them was real enough. Elizabethan and Jacobean preachers, social commentators and pamphleteers were convinced of the existence of an organized hierarchy of vagrants and rogues. John Awdeley's *The Fraternity of Vagabonds* of 1565 contained descriptions of such exotics as the ruffler, the abraham-man, the queer-bird, the Irish toyle, the kinchin mort and the doxy. Thomas Harman's *Caveat for Common Cursetors*, published two years later, portrayed a similar hierarchy of different species of rogue. These fictional vagrants rejected all the values of respectable society: they did not work, they rejected religion, they stole, they lived lives of sexual promiscuity, they were even seen, in times of war or civil commotion, as a coherent threat to national security. The Kentish JP William Lambarde, haranguing local jurymen in 1582, warned of the 'many of mighty, idle and runagate beggars wherewith we are much pestered', who 'continually by heaps and flocks increase upon us', and urged sharp action against 'these rotten members that otherwise would bring peril of infection to the whole body of the realm and commonwealth'. In 1654 Richard Young summed up a century of anti-vagrant sentiment when he declared that most rogues were 'an uncircumcized generation, unbaptized, not of the church, and so consequently without God in the world'.

Fortunately, the reality of vagrancy was very different from its image. Criminal vagrants certainly existed, some of them not unlike the professional rogues of pamphlet literature. But the typical vagrant, in Elizabeth's reign and beyond, was a much less threatening figure. Paul Slack, using various registers and returns, has analysed a sample of some 3000 vagrants recorded between 1598 and 1664. The sample includes a number of children and old people, but is composed overwhelmingly of young adults, perhaps 40 per cent of the sample being aged between 20 and 40. Most vagrants were single, and men predominated. Unmarried males formed 51.4 per cent of Slack's sample, single or separated women 24.9 per cent, married couples 12.9 per cent, and children younger than 15 formed 10.8 per cent. Rather than the organized bands of the pamphlets, most vagrants travelled in ones or twos, or at most in a family group. The distance they had travelled before being caught was usually limited: just over one-quarter were apprehended 20 or fewer miles from their place of residence, just under one-quarter between 21 and 40 miles. Vagrants were most often men or women who were down on their luck, and seeking work or the assistance of relatives in the area through which they were passing. Essex records from the early seventeenth century describe a number of such individuals. There was a 'verye poore man' from the London suburb of St Giles-in-the-Fields, who claimed he had come to Essex looking for work when he was apprehended for theft in 1623; the Suffolk man, charged with sheep-stealing in the same year, who 'hath noe abiding place but sayeth he worketh sometime in one place & sometime in another'; the ex-soldier, returning from the Low Countries, who in 1621 confessed to stealing some tools 'proposinge to have gone to London to have sould them,' to whome soever would have bought them'. It was isolated, if troublesome, people like these, rather than any organized 'fraternity of vagabonds', who constituted the reality of the vagrant problem.

Vagrancy is, as we noted in our discussion of law and order in the period, best understood as one aspect of the much broader problem presented by the pauperized mass of the poor, see page 117 above. Disorder, loose living, drunkenness, idleness and bastard-getting were by no means limited to the vagrant in contemporary imagination: increasingly, they were thought to be characteristic of at least some elements in the local resident poor. The dimensions of the problem were set out neatly in a petition sent to the Essex justices in 1640 from the weaving town of Bocking. The local officers complained about unlicensed and disorderly alehouses filled with 'journeymen and maides living out of services', by 'diverse wandering strangers which work within your towne', and 'idell loytring peopell who breake hedges, steale wood, use unlawfull games'. The poor had not only become more numerous: they were also becoming, and were perceived as being, more disorderly. In particular, it has been claimed, they tended to gather on heathland and in forest areas, outside or on the peripheries of the disciplinary forces afforded by the parish officers or the lord of the manor. This picture has probably been overdrawn: certainly, detailed research in a number of relevant counties has failed to confirm it in its entirety. Even so, in the course of the century before the Civil Wars, it seems clear that many parishes acquired a hamlet or street where immigrants and squatters lived, the rural equivalents of those suburbs which grew up outside the walls of so many towns at the same time. This rootless element, vulnerable to every economic depression, irregularly employed, existing largely independently of the agencies of church or state, provided a constant problem for law-enforcement officials and poor-law officers alike.

After about 1650 such people seem to have become less troublesome. Complaints about vagrants and masterless men, so strident over the previous century, became less marked. The poor, if not becoming tamed, were at least becoming institutionalized as the ending of population growth allowed a slackening of pressure at the bottom of society. The most famous poor-law legislation of the post-Restoration period, the Act of Settlements of 1662, was obviously enacted in a context where the poor were still mobile. But its basic objective was not to limit movement among the poor, but rather, given that the system of poor relief operated on a parish basis, to clarify the rules determining where settlement, and hence poor relief, might legitimately be claimed. The problem was not now that of dealing with the vagrant of Elizabethan trauma, but rather with those parish poor depicted in the Kentish sources with which we opened this section. The poor, both urban and rural, were numerous. Restoration hearth-tax returns present a number of problems of interpretation, but their tendency to show about one-third of households in many areas being exempted from taxation on the grounds of poverty is suggestive of the extent of the phenomenon. So are Gregory King's analyses of English society of the 1680s. These estimated that 364,000 families of labouring people and out-servants, 400,000 families of cottagers and paupers, and 85,000 families of soldiers and sailors, were decreasing the wealth of the nation in the sense that they were unable to survive without assistance. Yet by King's time this enormous body of poor people were familiar, a normal part of things. The hysterical fears of vagrancy and of the many-headed monster of poor people were now muted. The poor were an incon-venience, but they were not to be regarded as a threat again until the French Revolution let a new set of genii out of their bottles. By the late seventeenth century, a lasting equilibrium had been reached in English society.

Throughout the early modern period many schemes were mooted or set in motion for the relief of the poor, the most fertile time for such projects perhaps being the early years of the eighteenth century. There were, however, three consistent threads in the era's thinking on the poor. The first was fear: if the poor were not relieved, they might rise in despera-tion. The second was a notion that the poor would benefit themselves and perhaps benefit others if they were employed usefully: a notion probably not unconnected with the ever-developing capitalism of the period. The third, and perhaps most widespread, was a feeling that the better-off should do something for their less fortunate brethren. In the late seven-teenth century even such a paradigm of commercial success as Sir Josiah Child could think it 'our duty to God and nature to provide for and employ the poor', whether or not thus employing them should 'turn to present profit or not'. As the humdrum archives of the poor law demon-strate, a large proportion of people of property seemed willing, for whatever reason, to pay their assessed rates with minimal complaint and hence keep the system of relief going. This is not to suggest some sort of an idyllic situation: the safety net provided by the old poor law had many gaps, while occasional flashes of bitterness between the poor and those who were rated to help them have entered the historical record. Nevertheless, the poor law did help to alleviate both poverty and social tensions in early modern England. But we shall close this chapter with a brief overview of those tensions which did occur.

The steady increase in social stratification experienced in early modern England had important consequences. In the countryside there occurred a marked divergence in economic status and way of life between the upper stratum of rich yeomen and the mass of poor labourers. In towns, under similar pressures, the traditional concept of the corporate urban body politic was replaced by something like a class perception of urban society. In the peasant risings of 1549 the upper stratum of village society (Robert Kett is the obvious example) played their time-honoured role as the leaders of the village community. In the first half of the seventeenth century such people were still involved in lesser stirs like the Western Rising and the rioting in the fenland. By the 1760s their successors, the rich tenant farmers, were objects of hostility when the labouring poor rioted over grain prices: the sturdy yeomen of Tudor moralizing had become John Mordant's 'grasping farmers'. A profound transition had taken place: men of middling property, urban and rural, came to identify with those above them. What the poor made of it all is more difficult to establish.

Examining what the lower orders did or said when they confronted their betters, or when they tried to modify aspects of the socioeconomic system which they felt to be operating to their disadvantage, offers one avenue into this problem. By the late seventeenth century, as the grain riot replaced attacks on enclosures as the characteristic manifestation of rural plebeian discontent, towns and manufacturing areas in the countryside were experiencing a proliferation of industrial disputes. Setting out to find the first strike in English history would not, perhaps, be the most profitable of activities: the phenomenon, in one form or another, has probably existed as far back as people have been able to bargain collectively over their pay and conditions. One suspects that scattered references to such matters rest undetected in the archives of borough towns which contained an industrial workforce. One such, for example, can be found in 1635 at Norwich, when reports reached the town authorities about nocturnal gatherings at the 'Unicorn' inn involving journeymen working in one branch of Norwich's extensive textile industry. It was alleged that under the cover of communal feasting they were meeting 'onely to knowe howe the journeymen would holde all together concerning the mendinge of their wages & that they might have promised one another that they would have no lesse than vid [i.e. six pence] a weeke more than nowe they have if they could gett ytt'.

Lack of documentation makes it difficult to carry out a sustained study of labour relations and industrial conflict in any individual sector of the workforce before the eighteenth century, and we are all too frequently dependent upon intriguing shards of evidence like the one quoted above. For this reason, such studies as have been carried out on this topic are especially welcome. One such, focusing on Derbyshire lead-mining between the late sixteenth and mid-eighteenth centuries, has demonstrated how workers in that industry experienced processes which are more familiar to historians of the early nineteenth century. The growth of both national and international markets meant that lead-mining in Derbyshire, England's only major lead-producing area, became steadily affected by technological and organizational change, this change coinciding with the industry's becoming more heavily capitalized. Around 1600, the extraction of lead ore was carried out mainly by the free miners: independent workers who by 1640 still comprised half the total of 4000 men in the lead-mining workforce, the remainder being wage labourers. The free miners were gradually marginalized and proletarianized by the logic of the developments in their industry, but they put up a lengthy battle against the innovations which threatened their standards of living and their way of life.

Attempts to curtail free mining led to some 17 riots between 1608 and 1658, while this direct action coincided with attempts by the miners to defend their rights through the local barmote courts. These attempts created an interesting case history of a conflict between a local customary law, which defended the rights of the miners, and the national common law which, in its defence of big property, came to be seen as favouring the landlords and large-scale producers who were supporting and financing the new developments in the industry. The grand scheme of national economic development would portray the free miners as enemies of progress, but here, as so often, progress involved severe disadvantages for the lower orders. Detailed work on the petitions brought by the free miners, and the statements they made in court, demonstrate that this point had not passed them by, and that they were able to express opinions which, if only on a temporary or localized level, suggest the existence of something very like a class consciousness.

Indeed, historians have begun to embark upon a major reconsideration of the importance of custom in early modern England and, more particularly, of the importance of custom and the rhetoric surrounding it in offering an entry into what might be termed the plebeian political consciousness of the period. In numerous disputes between tenants and their landlords or artisans and their employers, custom was invoked to protect the lower orders against the men of property, in much the same way as, during the seventeenth century, the men of property invoked the English common law against what were perceived as the illegal demands of the Crown. Examples of disputes involving the invoking of custom are chronologically and geographically scattered, most of them involved in purely local matters, some of them occasionally reaching a broader significance as in the tumultuous early 1640s, when the outbreak of rioting and popular unrest which accompanied the disintegration of Charles I's regime included numerous examples of long-running customary disputes boiling over in the peculiar conditions of the times. As with the Derbyshire free miners, those invoking custom to defend their perceived rights were seen both by contemporaries and later historians as enemies of progress (it is interesting to reflect on why the propertied using the common law to protect their interests against central government have not, generally speaking, been regarded in this way), although it is worth reminding ourselves of what progress might mean for the lower orders in this sort of context. If we may extend our range of reference to the end of the eighteenth century, when a number of social changes already in progress in 1760 were much further advanced, we find a Shropshire reporter to the Board of Agriculture commenting that 'the use of common land by labourers operates upon the mind as a sort of independence'. Clearly, such 'independence' among this social class was undesirable: after enclosure, this reporter explained, 'the labourers will work every day of the year [and] their children will be put out to labour earlier'. More than two centuries before this means towards disciplining the agricultural workforce was being advocated, the manorial jurors of Southampton gave their views on why enclosures on the local commons should be destroyed: 'our ancestors of their great care and travail have provided that and like many other benefits for their successors, so we thinke it our dutie in conscience to keepe, uphold and maintaine the same as we found yt for our posteritie to come'. Such expressions of the importance, moral as well as economic, of customary rights were made frequently, and despite their usually being defeated, the defenders of such rights fought a surprisingly tenacious battle in the face of the advancing commercialization of agriculture and the old artisan-based forms of industrial production.

Despite the growing awareness of the importance of local disputes revolving around the defence of customary usages, little systematic work has been carried out on strikes or industrial riots before the eighteenth century, by which time they were very common. C.R. Dobson, who has completed some important preliminary work on what he terms the 'prehistory of industrial relations' has uncovered some 97 labour disputes in England between 1717 and 1760. Most of them were concerned with hours and wages, and the two biggest geographical concentrations were London, with 30 disputes, and the south-west, with 27. Obviously, with most industrial production still based on the small workshop, strikes in the modern sense, along with the type of consciousness and solidarity which underlies them, would not have been common: disputes and friction between individual masters and men were more normal. Nevertheless, in some trades recognizable prefigurations of modern attitudes already existed: such attitudes were not the product of some smashing of idyllic social relationships by the advent of the factory. 'It is a task above the strength of a few individuals,' declared a pamphlet issued in defence of organization on the part of London journeymen masons in 1748, 'nor can it be accomplished without uniting in great bodies, and unanimously joining to seek redress.' An awareness of the power of organized labour, however localized and imperfect, was evidently present in the mid-eighteenth century.

Often, however, labour disputes occurred not over pay, hours or conditions in the modern sense, but rather over those perquisites which traditionally were regarded as part of wages in many trades: we return to the importance of custom. Disputes over what constituted legitimate perquisites were endemic, as in the royal dockyards, where workers tended to be a little imaginative in their interpretation of what formed the 'chips' or waste wood to which they were entitled. The shipwright who, in the reign of Charles I, pleaded ancient custom when he was caught loading 9000 pieces of wood into a lighter is an extreme example of the tendency of dockyard workers to push their luck in such matters. More often, however, disputes arose out of short-term difficulties. Thus in 1757 Colchester clothiers demanded that the 'thrums', or weft ends left on a loom after the finished cloth had been removed, should be returned to them. These thrums were legally the clothiers' property, but were regarded as a customary perquisite by the weavers, more than 500 of whom struck, only going back to work when their piece-rates were improved in compensation for the loss of their thrums. Similar disputes occurred in the countryside. Traditional rights to collect firewood from forest, wasteland or common sometimes came under attack when landlords or tenant farmers adopted more modern attitudes to property rights. Similarly gleaning – the right of the poor to collect loose grain from the ground after harvest – led to a number of conflicts. The right to glean, vital in keeping a poor family in bread grain over the winter, was seen as a fundamental right in arable areas, even after a decision in the Court of Common Pleas in 1788 defined the practice as trespass.

Conflict between rich and poor took other forms. Many labouring people were, at some stage of their lives, on the wrong side of the law. Crime should not be romanticized into class resistance: yet it is evident that some forms of crime, notably subsistence poaching, might be interpreted as 'social crime', as acts where plebeian notions of right and wrong came into conflict with those enshrined in the statute book. In some trades, notably those dependent on putting-out, defrauding (or, to use the contemporary parlance, embezzling) materials legally the master's was endemic among the workforce. Poor-law records suggest that even paupers might not be as grateful or subservient as may have been wished. In 1708 a Kentish JP noted the refusal of goodwife Francis and the widow Curtis of Shoreham to wear the 'parish badge or mark' which those in receipt of parish support, there as in so many places, were meant to sport. The two women, despite their avowals when they came 'a Christmas-gooding' to the justice's house, continued to leave off what they probably regarded as a shameful mark of their poverty. They continued to do so when threatened with a cut in their poor relief and, if they persisted, a spell in the house of correction.

Running a workhouse could also have its problems. In Dartford, again in Kent, the keeper of the workhouse noted in February 1740 that 'Dame Bur is still very insolent', and that 'there is no speaking with Mrs String without her falling into such passion and raveing, scolding and defiing all the governors and their rull and orders'. A little later the same official was confronted by Betty Pinden, who had 'all the bad qualities that a child of her age [about 14] can have ... she does much mischief in the garden, beats the other children without provocation, steals when she has opportunity, money or what she likes, and is already most shamefully lewd'. The poor, as they demonstrated collectively in a riot or individually through the insolence of a goodwife Francis or a Betty Pinden, were far from totally subservient.

Yet it remains difficult to determine whether any of this adds up to something like class consciousness. Certainly, in times of extreme social tension, the lower orders were recorded as having voiced sentiments in which they demonstrated a clear sense of identity against the rich. In 1549 one of Kett's rebels declared that 'it were a good turn if there were as many gentlemen in Norfolk as there be white bulls'. In 1566 a Colchester weaver complained that 'we can get no work nor have no money, and if we should steal we should be hanged, and if we should ask no man would give us, but we will have a remedy one of these days, or else we will lose all, for the commons will rise'. The Oxfordshire rebels of 1596 planned 'to knock down gentlemen and rich men'. In 1643 a rioter in Northamptonshire hoped 'within this year to see never a gentleman in England'. Apprentices rioting over grain-marketing practices in Sheffield in 1675 declared that 'ye wild asse, is still the lyon's prey, soe doth ye rich feed on ye poor each day'. If such sentiments were an accurate reflection of widely held views, the lower orders clearly possessed something approaching a class consciousness. This may have been temporary and localized, but it must reflect some deeper attitudes. The common people's ideas about the social hierarchy of which they formed a part have still to be investigated systematically. Nevertheless, both their words and their actions show that they were perfectly capable of formulating grievances, and acting to redress them.

Conversely, even if some rioters had fond imaginings of a world without the rich, such a situation was clearly unobtainable and probably outside the ambitions of most of the lower orders. Realism dictated that both the rhetoric and the actions engendered by riots and labour disputes should be limited to gaining what was perceived as justice: thus a Somerset grain-rioter, in a not atypical instance, could declare 'I hope the justices of the peace will take order that we poor men shall have come without such violence'. Normally the justices, as aware of the rules of the game as the rioters, would indeed 'take order', and try to defuse the situation. This preservation of hierarchy in time of crisis was a counterpart of the everyday dialectic between deference and paternalism, a dialectic whose importance increased as the proletarianization of the lower orders proceeded. The poor labourer anxious to keep his family fed had to maintain the proper attitude towards his betters: from them came work, credit and poor relief. A Digger pamphlet of 1649 described how the poor would go 'with cap in hand and bended knee to gentlemen and farmers, begging and entreating to work with them for 8d or 10d a day, which doth give them occasion to tyrannize over poor people'. For many of the labouring poor this was not too far from reality: yet even when they were deferentially quiet, the poor retained their own view of things. A writer in 1657 remarked on 'laboring poor men which in times of scarcity pine and murmer for want of bread, cursing the rich behind his back; and before his face, cap and knee and a whining countenance'. Contemporaries were aware that the apparent passivity and deference of the poor did not imply an absence of social tension or plebeian discontent: historians would do well to follow their example.

Notes

1 Sources: Francis W. Steer (ed.) *Farm and Cottage Inventories of Mid Essex, 1635–1749* (Essex Record Office Publications, 8, Chelmsford, 1950); Peter Ripley, 'Village and town: occupations and wealth in the hinterland of Gloucester, 1660–1700', *Agricultural History Review*, 32 (1984), pp. 170–9.
2 John Rule, *The Experience of Labour in Eighteenth-Century Industry* (1981). Our discussion of labour conditions at this point depends heavily upon Professor Rule's findings.
3 Keith Snell, *Annals of the Labouring Poor: Social Change in Agrarian England, 1660–1900* (Cambridge, 1985), p. 104.

PART
III

THE SPIRITUAL AND MENTAL WORLD

|9|

Religion

Few historians would deny that religion was of central importance in the early modern period. Similarly, few would deny that attempting to encompass its social history within the limits of a short chapter is not an easy undertaking. Religion, then as now, can be studied on a variety of different levels. The first is the personal. Religion, ultimately, is about individual belief and, as we shall see, individuals in our period could reach very different conclusions about what they believed in. The second is social. Religion helps provide people with rules and assumptions about how they should interact with their fellow human beings. Moreover, the social aspects of religion might show themselves in differing attitudes to belief among people of different economic or educational levels, or in religion's effect on perceptions of the social order. Third, religion involves the extension of social relations beyond the frontiers of purely human society. Specific peculiarities complicated matters further in England between the mid-sixteenth and the mid-eighteenth centuries. The church, in its institutional sense, was of tremendous economic and political significance. Religion played a vital role both in attempts to maintain ideological control, and in attempts to rebel against such control. The period was also one of massive, perhaps unique, fragmentation in matters religious, one when the religious imagination of the English was at its most fertile. Arriving at any general conclusions about how this fertility manifested itself in the social realm is, as might be imagined, difficult.

One problem which must be confronted at the outset is the idea that there was some sort of causal relationship between religious and economic change. More particularly, the notion that there was a connection between the Reformation and the rise of capitalism is deeply embedded in general historical thinking. The differences in religious ideas between different social strata is a question which must be addressed at certain points: yet it is by no means the only issue and is rarely the most interesting one. The alleged appeal of Protestant ideas to the bourgeoisie, often based on a second-hand knowledge of the work of Max Weber and R.H. Tawney, refuses to go away, despite the best efforts of more recent scholars. It has, indeed, been modified and supplanted by some more subtle forms of economic, even environmental, determinism: some interpretations of the radical sects of the 1640s and 1650s, for example, suggest that the sectarian confronted by his Maker would not say 'Lord, I have sinned,' but rather, 'Lord, I come from a wood-pasture area in the highland zone.' Such notions would have made little sense to contemporaries, least of all the idea of a link between the Reformation and the 'middle class'. In fact, observers in the 1560s, that heroic decade of Calvinist expansion, would have seen connections between reformed religion and noble revolt in Scotland, France and the Low Countries, and between the reformed religion and noble faction in Poland and (in the form of the Earl of Leicester's patronage network) England, and come to the conclusion that the new religious ideas seemed to have a peculiar attraction for the nobility. In so doing, they would have raised some rather more intriguing questions about the connections between religious innovation and social hierarchy than those revolving around burgeoning capitalism. In any case, one suspects that English Protestants, rejoicing in the unexpected deliverance created by Mary Tudor's death in 1558, had some rather more urgent things to worry about than Luther's views on usury.

The progress of reformation

Without a doubt, Mary's reign had given the small body of enthusiastic English Protestants a very nasty shock. The end product of her reign was to harden many moderates against Roman Catholicism, and to create, largely through John Foxe's *Acts and Monuments* (more familiarly known as the *Book of Martyrs*) a Black Legend of papist oppression and intolerance which was to fortify later generations of English Protestants in their hatred of Romish antichrist. This legend was strong and enduring, as was the interpretation which saw sixteenth-century English religious history as a steady progress towards a Protestant reformation. Yet it is difficult to see any clear reason why, had Mary lived longer, and had the more active Catholicism of the Counter-Reformation been introduced, England should not have returned to Rome. Less promising areas, the southern Netherlands and Bohemia to name but two, were to be reconverted to Catholicism by a policy of the extirpation of heretics by fire and the extirpation of heretical ideas through education. It seems likely that similar policies would, in England, have won over a population which was, as yet, very unconvinced about the advantages of Protestantism. Perhaps the greatest obstacle to such an outcome, apart from Mary's early death, were the essentially traditionalist views she and her advisers held. Mary envisaged a return to some sort of pre-1533 Catholicism, rather than the more hard-edged Counter-Reformed faith which was being developed at Trent. In this, she was probably not far removed from most of her subjects. But this traditional Catholicism, despite its hold on the religious outlook of many, was somehow static, and lacked the dynamism to win the ideological war against the enthusiasm of the reformers. Nevertheless, if Mary had survived into old age, and if she had been able to engineer a Catholic succession, there is every chance that Protestantism would have been extirpated by a process of attrition.

In the event, it was the Elizabethan Settlement of 1559 which was to provide the framework within which future religious developments were to take place. To the more ardent reformers, the Settlement was a useful basis for further reformation. Elizabeth's personal religious credo, as many historians have commented, is somewhat difficult to pin down: at most, it seems, she supported a moderate Protestantism, while the position of England in international affairs early in her reign made caution, even procrastination, over any settlement of religion most advisable. From the start, however, she was pushed towards a more radical stance. The Marian bench of bishops, in an act of some courage, refused to accept the Royal Supremacy, and resigned. The Queen was thus pushed to the only other group of suitable candidates for the episcopate: those who had suffered exile or imprisonment under Mary and whose attachment to further reformation had been hardened accordingly. After some heart-searching, and considerable correspondence with their continental mentors, many of these accepted sees. Elizabeth therefore had not only to accept a religious settlement which inclined in some ways towards advanced Protestant theology, but also an episcopate consisting of men who were concerned to carry the work of reformation a good deal further than was the monarch. Problems were to arise from this: to take the extreme example, from 1576 the affairs of the Church of England were disrupted by a serious clash between Elizabeth and the Archbishop of Canterbury, the extreme Protestant Edmund Grindal, over the suppression of those clerical discussion meetings called prophesyings: a clash which led to Grindal being suspended until his death in 1583. A few of the more penetrating Protestant minds had envisaged such complications from the outset: more commonly, and more reasonably, the mood among English Protestants in 1559 was one of rejoicing. The settlement was theologically sound, and the church hierarchy headed by men that could be trusted. Moreover, the settlement emphasized one of the peculiarities of the English Reformation: the role of the godly prince. In 1537 *The Institution of a Christian Man*, an early Protestant tract, had envisaged the Crown as an agent of further reformation, a notion which obviously enjoyed considerable if short-lived encouragement in the reign of Edward VI. Despite Elizabeth's lack of enthusiasm for an ardent Protestantism, her rule, especially after England's involvement in war against Spain from the mid-1580s, inspired special devotion to the Supreme Governor as the divinely appointed protector of a national Protestant church. Elizabeth's reign established the principle that being loyal meant being a Protestant as defined in the 1559 Settlement.

The other great product of the Elizabethan period was that distinctive feature of the English Reformation known to some contemporaries and most modern historians as Puritanism. As any reading of the relevant literature makes clear, this term has been variously and widely defined: Thomas Fuller, in his *Church History of Britain* of 1655, expressed the wish that 'the word "Puritan" were banished common discourse, because so various the acceptations thereof', a view which has much to commend it. Some idea of contemporary attitudes on the use of the term was provided by John Shaw, preaching to some of parliament's Yorkshire forces at Selby in February 1643: 'the word Puritan, in the mouth of an Arminian, signifies an orthodox divine; in the mouth of a drunkard signifies a sober man; in the mouth of a papist signifies a Protestant'. The definitions employed by later historians, while usually less hostile than those noted by Shaw, have changed and will doubtless continue to do so.

The current consensus among historians working in the field is that the idea of Puritans, at least before the 1630s, as anti-episcopalian, separatist, or in any way revolutionary, must be rejected. The Puritan was content to work within the church as settled in 1559, conscious of the need for further reform, yet equally aware that real gains had been made in the Elizabethan Settlement, and unwilling to risk sacrificing them over such secondary matters as ceremonial or clerical attire. For such people, their views perhaps best summed-up around 1600 in the voluminous writing of William Perkins, the epithet 'godly' is perhaps more useful than 'Puritan'. The Reformation, for them, was something which began inside the individual believer. They stressed the need to study scripture as a means of understanding God's word, and the need to put that understanding into worldly action in their everyday conduct. Thus bibliocentrism was converted into worldly activism: for the Puritan, all aspects of life were subject to God's scrutiny, and the godly in all of their daily activities were to demonstrate God's glory. Idleness was anathema, and the idea of the calling was counterpoised against it. Thus even members of the gentry or the leisured classes in general could find a place among the godly if they put their time to good use in religious studies and served the commonwealth as godly magistrates or in other capacities. Puritans saw themselves as locked in a constant struggle against a very widely defined and all-embracing sinfulness. This struggle took place within the individual, and Puritan diaries are full of references to their writers' attempts to overcome sloth and all those other temptations to which the flesh is prone. The struggle also took place in the social context, as Puritan clergymen, magistrates, parish officers and, by their example, the godly in general attempted to spread the word among the masses.

Whether in the writings of theologians like Perkins, in diaries, or in the emergent popular Protestant consciousness, the concept of a providential

God was central to English Protestantism. To some extent this concept, by helping people to understand the workings of an unpredictable universe, did much to fill the gap left by the loss of the magical aspects of medieval Christianity: the Almighty was seen as making active and constant interventions in the affairs of human beings. The idea of direct divine rewards or punishments for good or evil behaviour was firmly established in the late medieval popular religious consciousness. Protestant theology and the popular press spread it more widely after 1558. Puritan diaries show how illness, good fortune and everyday accidents might be ascribed to divine providence and lead, as appropriate, to heart-searching over sinfulness or rejoicing over God's goodness. Godly tracts, concentrating on the wages of sin, made constant use of awesome examples of divine displeasure. Samuel Ward's *Woe to Drunkards*, to take a typical example of 1627, included a list of anecdotes showing how 'extraordinary judgements' commonly befell those given to alcoholic excess. Drunkards are depicted dying of mysterious illnesses, drowning inexplicably in shallow water, breaking their necks when falling off horses, receiving fatal injuries when falling downstairs, falling off 'an high and steepe rocke in a most fearful manner', or simply drinking themselves to death. English Protestants were also painfully aware that God judges nations as well as individual sinners. Richard Bernard voiced a commonplace when he declared in 1619 that God had honoured England 'above all places in the Christian World': but the obverse of this commonplace was the less comforting assumption that the Almighty's wrath would be especially unrestrained should the members of the elect nation prove sinful, and hence ungrateful.

Early Elizabethan Protestants, however thankful of the divine deliverance which Mary Tudor's early death constituted were, therefore, acutely conscious of how much needed to be done. The more reflective of them realized that convinced Protestants were a tiny minority. Such gains as had been made under Edward VI had been at best partial and, in so far as they had not been reversed in Mary's reign, were in any case essentially destructive. The old religion had been damaged under Edward, and perhaps discredited by Mary's persecutions and her Spanish marriage. The problem of planting the Reformation in its place remained. The advanced Protestant had friends at court, while the episcopate was trustworthy. Unfortunately, many of those other agents whose active assistance would be needed to plant the Reformation were potentially or actually hostile. Once more we return to one of the basic problems of government in this period: in both the ecclesiastical administration and the secular, the size of administrative units meant that authority had to be devolved, and that in consequence authority was exercised by local officials whose dedication might be suspect. Such problems were especially daunting for the Protestant Cause early in Elizabeth's reign. The compliance of the secular authorities was essential, but it was unlikely to be forthcoming from places like Lancashire, where only six of 25 justices were reported as being favourable to Protestantism in 1564, or Sussex, where at about the same time Catholic office-holders outnumbered adherents of the new religion by about two to one.

Further complications were caused by the familiar problem of low clerical standards. As we have noted, these were to improve massively over the century before 1642, although even by then perfection had not been attained. In 1559 the situation, from the point of view of proponents of the Reformation, was very worrying indeed. The episcopal bench might be filled with educated and enthusiastic reformed clergymen: but few such were to be found in the parishes of the realm. One of the key problems faced by the reformers, therefore, was that of providing the educated and devoted clergy upon whom the work of spreading true religion depended. The task proved a difficult one, made more so by the low value of many clerical livings and, in Elizabeth's reign at least, by the monarch's rapacious attitude to the church's economic resources. Some dedicated reformed clergymen, such as Richard Greenham, the Puritan divine who spent his life ministering to the poor parish of Dry Drayton in Cambridgeshire, did emerge, but such men were exceptional. Clerical deficiencies were made more serious by the emergence of an articulate laity who were only too willing to comment on low standards among the clergy. In Elizabeth's reign, complaints about innovation were, perhaps, more common than criticisms of insufficient clergymen: the Yorkshireman who responded to a godly minister by declaring that 'the preaching of the gospell is but bibble-babble, and I care not a fart of my tail for any black coat in Wensleydale', was probably voicing a fairly common conservative attitude. A generation later, however, another Yorkshire clergyman was described as 'a base priest and a base paltery priest and had no learning in him: he hath a ready tongue and can prattle & talke with his tongue, but he is noe scholler'. Thus the model Protestant clergyman would be criticized by conservatives, and the unlearned old-style clergyman by the model Protestant layman. It is interesting to note that anti-clericalism, so often adduced as a cause of the Reformation, probably received an enormous boost from it.

Even with an effective clergy, the problems faced by the reformers would have been daunting enough. Their main task was to overcome two apparently contradictory phenomena. First, there was popular attachment to the traditional Christianity of the pre-Reformation era. Although the late Middle Ages should not be sentimentalized as an 'Age of Faith', the strength of the religious belief experienced then should not be underestimated. It witnessed a flourishing of pilgrimages to shrines, of belief in saints, of religious confraternities, of enthusiasm for festivals, and an obsession with matters of death, hell and salvation. Ordinary Christians may not have been educated theologians, but they often had a clear idea of a set of religious fundamentals which were of great meaning to them, although perhaps laughable to the learned reformer. Such ideas were deeply offended by such Protestant doctrines as the denial of the efficacy of prayers for the dead, of the doctrine of purgatory, and of confession, while further disquiet was doubtless prompted by the destruction of images and the confiscation of church property. Above all, this late medieval Christianity seems to have provided a social ethic, a rationale by which people could live together. Such Puritan works as Arthur Dent's much reprinted *Plaine Man's Pathway to Heaven* constantly attacked what was regarded as the slack, but apparently disturbingly widespread, view that doing good by one's neighbours, following a decent personal morality, and going to church once in a while, was Christianity enough. In such a view the notion of charity, of achieving social harmony through Christian neighbourly behaviour, was of central importance. Reformed religion, with its emphasis on a much more intellectual approach to spiritual matters, on a more vigorous godliness in everyday conduct, and on the existence of a religious élite in the shape of the elect, offered a total challenge to the traditional, less austere, system of belief.

Overcoming an imperfect Christianity distorted by superfluous popish excrescences was bad enough. Confronting near total religious ignorance or indifference was even worse. Popular unbelief or uninterest in matters religious during this period has never been fully explored. Nevertheless, scattered comments on how many individuals, after more than a millennium of Christianity, seemed almost untouched by fundamental religious teachings, survive in large number. Puritan concern over spreading the word to the 'Dark Corners of the Realm' was but one facet of a more general, and Europe-wide, determination by ecclesiastical authorities and godly clerics to combat what was apparently a newly identified problem: that Europe was, by the new standards of the second half of the sixteenth century, at best a half-Christianized continent. Well into the seventeenth century, to go no further, godly Englishmen were distressed at meeting people whose grasp of Christianity was minimal. One old man, who at least demonstrated how the old mystery plays had provided some basic religious instruction, was asked around 1640 who Jesus Christ was. 'I think I heard of that man you spoke of once in a play at Kendal called a Corpus Christi Play,' he replied, 'where there was a man on a tree and the blood ran down.' The discontinuation of mystery plays precluded even this type of insight. Oliver Heywood, the Yorkshire nonconformist minister whose complaints about the ungodliness of the world around him were more or less continual, noted meeting an unusually ignorant boy in 1681. The lad 'could not tell me how many gods there be, nor persons in the godhead, nor who made the world nor anything about Jesus Christ, nor heaven nor hell, or eternity after this life ... yet this was a witty boy and could talk of any worldly things skilfully enough,' wrote Heywood. Spreading God's word among the English was evidently a lengthy and uphill struggle.

The struggle could, however, be carried on by a number of means. One was the printed word. The Reformation is virtually unimaginable without the invention of the printing press, and from the mid-sixteenth century England was flooded with books on reformed religion and editions of the Bible itself. Another medium was preaching: the Protestant notion of a preaching ministry was central to the objective of bringing the true word of God to the population at large. After the 1570s, when it became apparent even to enthusiastic Protestants that inculcating godliness was going to take time, catechizing also achieved a vital role. It was seen as a handy means of instructing in right religion, especially the young, and a much less risky method of bringing people to the true light than Bible reading. Emphasis was also laid on disciplining the population, not least through the ecclesiastical and secular courts.

The Reformation, as we have noted, coincided with the development of a more intrusive secular state, and it rapidly became axiomatic that the good and obedient subject should also be a good and obedient Christian. The ecclesiastical courts, attempting to enforce attendance at church, high moral standards, and religious conformity, experienced an upsurge of prosecutions over the years 1560–1642. There is some question as to the effectiveness of the church courts' main sanction – excommunication – but there is little doubt that it was seen as an important means of enforcing godliness. Records of the secular courts of the period also begin to include details of prosecutions not only of recusants and others failing to attend church, but also sabbath-breakers, bastard-bearers, fiddlers, drunkards and bear-baiters. One of the major outcomes of the English Reformation was a more active campaign against moral offenders: sin had become criminalized. Indeed, by defining what was correct religion and by emphasizing the powers of the devil, the Reformation gave a tremendous boost to fear over human sinfulness and depravity. As the witchcraft statute of 1563 suggests, advanced English Protestants, imbued with a sense of mankind's innate depravity, had no problem in accepting that humanity should seek diabolical assistance in its pursuit of evil.

Human depravity, or at least those sins of curiosity and disobedience which caused mankind's Fall, might also lead busy spirits to contemplate separation. One of the great achievements of the Elizabethan Settlement was to combine an advanced, neo-Calvinist theology with a traditional, episcopal structure of church government. By the end of Elizabeth's reign, however, and certainly by the end of James I's, a small but much-studied number of English Protestants were rejecting much of the system of church government and some of the theology. The most coherent challenge to what some were beginning to see as a church but half reformed came from the advocates of a Presbyterian system of church government, their most noted spokesmen being Thomas Cartwright and Walter Travers.

Presbyterian ideas attracted some attention in the 1570s and 1580s, not least from the authorities, who removed Cartwright from his theology professorship at Cambridge. But, despite Leicester's patronage of Cartwright, Presbyterianism failed to make much impact among influential laymen, and consequently fizzled out, only reviving when episcopacy was discredited in the 1630s. Others discontented with the Elizabethan church came to the conclusion that separation, rather than some sort of Presbyterian reformation from within, was the solution. Some groups shared notions that were present in earlier Anabaptist, perhaps even Lollard thinking: all of them were evidence of that centrifugal tendency which, despite the desires of English Protestant theologians, was probably inherent in the whole process of the Reformation. A few individuals, like Henry Barrow and Robert Browne, were very capable men, and a few groups, like the Family of Love, may have enjoyed a coherent theological position. The separatists, whether leading a precarious existence in England, or in exile in the Dutch Republic or, after 1621, New England, while constituting a complicating factor in English religious life were very few in number. Even so, they acted as a constant reminder to the Protestant mainstream of the threat from the left. Few could contemplate separatism without shuddering at the memory of the Anabaptist excesses at Munster, where in 1534 John of Leyden and his followers had demonstrated the dangers of liberty in religion by practising community of goods and polygamy.

Roman Catholics constituted a more consistent source of fear. Despite laws against recusancy, and the feeling that the Papal Bull of 1570 made every Catholic a potential traitor, a hard core of devotees to the old religion carried on in spite of dungeon, fire and sword. Yet their numbers, geographical base and social significance were all very limited. The best estimates suggest that there were 60,000 Catholics in England by the mid-seventeenth century. Their only stronghold was the fertile and advanced Lancashire plain, although there were important concentrations in the North Yorkshire dales, in Monmouthshire and Herefordshire, and substantial bodies of recusant gentry in the West Midlands and in an area centred on West Sussex and Hampshire. How far they saw themselves as the heirs to traditional religion is a subject of some controversy. John Bossy, author of the largest recent work on English Catholicism, has argued that it is impossible to speak of a 'Catholic Community' in England before consciousness of a separate identity, bolstered by the Post-Tridentine doctrines of the missionary priests who filtered into the country after 1571, became established. Others, notably Christopher Haigh, have argued for continuity. Certainly, such sentiments as those of Sir John Southworth, who told Archbishop Grindal that 'he will follow the faith of his fathers: he will die in the faith wherein he was baptized' demonstrate that English Catholics could preserve their self-consciousness without the assistance of continentally trained priests.

More agreement exists over the importance of the gentry as supporters of Catholicism. Once more, Dr Haigh has offered an important *caveat* by insisting on 'the relaxed, peasant Catholicism of the dales and the Fylde'[1]:

but in most areas Catholic belief, and missionary priests, were kept alive in gentry households. The priests led a precarious existence, but they kept on coming. Despite the execution of some 200 of them in Elizabeth's reign, there were still 300 at the time of her death, and perhaps twice that number by the outbreak of the Civil War. But their dependence on the gentry had an ironic result. Roman Catholicism, above all forms of Christianity, stressed the special nature of the priesthood, the mystical nature of its role: yet no other body of clergy were more dependent upon the support of influential laymen than were the missionary priests. By the middle of the seventeenth century there is every indication that English recusant gentry were quite happy to keep things that way.

The presence of a popish fifth column, the vision, after 1618, of a Catholic resurgence on the continent, and, above all, the knowledge that much of the work of reformation remained to be done, left the English Protestant activist of the latter years of James I's reign little cause for complacency. Nevertheless, some solid achievements could be numbered. The Elizabethan Settlement may not have provided a church organized on the most advanced continental models: yet it was doctrinally sound, and had done much to foster the general belief that being loyally English entailed being Protestant. Sin still abounded, and the elect were used to combating it both in their own person-alities and in other people: yet the ministry was better educated and more godly than ever before, newly founded grammar schools were inculcating right religion in the young, sermons and lectures were becoming more numer-ous and better attended, and a godly monarch sat on the throne. English Protestants in the 1620s found much to worry or even dismay them: but they had only to look at the Palatinate, at Bohemia, or at the Low Countries, to realize how much worse things might have been.

Above all, they could draw encouragement from the realization that Protestantism was clearly, if in some areas only slowly, making an impact on the religious consciousness of their compatriots. As we have noted, late medieval Christianity was a religion, as far as the mass of believers were concerned, very different from that being promulgated by reformed preach-ers. It had enjoyed limited mental horizons, and was dependent on a pattern of religious or semi-religious rituals and observances, all of them commu-nal in their message, some of them very local in character. The reformers, by attacking the shrines and relics upon which so much of this traditional faith had rested, and by downgrading the 'magical' aspects of both the old faith and the old notion of the priest, set out to destroy this religious system.

What they intended to put in its place remains a legitimate question. Certainly, Protestantism was not without its communal aspects. A sermon might seem a poor substitute for a parish ale, but in some towns, not least when they coincided with market day, sermons and lectures became occasions for displays of popular piety. Indeed, some town authorities remarked that these religious exercises, by encouraging an influx of visitors, had the added advantage of being good for business. Similar comments were made at the time of the Reformation about the old Corpus Christi plays. Interestingly enough, it has been argued that the popularity of Puritanism at Coventry may have been due not to the town's Lollard tradition, but rather to the local mystery plays which had created a taste for religious spectacle which was, in a sense, taken over by sermons. Yet it does seem, on balance, that Protestantism was a more exclusive religion than pre-Reformation Catholicism had been. Convinced Protestants did exist among the poor and, as events after 1640 were to indicate, a strong tradition of popular Protestantism existed by that date. But (and leaving the implications of the doctrine of election aside) Protestantism, with its emphasis on scripture, on the internalization of a religious system, on religion as a body of beliefs rather than a series of observances, was more likely to appeal to some social groups than others. Any easy assumption of a connection between reformed religion and a 'middle class' should be regarded with extreme scepticism. Yet it is evident that Protestant, and especially Puritan, notions were more likely to make sense to those that could read, had the leisure time to do so extensively, and had a place in the social hierarchy which made them sensitive to the need to preserve order in the face of man's rebellious and sinful nature.

Unexpectedly, after 1625 the challenge to the Protestant godly came not from the rude multitude, but from the agents of the central government and the establishment of the Church of England. From that date, as we have seen, 'Arminian' innovations, although attractive to Charles I, alienated many of his Protestant subjects (see page 17 above). Godly Englishmen were fearful of resurgent continental Catholicism and worried by the papists gathered around Henrietta Maria. They now saw in Arminianism's downgrading of predestination and its insistence on ceremonial evidence of a barely diluted version of that popery which they had been raised to fear from birth. Church court records show scattered opposition to Laudian innovations in the 1630s, and this exploded in 1640. Members of the Long Parliament, supported by large and vocal mobs of Puritan Londoners, attacked episcopacy: the idea of the 'Godly Bishop', a part of English Protestant ideology since the burning of Latimer, Hooper and Ridley, was discarded. Before the Long Parliament met, the summer of 1640 was punctuated by riots in which troops levied to fight the Scots joined with local people to break altar rails and other symbols of anti-Protestant innovation. Hostility to these innovations had produced a religious consensus which united Puritan peers and iconoclastic agricultural labourers; this unity was to be short-lived.

Gangraena

On 16 February 1646 Thomas Edwards, Presbyterian divine and experienced controversialist, published the first part of his *Gangraena*, described by the author as a 'Catalogue or Black Bill of the errours, heresies, blasphemies and pernicious practices of the sectaries of this time broached and acted in England in these last four years'. In a torrent of language which almost (but, as the publication of two subsequent parts demonstrated, not quite) exhausted the vocabulary of abuse, Edwards listed the heresies and other religious malpractices which had proliferated since 1642, and offered a slamming indictment of religious toleration. The book was a compendium of heretical ideas and, given the many letters from mainstream Protestant divines printed in it, of conservative fears, not the least of these being that social disintegration was the inevitable consequence of religious heterodoxy. Episcopacy had gone, but no organized national Presbyterian system had been created to replace it. Censorship had gone and so any opinion, no matter how ill-educated or low-born the man or woman voicing it, could find its way into print. What was published showed that from 1642 a twofold preoccupation had gripped radical critics of the *status quo*: the replacement of idolatry by true religion, and the replacement of tyranny by liberty.

It is obvious that, despite the label 'The Puritan Revolution' sometimes being attached to events between 1640 and 1660, the opinions castigated by Edwards and his fellow conservatives had already gone far beyond the mainstream Puritanism of William Perkins, Arthur Dent and Laud's critics in the House of Commons. The first heresy that Edwards noted was the denial of that most fundamental of Puritan beliefs: the acceptance of the authority of scripture. Scripture was regarded by some sectaries as 'but humane, and so not able to discover a divine God': greater emphasis was placed on the divine Spirit's impact on the believer. Similarly, Edwards recorded as the thirty-first of the heresies proliferating around him a denial of predestination, and an assertion that 'Christ died for all men alike, the reprobate as well as the elect'. Perhaps most disturbing for clerical observers was the way in which radicals were rejecting the importance of the godly minister in the Almighty's scheme of things. Overton the Leveller thought that the minister might be 'gifted with a black coat, an university dialect and the external advantages of arts and sciences', yet still be lacking in true religion. Moreover, the insistence on personal revelation and the working of the Spirit within the individual meant that the idea of a separate spiritual identity, already familiar in the doctrine of election, could be pushed to its logical conclusion. If traditional Christians of the early sixteenth century saw their religion essentially in terms of community values and shared ritual, the mid-seventeenth-century sectarian was only too willing to dare to stand alone. James Parnell, the Quaker saint who was to die as a result of a hunger strike in Colchester gaol before his twenty-first birthday, summed this up neatly in his *A Shield of the Truth* in 1655:

And now is the separation, the sheep from the goats, the wheat from the tares, and Christ is coming to set at variance father against son, and son against father, and the wife against the man, and the man against the wife, and to turn the world upside downe; and this is the cause why the world rages.

Another early Quaker, James Nayler, recounted how the word of the Lord first came to him: 'I was at plough, meditating on the things of God, and suddenly I heard a voice saying unto me, "Get thee out from thy kindred and from thy father's house".'

This willingness to accept the dissolution of many existing social ties if the Lord willed it, the collapse of episcopacy, the absence of any alternative discipline, and the presence of widespread literacy and an uncensored printing press combined to provide the context within which religious, and hence social, radicalism flourished. For many men, the experience of service in the New Model Army provided a powerful catalyst. The radicalism of this force should not be overstated: as Mark Kishlansky has reminded us, not every soldier was a psalm-singing visionary intent on tearing down antichrist. Nevertheless, some troops in some units experienced a genuine religious and political education during their military service. Like-minded spirits came together in a common cause, refined their views in debate with their fellows, and toughened their consciousness through the hardships of campaigning and the dangers of battle. From the outset of hostilities conservative parliamentarians were disturbed, and royalists delighted, by reports of roundhead soldiers disputing with ministers, smashing images and other popish baubles in the churches they passed, and eagerly debating religion among themselves. Richard Baxter, admittedly thinking back over a period of many years, was left with a strong impression of the mood of the New Model just before Leveller ideas gripped it. The troops, he remembered, were convinced that 'God's providence would cast the trust of religion and the kingdom upon them as conquerors.' But their most 'frequent and vehement discussions', according to Baxter, were 'for liberty of conscience, as they called it; that is, that the civil magistrate had nothing to do to determine of anything in religion by constraint or restraint'. Many of these men were unlikely to settle down easily to a civilian life dominated by traditional social hierarchies and a Presbyterian church discipline.

Thus the peculiar circumstances of the 1640s permitted the emergence of a wide variety of ideas about religion. Many of these may have been held, however incoherently or secretly, before the collapse of ecclesiastical authority, although attempts to trace them back to earlier, even Lollard, traditions have probably gone further than the evidence will allow. Even so, any church court act book for the half-century before 1642 will provide scattered, if often tantalizingly allusive, evidence that the lower orders held a number of beliefs at odds with those of official Christianity. These beliefs blossomed in the hot-house atmosphere of the 1640s. Millenarianism was one of their basic components. The tensions created by the Reformation, and the exegesis of such prophetic texts as the Books of Daniel and Revelation, had created a widespread acceptance among Protestants that the Second Coming, the end of the world, and the dissolution of all things, were imminent. This was a firmly pessimistic view, resting on the conviction that there was no real hope of any improvement of the earthly condition. It was especially firmly embedded in the mainstream of English Protestant thinking, and was not, in itself, radical. However, the series of extraordinary events which befell England in the 1640s invited millenarian speculation, and this speculation seems to have had great appeal for those outside the political nation. Numerous pseudo-prophets were appearing with unorthodox ideas about the nature of Christ's kingdom and the role of the lower orders in it. In the prevailing atmosphere of millennial excitement, they were often able to attract a following. A typical example was John Reeve, a London tailor, to whom God appeared early in 1652, informing him that he and his cousin, Ludowick Muggleton, were the two witnesses referred to in the Book of Revelation, the prophets of the Third Age, the Age of the Spirit. The two cousins founded a sect, called the Muggletonians, whose last known adherent died in 1979.

Quite apart from their heresies, the sects often preached an implicit, and in some cases explicit, social radicalism. Setting up Christ's kingdom involved the overturning of earthly hierarchies: Abiezer Coppe the Ranter warned that 'kings, princes, lords, great ones must bow to the poorest peasants; rich men must stoop to poor rogues, or else they'l rue for it'. To conservatives, one of the most disturbing aspects of radical sectarianism was the part played by women. The small independent congregations which proliferated after 1642 often allowed their women members to debate and vote. In others women were able to preach or, failing that, prophesy: as the Fifth Monarchist Mary Cary put it, 'all saints have in a measure a spirit of prophesie'. For the first time, women were allowed to use that spirit, and the enthusiasm for matters religious among women which was such a feature of the period was given full rein to express itself. Contemporaries remarked on the spectacle of 'bold impudent housewives, without all womanly modesty', preaching 'after a narrative or discoursing manner, an hour and more, and that most directly contrary to the Apostle's inhibition'. This was disturbing enough, but it was just one aspect of the more general spectacle of the lower orders developing ideas on religion whose immediate consequences were a direct attack on the social order.

Perhaps the most coherent grouping to emerge from the chaos of radical religious speculation were the Fifth-Monarchy Men. Their ideas were derived from millenarianism, their name from the Book of Daniel: scripture told how Daniel had a vision of the rise and fall of four successive empires, which were followed by a fifth monarchy which would endure for ever. The hectic events of the 1640s led to a re-identification of the four degenerating empires (the fourth was variously identified with the rule of Charles I, the Rump Parliament and Oliver Cromwell) and a conviction grew that the fifth monarchy, the reign of Jesus Christ and his saints, was at hand. This monarchy, or at least the period of transition leading to it, would obviously entail some basic changes in earthly affairs. The Fifth-Monarchy Men envisaged a purge of the clergy, the abolition of tithes, the reform of the law, the imposition of a puritanical morality, the reduction of taxes and a removal of the privileges of the rich. The sect's membership, perhaps 10,000 at most, was drawn mainly from artisans and other small property-owners: textile workers, as ever, formed a major element. Despite their artisanal support and the egalitarian implications of their programme, the Fifth Monarchists were not a democratic group. The saints were thought of as an exclusive spiritual élite whose rule, while shattering existing earthly hierarchies, would impose new ones. For a brief period at the time of the Barebone's Parliament in 1653 the Fifth Monarchists entered the political arena as a serious force. They declined thereafter, although Venner's Rising of January 1661 reminded contemporaries of the old vigour of the saints, as well as adding more fuel to fears of the sects.

An even more extreme position, in both religious and social terms, was taken by the Ranters. Unfortunately, much of what we know about this group was written either by their enemies, or by former adherents who were disclaiming their radical past. Further complications arise from the use of 'ranter' as a loose term of abuse which might cover a wide range of religious speculation. The most common Ranter belief was the conviction that God existed in both people and material objects, a conviction which led Ranters variously to either materialist or mystical conclusions. The belief in an in-dwelling God was related to an extreme antinomianism. One of the problems for the authoritarian wing of Protestantism was the tendency for sectarians who thought of themselves as being members of an elect to regard themselves as being unconstrained by the moral law. With the Ranters this view, if we may believe contemporary reports, was taken to its logical conclusion. Ranters rejected contemporary morality, especially sexual morality. As might be expected, they also rejected all but the most figurative conception of hell and, like other radicals, set the inner light above scripture as a source of authority. In so far as they can be said to have existed in anything like an organized group, they seem to have flourished briefly around 1650, their appeal being mainly to the lower strata of society, notably the London lumpenproletariat.

As the Ranters demonstrated, the Spirit might bloweth where He listeth at any time, but in the 1650s His listing was blowing Him in some very odd directions. Further evidence on this point is provided by the early history of the Quakers. From 1652 reports began to filter through to the government of a new group of religious radicals forming in the north. These gradually took coherent shape as the Quakers, their origins being in an association of separatists who envisaged a loose church fellowship. The early Quakers were young, and many of them, in both their personal conduct and their religious beliefs, were very radical. James Nayler was responsible for one of the most spectacular acts of blasphemy of the Interregnum when he parodied Christ's entry into Jerusalem by riding into Bristol on a donkey, while the court records of the 1650s are littered with Quakers being prosecuted for disrupting church services and insulting secular magistrates and clergymen alike. By 1660 the Quakers were losing this radicalism, but they had established their presence by publishing perhaps a thousand pamphlets and gaining 35,000–40,000 adherents. Unlike many of the sects, they had considerable support in the provinces and in rural areas. Typically, their membership came from the middling sort: at Terling in Essex, at a slightly later date, the Quakers numbered two yeomen, a husbandman, an innkeeper, a millwright and a grocer. Their views, as they emerged in the 1650s, give a better idea of what they were against (notably predestination) than what they were for. Perhaps their clearest tenet was their insistence on the primacy of the spirit over scripture, a belief which, here as with other sectaries, was the uneducated person's rejection of the spiritual authority of the learned. Socially, Quaker demands included such familiar sectarian objectives as law reform, the abolition of tithes, and the disestablishment of the church. Whatever their later attachment to quietism, the early Quakers were an active and radical force, as alarming to contemporaries as were the Ranters with whom they were so often confused.

The explosion of sectarian activity and religious speculation in mid-seventeenth-century England has, deservedly, attracted considerable attention from modern historians. Yet the activities of the radicals should not obscure the fact that they were a small minority of the population. So far, little attention has been given to that vast bulk of the population which did not turn to Muggletonian, Baptist, Fifth-Monarchist, Ranter or Quaker teachings. Certainly, there is some evidence of attachment to pre-1640 Protestantism. Many moderate episcopalian clergy swallowed their scruples and continued to officiate throughout the Interregnum: thus a newsletter reported in 1653 that 'the clergy of the old model begins to be very dear to the people in many parts of the nation: conventicles for the Common Prayer are frequent and much desired in London'. Other episcopalian clergymen doubtless did what Roman Catholic priests had done for some time, and found support and succour in gentry households. On a more popular level, there are signs of public resentment of the sects in general and of Quakers in particular. The Quakers doubtless suffered from having hatred drummed-up against them by the gentry and Presbyterian clergy, but it is clear that by the late 1650s that hatred was present and very amenable to being encouraged. The early Quakers were bizarre enough in their conduct, and it was easy to blacken them with charges of immorality, incest, buggery or witchcraft. Quaker meetings and individual Quakers were attacked, sometimes violently, both before and after 1660. The hostility against them, at all levels of society, can only be interpreted as part of a profound and widespread desire to see the world turned the right way up again.

Towards religious pluralism

The Restoration, as we shall see in the concluding chapter of this book, restored more than just the monarchy. Among other institutions which returned in 1660 was an episcopal Church of England, reimposed with the enthusiastic support of the political nation in general and of gentry members of the House of Commons in particular. The history of religion should not be confused with the history of legislation about religious matters, but the Clarendon Code which followed 1660 furnishes striking evidence of the hostility of those now in power to the sects, even to those moderate Presbyterians who had helped engineer the return of the House of Stuart (see pages 338–9 below). The Clarendon Code formed the framework for enforcing religious uniformity down to the Toleration Act of 1689. The implementation of this code was, as ever, subject to modification or intensification by local officials, while occasional moves towards greater toleration by Charles II or James II might create a temporary amelioration of the dissenters' lot. But, in general, the period was a difficult one for them. The accession of William and Mary heralded an easier period, but the Tory reaction under Anne brought the Occasional Conformity Act of 1711 and the Schism Act of 1714, both very detrimental to dissent. These Acts were, however, repealed in 1718, and the Whig Ascendancy in early Hanoverian England, despite sporadic attentions from hostile mobs, proved to be an era of gradual improvement. Full civil liberties were not to be achieved until well into the nineteenth century, but by the mid-eighteenth a new mood was obviously present. Thus Lord Mansfield, in his comments on a test case of 1767, could remark: 'It is now no crime for a man to say he is a dissenter; nor is it a crime for him not to take the sacrament according to the Church of England; nay, the crime is if he does it contrary to the dictates of his conscience.' The impossibility of a senior member of the legal establishment saying such things in 1550 demonstrates how much attitudes to religious conformity had changed.

Compared to the pre-1642 church, or post-Restoration nonconformity, the Church of England's history in the century after 1660 has received little attention. Yet it was that century which saw the arrival of a distinct body of thought and practice which can be described as Anglicanism, and which identified that Anglicanism as a conservative force. There is also a tradition that this conservativism was accompanied by considerable intellectual inertia. Certainly, in the age of Walpole bishops tended to be placemen rather than scholars or theologians, while country parsons, although graduates, have normally been thought of as intellectually limited. But recent research has challenged that stereotype, while after 1660 Anglicanism developed a style which is indicative of a certain vigour. Educated Anglicans came to regard themselves as heirs to a religious tradition which had the early Elizabethan, John Jewel, as its earliest apologist and the late Elizabethan, Thomas Hooker, as its greatest. This tradition was based on a unique blend of scripture, reason and custom, all of them emanating ultimately from the Almighty. Scripture, reason and tradition were thus seen as unconflicting, and it was from their ability to appeal to all three that Anglicans derived their particular position and their peculiar strength. Despite the ideological difficulties with the Glorious Revolution which led to the defection of the nonjurors, despite its association with Toryism, despite its downgrading after the discontinuation of Convocation in 1717, Anglicanism cannot be written off as a timeserving or weakly deistic religion. Something of its quality was revealed when William Grimshaw, an Anglican minister, told John Wesley that he 'believed the Church of England to be the soundest, purest, and most apostolical, well constituted national church in the world'.

Despite the develoment of such convictions, and of the emergence among theologians and leading ecclesiastics of an assured Anglican style, it remains clear that the changing religious climate of the late seventeenth and eighteenth centuries was providing intellectuals within the Anglican mainstream with some new problems. The presence of entrenched and legalized nonconformity meant that relationships and alignments with another religious grouping had constantly to be borne in mind. Historians are now less certain of the coherence or importance of Latitudinarianism, a tendency among at least some churchmen to take acceptance of nonconformity a little further than the letter of the law prescribed, but there were obviously some highly placed ecclesiastics who were willing to maintain a dialogue with the nonconformists. More worrying, for the theogically concerned Anglican, was the growth of a looser form of religious belief among the educated which was normally described as deism. The atheism which clerical observers of the period so feared was hardly widespread before the middle of the eighteenth century, and even after that date there were very few people willing to reject Christianity altogether. But early Enlightenment thinking was leading at least a few people towards deism. Theologically, this was not a very well-defined religious position, but in essence it rejected the belief in revealed religion and the acceptance of a scriptural basis that were fundamental to Anglicanism, and replaced these with a belief in an abstract deity which presided over a natural order and which was to be worshipped in conformity to that order. Deists thus took the concepts of 'reason' and 'nature' in religious matters to extremes, tending to reject any signs of 'enthusiasm'. It is no wonder therefore that that most enthusiastic of Christians, John Wesley, should single out deists and deism for special stricture when decrying the slackening religious standards of the eighteenth century.

Establishing the evolution of a distinctive Anglicanism among the élite, or the spread of such essentially intellectual tendencies as deism, is easy enough: assessing the impact of the beliefs of the restored church is more difficult, not least because the topic is under-researched. The eager participation of 'Church' mobs in the Sacheverell riots of 1710 suggests an active pro-Anglican popular reaction, but the attachment of the lower orders to Anglicanism under more orderly circumstances remains an elusive issue. Even those institutions which might have done most to enforce Anglican doctrines, the ecclesiastical courts, have received little attention for the period after 1660. Indications suggest that they were less effective, and less used, than before 1642, but the current level of research leaves the question open. Similarly, the provision of services and the attendance at them seems to have been very low in some areas. Pluralism was still common, especially in the rural south, so that many parishes (four-fifths of those in the Archdeaconry of Colchester in 1724, for example) enjoyed only the bare minimum of a Sunday service each week. Others, notably in the north, where perhaps Anglican clergy thought they had to try harder, had more: at Leeds, for example, daily services were held in the parish church by 1764. Variations in the number of regular communicants were equally striking. In some parishes this could be very low, as little as eight on an average Sunday. In others, such as Clayworth, Nottinghamshire, or Goodnestone, Kent, in the 1670s, the proportion of parishioners attending communion could be very high. But such success stories were almost invariably due to an unusually active parish priest rather than to any national, or indeed regional, trend.

It was, in fact, the presence of such priests which destroyed the old stereotype of the eighteenth-century parson as a being whose greatest interests were drinking port or foxhunting with the squire. One such, to whom we have already referred, was William Grimshaw of Haworth, Yorkshire. Grimshaw's ministry, dating from around the middle of the eighteenth century, recalled the godly standards of the Puritan era. He played an active role in suppressing such ungodly activities as football, and was reputed to have encouraged sabbath-day loafers in alehouses to get into church with his whip. These methods, and the strength of his convictions and the personal example he set, allowed Grimshaw to claim that he had increased the usual number of communicants from 12 to (in the summer months at least) 1200. Regional studies provide further evidence that the Church of England was far from somnolent. In Devon, for example, the Church was quietly going about its business of education and charity, its clergy setting a pattern of piety and pastoral care. In Cornwall, enthusiasm for the new evangelical ideas which spread in the early eighteenth century led to the foundation of the Clerical Club. Above all, there was a lively awareness running through the Church of the need to spread God's word. Anglican activists were in some measure inhibited by the risk of being labelled as 'enthusiasts', and of being equated with contemporary dissenters and earlier sectaries. Such prejudices were largely responsible for hamstringing the Societies for the Reformation of Manners, founded from the late seventeenth century in response to grass-roots dismay at prostitution, drunkenness and profanation of the sabbath. More durable were the Society for Promoting Christian Knowledge (founded in 1698), the Society for the Propagation of the Gospel (founded 1701), and the charity-school movement. Despite their essentially high-church position, supporters of these organizations showed a real desire to spread a practical and useful Christianity.

This evangelical Anglicanism, developing from around 1700, was the root of the greatest religious success story of the eighteenth century: Methodism. Despite its eventual separation, the movement's founder, John Wesley, was insistent on his desire to keep it within the Church of England. Methodism's origins lay in a 'Holy Club' of undergraduates who, from 1729, gathered around Wesley at Oxford, where he was a fellow of Lincoln College. Wesley, while remaining faithful to Anglican orthodoxy, wanted to revive apostolic usages and impose a stricter discipline than that generally obtaining in the Anglican church. Above all, his faith was an active one: as the greatest Methodist orator, George Whitefield, put it, 'a true faith in Christ Jesus will not suffer us to be *idle*'. Accordingly, the history of early Methodism is more redolent of the enthusiasm of the 1650s than of eighteenth-century rationality. From about 1739 Wesley encouraged preaching in the open air, and the task was increasingly carried on by lay preachers rather than ordained ministers. Groups hitherto little touched by formal religion, like the 'rough colliers' of Plessey, Northumberland, or Cornish tin-miners, were brought to hear and love the word of God. Conversion on hearing the word was often accompanied by hysteria. One of Wesley's early hearers, Thomas Maxfield of Bristol, underwent conversion in 1739, roaring and beating himself so much that it took six men to hold him down, and Wesley's journal records similar conversions well into the 1780s. Moreover, like the Interregnum sectaries and their Puritan predecessors, the newly converted Methodists lost no chance to criticize the less godly. Thus in 1747 it was reported that the Redruth Methodists not only led exemplary lives themselves, but 'if they see any person drunk, swearing or the like, they reprove him, and are apt to tell him, he is in the way of damnation'.

All this prompted a predictable reaction. As early as 1739, 100 tracts were in print criticizing the Methodists for their enthusiasm, while by 1743 Methodist preachers could expect to find themselves on the receiving end of mob violence. Above all (and despite the support of that great patroness of evangelicalism, Selina, Countess of Huntingdon) the comfortable, sedate and formally religious feared the socially subversive overtones of the Methodist impact among the poor. Curiously, though, despite the enthusiasm of Wesley, his brother Charles, Whitefield and their early plebeian supporters, Methodism moved towards a formal structure of organization and discipline. By the late eighteenth century it offered a complete substitute for the parish church and the Anglican ministry. Indeed, by 1770 Methodism was demonstrating its maturity by experiencing schism: on the one hand was Whitefield, supported by the Countess of Huntingdon, with his staunchly Calvinist views on salvation; on the other the Wesley brothers, with more Arminian attitudes to the availability of grace.

Tracing the fortunes of the various dissenting churches is a more difficult process. As might be imagined, the Restoration and the Clarendon Code caused massive dismay from which it took some time to recover. Nevertheless, the nonconformists survived, and in the face of adversity displayed that gritty godliness which was one of the more appealing facets of pre-1642 Puritanism. As persecution waned, a number of distinct strands of nonconformity emerged. The Presbyterians maintained their image as a respectable and solid body with an educated and efficient ministry. The Independents (or Congregationalists) and Baptists had rather more problems in achieving respectability: they were associated in both the official and the popular mind with the radical sects of the Interregnum. But they too survived into the era of toleration, although probably in a less coherent form than did the Presbyterians. By about 1715 adult Presbyterians, Independents and Baptists probably numbered about 300,000 nationally, although the strength of nonconformity was great in some areas. Generalizing about the social profile of nonconformist groups is also complicated by regional variation, but some sort of pattern can be traced. The tone for the Presbyterians, as befitted their respectable image, was set by their solidly bourgeois leadership and their educated ministry. Independents seem to have been drawn from a slightly lower stratum: shopkeepers, tradesmen and artisans. The Baptists, on the other hand, seem to have attracted the poor, and were also unusual in making an impact in rural areas.

Ironically, just as the more tolerant attitudes of the Hanoverian period arrived, the number of adherents to the Old Dissent fell. Nationally, the number of dissenting congregations dropped from 1107 in 1715 to 702 in 1772, while in some localities the fall was even more marked. In Devon, for example, the number of meeting-houses dropped from 80 to 57 between the early eighteenth century and 1764, while the number of parishes reporting dissenters fell from 175 to 60. Some new dissenting groups, such as the Ebeneezer Baptists of Scarborough, did establish themselves in the third quarter of the eighteenth century: but by that time the number of dissenters was declining, and smaller sects, such as the Seventh Day Baptists, faced total eclipse. The reasons for this decline are varied. Certainly the very rejection by many of the sects of an educated clergy and a formal church hierarchy was self-defeating in the long run. Extraordinary motions of the spirit encouraged short-term enthusiasm, but there are manifest difficulties in maintaining the impetus of such motions over long periods. Moreover, by the second quarter of the eighteenth century alternatives to Old Dissent were being offered to those seeking, or capable of being touched by, a heightened sense of Christian awareness. The pietist movement, associated with the Moravian church, had reached England by that point, and there was also the related Anglican evangelicalism. Methodism was also attracting the more enthusiastic believer: an instructive comment was made by a Devon parson in response to visitation articles in 1764: 'There is indeed a Meeting-House, formerly occupied by Presbyterians, but of late it is frequented by the new sect of Methodists.' Nonconformity had weathered persecution, but it seemed unable to cope with the Wesleyan challenge.

Not even the Quakers were immune from the problems of declining numbers and, in a certain sense, stagnation. The fortunes of the Friends, like those of other groups, varied from area to area. It seems that they flourished despite the sometimes severe persecutions of 1660–88, to reach a peak, from which they slowly declined, of about 50,000 members in 1715. By that date they had long lost the radical edge which had so animated respectable fears in the 1650s. The Quakers were still readily identifiable by their speech, their dress, and their manner of greeting, while their refusal to doff their hats or take oaths was subversive enough by contemporary standards. Yet they, too, had acquired both church discipline and a hierarchy. Thus a sect which had included James Nayler among its early adherents could, by 1676, exclude a man from the Buckinghamshire meeting for dancing and 'prophane carriage'. In addition, their increasing tendency to do business by committee meant, as seems to be the nature of things in such matters, that the more businesslike should take control: thus meetings for church affairs took a more respectable, perhaps even more bourgeois, tinge than the membership as a whole. The composition of this membership was still drawn overwhelmingly from artisans, farmers and other small property-owners, both urban and rural: there was a steady decline in the number of gentry Quakers, a noticeable minority in the movement's early days. By the end of our period, only a small proportion of this membership, varying from 10 per cent to 25 per cent by region, was formed of new converts: most Quakers were the descendents of Quaker parents. A stability had set in, symbolized by attempts at a major national reorganization in 1737 and the commencement, by about 1760, of something like a systematic membership list by the various meetings. The Spirit was moving a good deal more sedately than He had a century before.

The Catholics showed a better capacity for survival, at least on the strength of their membership numbers, than did the sects. Despite the rhetoric of the period, there is little evidence that Catholics were systematically persecuted in the Interregnum, and after 1660 many of them must have been confident that a similar situation would continue to obtain. The Popish Plot of 1679 demonstrated the strength of old fears, while the reign of James II created some new ones. Popular anti-Catholicism emerged regularly in times of stress, and was revived annually on November the Fifth. Modern Bonfire Night, outside a few favoured places like Lewes, is a pale affair compared to those old celebrations, when the effigies of Guy Fawkes, his fellow conspirators and the Pope were burnt (sometimes with live cats inside, to achieve appropriate sound effects) to remind the English of the popish threat.

Generally, however, the Catholics, who had long since given up hopes of a national restoration of their faith, progressed towards acting like, and being accepted as, just another sect. The political conduct of Catholics in the reign of James II, indeed, showed both their lack of ambition and their common sense. Their upper-class leadership realized that a full-scale revival of their faith would simply alienate most of their compatriots and (scarcely less desirably) increase the power and status of the clergy. Lack of Catholic aggression at this point probably did much to foster the gradual toleration they experienced over the eighteenth century. There was also a dilution of religious observances. Before the late seventeenth century, Catholics had been remarkable for their attachment to religious practices which were private and virtually outside the field of legislation: days of fasting and feasting, for example. But after about 1700, these practices lost their hold: English Catholics, like their Anglican and nonconformist compatriots, entered the world of rational Christianity. This, and much else, shows how the 80,000 or so Catholics who lived in England at the end of our period were affected by the wider culture in which they existed.

The religious pattern was further complicated by the emergence of the Jewish community. The key figure in the story of the re-entry of the Jews to England was Menasseh ben Israel (alias Manuel Dias Soeiro). Menasseh ben Israel was a typical example of those Iberian Sephardic Jews who in the sixteenth and seventeenth centuries underwent a Diaspora which scattered them through much of the Mediterranean world and northern Europe. He was born at Modena in 1604, but settled early in life in Amsterdam, where he made contact with an English embassy in 1651. An increased interest in Hebrew studies, as well as the more general Puritan emphasis on the importance of the Old Testament, had created a receptive attitude towards the Jews: Cromwell himself was interested in the possibility of their being readmitted to England. Events overtook the deliberations of the official committee on the matter, however. A Jew living in England, Antonio Rodrigues Robles, established the right to Jewish residence in a test case. In December 1656 a synagogue was established on London's eastern fringes, followed by a Jewish cemetery at Mile End. The Jewish presence after the Restoration was strengthened by a number of influential Marronos who accompanied Charles II's queen, Catherine of Braganza, and by a number of judicial decisions which helped establish the civil rights of Jews. There was some petty harassment, but a viable

Jewish community, perhaps the least persecuted in Europe, emerged. Many of its members were involved in trade, but an influx of Ashkenazic Jews escaping from pogroms in eastern Europe modified the traditional stereotype that would connect Jewishness with merchant wealth: indeed, worry over their poor became one of the dominant concerns of the Jewish community. By the end of our period Jews, and especially Sephardic Jews, were beginning to assimilate, and their solid adherence to the Hanoverian cause in 1745 did them little harm. That their position had its limitations was, however, demonstrated in 1753, when a parliamentary Bill proposing the naturalization of a few of the richer Sephardi prompted violent popular opposition. A General Election was near and the Bill was dropped. Nevertheless, despite mob action and the intemperance of some of the language used, there seems to have been little active violence against Jews or their property. If the toleration of the English had its limitations, so did their anti-semitism.

Before the Reformation Christianity in England had been wholly in theory and (a few Lollards excepted) wholly in practice a unified system. By 1760 this was no longer the case. Most people, some of them very reluctantly, were forced to accept that they lived in a religiously pluralistic society and were prepared, most of the time, to accept this. Yet as well as this readily discernible vertical fragmentation of religion there existed, in Christianity, more elusive horizontal divisions: people had different ideas about the nature of Christianity, and certainly of the Christian God, and for some people some of these differences were determined by social stratification. The shrine of Our Lady of Walsingham, probably the most visited in Europe, had, in Henry VIII's reign, numbered the Duke of Buckingham and Cardinal Wolsey among its visitors, while the King himself had paid for a candle there as late as 1538. The Countess of Huntingdon apart, such élite involvement in the more enthusiastic aspects of religion was rare two centuries later: it is difficult, for example, to imagine Walpole undergoing an hysterical conversion at a Methodist field meeting. Recent writing has stressed the attachment to high-church ceremonial shown by some Hanoverian bishops, and doubtless there was more adherence to traditional usages among the élite than has sometimes been claimed. Nevertheless, the early enlightenment increased the importance of reason as an aspect of religious belief, and in 1748, with David Hume's *Philosophical Essays Concerning Human Understanding*, the first work written by an author to challenge rational, as well as revealed, religion appeared. Generally, by that time believers among the élite tended towards a view of Christianity which was rather different from that of the masses. The God of Isaac Newton was a deity less accessible to the popular mind than that of John Foxe.

Perhaps the most important divergence came with the rejection or downgrading among educated sophisticates of that most important component of early Puritanism: the providential, interventionist Almighty. Again, we are discussing a relative, rather than an absolute shift. The idea of a providential God was never entirely lost among the élite and, as reactions to the Lisbon earthquake of 1755 demonstrate, the old notion of a vengeful God could still be mobilized on appropriate occasions at the end of our period. On the strength of a lively and as yet little studied popular literature, however, it would seem that such notions were consistently attractive to and in some measure held by the lower and middling sorts. Certainly, with the onset of the more rational Christianity of the eighteenth century, such views were thought more typical of nonconformity. The writings of Oliver Heywood, compiled mainly in the 1670s, contain many 'observable providences relating to others', in which yet more true stories describing the dreadful accidents which awaited drunkards and other sinners were recorded. At the beginning of the eighteenth century the religious life of London was rendered more complicated and more lively by the arrival of the French Prophets, at their core a group of newly arrived Huguenot refugees, who gave a boost to the old phenomena of prophesying doom, levitation, going into religious trances, faith-healing, and speaking in tongues. Early popular Methodism also accepted the reality of divine providence and the importance of making God's glory manifest by the godliness of everyday conduct. Thus a critic of 1761 wrote of Methodists:

> The Lord is in all their doings ... whether they are at home or abroad, in good or evil plight, whether it rains or clears up, whether they escape a shower or are wetted by it, it is all owing to some divine direction, and made to answer some great purpose.

Methodism in particular harked back to the old godly activism, to the old vision of a general reformation. 'What may we reasonably believe to be God's designs in raising up the preachers called Methodists?' asked the 'Large Minutes' of 1783: the answer was 'To reform the nation, and in particular the church: to spread scriptural holiness over the land'. It is striking that for these most enthusiastic of Protestants the work of reformation, well over two centuries after the break with Rome, was still woefully incomplete.

Behind such problems as plebeian belief in a providential God and plebeian notions about godliness there lurks a more general question: what did religion actually mean to the bulk of the population? As the shrewd reader may have noticed, the term 'popular religion' has been used very sparingly in this chapter. This is not merely because of lack of evidence. It also follows from severe doubts about the usefulness of the term, doubts founded mainly on the fact that the religious beliefs of the populace at large showed a dazzling range of variations, from the enthusiasm of the Ranter to the indifference of which so many clerical intellectuals complained. In 1550 the phrase might have meant something, but developments over the next two centuries render its employment difficult. Were the custodians of popular religion the churchwardens who hid church ornaments in the reign of Edward VI, or the Protestant iconoclasts who wanted to smash them? Were they the people who eagerly accepted the Quaker message in the 1650s or the Methodist message in the 1740s, or the people who beat up Quakers and Methodists?

Against this bewildering chaos of evidence and questions, it would seem that the one tenable conclusion is that for most people Christianity meant much the same in 1760 as it had two centuries before, certainly as far as its social aspects were concerned. It provided a number of explanations, however partial, for a number of otherwise inexplicable problems, ranging from why everyday accidents occurred through to the origins and moral purpose of mankind. What it had to say about birth, death and marriage helped to make sense of those vital rites of passage through which people went. It was still something mystical and awesome, otherworldly in a very real sense. Above all, Christianity reinforced a general value system which it had probably helped form: the idea that being a worthwhile human being involved respecting a basic morality of doing as you would be done by and, via charity, doing a bit more than that. Whatever the complications imposed from above, and despite (or perhaps ultimately because of) the complications inherent in living with Catholic, Quaker, Presbyterian or Methodist neighbours, most people over the timespan with which we are concerned believed that Christianity was essentially about behaviour as much as belief.

Notes

1 Christopher Haigh, 'The continuity of Catholicism in the English Reformation', *Past and Present*, 93 (1981), p. 69.

|10|

Education and literacy

In the modern world, one of the standard indicators of the level of a society's development is the extent of the educational facilities it enjoys and the extent to which its population is literate. It is, moreover, a commonplace that literacy and education flourish in societies which are large and complex, and in which industry, trade and commerce are well established. At the very least, the exposure of a large part of the population to formal education presupposes that the society in question has reached the level of prosperity required to allow it to free children and adolescents from the labour process for a few years. These assumptions are of obvious relevance to early modern England. If, as we have argued, English society was becoming more complex and more commercial, we would expect to see rising levels of literacy and an increase in the provision of educational facilities. There is considerable evidence that this was the case. To take the most obvious indicator, the output of the printing press, introduced into England in the late fifteenth century, suggests a growing demand for the printed word. It has been calculated that between 1576 and 1640 an average of 200 titles was published each year, amounting to an annual production of perhaps 300,000 volumes. The political debates of the 20 years that followed 1640 witnessed a massive rise in publication, with as many as 2000 separate titles being published in some years. The sheer statistics of book production demonstrate the existence of a wide reading public.

A number of these books dealt with education: some, indeed, were written by educationalists. From these, we can begin to discover what contemporaries thought education was about, what they thought the uses of literacy were. What rapidly becomes evident, perhaps more so in the years before 1640, was that the most consistent theme was that the main object of education was the inculcation of correct religious views. John Brinsley, an experienced schoolmaster, writing in 1622, felt that 'onely he who is endued with right knowledge and understanding' could 'give God that glorie for which he was created, and redeemed from hell, or can in anie measure honour him as he ought to do to his owne salvation'. John Dury, a would-be educational reformer writing in the heady days of 1649, declared that 'the main scope of the whole work of education, both in boys and girls, should be this: to train them to know God in Christ that they may walk worthy of him and become profitable instruments of the commonwealth'.

The ideals of such writers were reflected in the reality of the educational system: formal education was, in large measure, controlled by the Church. The two universities were largely under ecclesiastical control, while all schoolmasters were, at least in theory, licensed by the local bishop. Such control seems to have been in keeping with wider attitudes: the statutes of countless grammar schools founded in the period, for example, agree in making it a priority that schoolmasters should be men of sound religion and godly behaviour, and that their pupils should receive sound instruction in matters spiritual. The consequences of failure in this were almost too dreadful to contemplate: the ignorant and uninformed might fall prey to the blandishments of popish propaganda. Thus John Brinsley, when encouraging the Protestant English to a higher level of awareness over matters religious through education, added weight to his argument by insisting that the forces of international Catholicism were already very active in that respect. In particular, the Jesuits, 'the principal plotters of the ruine of all the churches of Christ', had, with characteristic efficiency, devised an international syllabus which was perverting the minds of countless young Europeans.

Education was not, however, advocated purely on religious grounds. Some educationalists and, we suspect, rather more of the public at large, were convinced that it would prove useful to many as they went about their daily affairs. In a world increasingly involved in credit transactions, with debt, with business deals, even with public service and court attendance, literacy would be considered an asset and educational facilities would be in some demand. A writer of 1618 put into the mouth of a 'countryman' the opinion that education, as well as aiding religious edification, helped 'set down common prices at markets, write a letter and make a bond, set down the day of our birth, our marriage day, and make our wills when we are sick for the disposing of our goods when we are dead'. Literacy was also of growing relevance to leisure. From about the middle of the sixteenth century the printing presses of London produced not only a stream of books, but also a whole flood of almanacs, pamphlets, ballads, broadsides, chapbooks and jestbooks, a popular literature intended to instruct, amuse and occasionally shock what was a very wide reading public indeed. Assessing the extent of this output is difficult, for much of this popular literature was of an ephemeral nature. We know, however, that almanacs were selling at the rate of perhaps 400,000 a year in the mid-seventeenth century, or one for every 12 or so of the population.

There are, therefore, strong signs of a forward thrust in education and literacy over our period. Indeed, by the early seventeenth century it is possible to find observers claiming that there was too much education in England. As early as 1611 Sir Francis Bacon was complaining that there were 'more scholars that the state can prefer and employ', and those trying to analyse the origins of the Civil War, both in the seventeenth century and more recently, have seen an excess of educated people as a relevant factor. Thomas Hobbes, to take a well-known example, felt that the outbreak and progress of the political crisis could be partly attributed to an over-supply of scholars imbued with classical texts advocating republicanism, while one modern historian has postulated the existence of a body of 'alienated intellectuals' just before the wars.[1] More general claims have been made about the significance of educational change before the 1640s. The most noteworthy came in 1964 when Lawrence Stone suggested that the 80 years before 1640 witnessed an 'educational revolution' of far-reaching importance. After assembling information about entry to higher education, about the increase in the number of schools, and about literacy rates, Stone argued that there had occurred 'a quantitative change of such magnitude that it can only be described as a revolution ... it may well be that early seventeenth-century England was the most literate society the world had ever known'.[2] Contemporary views on the importance, and possible dangers, of education, Professor Stone's arguments, and the claims of other recent historians all combine to suggest that the problems of education and literacy are well worth further investigation.

Higher education: the universities and the Inns of Court

One of the most marked educational trends in the century before 1640 was an increase in the number of entrants to England's two universities. As ever, basing statistics on early modern materials involves a number of pitfalls. Source materials for reconstructing details of entrants are deficient, especially for Cambridge, before the 1580s, while the usefulness of one of the principal sources, matriculation registers, is impeded by the knowledge that a number of students who did not matriculate were present at the universities. Nevertheless, the overall pattern, as set out in Figure 10.1, is a clear one. Admissions were low around 1550, but seem to have picked up after that date, and rose rapidly to reach a peak in the 1580s. A subsequent decline, probably a response to the somewhat difficult economic conditions of the 1590s, was followed by a recovery in the early seventeenth century, and an absolute peak of about 1000 entrants was reached in the 1630s. The Civil Wars, understandably, resulted in a

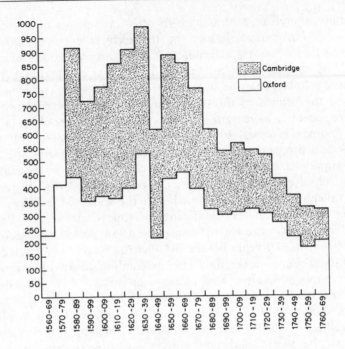

Figure 10.1 Estimated annual freshman admissions to Oxford and Cambridge (decennial averages), 1560–1769. *Source*: Lawrence Stone, 'The Size and Composition of the Oxford Student Body, 1580–1909', Table IA and IB, in Lawrence Stone (ed.), *The University in Society*, 2 vols. (Princeton and London, 1975), vol. 1, pp. 91–2.

drop in numbers, but admissions for 1650–79 were fairly buoyant, roughly on a level with those obtaining early in the seventeenth century. Thereafter, a fall set in: levels were low in the period 1680–1729; then a real slump came towards the mid-eighteenth century, which continued for some decades after 1760. At least some sections of English society had greater access to higher education in the late sixteenth and early seventeenth centuries than ever before. On Stone's calculations it would seem that just before the Civil Wars a higher proportion of male adolescents was entering higher education than at any time before the twentieth century: about 2.5 per cent of youths aged 17 (the normal age for university matriculation at that date) entered Oxford, Cambridge or an Inn of Court in the 1630s.

The changes in numbers of entrants over the period 1550–1760 were accompanied by changes in the social composition of the student body. Despite technical problems inherent in the relevant sources the pattern, once again, seems clear. In the late sixteenth and early seventeenth centuries the largest single element in the student body, at Oxford constituting over half of undergraduates between the 1570s and the 1630s, were youths whose fathers were described as plebeian. College registers reveal that, although there were few representatives of the labouring poor, the fathers of many students came from a relatively humble station: husbandmen, clothworkers, glovers, and other tradesmen or craftsmen. Access to a university education was, apparently, not impossible for youths of a fairly lowly background. Gradually, however, students of plebeian origin were outnumbered by the offspring of the gentry. As we have seen, ideas on what constituted proper aristocratic behaviour were changing, and the Renaissance concept of the gentlemen had placed a considerable emphasis on the virtues of education in general, and of a classical education in particular. As a desire that their sons should acquire a university education became fashionable among the élite, so those sons appeared more frequently in college registers. Oxford and Cambridge were, by 1600, providing for the educational needs of two groups of students: the plebeians, most of whom were destined for a career in the Church, who actually took degrees and, so far as can be seen, worked hard for them: and the sons of the gentry who, despite the presence of a number of real scholars among their ranks, were mainly there to acquire polish and cultural accomplishments.

After the Restoration, the proportion of plebeian students fell. They had formed 55 per cent of matriculants at Oxford in the years 1577–79, a proportion which had already fallen to 37 per cent by 1637–39, and was to fall further to 27 per cent in 1711, 17 per cent in 1760, and to a mere 1 per cent by 1810. Thus not only did the total number of entrants fall over the second half of our period: those who did enter the universities were drawn from an increasingly narrow social base. The costs of education had risen, and many plebeians were now unable to work their way through college, as they had done before, as sizers or servitors waiting on the dons or the gentleman-commoner undergraduates. Moreover, many of the scholarships originally founded for the support of poor scholars had become the preserve of the gentry or the clergy. Indeed, one of the most marked trends in the changing social composition of the student body was the increase in the proportion of sons of the clergy who were matriculating, from perhaps 1 per cent at the beginning of our period to 15 per cent at the end. The absolute (but by no means relative) drop in the number of gentry entrants after the late seventeenth century suggests that the landed orders were now unwilling to send their sons to university. The Renaissance insistence on the virtues of a classical education had been replaced by a feeling that the graces needed by a man of quality might be acquired elsewhere than at university. Moreover, given the harsher agricultural conditions which followed the Restoration, many minor gentry were unable or unwilling to spend the money needed to support a son there.

The curriculum to which the university student was exposed was essentially conservative and non-utilitarian. What were studied were the 'liberal arts', basically the education appropriate to the free man of a Greek city-state in the fourth century BC. The subjects comprehended the 'trivium' of grammar, dialectic and rhetoric, and the 'quadrivium' of arithmetic, geometry, astronomy and music. At Cambridge, under the University Statutes of 1570, the arts course took seven years: four years to Bachelor of Arts, then another three years to Master of Arts. The student would study rhetoric, logic and philosophy up to his BA, and would then progress to his MA through the study of natural, moral and metaphysical philosophy, drawing and Greek. The system was probably more flexible in practice than it was on paper, but its objective was clearly to send the student along a series of clearly marked progressions, the subjects being studied consecutively, not simultaneously. The syllabus did change a little during our period, with some limited addition of new subjects, while it was also possible, then as now, for the keen or gifted student to follow interests outside the curriculum. Moreover, the new role of the universities as finishing schools for the sons of the landed orders meant that the colleges attracted a penumbra of tutors giving instruction in extracurricular subjects. By 1700 the student who was willing to pay for it could obtain private tuition in chemistry, physics, anatomy, botany, mathematics, French, Spanish, Italian, music, dancing, riding and other physical exercises.

If, officially at least, there seems to have been little change in the curriculum, marked changes occurred in the method of teaching. The second half of the sixteenth century witnessed two of the more significant and long-lasting developments in the history of Oxbridge: the rise of the college and the rise of the college tutor. The normal medieval assumption was that colleges were essentially communities of graduate fellows: students working for the BA usually lived in halls or hostels in the town. But from about 1550 undergraduates, plebeians on scholarships and gentleman-commoners alike, began increasingly to lodge in college. Moreover, from about 1570, at Oxford at least, a regular practice was institutionalized when it was ordered that every commoner should be assigned to a college tutor. This system helped to assure parents that their sons were under some sort of control at a dangerous age, and also convinced the parents of gentlemen-commoners that they were getting some sort of value for their money. Scholars, too, were increasingly the recipients of tutorial teaching and, since the sons of the wealthy needed servants, became integrated into college life as sizers and servitors. The rise of the tutorial system meant that the older forms of university teaching, the lecture and disputation, fell into disuse. It also meant that the focus of an undergraduate's attention, and perhaps of his loyalty, became his college. It is probably no accident that this period witnessed a massive increase in building in colleges. In Oxford, between 1610 and 1670, although only one new college (Wadham) was actually founded, most colleges experienced extensive building operations, mainly to provide new quadrangles to accommodate undergraduates. Much the same situation obtained at Cambridge.

But this expansion and innovation was not sustained. As we have seen, the boom in admissions of the 80 years before the Civil Wars gave way, from the late seventeenth century, to a decline which degenerated into a slump, while the student body became more socially exclusive. There is a considerable tradition that this decline and narrowing in student intake was accompanied by a similar decline in and narrowing of intellectual activity. By far the most vivid account of what it was like to be an intelligent and lively undergraduate in this slump period is to be found in the *Autobiography* of Edward Gibbon. To the future chronicler of the fall of the Roman Empire, his 14 months at Magdalen College, Oxford, in 1751–52 were 'the most idle and unprofitable of my whole life'. Gibbon wrote:

> The schools of Oxford and Cambridge were founded in a dark age of false and barbarous science; and they are still tainted with the vices of their origin. Their primitive discipline was adapted to the education of priests and monks; and the government still remains in the hands of the clergy, an order of men, whose manners are remote from the present world and whose eyes are dazzled by the light of philosophy. The legal incorporation of these societies of popes and kings had given them a monopoly of public instruction; and the spirit of monopolies is narrow, lazy, and oppressive.

In Oxford, according to Gibbon, 'the public professors have for these many years given up altogether even the pretence of teaching'. The dons did not debate intellectual matters, and their conversation rather 'stagnated in a round of college business, Tory politics, personal stories, and private scandal'. Such men gave scant encouragement to the aspiring young scholar. Dr Waldegrave, Gibbon's first tutor, was a man whose 'learning was of the past, rather than of the present age', and who 'like his fellows' was satisfied with 'the slight and superficial discharge of an important trust'. An institution of higher education should not be damned on the criticism of one, even if very bright, undergraduate: it is difficult, however, to achieve any more than a partial rejection of Gibbon's portrayal of mid-eighteenth-century Oxford.

That things had been more promising a generation or two earlier is suggested by the university's attempts to get to grips with new scientific ideas. Individuals at the universities had been involved, from the mid-seventeenth century, with developing new approaches to what the age knew as 'natural philosophy': but these new approaches were to make little lasting impact on either the syllabus or the formal provision of teaching. At Oxford, a Readership in Chemistry was set up in 1704, and the first incumbent, John Friend, lectured to large audiences. A number of distinguished scholars held the Savilian Chair of Astronomy, while in 1728 the Sherardian Chair of Botany was established. At Cambridge, too, new professorships were created and capable men appointed to fill them. But despite this evidence of intellectual vitality, only a very small proportion of undergraduates actually came into contact with the new science, while the creation of new chairs, even George I's Regius professorships in history and modern languages, had little impact on the entrenched indolence of the dons. Attempts to inject new ideals and a more rational view of education foundered on the tradition of non-lecturing.

The fortunes of the Inns of Court, the equivalent of the third university of the realm in this period, were in many respects similar to those of the universities. The Inns too experienced a dramatic rise in admissions from the mid-sixteenth century. Admissions totalled about 100 a year in 1550, about 250 in 1600, and reached peaks in the middle years of James I's reign and the 1630s. From the start, the Inns were more socially exclusive than the universities: there were no scholarships to support poor students, and no opportunities for working one's way through as a part-time servant. Analysis of those admitted shows the landed orders firmly established in the student body. There were 12,163 non-honorific admissions to the Inns between 1590 and 1639, of which 40.6 per cent were the sons of peers or esquires, and 47.8 per cent the sons of mere gentry. The overwhelming majority of these entrants did not come to an Inn to acquire a legal training: only about one in six of them were actually called to the Bar. Although the idea that a smattering of legal training might be useful to their heir might have influenced some fathers when sending their sons to an Inn, the main objective was to provide them with polish and social graces. Even more than the universities, the Inns in this period functioned as finishing schools for the male offspring of the landed élite.

In the absence of a proper tutorial system, many of the students at the Inns must have succumbed to the sexual and other leisure facilities offered by London: it is probably no accident that the dissolute young Inn of Court man was a figure frequently satirized in contemporary literature. As with Oxford and Cambridge, however, the landed orders obviously felt after 1660 that their money could be better invested than by supporting their sons at the Inns. By the early eighteenth century admissions had fallen considerably (to 1209 for the whole decade 1700–9), while the proportion of gentlemen-students had fallen, their near monopoly being eroded by the sons of merchants and professional men. By the time the great legal writer Sir William Blackstone delivered his first series of lectures at Oxford in 1758, the Inns' function as a finishing school for the sons of the gentry was more or less dead. For those investing in providing their sons with social graces, the grand tour was probably thought of as more appropriate and, given that the young gentlemen would be accompanied by a tutor, less morally dangerous than a spell at an Inn of Court.

Those who were actually studying law at the Inns encountered an intellectual regime, and studied a discipline, which were almost brutalizing in their nature. Despite the claims of Coke, the English common law simply did not exist as an intellectual system. Learning the law was essentially tedious, involving the rote learning of details rather than the confrontation of general principles, and was especially disliked by those coming to the Inns after acquiring a grounding in classical education at a university. Littleton's *Tenures*, in many respects the cornerstone of the common law, was described as 'undoubtedly the most crabbed author to begin with any science in the world'. Coke's *Commentary* on Littleton's work, according to Roger North, bred 'more disorder in the brains than any other book can', yet was widely recommended as the basic text for legal studies in the seventeenth and eighteenth centuries. The student would be admitted to the Inn as an Inner Barrister, and would probably have to study for 10 or 12 years before emerging as a fully-fledged member of the profession. There were three traditional teaching methods: the bolting, in which the student argued about cases and questions put to him by a Bencher and two Barristers; the moot, a public disputation between a Reader and two other Benchers, intended for the edification of all ranks of the profession; and readings, a more advanced form of instruction given in Law French. All these teaching methods declined in importance. Those meant to be teaching had discovered that the law offered far more profitable ways of passing the time than instructing in the subject. At the same time, students drew the obvious conclusion about the quality of the teaching they were receiving, and sought to remedy the situation by private study: the place of formal exercises was in some measure taken by the printed treatise. But in the absence of a tutorial system, this retreat into individual reading meant that many who were eventually called to the Bar had only patchy formal training: many barristers must have gained their training as they practised.

The histories of the universities and the Inns of Court, therefore, illustrate both the evidence supporting Stone's 'educational revolution' and some of the problems which preclude total acceptance of it. The first of these is the conclusion that there was very little that was 'revolutionary' in the syllabuses of either the universities or the Inns, although, as we have seen, both may have experienced a change in teaching methods in the century before 1642. But the biggest difficulties with the educational revolution come when post-1660 developments are taken into consideration: there, if anything, it is possible to trace a counter-revolution, or at least a change in fashion. Could it not be, therefore, that as far as what we would now term higher education is concerned, what we are confronting before 1640 is not so much a revolution, as a symptom both of current fashions in education, and particularly upper-class education, and an aspect of the economic buoyancy of the landed orders? These were doing well, and were able to send their sons into higher education or (albeit more rarely) found a scholarship that might allow a boy of more modest fortune to study at Oxford or Cambridge. After 1660 a new stability set in: a stability which affected higher education as much as everything else. Money was tighter among the gentry and yeomanry, and with the gentry in particular there were new ideas about how such of the family's resources that were to be invested in education might best be used. Moreover, those Renaissance and Reformation ideals on the importance of education which had been so persuasive before 1642 were no longer fashionable. Oxford, Cambridge and the Inns of Court reflected that change from an expansionary world to a static one which we have so often traced in this book.

The grammar schools and their rivals

The endowed grammar schools, 'the nurseries of all learning, and vertue' have long been regarded as one of the glories of the English education system. Yet they coexisted with a number of other, and potentially rival, educational institutions. For the population at large, most noticeably outside the towns, a number of schools existed, some of them offering Latin grammar, others basic instruction in English. Parsons, lay graduates and others might offer to teach on a more or less *ad hoc* basis in remote areas, and many people took their first steps in literacy under the instruction of such teachers. For the rich, the private tutor might have been considered more suitable than the grammar school. Defoe might refer to 'those murtherers of a child's morals, call'd tutors', but as early as 1670 a writer could comment that the gentry 'now frequently judge themselves under the necessity of entertaining a tutor at great charge in their own houses'. Indeed, that great classic of Renaissance educational theory, Roger Ascham's *Scholemaster* of 1570, was written with the private tutor to the great in mind.

But our main concern initially in this section will be the endowed grammar school. There is every indication that this institution, like the universities, was experiencing a boom between the mid-sixteenth and the mid-seventeenth centuries. One hundred and thirty-six grammar schools were founded during the long reign of Elizabeth I, another 83 under James I, 59 under Charles I, and 80 under Charles II. Many of these foundations failed over time: but Christopher Wase, who set out upon a national survey of grammar schools in 1673, found 704 in existence at that date. Large amounts of money went into endowing grammar schools: just over £383,594 went into English education from charitable or philanthropic sources in the 40 years after 1603, of which nearly £220,600 was spent on endowing grammar schools. The impetus behind this boom was largely religious: as a petition requesting permission to endow a new school in Elizabethan Derbyshire put it, without the right education the people would not only neglect the Queen's laws and fall into vice, but also 'cleave to papistry, rather than the gospel'. Some of these schools were to become powerful and successful educational institutions. But the social background of the boys attending them (grammar schools, like the universities, were a male preserve) has so far received little systematic attention. Many founders of schools intended them to provide at least some free education for poor boys. Abraham Colfe, for example, founded a school at Lewisham in Kent in 1647. He envisaged that its pupils would be drawn from the neighbourhood, and would consist of orphans, the children of parish pensioners, and the offspring of 'day labourers, handy-crafts men, mean tradesmen, painful husbandmen, or of any other honest and godly poor persons ... so that the children be of good wit, and capacity, and apt to learn'. Entry to Colfe's foundation remained true to his original intentions until the 1970s, but even as he wrote other schools were well on the way to social exclusivity. Eton and Westminster already had an upper-class tone to them, while up in Yorkshire Pocklington Grammar School could number 76 sons of the local gentry in its register by 1650. Like the universities, the grammar schools were evidently regarded as desirable institutions by the gentry.

Given this, it is interesting to note that the education offered in these schools, again like the universities, was essentially classical and non-utilitarian. Latin grammar dominated the syllabus, and was taught largely through memorizing and repetition ('gerund grinding' as Milton called it) which were obviously seen as handy checks on youthful spontaneity. A boy normally entered grammar school aged seven or eight, and stayed there for another six or seven years if he was to complete his education. His school day began at six or seven in the morning, and continued until five, or in summertime six, in the evening, with breaks for breakfast and dinner. This regime was varied by between five and eight weeks holiday a year, although holiday tasks might be set. It was intended that by the end of his schooldays the pupil would be sufficiently well grounded in Latin grammar to allow him to enter the university. The exact system of learning varied from school to school, although from 1542 *A Shorte Introduction of Grammar*, known familiarly as *Lily's Grammar*, became something of a standard work of instruction. It was published at the rate of 10,000 copies a year in Elizabeth's reign.

The basic diet of Latin might be varied but, given that the usual variations were Greek or Hebrew, one suspects that most schoolboys derived little comfort from them. Even so, there are signs of a broadening of the curriculum to meet new expectations of what education should be about after 1640. Certainly, by the late seventeenth century the masters of many grammar schools must have been aware that they were losing custom to the non-endowed schools and academies which were often offering instruction in more utilitarian subjects. So, although Latin was to remain the major element in a grammar-school education until well into the

nineteenth century, some of the grammar schools, facing the realities of
the post-Restoration world, offered a wider range of subjects. Dartford
Grammar School, founded in 1679, employed two masters: one to teach
Latin, the other English, mathematics, and, as befitted a school in that
town, navigation (by 1700 geography had been added to the syllabus).
Schools which were able and willing to adapt in this fashion often did
well. Thus at Manchester Grammar School of the 196 boarders and 476
day-boys who attended between 1740 and 1765, only 100 (of whom only
16 were day-boys) went on to university. The remainder went into trade
or commerce locally, and it is inconceivable that these youths had not
taken advantage of more utilitarian subjects than Latin.

But in general the grammar schools, so active before the Civil Wars,
seem to have entered a decline in the century after 1660. The reasons for
this are manifold. Although some, like Manchester Grammar School, were
able to adapt, others were clearly left behind as educational tastes
changed. Yet others declined in line with the overall economic decline of
the region in which they were located: schools in East Anglia, for example,
that great region of educational foundations in the years 1550–1660,
suffered hard times as the national economic centre of gravity moved away
from the east. Some schools suffered because the master was a pluralist
clergyman who allowed his school to fall into neglect, and some, as an
early nineteenth-century historian of the grammar schools put it, suffered
from 'the negligence or cupidity of the ignorant and unprincipled trustees'.
Yet it is difficult not to interpret all this as symptomatic of that general
change in educational priorities which we have traced with respect to the
universities: the Renaissance emphasis on the virtues of a classical education were passing away. If the universities were suffering as a result of
this, little wonder that the grammar schools, whose traditional function
had been to provide entrants for the universities, were also suffering.

It is difficult to assess how far these Renaissance ideals were ever translated into practice in the early modern English grammar school.
Conditions in the classroom must have been chaotic. The usual idea was
that all pupils in a school would be taught in one room, where the normal
teaching staff of two (the master and an usher) might find themselves
confronting as many as 140 boys. Some woodcut illustrations of school-
rooms survive and, if they are to be trusted, teaching must often have been
carried on in an atmosphere unconducive to reflective study. Boys were
taught in groups, probably one for each form, and one woodcut of 1592
shows how they might be scattered around the schoolroom doing their
lessons with or without the supervision of the master. This print also
demonstrates the range of visual aids which were used in the period:
pictures, diagrams, and even a music score are stuck on the walls.

The schoolmaster was a figure of authority, and this authority was
backed by frequent application of corporal punishment. The educational
theorists – Roger Ascham, Richard Mulcaster, John Brinsley, Charles

Hoole, Christopher Wase and the rest – were insistent that schoolmasters should be men of high quality and considerable dedication who should teach through encouragement and example. For such men corporal punishment, as an aid to discipline and an antidote to idleness, should only be used a last resort. But here as elsewhere, the gap between the recommendations of educational theorists and actual practice in the class-room was a wide one. Many schoolmasters, to use the contemporary expression, were 'insufficient', and had far too ready a recourse to the rod. Brinsley, writing in 1622, thought that over-severe discipline alien-ated children while at school, and that in later years former pupils might claim that 'by our blowes they were made dunses or deafe ... or to hate all learning'. As Ascham recorded in the preface to his *Scholemaster*, the idea of writing it first came to him when news reached a dinner party he was attending in 1563 that 'diverse scholars of Eaton, be runne awaie from schole, for feare of beating'. Despite the presence of humane figures at the top of the teaching profession, most contemporaries were agreed that regular beating was an intrinsic part of the schooling process. A former pupil of Eton, writing about a century after Ascham's dinner party, commented that at that establishment 'many a brave and noble spirit there has been broken' by brutal corporal punishment. Part of the problem was a complete lack of teacher-training: as Brinsley remarked, 'so few of those who undertake the function, are acquainted with any good method, or right order of instruction, fit for a grammar school'. Even if they were, it would still probably have been an exceptional teacher who, helped only by an usher, could impose order on a room of more than 100 boys.

Conflict between master and pupils was always latent and, during this period, was sometimes allowed to express itself ritually through the process known as 'barring out', 'shutting out', 'penning out', or simply 'the exclusion'. This custom, apparently well known by the mid-sixteenth century, normally took place just before Christmas, or sometimes at Shrovetide. It was fundamentally a ritualized, sometimes very tamed, safety-valve through which the pupils were allowed to let off steam. The teacher would be excluded from the school, and the pupils would meet together, formulate their demands over holidays and conditions within the school, and pass them to the master for his consideration. These displays of pupil power do not normally seem to have been very threatening or particularly rowdy: it was apparently not unusual for the governors to come and watch the barring-out, after which a feast might be held or refreshments provided. At times, conversely, things could get out of hand. At Manchester Grammar School, the pupils were reputed to have held the school for a fortnight in the 1690s, aided by the townspeople who provided them with food and firearms. At King Edward's School, Birmingham, attempts to end the custom resulted in a serious disturbance in 1667 in which the scholars, again aided by local townspeople, not only excluded the master but also threatened to kill him. A master at Coventry was shot in the leg during a barring-out in 1629, while a master at Shrewsbury was wounded in the course of another in 1671. Despite such excesses, and occasional attempts at suppression, the custom continued, perhaps most strongly in the north of England, until well into the nineteenth century.

As barring-out suggests, the everyday experience of schooling was rarely as orderly and disciplined as the writers of books on education would have hoped. In reality, few schools can have been those centres of godliness, discipline and sound learning which contemporary theorists prescribed. Some were very remote from the ideal. Sir John Bramston remembered such an establishment when he described his schooldays in the early 1620s at Blackmore in Essex. The master there was a 'popular preacher', the local vicar. Bramston recalled he was 'a very meane superficiall schollar, and I believe did his best', but he was incapable of giving his pupils a sound grounding in grammar, 'the want thereof was a great miserie to me ever after'. The master was a violent man 'of a temper very unfitt for a scholemaster', who was 'like a furie to wife, children, servants, schollars, all the house'. Despite his being a much admired preacher and 'a great pretender to sanctitie and religion', he encouraged his pupils to rob ponds of fish, and to kill the pigeons of his neighbours. It is little wonder that when the young Bramston wrote home describing conditions at this school, his father quickly removed him and his brother, and sent them to a more suitable establishment.

The Reformation had given the endowed grammar schools a tremendous impetus. Although the chance to achieve something approaching universal male education, which at least some enthusiasts were advocating at the time, was lost in the reign of Edward VI, it is obvious that the Dissolution of the Monasteries and the later Dissolution of the Chantries were not disasters for English education. Although the opportunity to turn massive resources over to education were lost, a number of new schools were founded out of the spoils of the plundered church, while proponents of the new religion were only too willing to invest in Protestantism's future by endowing grammar schools. Indeed, by 1708 a commentator felt that the Tudor founders of grammar schools 'began to run into a sort of excess and almost bordered on the former superstition of founding cells and monasteries'. But by that date, as we have noted, fashions in what would now be described as secondary education had changed: there were other objectives than the entry into the priesthood which eight years in a grammar school and seven years at university prepared boys for.

By the late seventeenth century the alternatives to the grammar school were becoming increasingly attractive. Parents were sending their sons increasingly to private academies, where they would acquire not only a knowledge of Latin grammar, but also a grounding in more utilitarian subjects, as well as such accomplishments as riding, fencing and dancing. In a sense, therefore, these academies constituted an educational advance:

they offered a more 'useful' curriculum than did the grammar schools. Conversely, they contributed to that process of social exclusiveness which we have already seen developing in the universities and in many grammar schools. By 1760, accordingly, many grammar schools were in decline, others had become the preserve of the privileged, and the growth of the academies and other private institutions had done nothing to alleviate the lot of children barred from formal education because their parents could not afford to meet its costs. But many children of the lower orders, either through good luck or high motivation, were acquiring literacy and an education which sometimes went beyond the basic.

Literacy and education: the wider picture

Measuring literacy in the past is another of those statistical exercises which is beset by problems. Literacy is, moreover, in many respects a relative concept: it is rarely an abstraction, but rather something which should be measured against specific needs. Even so, there is every indication that literacy was increasing steadily throughout our period. The most usual method of measuring this process is by counting how many people had the ability to sign their name at any given point. There are several problems with this method: a person might, to take the most obvious of them, be able to sign their name, but otherwise unable to read or write. Doubts on this point are, however, stilled by the educational textbooks of the period and such autobiographical details of early schooldays as have survived from them. These agree that reading was normally taught before writing, so that most of those able to write their name would have acquired basic literacy before being taught that accomplishment. Moreover, lists of signatures are the only sources we possess which allow us to measure changes in literacy over time, between social groups, and between the sexes: at least when we compare the ability of various groups of our ancestors to sign their names, we compare like with like. We do not know how many of those who could make their signature could also master Newton or Milton, or how many of them could do little more than puzzle their way through a chapter of the Bible or a popular ballad: but the ability to sign does at least provide a concrete basis from which to discuss changes in literacy.

Recent research, notably David Cressy's, has demonstrated the pace and extent of the rise in literacy. Overall figures must be accepted for the approximations that they are, while it should be noted that the process was not one of steady advance: in particular, there was a stagnation in the period c.1590–1615 when, interestingly, admissions to the universities also lost their buoyancy. Yet the general pattern of advancing literacy is clear enough. In the mid-sixteenth century, perhaps 20 per cent of men and 5 per cent of women could sign their names; by the mid-seventeenth century, this accomplishment had been learnt by 30 per cent of men and 10 per cent of women; by about 1715 the proportions had risen to 45 per cent of men and 25 per cent of women; while by 1760, some 60 per cent of men and 40 per cent of women were able to sign their names.

Naturally enough, these overall figures mask some important geographical variations, although these were fairly unpredictable. London maintained a high level of literacy throughout, but outside the capital variations did not follow any set pattern, and certainly did not fit any simplistic model of regional economic development. The signatures on various returns, petitions and protestations of 1641–44 illustrate this point. Norfolk was exceptional with 55 per cent adult male literacy, and there was a grouping of other counties in the south-east with above 30 per cent. Conversely, county scores of that order were by no means restricted to that area, while widely separated counties might have very similar adult male literacy rates: 28 per cent in Cornwall, 29 per cent in Sussex, 26 per cent in Yorkshire, and 28 per cent in Suffolk. Geographical variations in literacy, in fact, seem to have been less obvious on a county basis than between various parishes within the same area: the impression is one of isolated, even random, pockets of greater literacy against a background of high illiteracy.

Variations between social groups are easier to trace. The gentry and peerage were almost universally literate by 1550, and were to remain so. Literacy among the yeomanry seems to have increased, from about 40 per cent able to sign their names in the mid-sixteenth century to 60 per cent by the early eighteenth. Tradesmen, on a sample from the diocese of Norwich (admittedly an unusually literate area) were 20 per cent able to make a signature in 1530, and 65 per cent in 1710. Social groups beneath these were apparently denied any but a limited access to educational provision throughout the period. Husbandmen's ability to sign their names fluctuated between 10 and 20 per cent, and showed none of that tendency to increase which was so marked among yeomen. Literacy rates among the labouring poor were very low indeed.

Most commentators, indeed, were convinced that education was something which it was dangerous to offer too much of to the poor. Even the proponents of mass education were more concerned with promoting godliness than with liberating the intellectual potential of the population at large. John Brinsley, in his *A Consolation for our Grammar Schools* of 1622, stated what was probably the standard position. It was possible, and desirable, that a few men of exceptional talents might rise from the lower orders: but, for the most part, the masses, even if exposed to a little education, should be encouraged to follow the callings appropriate to their station in life. Otherwise, wrote Brinsley, 'we should be left destitute of husbandmen to till the ground and much more of meet supplies to furnish all other callings'. After the Civil Wars, the spectre of the world turned upside down meant that the education of the poor was seen as intrinsically risky. Edward Chamberlayne, in the 1682 edition of his much read *Angliae Notitia*, thought that 'the little smattering of learning got at the grammar schools' made tradesmen 'commonly proud, stiff necked, self-conceited, unapt to be governed, apt to embrace every new doctrine, heresy, schism, sect and faction': 'our late unhappy troubles' had demonstrated that letting such people into universities had even worse consequences. Even the allegedly radical reformers of the Interregnum did not see mass education as a levelling force. Samuel Hartlib's scheme for renewing English society through a national school system envisaged a rigid educational hierarchy. His schools were of 'four several kinds or degrees', of which the first was for 'the vulgar, whose life is mechanical'. The other three were for the gentry and nobility, 'who are to bear the charges in the Commonwealth', for scholars, and for 'the sons of prophets, who are a seminary for the ministry'.

Generally, educating women was seen as being as superfluous, and only a little less dangerous, than educating the male poor. As we have seen, women were excluded from the universities, the Inns of Court, and the grammar schools, a situation which provoked little adverse comment from male educationalists. The careers which these institutions educated men for, the priesthood, affairs of state, and the law were in any case closed to women. A few gems of Renaissance womanhood, such as the daughters of Sir Thomas More, Lady Jane Grey, or Queen Elizabeth I herself might be adduced by the apologists for women's education, but they were usually regarded as objects for wonder rather than patterns for emulation. The common attitude was attacked by Bathsua Makin, a proponent of education for women and the proprietress of a private academy for the education of girls at Tottenham. She remarked on how it was widely believed, 'especially among a sort of debauched sots', that 'women are not endued with such reason as men, nor capable of improvement by education as they are ... a learned woman is thought of as a comet, that bodes mischief when it appears'. Those holding such views regarded educating women, like educating lower-class men, as something which would subvert the natural order of things. As with the lower orders again, if education were to be given to women, it should be limited in its nature, and designed to fit their inferior station. Thus John Amos Comenius, the Czech educational reformer whose opinions enjoyed something of a vogue during the Interregnum, can be found agreeing with the general proposition that women should be educated in very limited ways. He held that women should be educated, for they, like men, were formed in the image of God, were often furnished with 'equal sharpness of mind and capacity for knowledge', and had on occasion been called by God to rule nations, and even to the office of prophesying and 'of inveighing against priests and bishops'. Comenius, however, rather spoilt his liberal position by stating that the object of educating women was not that 'their tendency to curiosity shall be developed', but rather that they should be directed 'chiefly in those things which it becomes a woman to know and to do: that is to say, all that enables her to look after her husband and to promote the welfare of her family'.

Education was not seen as a restricting rather than a liberating force purely in relation to women: as the insistence on the connection between schooling and the acquisition of right religion implies, there was a general feeling that education was one of the means by which a well-ordered state would socialize its subjects. Education was already seen as an agent of social control. Ascham, for example, wrote in 1570 that there was 'much presumption in youth, small authority in age, reverence is neglected, duties be confounded, and to be short, disobedience doth overflow the banks of good order, almost in every place, almost in every degree of man'. Education, Ascham insisted, was one of the remedies for this. Most other observers in our period agreed. Just over a century later, Robert Neville declared that 'the want of knowledge is an enemy to the peace of a kingdom', since 'ignorance makes men stubborn and mutinous'. In 1663 Marchamont Needham, in turn apologist for Charles I, Oliver Cromwell, and the restored monarchy, held that a strict early education helped keep people 'in obedience to their prince' and 'in a quiet and just demeanour towards one another'. In the early eighteenth century the supporters of the charity-school movement made their position clear: 'children are made tractable and submissive by being early accustomed to awe and punishment and dutiful subjection. From such timely discipline the public may expect honest and industrious servants.'

Against such opinions, the accounts that have come down to us of how members of the lower orders became literate sound almost subversive. Those who recorded what Margaret Spufford has called their 'first steps in literacy' have left a lively impression not only of the breadth of informal educational facilities which were available in early modern England, but also of a widespread desire for literacy among the lower orders. Oliver Sansom, born in 1638, related how he was 'put to school to a woman, to learn to read', a skill which he acquired rapidly. John Evelyn, the diarist, joined the other children of his native village for instruction in the church porch at the age of four. James Fretwell, son of a Yorkshire timber merchant, was educated in the early years of the eighteenth century. He was sent to 'an old school dame' who proved unsatisfactory, and was then taught the basics of reading by his mother, 'untill I could read in my bible'. He was subsequently sent to school, 'my dear mother being desirous that I should have a little more learning than she was capable of', and showed himself to be a precocious scholar.

Schooling was more readily available, and perhaps deemed more relevant by parents, to the children of yeomen, merchants and craftsmen. The children of the labouring poor and, to a large extent, of husbandmen were needed in the labour force as soon as they were strong enough to make a contribution to the family economy. Even many of those children who did go to school experienced an intermittent education, interrupted by the rhythms of the economy. William Stout, for example, remembered that in the rural Lancashire of the 1670s schooling was disrupted by the demands of agriculture. Boys aged 10 or 12 would be kept from school 'especially in the spring and summer season, plough time, turf time, hay time and harvest, in looking after the sheep, helping at the plough, going to the moss with carts, making hay and shearing in harvest'. Yet many plebeian autobiographers, like Stout, recorded how their parents, whatever their circumstances, were willing to do whatever they could to give their children at least a basic education. The point was not lost on contemporaries: a disgruntled royalist wrote in 1651 that one of many signs that the lower orders were getting uppity was that 'the cobbler will clout it till midnight, the porter will carry burdens till his back crack again, the ploughman will pinch both back and belly to give his son learning'.

This last comment reminds us that learning was widely regarded as something best reserved for one's son. Yet women, too, were showing a desire for education, and an ability to gain some sort of access to it. One remarkable development was the growth of the girls' boarding school. This had its origins in the early seventeenth century. There was apparently a 'Ladies' Hall' at Deptford in 1617, whose pupils performed a masque at the Jacobean court. In 1628 another institution on the fringes of the capital, Mrs Friend's school at Stepney, provided instruction in writing, needlework and music for an annual fee of £21. Such institutions blossomed around London as the century progressed, there being a particular concentration of them in the Hackney area after the Restoration. By then most large provincial towns would also have a girls' boarding school. But the education offered by these establishments was usually very much directed towards producing women in the conventional stereotype: although most offered at least some academic subjects, the emphasis was upon 'accomplishments' which would improve the young woman's prospects on the marriage market, and make her a more agreeable wife after her wedding. Moreover, the girls attending these schools were the daughters of the well-to-do: educational provision for the daughters of the lower orders was much less advanced.

Nevertheless, female literacy was increasing, and the chances of a girl receiving an elementary education were getting better. As early as 1581 Richard Mulcaster envisaged that girls would go to the local petty school as well as boys, and probably many had access to those informal local educational facilities to which we have alluded. As with the sons of husbandmen and labourers, appreciation of the need to educate girls might be limited, and opportunities might be denied or restricted by the demands of the family economy. But in some plebeian circles at least female literacy seems to have been taken for granted. Oliver Sansom, a Quaker yeoman in his adult life, noted that his wife was of 'a good yeomanry family and had been brought up in a sober and suitable way of education', while her relatives were 'greatly affected' with 'reading good books, the holy scriptures especially'. The literacy of his wife and her family allowed him to keep in touch with them during his lengthy spells in prison, and when he abjured his wife's company after contracting smallpox.

There were, therefore, a number of individuals who would help a boy or girl through their first steps in literacy. But many of these teachers were far removed from the standards prescribed by educational theorists. Teaching in a petty school, like keeping an alehouse, was apparently often thought of as a type of out relief, fit for 'poor women, or others, whose necessities compel them to undertake it, as a meer shelter from beggary'. Thus in 1661 we find John Bagford, 'a very sickly weak and impotent person, by reason whereof incapable to follow any other employment' than that of elementary schoolmaster. A little later we come across Richard Roach, an ex-sailor, who had suffered a broken back and other injuries while in the Royal Navy. Roach was 'forced to betake himself to keep a small school, thereby to assist towards the support of himself, his wife, and two small children'. The aid that these teachers could give must have been very basic indeed: yet they undeniably provided a service which was much in demand, and any talk of an 'educational revolution' has to address the significance of these men and women and their customers. Long after Oxford and Cambridge had ceased to be fashionable among the gentry, the lower orders in small-town and village England were evidently willing to spend the few coppers needed each week to obtain a grounding in the basic educational skills for their children.

The motivations behind this desire for education are difficult to assess, and in any case were probably very varied. For some workers, even those in basically manual occupations, literacy might have been seen as potentially useful. Once upward social mobility was seen as possible and desirable (and we have no way of telling when this occurred) education might be seen as a means to an end. Some might be drawn to literacy for religious motives, or were at least willing to turn such abilities as they acquired towards spiritual ends. Josiah Langdale, from an East Riding farming background, recounted how, in the late seventeenth century, 'I had not time for much schooling, being closely kept to what I could do in our way of husbandry ... I endeavoured, however, to keep my English, and could read the bible, and delighted therein.' Others read less edifying works purely for entertainment. John Bunyan who went on to read (and, indeed, write) better things, remembered how, as an adolescent, his attitude was 'give me a ballard, a news book, *George on Horseback* or *Bevis of Southampton*, give me some book that teaches curious arts, that tells old fables'. Others were motivated to acquire literacy by a simple desire to learn. There is no single completely convincing explanation of why individuals choose to become literate.

By the end of the seventeenth century, however, there was at least one body of opinion which was unwilling to leave the education of the masses to the sort of haphazard influences we have described. The Society for Promoting Christian Knowledge was founded in 1698, and rapidly set about encouraging the foundation of charity schools. Many were opened, with the support of the SPCK, by public subscription, with the intent of spreading Christianity among the godless poor. These schools were meant for the very poorest children, and a curriculum appropriate to their pupils' station was devised: reading and writing, with perhaps some elementary accounting for the boys, and sewing for the girls. The essential objective was to inculcate moral and religious discipline. The hymns the children sang, the prayers they recited, and the sermons they listened to all reminded charity schoolchildren that they owed deference not only to the Almighty, but also to their social superiors. The charity-school movement enjoyed a considerable vogue up to the 1730s, its influence being most marked in London. In 1704 there were 54 charity schools in the capital, with some 2000 pupils: by 1729 there were 132 schools with 5223 pupils. There were also numerous foundations of charity schools in the provinces. At York, for example, charity schools were founded for 40 boys and 20 girls in 1705, patronage being provided by the Archbishop, the Dean and Chapter, and the Lord Mayor and Corporation. The pupils were to be the children of freemen with unusually large families, or orphans. They were to receive free board and lodging as well as tuition, the assumption being that they would be apprenticed to local tradesmen at an appropriate age. That these York children were to be clad in distinctive coats, the boys in blue, the girls in grey, reminds us of one of the most lasting legacies of the movement to the English educational scene: school uniform.

Throughout our period, society at large was expressing a desire for education, and this desire was being accommodated in a variety of different ways. Among the rich, a son might be sent on the grand tour, or to a Scottish or continental university, or be educated at home by a tutor, rather than being sent to a university or an Inn of Court, these latter options still being open. The moderately well-off might send their sons to a traditional endowed grammar school, or might send them, as well as their daughters, to a private academy teaching more immediately 'useful' subjects. The lower orders had access to what was almost an educational underworld, while even the very poor might be swept into the educational net by the charity-school movement. Many schools were in existence. In 1743 Archbishop Herring carried out his primary visitation of the diocese of York. This revealed that, out of a sample of 645 parishes, 379 (or about 58 per cent) possessed a school of some sort: 'charity', 'free', 'endowed', 'public', 'private', 'English', or 'petty'. By 1760, England had a very variegated educational system, of which the population made considerable use. Yet problems remain in interpreting this: in particular, the links between educational provision and economic change and industrialization.

Even if there are doubts about the validity of the concept of an educational revolution, it is nevertheless obvious that England made considerable progress towards being a more educated and more literate society between the mid-sixteenth and mid-eighteenth centuries. It could, therefore, be argued that the English as a nation were becoming more educated and literate at the same time as their economy was becoming increasingly commercialized. But though this can be asserted in general terms, it is difficult to demonstrate it in any precise way, and the exact nature of the links between increased educational provision and economic change are elusive. As we have seen, economic motivations were not the only, or even the most important, ones which made people desire education. Conversely, although it can be argued that commercialization and later industrialization created many jobs to which literacy was essential, these processes also created many others to which it was not.

Different individuals and different groups in society obviously had different reasons for wanting education for themselves, for their sons, even for their daughters. Even so, there were a number of factors other than economic ones which provided the context within which they made their decisions about education. The desire in official circles that the masses should acquire godliness through education, and the wish of many individuals to read the word of God themselves, was probably a greater incentive towards educational expansion. Certainly, several countries much less economically developed than England, notably Sweden and Scotland, enjoyed much higher literacy rates than England by the eighteenth century, mainly because of the energies of their clergy. Likewise, the growth of the state placed a growing premium upon literacy. From the Middle Ages, the employment of bureaucrats and the keeping of written records by the state's administrative machine not only provided a career avenue for the literate, but also created a familiarity with the written word, and perhaps a need for literacy, among the population at large. We can sense something of this in the evident exasperation of a group of Cambridgeshire villagers who in 1579 complained that their parson, among other irritations, had made his brother parish clerk, 'whoe is unlearned at all, and we think him not sufficient to serve that place'. And among the Tudor and early Stuart élite, it was fashion as well as job opportunities in the state which made the acquisition of a classical education so desirable. Yet it is undeniable that the decline of those great centres of non-utilitarian education, the universities and the grammar schools, was setting in just when the commercial life of the nation was quickening. In general, the link between increased educational provision and economic advance, although clearly not to be taken simplistically, is undeniable, and it is possible that for some people the desire for education was linked with a desire to take advantage of the opportunities offered by an ever more complex economy.

But we must beware of looking at the problems of education and literacy from a twentieth-century viewpoint. People who write history books and, in general, the people who read them, have normally attained a fairly high level in the educational system. They are, therefore, generally convinced that formal education is a good thing, of great benefit to both the individual and to society, however difficult it may be to describe those benefits in precise terms. Conversely, in the early modern period many people were able to cope perfectly happily with life despite being illiterate, or at best only partially literate. For most people, even in the eighteenth century, literacy and education were things which were conceived of in functional terms, things from which skills appropriate to the needs of the individual concerned might be derived. This education at the grass-roots had little place in the discussions of educational theorists of the period, and was far removed from the world of Oxford and Cambridge. Yet there were many people who remained indifferent to schooling even of this informal nature. Above all, people were capable of rational action, of acquiring and digesting information, without literacy or formal education. Illiteracy was not, even in 1760, a bar to economic advancement. Nor was it any impediment to common sense. Most people, most of the time, could survive happily enough in a predominantly oral culture, with its own traditions and tales, proverbs and jokes, customs and ceremonies. Even for those who had taken their first steps in literacy, it seems likely that this oral culture was of greater importance than the literate culture on a day-to-day basis.

Notes

1 Mark H. Curtis, 'The alienated intellectuals of early Stuart England', *Past and Present*, 23 (1962), pp. 25–43.
2 Lawrence Stone, 'The educational revolution in England, 1560–1640', *Past and Present*, 28 (1964), p. 68.

|11|

Culture, popular and élite

In 1976 the author of a book on the English Baroque opened her work by castigating her colleagues: 'historians are notorious,' she wrote, 'for their ability to shirk fundamental issues, and nowhere has this ability been made more manifest than in their reluctance to write histories of culture.'[1] This reluctance is quite understandable. Explaining cultural developments is a peculiarly difficult task. There are the problems of deciding what exactly cultural history embraces, of developing appropriate methodologies for approaching it, and those arising from the awareness that many aspects of the subject are the field of specialist research. Any account of cultural developments must involve simplification, yet the historian must remain cautious about lumping a number of varied, even contradictory, artistic styles and individual artists together under some umbrella term like 'Renaissance' or 'Baroque'. Nevertheless, the historical description of any society will be incomplete if it ignores that society's characteristic forms of self-expression. At one level, the influence of the existing social structure or level of material conditions upon the artist are obvious enough: even artists have to make a living, and are therefore dependent upon the society around them. But moving beyond this truism is difficult, not least because it seems that artistic developments at many times possess a logic of their own, a sort of 'aesthetic autonomy' which defies connection with trends in the socioeconomic base.

Yet more complications arise from the tendency of historians to interpret culture in an increasingly less limited way. Recently, they have been attracted to an anthropological definition of culture. This definition is very wide: it incorporates the whole context within which the individual human being exists. Thus to Bronislaw Malinowski the word 'culture'

> comprises inherited artefacts, goods, technical processes, ideas, habits and values. Social organization cannot be really understood except as part of culture; and all special lines of inquiry referring to human

activities, human groupings and human ideas and beliefs can meet and become cross fertilized in the comparative study of cultures.[2]

It is a society's culture, in this broad sense, which transforms the individual into a member of an organized group, and it is culture which provides continuity if a group survives. Culture in this sense includes not only artefacts and buildings, but also religious beliefs, customs, and those bodily and mental habits which work, however indirectly, towards the fulfilment of social and individual needs. It is culture which makes society possible, because it provides individuals with a common knowledge and a set of common expectations about how they ought to behave towards each other. Culture, in its anthropological sense, is essentially the organized behaviour of humankind.

When the first edition of this book was published, I noted that some historians had already begun to try to study behaviour in the past in these terms, and it is possible that work could be carried out on early modern social history using the anthropological definition of culture as an organizing theme. Anthropology has indeed continued to inform early modern history, but it has perhaps been more important as constituting one of the major influences on a new sub-discipline which has emerged in the 1980s and 1990s, cultural history. Those considering themselves to be exponents of this new approach to history have been a little reticent in defining exactly what this term means and have, in fact, celebrated the conceptual and thematic eclecticism which seems to characterize it. Its subject matter does appear to begin with an awareness of 'culture' defined in more or less anthropological terms, that is as a generalizing force in society rather than something in which the élite are concerned. Conceptually, the framework of this new cultural history would seem to flow from two main sources. The first of these is French. In 1929 the historical journal *Annales* was founded, and from the 1930s a number of historians, including many in the English-speaking world, were influenced by the writings of the so-called 'Annales School': in effect a loose grouping of French historians who were responsible for major advances in, especially, approaches to social history. One of their main areas of interest was the history of *mentalité*, a term which it is difficult to translate into English, but which entails the study of the mental world of people living in the past. Equally, there has been, largely under the influence of historians from the United States, an interest in more recent social theory, most obviously recent writings in anthropology, in linguistic theory, and the challenges to accepted historical method supposedly posed by the French philosopher Michel Foucault.

Although the arrival of this 'new' cultural history has to be noted, what it will add up to remains problematic. Obviously any serious widening of the intellectual debate within the discipline should be welcomed but, on our current understanding of its main features, two major problems remain with cultural history as currently practised. The first is a concern about the theoretical eclecticism of the exponents of the new cultural history. Perhaps the basic problem here is that, since the discrediting of Marxism or, perhaps more accurately, the extension of social historians' interests to area where Marxism does not provide a helpful conceptual framework, those interested in the interplay between history and social theory have lacked a unified frame of approach. The idea of an 'intellectual tool-box', from which the historian can take and use different social theory when and as appropriate for different tasks might be a useful one, but it does mean that there is nothing like the intellectual coherence which Marxism, whatever its faults and limitations, provides. For example, as one of the leading French exponents of cultural history, Roger Chartier, has commented, there is a basic cleavage between the use of American symbolic anthropology in writing history and the models provided by French sociocultural history. Second, cultural historians, in exploring the mental world of people in the past, seem to be doing what a fair number of social historians have long been doing anyway. There is, perhaps, more use of theory, and as a consequence more use of technical terminology, but a number of the approaches to the past now being championed by Anglo–American cultural historians have for some time been familiar to readers of historians from the 'Annales School', from a number of other European traditions, and from at least some historians from the English-speaking world.

At its best the new cultural history does both challenge orthodoxies about the mental world of the past and emphasize the importance of that world. If we may quote Roger Chartier:

> Structures of the mental world are not an objective given, any more than intellectual and psychological categories. They are all produced historically by the interconnected practices – political, social and discursive – that construct their figures. It is such differentiations and the schemata that fashion them that are the objects of a cultural history that has come to rethink completely the relation traditionally postulated between the social realm (identified with a very real sort of reality, existent in itself) and the representations that are supposed to reflect or distort it.[3]

As we have noted when discussing anthropological perspectives, a more overtly theoretically informed approach to the history of 'culture' might lead to a fundamental rewriting of history. If, however, we may return to a less grandiose level, we find that historians of early modern England have become increasingly familiar with and had their approach to the period informed by the notion of popular culture, a concept which impinges upon the anthropological definition of culture at many points. Yet studying this popular culture is itself beset by many difficulties. The most obvious of these are evidential: this popular culture was predominantly oral, and hence is now largely lost to us: even its festivals and ceremonies are essentially impermanent. The historian of popular culture is dependent upon scattered evidence, much of it filtered through hostile or indifferent sources. A great deal of what we know about early modern popular culture has come to us via the strictures of Puritan or gentry observers, or in the form of incidental details found in court records or diaries. An even bigger problem, perhaps, is the definitional one. As far as I can see, no totally adequate definition has yet been produced of what 'popular culture' actually was. Most commonly it is regarded as some sort of residual category, as the unofficial culture, as the shared attitudes, values and assumptions of non-élite groups. This is probably an adequate working definition but, as we shall see, it leaves a few complications unresolved.

Popular culture: an exploration

If culture is an expression of shared values, it is perhaps logical to begin our analysis of popular culture by examining expressions of common sociability. The most important of these, for many communities, was the parish feast, known variously in different parts of the country as the wake, the revel or the ale. These were usually celebrated around the time of the feast day of the saint to whom the parish church was dedicated, with the Sunday after that anniversary initiating a week of celebrations, although there were also significant groupings of wakes in the late spring and early summer, and the first half of the autumn. These feasts were accompanied by 'all sorts of rural merriments', which might involve communal eating and drinking, races, dancing, all sorts of local sporting contests and such pastimes as bull-baiting. They constituted a regular focus for community life over the whole of the period with which we are concerned: the wakes described by gentry observers in the mid-eighteenth century were manifestly the descendants of those parish ales which the Puritans had tried so hard to eradicate.

Sentiments of communal solidarity were also expressed in the regular round of calendar customs. Although the modern idea of Christmas is essentially a Victorian invention, the festival had already acquired a largely secular character: as an observer put it in 1754, 'with the generality Christmas is looked upon as a festival in the most literal sense, and held sacred by good eating and drinking'. Christmas, traditionally, was followed by 12 days of celebration. Lords of misrule presided in the houses of the great, in counties as far apart as Yorkshire and Oxfordshire mumming plays and ritual dances were performed, while wassailing took place in Somerset. There were also celebrations on New Year's Night, and on the first Monday after Twelfth Night, still known as Plough Monday.

As John Aubrey remarked, notwithstanding the 'change in religion', the plough-boys 'will keep up and retaine their old ceremonies and customes and priviledges', which meant that in many places they dragged a plough around the parish on Plough Monday, demanding food and drink or money, and performing mumming plays or dances.

Easter was not generally celebrated so enthusiastically, although Shrove Tuesday was one of the big occasions in the traditional calendar, being regarded as the great holiday for apprentices. May Day, on the other hand, was the occasion of widespread celebrations, many of them sufficiently indecorous to have attracted adverse comment from the Puritans. Similarly, Whitsun was a great popular holiday, and was still the occasion for the parish ale in many villages in the late eighteenth century. Midsummer's Eve was celebrated in many areas, at times in a somewhat macabre fashion: there was a tradition that those sitting in the church porch throughout Midsummer's Night would see the apparitions of those members of the parish who were going to die over the next 12 months come knocking on the church door. The early summer witnessed sheep-shearing and attendant festivities in many areas (Aubrey noted them 'on the downes in Wiltshire and Hampshire'), while the onset of autumn was marked by harvest-home festivals, when 'a barell of good beer is provided for the harvestmen, and some good rustique cheer'. November brought Guy Fawkes' Day, the subject of popular celebration very quickly after 1605, while by December preliminary festivals for Christmas were celebrated: on 6 December, for example, many schools took a holiday in honour òf St Nicholas, the patron saint of schoolboys.

For most of the lower orders, England was only merry on selected and well-separated occasions. Nevertheless, these feasts and customs not only provided an occasion for general enjoyment and the letting-off of steam, but also gave the lower orders a sense of the rhythm of the world in which they lived, and perhaps helped foster a sense of belonging. Similar functions were performed by those customs which attended the rites of passage of birth, marriage and death. These were imbued with those magical beliefs which are discussed at length in the next chapter. Christening was still regarded as a quasi-magical rite essential to the child's welfare, while the ceremony of churching had obvious parallels with the post-natal purification rites recorded in many non-Christian and pre-Christian cultures. A christening was also an appropriate occasion for celebration, when the women of the parish might 'bring their cakes at a gossiping', or when godparents might bring such gifts for the child as apostle spoons, porringers, bowls or mounted corals. Weddings were accompanied by all sorts of celebrations. In Oxfordshire, so White Kennett noted in 1695, running at the quintain was a popular sport at weddings, there being 'seldom any public wedding without this diversion on the common green with much solemnity and mirth'. Some 50 years previously, Ralph Josselin, his Puritan sensibilities obviously a little ruffled, noted attending 'a strange vaine wedding', where 'a poore man gave curious ribbands to all, gloves to the women and the ringers, yett there was very good company'. Death was attended with more curious ceremonies, many of them pagan in origin. Aubrey noted that when he was a boy in Wiltshire a penny would be placed in the mouth of the deceased before interment as a gift for St Peter, a custom which he thought was still current in Wales and the north country. He also recorded that in Yorkshire 'they continue the custome of watching and sitting up all night till the body is interred', during which time 'some kneel down and pray (by the corps), some play at cards, some drink and take tobacco: they have also mimic-all playes and sports'. Funerals might be accompanied by 'sin-eating', in which one of the poor of the parish, in return for a dole of food, drink and a few pence, would offer to assume the responsibility for the sins of the deceased.

Popular culture comprehended popular pastimes and recreations. Football was, by the early eighteenth century, already well established, although it was very unlike the modern game. A football match might be a contest spread over two miles of countryside, played by two teams of indeterminate (and often very large) numbers drawn from neighbouring parishes or from rival parts of the same village. Cricket was already acquiring a genteel following by 1760, as was bare-knuckle boxing, although the lower orders remained attached to wrestling matches, those forms of duelling with simple sticks known as cudgelling, backsword, or singlestick and, in the Elizabethan and early Stuart periods at least, archery. Less appealing (if a powerful corrective to any desire to idealize the pastimes of our ancestors) were those sports which involved torment-ing animals. Bears, bulls and badgers were baited by dogs, evidence of a low level of sensitivity to animal suffering. Further evidence of this was provided by the custom of throwing at cocks, the great Shrove Tuesday sport. This involved tying a cock to a fixed point with a string five or six feet long, and then charging all comers (three throws for two pence seems to have been the going rate in 1760) for throwing cudgels or broomsticks at it until it was killed, the dead bird going to the person administering the blow which killed it. Cock-fighting was another popular sport as, less distastefully, was horse-racing, while all classes also indulged in hunting.

The most common recreation, however, was going to the pub. By the middle of the sixteenth century the alehouse was an established part of social life. Legislators tried to regulate the alehouse; preachers fulminated against it; justices of the peace and parish officers eyed its customers with suspicion; yet the population at large continued to go to it. Many of the social ills identified by its opponents existed in reality: alehouses might be centres for receiving stolen goods, vagrants lodged in them, they were often the scenes of violence, prostitutes plied their trade in them, and they constituted an encouragement to poverty and a threat to family life. Yet they also offered the lower orders their sole recreational institution and, moreover, served a number of useful functions, as pawn shops or labour exchanges, for example. Thus the alehouse was not only a place to go and drink, but also a location where neighbourly and communal solidarities might be reaffirmed. Aubrey, for example, noted that in one North Yorkshire village it was 'the custom for the parishioners after receiving the sacrament, to goe from the church directly to the ale house, and there drink together as testimony of charity and friendship'. Ironically, the Puritan attack on the communal, 'recreational' functions of medieval Christianity, and on country pastimes, had the consequence of making the alehouse more popular and more obviously a rival focal point to the church.

Another element of popular culture which was clearly discernible in 1550 was popular literature: pamphlets, almanacs, chapbooks, broadsides and ballads. Such materials were readily available in London, enjoyed ever increasing sales in the countryside through the activities of petty chapmen and, after the growth of provincial printing after 1695, might also be produced locally. The content of this literature was very mixed. Much of it was religious, while some of it, notably the almanac, was more or less utilitarian. Much of it, conversely, was clearly sensational in its tone, with descriptions of 'late horrid murders', 'monstrous births', or of such disasters as floods, earthquakes or fires. By the late seventeenth century, much of it was concerned with news, especially with accounts of or comment on high politics or foreign wars: the way was obviously being paved for the newspaper, which emerged in something like its modern form in the early eighteenth century. Overall, the salient feature of this popular literature was that it was normative, didactic, and supportive of the existing social order: on those rare occasions when social injustices were discussed, it was along inoffensively traditionalist lines, and even the sensational events which were so frequently described were recounted in the context of a conventional Christian world view.

There is thus little doubt that this popular literature helped reinforce what modern observers would think of as the irrational and superstitious elements in the belief system. Aubrey recorded many of these, as did Sir Thomas Browne, who in his *Pseudodoxia Epidemica* (1646) noted many 'questionable customs, opinions, pictures, practices, and popular observations' which were commonly held. This was a mental environment where superstition, although coexisting with and in large measure integrated into a traditionalist Christianity, reigned supreme. Aubrey showed how people generally accepted the reality of good and bad luck, and were therefore concerned with 'omens, portents and prognosticks'. Aubrey also discussed beliefs in ghosts, apparitions, 'knockings', the meaning of dreams, conversing with angels and spirits, plantlore, and traditions about Robin Goodfellow and fairies. Belief in these last was, it seems, widespread in the earlier seventeenth century. 'When I was a boy,' remembered Aubrey, our country-people would talk much of them: they were wont to please the fairies, that they might do them no shrewd turns, by sweeping clean the hearth, and setting by it a dish whereon was set a messe of milke sopt with white bread.

Here we catch a glimpse of culture in something like the anthropological sense: a total belief system, a way of looking at and explaining the world, reinforced by traditional stories and jokes, proverbs, and even the products of the popular press.

Not enough survives to permit a total reconstruction of this culture, or to delineate those sub-cultures which might form elements within it. Some occupational groups, notably ploughmen, shepherds and sailors, had their own customs and beliefs. There were also doubtlessly variations along the lines of gender. Women were debarred from many customs and rituals, and it seems to have been assumed that their role in many of the sports of the period was limited to that of spectator. But they probably had their own recreations, customs and circles of sociability. Unfortunately, sources dealing with female single-sex conviviality are more limited than those for male sociability, but there is little doubt that women did meet to socialize. Indeed, as no doubt with men, the sexual division of work meant that women came together in groups to carry out such tasks as raking, gleaning or milking, while the lack of a clear dividing line between work and sociability meant that they might indulge in broadly cultural activities while working. Certainly, contemporary jokes about marriage normally assumed that wives had their own circle of friends, 'gossips' as they were called, with whom the trials of wedlock, including any deficiencies in their husbands' performance in the marital bed, might be discussed.

Female bawdy outside marriage also found means to express itself. Aubrey recounted how 'young wenches have a wanton sport, which they call moulding of cockle-bread', in which the girls would stand on top of a table, pull up their skirts, and 'wabble to and fro with their buttocks as if they were kneeding the dowgh with their arses', reciting an appropriate rhyme while they did so. Aubrey also thought that women played a vital role in the transmission of popular culture. He was insistent that 'the women have several magical secrets handed down to them by tradition', and also held that 'in the old ignorant times, before women were readers, the history was handed down from mother to daughter'. Indeed, by the end of our period, much of the old folklore of fairies, magic, charms and omens was increasingly regarded as the territory of children and of women from the lower orders. 'She took so much pains from my infancy, to fill my head with superstitious tales and false notions,' wrote the ever urbane Lady Mary Wortley Montague of her childhood nurse, 'it was none of her fault I am not at this day afraid of witches and hobgoblins or turn'd Methodist.'

This observation catches one of the major cultural shifts which are supposed to have taken place in our period. In 1550, or thereabouts, popular culture, it has been claimed, was everybody's culture: the élite might participate in a learned culture as well, but the cultural forms and attitudes of the masses, their sports, belief systems and so on would be shared by the aristocracy and the remainder of the upper orders. Yet by 1800 the élite had withdrawn from the culture of the people, and had developed a distinctive culture (or perhaps number of cultures) of their own. The new concepts of aristocratic behaviour, and the growth of bourgeois susceptibilities which came some time after them, made members of the élite unwilling, perhaps even unable, to participate in the robust pastimes, the indecorous ceremonies, and the superstitious customs of the lower orders. As we shall see in the next chapter, this was part of a far-reaching change in the general intellectual climate: for the present, it is enough to note that from about 1650 participation in popular culture by a member of the élite was likely to be an attempt to gain or reinforce popularity, an adventure, or a precursor of what a later age was to know as slumming. By the mid-eighteenth century, Lord Chesterfield was advising his son to avoid 'common proverbs', as these were 'proofs of having kept bad and low company', while by that time more purposeful objections to some aspects of popular culture were being voiced. Such popular blood sports as throwing at cocks were attacked, a development with which the modern historian cannot but sympathize. Other targets of élite censure, such as the old-style football or the country wakes, although undoubtedly rough enough occasions, were more legitimate forms of self-expression by the lower orders, and it is significant that these were now offensive to respectable opinion.

Something like an organized campaign against popular pastimes, indeed, had already occurred in the period c.1550–1660. We have already noted the Puritan attack on the 'common country disorders': parish ales, country dances, maypoles and the like. This was part of the English dimension of an attempt to tame popular culture which was spread over most of western Europe, a taming which has been characterized as the triumph of godly culture, of Lent over Carnival. These 'godly' values were by no means restricted to Puritan preachers, but were widely diffused among the local élites of Elizabethan and early Stuart England. To these élites, some of the rougher aspects of popular culture, and especially those which involved an inversion of norms, came to be viewed as symptoms of disorder and hence as something to be suppressed. Nevertheless, there is considerable evidence of survivals, while many parsons, country gentry, and yeoman farmers tolerated or even encouraged the old customs. Thus when Nicholas Blundell, that Lancashire recusant gentleman, marled some fields in 1712, he not only gave a celebration for his workers at the end of the job, but also taught a sword dance to eight villagers to be performed there. Many of the festivities to which the Puritans had objected were still taking place in the middle of the eighteenth century. John Bridge, for example, collector of material relating to country life in Northamptonshire between 1719 and 1724, recorded that wakes were still being held in 198 of the 290 parishes he investigated.

Thus a vigorous and varied popular culture existed throughout our period. Many of its aspects – the heavy drinking, the frequent undertones of violence, the cruelty to animals, above all the sometimes almost total-itarian insistence on conformity – might well be repugnant to the modern observer. Yet this popular culture, together with religion, was vital in helping people to place themselves in the world around them, and in providing fixed or casual opportunities for recreation or festivity. The very resilience of this culture demonstrates its crucial importance in the life of the lower orders. Yet it was not static and immutable. Despite what those attached to the notion of a vague something called 'the traditional world' might think, popular culture is dynamic and changes: as Peter Burke has argued, the idea of an unchanging popular culture is 'a myth created by the educated townsman who sees the peasants [Burke is writing in a European context] as part of nature rather than part of culture, as animals rather than men'.[4] Tracing changes in preindustrial popular culture is an urgent item on the historian's agenda: certainly, some contemporaries were aware of change. Aubrey, to take a pertinent example, constantly refers to customs being 'rarely used in our dayes', and saw the Civil Wars as the great watershed in popular superstition. Investigation of changes over time, along with the differences between occupational groups, age groups, and the two sexes, will all be necessary before a fully rounded impression of early modern popular culture can be formed.

A limited renaissance

If popular culture has only just begun to receive attention from the gener-ality of historians, they have long been familiar with the élite culture of the Elizabethan and Jacobean periods. Throughout these periods (and, indeed, down to 1760) most artistic activity was carried on by local crafts-men, artisans and performers. These produced vernacular architecture, interior decorations, furniture and musical performances which often owed a little to outside influences, and which were probably often deeply rooted in the local, even popular, culture. Yet historians have tended to focus their attention on those at the top of the artistic ladder, and have made some extravagant claims for the extent and significance of their achievements. Befuddled by the old view of the Elizabethan period as one of glorious and successful enterprise, some have spoken of an 'English Renaissance', an era of artistic attainment which, by implication if nothing else, equalled those continental developments to which the label 'Renaissance' is more generally applied. Doubtlessly, the arts in the

Elizabethan and early Stuart periods did experience considerable advancement: an age which produced the greatest English playwright ought logically to have been one of more general artistic achievement. Yet few Englishmen of 1600 or 1640 would have argued seriously for any great pre-eminence of the arts of their native country: those best equipped to comment on such matters were distinguished by the avidity with which they acquired works of art, and ideas on artistic styles and cultural attitudes, from abroad.

It has been claimed that the sixteenth century was the greatest in the history of European painting. England contributed little to this, and English-born painters practically nothing. The English Reformation curtailed that ecclesiastical patronage which was to be so important on the continent: it could be argued that, given the iconoclasm of the reign of Edward VI and the early years of Elizabeth, the Reformation's contribution to English visual and plastic art was a negative one. The Elizabethan court was in many respects still medieval in its tastes, and outside of having their portraits painted courtiers showed little interest in painting. Even in portraiture the overwhelming influence was foreign. The first painter of note in Tudor England, flourishing there between 1532 and 1543, was Hans Holbein, a native of Augsburg. Later portrait painters doing well in Tudor England were normally European: Germans, Netherlanders or Italians. Their collective influence did little to found a native school of painting, and Elizabethan visual art was characterized by a fairly even level of mediocrity. There was little sign of individual genius and most painting was carried out by craftsmen painters. A major exception was Nicholas Hilliard. Born in Exeter around 1547, Hilliard had visited the French court, and had absorbed the more advanced continental styles. He was essentially a miniaturist, but the miniature portraits produced by him and his great rival, Isaac Oliver, did much to influence contemporary full-size portraiture.

The achievement in music was more impressive. Church music did not suffer as badly from the Reformation as did church decorations, a fortunate state of affairs epitomized by the most talented English composer of the mid-sixteenth century, Thomas Tallis. The next great name in English music, at one time an associate of Tallis's, was William Byrd. Similarly primarily a composer of church music, Byrd was a Roman Catholic, and his success under Elizabeth is a neat demonstration of how genius and royal patronage could protect the individual from the consequences of recusancy. The English church was not, however, to find its first true composer until the maturity of Orlando Gibbons in the next reign. Meanwhile, musical life was developing outside the church. A massive upsurge in secular music occurred late in the reign of Elizabeth, the crisis of 1588 apparently acting as a psychological turning point. Only one song book had been produced between 1530 and that date, yet 80 vocal collections containing between 1500 and 2000 pieces, most of them secular, came into print between 1588 and 1630. This period is particularly associated with the rise of the madrigal. Originally an Italian form, this was accepted in England during the 1560s as part of a more general vogue for things Italian, and later became fully anglicized. Another vocal form of the period was the 'ayre', a song performed to a lute accompaniment, John Dowland being the master of this genre. English music was therefore in a very active state between 1580 and 1620, and had considerable influence in northern Europe. Yet there is little indication that English composers were in touch with the most advanced influences, notably those of the Italian Baroque.

Significantly, the most marked advances were made in that most insular of the arts: literature. The century before 1660 was one of the great formative periods of the English language. By 1760 the conventions of English grammar, style, pronunciation and (despite some aberrations even in the best circles) spelling were very similar to what they are today. But in the mid-sixteenth century English was still an obscure and in many ways unformed language. Nobody but the English felt any need to speak it. Whereas the twentieth-century Briton or North American assumes that their language will be spoken wherever they go, Englishmen of the sixteenth century had to conduct their diplomacy, international commercial transactions, intellectual debates, and tourism in other languages: Latin but also Italian, French or Spanish. English writers were aware that their native tongue was of only marginal importance, and a number of them felt moved to justify the employment of English as a language in which intellectual or scientific matters could be debated satisfactorily. The foundation of the *Academie Française* in 1635 convinced many writers of the need for a similar body to set a uniform standard for English usage, and a number of schemes were proposed towards that end. But by about 1700 any feelings of linguistic inferiority were vanishing. English was, by that date, a less vital tongue than it had been around 1600, but it was fully adapted to provide the means of communication in a society where literacy was broadly based, in which the prevailing taste was for order, common sense and rationality, and where a large fashionable market for literature was emerging.

Around 1600, however, the most striking aspect of the English language's development was far removed from the measured rationality of the Augustan Age. Between about 1580 and 1620 a remarkable flowering of the English drama occurred. This is most often associated with the towering genius of William Shakespeare, but the Bard of Avon's deserved fame should not obscure the talents and importance of a number of other playwrights working in the period. There were Christopher Marlowe, Ben Jonson, and a number of less familiar figures, now best remembered in connection with the bloody revenge tragedies which were so popular in the period: Cyril Tourneur, John Webster, Thomas Middleton and their fellows. Together, their efforts made the 40 years after 1580 the most exciting the English drama has ever known. Yet the drama, for all the forcefulness and vitality it displayed, was essentially conformist in its tone. If its main concern was with the place of the individual in the social and moral order, its basic assumption was that such an order did, and ought to, exist: even the corpse-strewn revenge tragedies conformed to prevailing values in being consistent demonstrations of the triumph of the moral law. Moreover, this drama essentially reflected the values of contemporary élites, of the aristocrats who were Shakespeare's patrons or of the London merchants whose morality provided Jonson's basic frame of reference. Many English literature scholars have argued for the broadly based appeal of drama in Shakespeare's day, yet it is noteworthy that the lower orders rarely appear in his plays except as figures of fun or threats to social hierarchy.

A second great development in literature was created by the poetry of the two generations after 1600. The poets of the mid-sixteenth century were essentially minor figures, while the work of such Elizabethans as Spenser and Shakespeare, despite its value, did not demonstrate a full maturity. Arguably, this came with the metaphysical poets, notably John Donne. Another school was formed by the cavalier poets, Robert Herrick, Thomas Carew, Sir John Suckling, and Richard Lovelace, closely connected to the court culture which flourished under Charles I and Henrietta Maria. These were swept away after 1642, but the mid-century upheavals produced two more substantial figures: John Milton and Andrew Marvell. Marvell, as a poet, was the lesser of the two, and after the Restoration turned much of his energy to politics. With Milton, however, we have an artist of genius, a writer of great poetry and prose, a man who had a sense of vocation both as an author and a religious being and who managed to combine his Puritanism with humanism. We have only to compare his verse with that of Sir Thomas Wyatt to realize how far the English language had progressed in the century which divided the two men.

Milton was a convinced Puritan, writing during the ascendancy of parliament and Cromwell. Arguably, however, the biggest contribution to the arts in the early seventeenth century had come from the court. The courts of medieval Europe had always provided patronage for artists and acted as focal points for élite culture. With the Renaissance these processes became more marked, and even the splendours of the fifteenth-century Burgundian court were surpassed by the grandeur of the courts of Lorenzo de Medici in Florence and those of the houses of Gonzaga, Este and Montrefeltro in Mantua. England, as we have noted, was not untouched by these developments. Under Elizabeth the court, although becoming more bureaucratized, was still essentially an overgrown aristocratic household, and accordingly continued to act as a centre of artistic patronage. This was encouraged under Charles I, who was one of the foremost collectors of his age. As early as 1622 the Venetian ambassador reported that the young prince 'loves old paintings and especially those of our province and city', and Charles's reign after 1625 saw the steady acquisition of paintings and other works of art.

The conscious drive towards what might be described as 'art for absolutism' at the court of Charles I involved the talents, among lesser figures, of two great men. The more familiar of these was Anthony Van Dyck. Born at Antwerp in 1599, Van Dyck first came to England, probably at the instigation of Arundel, on a quasi-diplomatic mission in 1620. His major contribution to English culture, however, came after 1632, when he settled in London for a long period. His work, although restricted mainly to portraiture, meant that painting being performed in England was at last on a level with the best continental work, and his example and the encouragement he received from Charles and other patrons did much to raise native standards. Much wider talents were displayed by that other genius, Inigo Jones. Architecture in England had been developing steadily under Elizabeth, and the 'Great Rebuilding' of her period had produced a few noteworthy achievements. None of them could rank with Jones's best work, which includes the Queen's House at Greenwich, and the Banqueting House for Whitehall Palace, the ceiling of which was decorated for the glorification of the House of Stuart by Rubens. Further artistic support for the Stuarts came from court masques: Jones was responsible for designing the scenery and staging over 30 of these between 1605 and 1640. The masque was, in modern terminology, a multimedia event, combining drama, music, poetry, dancing and visual effects. Because of this, the masque made considerable demands upon both the taste and the expertise of its contriver. It also possessed an essentially political function: it was concerned with both the public image of royalty and with controlling public reactions to royal policy. The storyline of the masque normally took the form of the thwarting of an attempt to establish chaos, with a subsequent restatement of the virtues of order, hierarchy and loyalty to the monarch. But events after the summer of 1642 demonstrated the limitations of the masque's ability to teach obedience. The courtier poets were dispersed, the royal picture collection sold off between 1649 and 1652, and Inigo Jones dismissed by a parliamentarian newsletter of 1645 as the 'contriver of scenes for the Queen's dancing barne'.

The Civil Wars marked a setback not just for royal involvement in the arts, but also for the aristocracy's. As we have seen, the changing style of noble behaviour had encouraged courtiers to become connoisseurs, and by 1640 England could boast such collectors as Arundel and Northumberland. The Interregnum, although by no means the cultural disaster which it is sometimes portrayed as, and which some of the more extreme Puritans desired it to be, did not see much official encouragement of the arts. The attempts made by Charles to mobilize the skills of visual and other artists to glorify his regime through architecture, interior decoration, portraiture and the masque were not emulated by parliament or by

Cromwell: indeed, a scheme proposed by a group of painters early in the 1650s to produce a series of paintings representing parliament's achievements since 1642 aroused little enthusiasm. At the same time, aristocratic interest in the arts waned. Several of the leading collectors of the Caroline period had died or gone into exile, and those that remained, sensing the mood of the times, were comparatively inactive. In 1660, at the beginning of Charles II's reign, Louis XIV wrote to the French ambassador in London and asked him who the prominent writers and artists were in England: he received the answer that there were none. In cultural terms, the influence of England in Europe was minimal: yet the century which followed 1660 was to be one of the most fruitful periods which the arts in this country have ever experienced.

The triumph of taste

The most impressive demonstration of this assertion came in architecture. Inigo Jones, his work out of fashion anyway, had died in 1652, and English architecture lost direction. But his ideas and style enjoyed a dramatic revival after about 1715. In that year Colen Campbell published his *Vitruvius Britannicus*, a work which celebrated the Palladian style that had been Jones's inspiration, and which was to become fashionable in early eighteenth-century Britain. The style was based on that of Andreas Palladio, an Italian architect best remembered for his work in Venice. Palladio made considerable use of Roman models, and it was felt that the classical, indeed republican, values that these models were thought to represent were appropriate to the era of the Whig Ascendancy. The Palladian style, under the active patronage of such Whig aristocrats as Richard Boyle, fourth Earl of Cork and third Earl of Burlington, became dominant. William Hogarth commented acidly in 1753 that 'were a modern architect to build a palace in Lapland or the West Indies, Palladio must be his guide, nor would he dare stir a step without his book'.

Yet the impact of Palladianism should not obscure the massive achievement of the period 1660 to 1730, when a number of buildings were constructed in that very different style which is best known as English Baroque. This style is associated with three great architects. First, there was Sir Christopher Wren. After initially coming to prominence as a mathematician at Oxford, Wren later turned to architecture, at first as little more than a gifted amateur. But after 1669 he was virtually chief architect to the Crown, in charge of the Board of Works with its extensive building staff. It is doubtful if the extent and variety of Wren's executed works can be rivalled by any other architect. The second major figure was Sir John Vanbrugh. Like Wren, Vanbrugh had little architectural training: he always claimed, indeed, that he owed the contract to build his masterpiece, Blenheim Palace, to a chance meeting with the Duke of Marlborough at the theatre. He began his adult life as a soldier, and then became a writer of comedies, before turning to architecture. The careers of both Wren and Vanbrugh are linked to that of a third architect, Nicholas Hawksmoor. A more obscure figure, Hawksmoor became Wren's clerk at the age of 18, and subsequently became Vanbrugh's right hand man. He was Assistant Surveyor at Greenwich between 1705 and 1709, and later became Clerk of the Royal Works until his suspension in 1733.

The buildings associated with this trio make an impressive list. Wren's great achievement was St Paul's Cathedral. The destruction of old St Paul's in the Great Fire had made the rebuilding of the City's cathedral, and of other churches destroyed in the conflagration, a matter of urgency. The foundation stone of St Paul's was laid in 1675, and its structure was completed in 1711: few, if any, buildings of such magnificence were raised by a single architect in his own lifetime. Wren was involved in the rebuilding of the city churches, a process which also gave employment to Hawksmoor and another talented architect of the period: James Gibbs. Greenwich Hospital, built between 1696 and 1705, was worked on by Wren, Vanbrugh and Hawksmoor, and made a gesture towards an earlier age by being designed to provide a frame for Inigo Jones's Queen's House when viewed from the Thames. The universities contributed to the English Baroque, with the Senate House, built by Gibbs, at Cambridge, and Wren's Sheldonian Theatre at Oxford. The style also produced the two most visited English country houses: Blenheim Palace, the gift of a grateful nation to the Duke of Marlborough, built by Vanbrugh between 1705 and 1722; and Castle Howard, built between 1705 and 1722 by Vanbrugh and Hawksmoor. These and a number of other less magnificent structures make the years 1660–1730 one of the most remarkable periods in English architectural history. Yet despite its splendours, the English Baroque coexisted with a number of other styles. Quite apart from Palladianism, a number of works were executed in the old Gothic style. Horace Walpole's house at Strawberry Hill in 1747 pointed to a revival of the Gothic, while the house Vanbrugh built for himself at Greenwich in 1717, Vanbrugh Castle, almost defies having a stylistic label placed upon it.

In painting, the immediate post-Restoration period was dominated by Peter Lely. Born in 1618 in Westphalia of Dutch parents (his father was an army officer), Lely settled in England in the 1640s, and earned his living by painting portraits, notably those of a group of 'Puritan peers': Northumberland, Leicester, Salisbury and Pembroke. Business picked up after 1660. Lely became official painter to the Crown in 1661, and was later knighted. He ran an efficient workshop: some 500 portraits can be more or less attributed to him, while studio replicas and copies run into thousands. His successor was Godfrey Kneller, who came to England in 1674, having been born at Lübeck in the late 1640s. Kneller, too, was knighted, and in 1715 became the first painter in England to be made a baronet. Like Lely, he restricted himself to portraiture, and ran his workshop on production-line principles, peak production being 10 paintings a day. Landscape paintings, or those depictions of classical, historical or religious themes which were known to contemporaries as history paintings, were rarely produced in late seventeenth or early eighteenth-century England. The demand was for portraits. Partly, this was because of a widespread feeling that these were all English-based artists were capable of: there was a story current in the 1760s of a gentleman telling his son 'you surely would not have me hang up a modern English picture in my house, unless it were a portrait'. Second, as the output of Lely and Kneller suggests, the artists were making far too much money out of portraiture to feel compelled to experiment with different themes. 'Painters of history make the dead live,' commented the hard-headed Kneller, 'and do not begin to live themselves until they are dead. I paint the living, and they make me live.'

Understandably, opposition grew to such attitudes, and to what was increasingly regarded as a stultifying style. At the very end of our period the accession of George III, the first monarch with a real sympathy for the arts to sit on the English throne since 1688, heralded a golden age of English painting. This age was symbolized by the founding of the Royal Academy in 1768, and it is most readily associated with Sir Joshua Reynolds. Reynolds had returned from a visit to Italy (such visits were a necessity for aspiring English artists at the time) in 1752, and was laying the foundations for his later style. A more immediate challenge to the Kneller approach was offered by William Hogarth. He had been trained as an engraver, which was to have a tremendous influence both on his later style and his later popularity. He began by producing portraits, groups and conversation pieces, but later hit on what he described as 'modern moral subjects', and began to produce those series of narrative prints for which he is so well remembered: *The Rake's Progress* of 1735, for example, or the *Marriage à la Mode* of 1743–45. Although it is Hogarth's work which has entered the general cultural consciousness (our visual images of mid-eighteenth-century society owe almost everything to him) he was merely the most gifted of a number of printmakers who met an ever-increasing demand as the eighteenth century progressed. The gentry had their portraits, but shopkeepers and tradesmen liked to have a print or two on the wall. Art was entering the age of consumerism and mass-production: Hogarth noted that his prints sold most rapidly at Christmas.

Music did better in the Interregnum than the visual arts. Cromwell's enjoyment of music is well established and there was a lively musical life in the capital in the 1650s. Certainly, it was that decade which saw the introduction of Italian-style opera into England, an unlikely arrival in the period of Puritan ascendancy. The Restoration, however, witnessed an impressive flowering of English music. Charles II himself was musically inclined (one of the first services which Samuel Pepys performed for the House of Stuart was to convey the royal guitar across the channel), and after 1660 the Chapel Royal became established as the centre for English music. Its most famous, and probably most prolific, product was Henry Purcell. Despite the presence of a number of other good musicians, notably Jeremiah Clarke, Purcell left no obvious successor after his death in 1695, and English music did not assume its vitality again until the impact of George Frederick Handel. After working in various German courts, Handel first came to England in 1710, and was to spend the bulk of his subsequent 49 years there, eventually becoming a naturalized Englishman. His first love was opera, but his oratorios have made him the composer who left the biggest impression on English music. Yet it is ironic that this impression was made by a German composer who was an active proponent of an Italian art form, while it is indicative of the waywardness of English taste that Handel should be cherished in his adopted home at a time when the rest of Europe was coming to regard his compositions as outdated.

The ability to play music and sing was fairly widely diffused throughout society. It was one of the necessary accomplishments of the gentleman or gentlewoman, and was also widespread among sub-gentry groups. This has led, especially when Elizabethan England is being discussed, to some extravagant claims for a high degree of cultural unity: yet even in the sixteenth century, society was divided in its music as in most other things. Renaissance gentlemen were well aware that the lute and virginals were for them, and that the bagpipes, trumpet and other harsh-sounding instruments were appropriate for the lower orders. Nevertheless, an interest in music permeated all social groups. John Playford, the first English publisher to devote himself wholly to music, set up shop in 1651, and in 1655 published the first edition of his much reprinted *An Introduction to the Skill of Music*, the most successful of a number of such manuals which were printed during the later seventeenth century. Ownership of instruments was common among all groups but the very poor: thus in 1666 Pepys, watching the boats that ferried household goods across the Thames at the time of the Great Fire, noted 'hardly one lighter or boat in three ... but there was a pair of virginalls in it'. But by about 1700 music in England was moving away from being an essentially participatory activity towards something like the modern system of concerts and other forms of performance before an audience of cultural consumers. Concerts in the modern sense probably came with the Restoration, and by 1740 were a regular aspect of the attractions of that most famous of contemporary leisure establishments: Vauxhall Gardens. By that time, the commercialization of leisure was advancing, and something like the modern variety show was in existence: London audiences were regaled by Christopher Willibrand Gluck offering 'a concerto upon twenty-six drinking-glasses tuned with spring water, accompanied by the whole band', or Miss

Robinson playing the harpsichord with her feet. The way towards modern mass culture had been signposted.

Significant developments were also taking place in literature. The period 1680–1760 is often described as the Augustan Age, the age when English literature reached its highest level of refinement. This refinement is normally measured in terms of the attainment of a regularity of style, and of the ability to obtain sensuous or intellectual pleasure from the form of the literature, in large measure irrespective of its content. In certain respects, however, for all their undoubted polish the products of the Augustan Age seem less impressive than what had gone before. Sir George Etherege, William Wycherly, Sir John Vanbrugh, William Congreve and George Farquhar all wrote amusing enough comedies, but they were hardly capable of dramatic work on the same level as Shakespeare or Jonson. Whatever the good taste deployed by Ausgustan poets, they produced little that could stand beside the best work of Donne, Marvell or Milton: Pope entertains and occasionally shocks his readers, but he rarely moves them. But the great achievement in the literature of the period was the development of the novel. Various prototypes of the novel had been in existence since the Elizabethan period, but it first appeared in something like its true form in 1719 with the publication of Daniel Defoe's *Robinson Crusoe*. Defoe published a number of other novels in the early 1720s, and by the 1740s the form was firmly established by the works of Samuel Richardson, notably *Pamela* (1740) and *Clarissa* (1747), and of Henry Fielding, who published *Joseph Andrews* in 1742 and *Tom Jones* in 1749. With the novel, English literature began to gain wide recognition in Europe: Richardson's work, for example, influenced writers as diverse as Rousseau and Goethe.

More generally, the ability to put down thought in writing was higher in the early eighteenth century than ever before. The years between 1680 and 1760 witnessed the emergence of an identifiable and, in many respects, organized profession of writers, whose greatest encouragement came from that other great novelty of the early eighteenth century, the periodical essay. In 1709 Joseph Addison published the first edition of *The Tatler*, and from that date that journal and its rivals, the most notable of these being *The Spectator*, sought to spread the values of Augustan culture among the reading public at large. Yet despite the polish of many of these essays, one attribute which the writer of the period needed was toughness. The English literary world had produced more writers than it could support and, if French literature was tuned to the standards of the *Academie Française*, English literature was tuned to the standards of Grub Street. Many second- and third-rate writers tried to continue wars of words, or perhaps just scratch a living from writing, in garrets in the seamier slums of the metropolis: for them, life was precarious and the pretensions of the great writers of the age far distant.

Not all artists were eking out a precarious existence in Grub Street: some were doing very well indeed. On a European level, the early modern period saw a general rise in the social status of the successful artist. Certainly, by the late sixteenth century, artists figured regularly on what might be described as the 'honours lists' of European states. In this respect, as in so many others, England lagged behind continental practice, but by the late seventeenth century the successful artist could command both respect and a good income. Isolated examples demonstrate the latter point. Rubens (who priced himself out of the English market) received £3000 for his ceiling to the Banquetting House, Inigo Jones died worth £4150, the printer Thomas Guy, benefactor of Guy's Hospital, died worth £200,000, and Alexander Pope made something like £8500 between 1715 and 1726 from his translations of *The Iliad* and *The Odyssey*. The rise of a particular artist could sometimes be traced by the prices he was able to charge for his work. Lely, for example, charged £5 for a head and £10 for a half-length portrait in the 1650s, prices which rose to £15 for a head and £25 for a half length in 1660, and £20 for a head, £30 for a half-length, and £60 for a full-length portrait by 1671. From the reign of Charles I the successful artist might expect not only financial reward, but also a title. Rubens and Van Dyck were knighted by Charles I, Lely by Charles II, Kneller by William III, and James Thornhill, who painted the interiors of both St Paul's Cathedral and Blenheim Palace, by George I. Wren, Vanbrugh and Roger Pratt were among the architects who received a knighthood. By the end of our period, the successful artist might well pass as an honorary aristocrat, able to mix freely with the socially elevated.

By the time of Hogarth an artist's success might be gained by commercial attractiveness to the public at large. Yet for most artists success, or at least the initial steps towards it, depended on obtaining and retaining patronage. The English Reformation, as we have noted, ensured that the Church was to play a less active role than in some Catholic countries. The royal court provided avenues for advancement, although these were precarious and much less useful after 1688. Odd windfalls might come the way of the artist as the result of peculiar circumstances, as between 1731 and 1741, when Walpole spent £50,000 of the secret service funds on writers and printers, turning several promising talents into hack writers in the process. But by far the most common means by which artists attempted to advance themselves was by seeking the favour of a great man, and a number of the major talents of the age made their way forwards by calculated obsequiousness. Fortunately, the great were generally convinced that it was part of their function to patronize the arts, and usually prided themselves on having a good literary, artistic and musical taste themselves. This, however, created problems for the artist: the English patron might respect artistic genius, but they rarely displayed humility before it, and many artists had their creativity hampered or deflected by the caprices of their patrons. An extreme example was Sir John Vanbrugh while he was building Blenheim Palace. His plans were constantly being thwarted by Sarah, Duchess of Marlborough, who has been described as the average artist's nightmare patron. She was convinced that she knew better than Vanbrugh, and was almost neurotically hostile to spending money on the arts. Sarah was opposed to the whole idea of building Blenheim on the grand scale envisaged by Vanbrugh: the magnificent structure covering three acres, the enormous landscaped gardens that surrounded it, the long walks and avenues flanked by transplanted full-grown trees, the whole designed to be a source of pride to Britons and envy to foreigners. While the architect set about building his masterpiece, Duchess Sarah expressed her preference for 'a clean sweet house and garden, though ever so small', and did everything she could to obstruct and confuse Vanbrugh and his workforce.

But as mention of an operation on the scale of Blenheim Palace reminds us, artistic achievement in this period was not just dependent upon a few men of genius, but upon a whole army of lesser figures whom the great trusted to realize their schemes. Most building would not involve a Wren or a Vanbrugh, but rather local craftsmen, who would often build in styles grounded firmly in traditional forms. Some of these did very well. The exceptional circumstances of the rebuilding of London after the fire presented many opportunities to masons and builders in and around the capital. One who profited spectacularly at this time was the mason Samuel Fulkes. He was earning 2s 6d a day in 1664, but after the fire began to pick up small contracts, which grew ever larger, until he acquired two worth more than £3000 in the 1670s. The York firm of Etty prospered in the early eighteenth century, not least from contracts arising from the building' of Castle Howard, while a number of individual craftsmen attained prosperity from humble beginnings: thus William Caslon, one of the most famous printers of the mid-eighteenth century, began his career engraving gun locks. But for every celebrity there were hundreds of craftsmen and artisans, working not only on small projects but also on the great ones. Maybe 200 men were employed on the building of Castle Howard, while the building of Blenheim Palace, at its peak, may well have kept a workforce of 1000 active. It should not be forgotten that such structures were built not only by the sweat of a large and essentially anonymous workforce, but also took their toll in blood, broken bones – even lives. The accounts of the building of St Paul's, to take a well-documented example, contain numerous references to disbursements occasioned by industrial accidents. Between 1707 and 1711, £187 3s 10d was spent on fees for surgeons and apothecaries, £12 4s 6d was spent on coroners' fees and funeral expenses for those killed, £30 went to their widows, and another £35 was given to men who had been crippled.

Such casualties could at least have derived some satisfaction from the knowledge that they had contributed to the formation of a national artistic style. By the mid-eighteenth century, England was contributing to the wider European culture from the firm base of an established and self-confident artistic culture. This had survived the Francophilia of the Restoration when, as one contemporary put it, no dramatic performance seemed complete without a 'troop of frisking monsieurs'. It had survived the influence of Dutch culture after 1688. It was even, by the time of Pope, less slavish and more discriminating in its employment of classical models. The contribution of foreigners to the arts in England had been immense, the country had always been responsive to foreign vogues, and there was, perhaps, still a lingering sense of cultural inferiority in the best circles in 1760. Yet by that date something like an English style had evolved: aristocratic patronage had spread a common style in art and architecture, while *The Tatler*, *The Spectator* and the novel were spreading a polished literary style and what was consciously regarded as English attitudes among a broadly based reading public.

As was suggested at the beginning of this chapter, attempting to pull cultural developments together and relate them to social change is very difficult. Nevertheless, it is possible to delineate some broad changes over the period with which we are concerned. It is obvious that élite culture was better defined, and far more consciously adhered to, in 1760 than in 1550. Despite the standards imposed by Renaissance notions of gentility, it does seem that the notion of what constituted a man or woman of taste was much more developed by the middle of the eighteenth century. Moreover, this élite culture, these notions of what constituted fashion or good taste, was, at its highest levels, essentially aristocratic. It was this group which set fashions down to, and well beyond, 1760. As Hogarth's prints and the popularity of the periodical essay demonstrate, it is possible to discern the origins of a middle-class culture by the mid-eighteenth century: yet taste was established and fashions set in circles where social distinction, good birth and political power counted. The situation of popular culture, the study of which is complicated by so many problems of evidence and conceptualization, is more obscure. The old recreations, customs and beliefs seem to have been in decline by 1760, but it is worth pondering that the 'decline of popular culture', like the 'rise of the middle classes', is probably one of those phenomena which can be found in any period where historians seek it determinedly enough. Popular culture is something which changes, adapts and assimilates, and it would perhaps make more sense to approach its history in those terms rather than by using any simple model of decline.

It is, perhaps, in the study of popular culture that some of the biggest problems for future research and future conceptualization reside. As we have suggested, historians of popular culture have usually had to base their researches on scattered materials, in many cases the product of observers or institutions hostile to that culture. The nature of source materials provides even more problems when we attempt to turn to that most fascinating of subjects: the material culture of the middling and lower orders in the early modern period. There is no single method of analysing the relationship between material and social or cultural life, and here again the historian is confronted by a topic where the theoretical insights have been heavily developed in other disciplines, notably anthropology and archaeology.

In examining the material culture of non-élite people in early modern England, however, any theoretical problems have to be set aside in the face of a much more concrete one: that of a lack of survival of artefacts from the period, or even of pictorial depictions of, for example, the interior of the dwelling of a labourer's family. Probate inventories provide us with a basic listing of what people might have owned when they died, but it is difficult to reconstruct what cultural significance was placed upon the pots, pans, furniture and other utensils with which their households were equipped. Obviously, as wealth and consumerism spread among at least the middling groups at the beginning of the eighteenth century the possession of non-essential material goods increased: on one major sample of probate inventories, for example, between 1675 and 1725 the proportion of households with clocks apparently increased from 9 to 34 per cent, with looking-glasses from 22 to 40 per cent, with window curtains from 7 to 21 per cent. Such figures help support the economic historian's contention that early eighteenth-century England witnessed the birth of a consumer society, but it is difficult to understand what exactly this proliferation of goods and artefacts within the yeoman farmer or middling tradesman's house meant in cultural terms.

Indeed, the very history of housing illustrates yet further problems. The construction of houses by the nobility and gentry in the early modern period was a major phenomenon, and enough of these houses survive in good condition and are open to the public to allow us to gain some grasp of what life in them was like. Comparatively little attention has been paid to those dwellings of more lowly individuals which have survived from the period. Yet there is no reason to believe that housing as a cultural phenomenon or the allocation of social space within houses had any less import or cultural meaning in the early modern period than it has today. Certainly, enough dwellings survive to allow us to get a basic idea of floor-plans, while it would also seem that the two-storey dwelling, with chambers above an entrance hall and two or three rooms on the ground floor, became more common from about 1600 onwards. There was also a greater propensity to build in brick or stone, to make slate roofs, and to introduce chimneys in place of open hearths and air vents. There is also some evidence of improvements in interior decoration, even among the middling sort. A commentator on dwellings at Hatfield, South Yorkshire, at the very end of the seventeenth century noted that 'tho many of the houses be little and despicable without, yet they are neat, well furnished, and most of them ceiled with the whitest plaster within'. Obviously, more research is needed on the material culture of the poor and the middling orders of the period. What even these preliminary remarks demonstrate, however, is how cultural history interacts with economic history and, once we begin dealing with the availability and desirability of artefacts, not just with the history of manufacture but with the history of transport, design, consumption, taste and fashion.

And yet it is possible, by 1760, to see the early manifestations of a new cultural form: modern mass culture. By the middle of the eighteenth century people could decorate the walls of their houses with mass-produced prints; they could have their opinions, tastes and prose style sharpened by reading periodical publications; and they could forgo music-making at home in favour of going to a concert. Something was emerging which lay between élite and popular culture, and which was essentially the product of widespread literacy and widespread prosperity among the middling ranks of society: it is no accident that the Marxist interpretation of culture should regard the novel as a bourgeois art form. Nor was this trend confined to the capital: the general rise in levels of material culture and the origins of consumerism can also be traced in the provinces, particularly in connection with that burgeoning of urban life which set in about 1700. Local artists and craftsmen experienced a new impetus, and wood-carvers, stucco-artists, cabinet-makers, goldsmiths, coach-builders, clock-makers and other craftsmen producing fine wares benefited from the more refined taste of provincial gentry and town-dwellers. Broader evidence of provincial artistic vitality can be traced in such eighteenth-century developments as the emergence of a school of water-colour artists at Norwich, and the Three Choirs Festival, linking the cathedral towns of Worcester, Gloucester and Hereford. In their patterns of cultural consumption, as in so much else, the English were showing by 1760 how far they had moved towards the status of a developed nation. Indeed, they were confident that they lived in a new age, one which was more civilized and enjoyed a greater refinement of taste, than any which had gone before. Their country was experiencing not only an economic expansion, but also a cultural and intellectual one. It is to the achievement in the intellectual realm that we turn next.

Notes

1 Judith Hook, *The Baroque Age in England* (1976), p. 7.
2 Bronislaw Malinowski, 'Culture', in Edwin R. A. Selgin and Alvin Johnson (eds), *Encyclopedia of the Social Sciences*, 16 vols (New York, 1937 edn), vol. 2, p. 621.
3 Roger Chartier, *Cultural History: Between Practices and Representations* (Oxford, 1988), p. 14.
4 Peter Burke, 'Oblique approaches to the History of Popular Culture', in W.E. Bigsby (ed.), *Approaches to Popular Culture* (1976), p. 81.

12

Magic, witchcraft and natural philosophy

Religion, as we have seen, was of fundamental importance in explaining how people in early modern England saw themselves and the world around them. In this chapter we examine (in so far as they can be separated) some of the non-religious beliefs which people held. Our central concern is with that conglomeration of intellectual changes which occurred in the second half of the seventeenth century and which is known as the Scientific Revolution. There is a second, and connected, major theme: the decline of that category of beliefs called magic, and its replacement by that other category of beliefs which these days would be known as science, but which would usually be called natural philosophy in the seventeenth and eighteenth centuries. Arguably, the most important changes in the period covered by this book came not in the realms of economic or social structures, but rather in the intellectual field. Such a change is too important to be placed in a box marked 'The History of Ideas' and ignored by the social historian: as we shall see, investigation of this intellectual change involves considering phenomena as disparate as the village conflicts which underlay a witchcraft prosecution and the activities of scientific virtuosi operating under royal patronage.

An initial problem is that of defining magic. To do so involves overcoming modern rationalism, and accepting that ideas which seem ludicrous to us made considerable sense to our ancestors, and ought to be studied on that basis. There is also the in many respects insoluble problem of determining where magic ends and where science on the one hand and religion on the other begins. The type of Christianity being promulgated by English Protestant thinkers from about 1558 onwards was insistent that magical beliefs should be pared away from true religion. Thus there was at least a theological boundary between religion and magic, however imperfectly that division was grasped by the bulk of the population. On this level, the basic difference between magic and religion was one of control. People could attempt to contact God through prayer, but their attempts were purely supplicatory: God could not be coerced. Magic, conversely, was about the control and use of mystic forces. The magician understood these mystic forces and the remainder of the natural world of which they were part, and exercised control over them through this understanding. Unfortunately, much the same could be said of science. This also (and not least in the sixteenth and seventeenth centuries) was concerned with the understanding and, to some extent at least, controlling of natural phenomena. Most magic in England at this time was instrumental: it was directed towards specific ends, ends which might be positive changes (for example, transmuting base metal into gold) or simply protection (charms against witchcraft, for example). But magical acts and beliefs were not simply isolated phenomena: at all levels magic was integrated into a wider belief system, and it is from this that much of the difficulty in dividing magical from scientific beliefs derives. Our first step will be to examine this issue in greater depth.

The old belief systems

In the early sixteenth century, and over much of the two centuries that followed, the dominant system of scientific thought was that bundle of notions known as Aristotelianism. As the name implies, this system owed most to the thinking of Aristotle, but it also incorporated the ideas of other classical thinkers, notably those of Galen in medicine and Ptolemy in astronomy. These authors and later ones working in their tradition had provided the basis not only for a view of science, but also for a system of metaphysics, ethics and logic. In Aristotelian science the fundamental metaphor was an organic one, the dominant model was one of natural growth. Aristotelian cosmology was geocentric: the earth was the centre of the universe, and the sun and the planets revolved around it. The sun and planets existed in a separate world, incorruptible in their composition. On earth, where different physical rules obtained, matter was corruptible, and hence change might occur. All earthly substances were composed of a compound of the four elements: the heavy elements, earth and water, and the light ones, air and fire. Bodies tended to move towards their natural place in the universe not according to gravity, but rather according to which element predominated in their composition: hence heavy bodies moved downwards, while light ones, like smoke, moved upwards. In chemistry, change was explained in terms of alterations in the share that each of the elements had in the substance under consideration. There was not just a material change, however. There was also a change in 'substantial form': that is, a qualitative difference. Thus 'mechanical' change, in the sense of changing atomic forms, was precluded, and a 'purposive', almost moral development was thought to have taken place. This connected with the organic analogies which were basic to

Aristotelianism: substances and objects were held to have a moral capacity, almost a will, of their own when they behaved 'naturally'.

Despite mounting doubts with Aristotelianism, there was no real alternative to it as a universal system until Descartes published his *Discourse on Method* in 1637. It had, moreover, gained additional strength from being incorporated into Christianity. Some elements of Aristotelianism defied integration with Christian belief, but its moral basis, the ideas about final causes, tied in neatly with the theological concept that the will of God could be revealed in the working of the universe. Thus the Christian God, as reinterpreted by Aristotelian thinkers, was a kind of master logician whose premises could be explored through logical analysis. Aristotelianism was therefore the core of medieval Christian philosophical and scientific thought, was central in the teaching of most universities, Roman Catholic and Protestant alike, and received a tremendous boost in countries experiencing the Counter-Reformation by being adopted by the Jesuits. But by the sixteenth century Aristotelianism had ossified. Although many working in the tradition had carried out empirical, 'scientific', research, the dominant method of proof was not experimentation, but rather that curious form of oblique arguing, the syllogism. The syllogism was of central importance to that mode of thinking, arguing and teaching which was known as scholasticism, which was, in effect, simply the type of thinking taught in the Christian schools (i.e. universities) of the Middle Ages. By the sixteenth century some thinkers were coming to regard scholasticism as an outdated and constricting system obsessed with the sterile subtleties of the syllogism and expressed in bad Latin.

Yet the first challenge to Aristotelianism came not from experimental science but rather from another intellectual system which seems very odd to the modern thinker: Neo-Platonism. The teachings of Plato and later Platonic thinkers were little known in the Christian west until the fifteenth century, when they became increasingly influential. The Neo-Platonic tradition thought the material world 'unreal' because it was mutable and corrupt. It was, in fact, considered to be the last and lowest realm of existence: true perfection lay in the spiritual world. Matter was a link with this spiritual world, and the material world was thought to reflect the more perfect spiritual realities: thus there was a whole system of correspondences, with the earth, for example, forming a microcosm of the macrocosm of the spiritual world. By the sixteenth century, two other strands of thought had been woven into Neo-Platonism. First, when hitherto unknown manuscripts came west after the fall of Constantinople in 1453, European scholars became increasingly influenced by a body of writing ascribed to an apocryphal ancient Egyptian, Hermes Trismegistus. Hermetic ideas were essentially mystical. The world was conceived of as a place full of magical powers and hidden meanings, whose secrets might be unlocked by a chosen few. Such notions were bolstered by a second development, the absorption and Christianization of the Jewish Cabbala (literally, 'tradition'). It was thought that study of the Cabbala would reveal the hidden secrets of the Old Testament, and thus of the world, by the contemplation of cyphers. This ensured that even mathematics as practised by those influenced by Neo-Platonic ideas, was an activity which involved mystical contemplation as much as empirical calculations. Those wishing to portray the Renaissance as 'modern' or 'progressive' might like to ponder that its greatest direct contribution to western thought was to provide a massive reinforcement to magical and mystical beliefs.

Neo-Platonic ideas never replaced Aristotelianism as the official belief system, yet they enjoyed a considerable impact in Europe. Much of their attraction lay in their tendency to be idealistic and spiritually uplifting, in contrast to the sterile traditionalism of scholasticism. The Neo-Platonic scholar had to begin his work in a state of almost religious purity if he was to achieve meaningful results, and it was genuinely believed that such work would lead to a complete understanding of the universe, of those morally and spiritually perfect worlds of which the earth was but an imperfect microcosm. England, although essentially on the peripheries of European intellectual currents in the early sixteenth century, began to be affected by these mystic and occult ideas. Neo-Platonic works, notably Cornelius Agrippa's *De Occulta Philosophia*, appeared in English libraries from about 1550, and mystical and occult references, ultimately traceable to Neo-Platonic thinking, began to appear in the broader literature: Shakespeare's Prospero, for example, is a perfect epitome of a Neo-Platonic magus bringing order to an unharmonious and chaotic world. Even the Gloriana cult which surrounded Elizabeth I owed much to the Neo-Platonic insistence on perfectability. Protestantism joined the process. The more optimistic streak in English Protestantism, which saw the Reformation as an initial step towards a higher spiritual perfection, could easily connect with the idealistic Neo-Platonic striving for a greater understanding of the perfect world of the spirit.

The key figure in Neo-Platonic scholarship was the magus, the ascetic and isolated searcher for the truth. Elizabethan England provides us with a perfect example of the magus in the shape of John Dee. Probably of Welsh descent, and probably the son of one of Henry VIII's lesser court officials, Dee displayed many traits distinctive of the magus. He was unstinting in his devotion to the quest for knowledge: he recalled in his later life that as an undergraduate he worked 18 hours a day, devoting four to sleep and two to recreation and eating. He was also a polymath, pursuing wide-ranging intellectual interests. His most consistent field of study was alchemy, but he was also an expert in astrology and mathematics, and contributed to the medical knowledge of the day. His learning was firmly set in a European context. He went to the Low Countries to make contact with learned men there in 1547, studied at Louvain, and was offered a professorship at Paris. Later in life he travelled as far as Hungary, Poland and Bohemia, and achieved so much fame that in 1586 he was offered very remunerative employment with the Tsar of Russia (Dee refused the offer, although his son, Arthur, was to spend 14 years in Russia as physician to the Tsar).

Above all, Dee's activities show how far the scientists of the period were imbued with mystical and magical ideas. In his preface to Billingsley's translation of Euclid's works, published in 1570, Dee demonstrated his attachment to the Neo-Platonic ideal that mankind might rise to a state of revelation of the Almighty's purposes through the contemplation of numbers. Moreover, through his references to Vitruvius, Alberti and Dürer he showed that he shared the view of the human being as the *Imago Mundi*, the microcosm of wider ideal proportions. More dangerously, Dee and his associate Edward Kelly spent many hours trying to make contact with the angels and with other denizens of the spiritual world. These last activities fuelled the popular fear, so often encountered by the Renaissance magus, that he was a conjurer of demons. In 1583 Dee's house was sacked by a mob in his absence, and his scientific collection dispersed.

The nature of Neo-Platonic science, as well as the impossibility of separating scientific from magical thinking in this period, is demonstrated by alchemy. The main objective of the alchemist was to achieve the transmutation of matter, above all the transmutation of base metals into gold. But alchemists were insistent that theirs was no mere pecuniary endeavour. Alchemy was a philosophy of life expressed in chemical reactions. Its underlying notion was that everything in the world was alive and striving for perfection. It was, therefore, a deeply optimistic science, owing much to the Neo-Platonic concepts of the magus and of the possibility of unlocking the secrets of the universe. The alchemist saw himself as a spiritual thinker, pursuing truth on its highest level: thus Robert Fludd, the late sixteenth- and early seventeenth-century physician, alchemist and Rosicrucian, could write that 'the practice of vulgar chemists is nothing but a shadow and enigmatic image of true chemistry'. There was even a tendency among Calvinists to equate the master alchemists with those elected to God's grace. Yet alchemy, for all its peculiarities, made a real contribution to what the modern world would regard as scientific method. Whatever its underlying assumptions, the basic methods by which alchemic investigation was carried out were remarkably like modern scientific experimentation. The alchemist was working without thermometers or effective scales, but there was already the notion that exactly weighed and measured materials should be subjected to repeated and observed experiments at the same temperature. The debt of later generations of 'sooty empirics' to the alchemic quest was much greater than idealists like Fludd would have liked.

The practice of alchemy, dependent as it was on the leisure to acquire knowledge and the means to equip a laboratory, was essentially an élite occupation. Other areas where science and magic fused were not, and had a considerable popular impact. Perhaps the most remarkable of these was astrology. This was regarded in the sixteenth and seventeenth centuries as an exact science, virtually indistinguishable from what would now be called astronomy. Given contemporary ideas about the existence of different, but related, spheres of being, and of the microcosm and the macrocosm, it was self-evident that the movements of the stars and the planets should have an influence on human life. Astrology thus exercised some of the best minds of the period, and had a fair claim to being the most systematic attempt to explain natural phenomena according to the rigorous scientific laws then in existence. But astrology also had a considerable impact on the popular consciousness. By the seventeenth century handbooks were being published setting out the basic premises of astrology in clear and simple language, while astrological terms were passing into common usage. The most important medium for popularizing astronomy was the almanac. The almanac contained much of practical value, details of fairs, highways and phases of the moon, for example, as well as notes on such topics as medicine and farming, and a calendar. But it was also full of astrological information, and contained prognostications, involving political, religious and social speculations, for the year in which it was issued. The existence of a popular press and the spread of literacy ensured that almanacs enjoyed a very wide currency.

There was always a current of scepticism about astrology, and by the late seventeenth century, at the very point when astrological lore was enjoying its heyday on a popular level, belief in it among the élite, although never extinguished, was weakening. Nevertheless, astrologers enjoyed a lively trade throughout the seventeenth century. Some of the leading astrologers of the period wrote almanacs primarily to publicize their talents, and a few of them made a very good living. William Lilly, perhaps the greatest English astrologer, was reckoned to be making £500 a year in 1662, despite his custom of giving advice to the poor for a minimal fee or even for free. John Partridge, a writer of astrological almanacs who was heavily involved in disputes with Lilly, began adult life as a cobbler but died worth £2000. As such careers suggest, astrology not only offered solid financial rewards, but was also much in demand. Lilly, at the height of his career, might be giving advice to 400 people a year, and astrology was obviously an area where the élite magic of the Neo-Platonic magus made contact with the popular magic of the masses. Occasional tantalizing glimpses have come down to us of figures who connected the two worlds. Thus in 1687 the Essex JP Sir William Holcroft apprehended a female 'fortune teller' and her accomplices who had been living rough in Waltham Forest. Among her impedimenta were two works by Cornelius Agrippa, Reginald Scot's *Discoverie of Witchcraft*, and a treatise by John Gadbury, one of the period's most prolific authors of almanacs and popular works on astrology. Such figures, however rarely they surface in the historical record, raise important questions about the transmissions between élite and popular ideas on magic.

Insights into popular magic are impossible to come by other than on an anecdotal level; difficulties are further compounded by our knowledge of it being based on records kept by its enemies. Presentments before the Yorkshire church courts between 1567 and 1640, for example, include 117 cases of witchcraft and sorcery. Sixty-two of these are unspecified. Of the remainder, 18 were concerned with casting or lifting spells on cattle, and a further 18 with similar activities concerning human beings. The archives of other courts show the suppression of folk medicine, whose practitioners often used charms or magic formulae to supplement their herbal remedies, these in turn being prepared when the moon or the constellations were in their most favourable phase.

The writings of a few sympathetic observers afford wider insights into this world of folk magic. John Aubrey, to take perhaps the best example, described the common people as living in a world more or less imbued with supernatural beliefs. Young girls might use magic to ascertain the identity of their future husbands, pregnant women would go to the village wizard to determine the sex of their future child, the rites of passage of birth, marriage and death were all surrounded by customary practices whose roots lay in magic. For the poor or élite practitioner alike, magic provided a sense of being to some extent in control of nature, or at least created a feeling that the otherwise insoluble problems or uncertainties of a hazardous world might be overcome. There were sceptics at all social levels, and their comments sometimes provide instructive criticisms of contemporary occult customs and beliefs. Even so, the overwhelming impression is that the majority of the population, certainly before 1700, to a greater or lesser extent accepted magical beliefs as part of their world view. But two major issues arise from this assertion. First comes that of the connections and divergences between the ideas about magic held by the educated élite and those of the masses. And, second, there comes the problem of change over time and, in particular, of the retreat from belief in magic which, by 1760, apparently characterized the thinking of the élite. To study these problems further we must turn to an area where the changing belief system of the élite experienced a violent and tragic fusion with that of the masses: the persecution of witches.

The rise and fall of English witch trials

Before witches can be prosecuted, witchcraft has to be legally defined as a crime. Until just before our period, witchcraft was tried at the church courts, was subject to fairly light penalties and, as far as the current level of research allows any impression to be formed, was very infrequently prosecuted. The fifteenth century, that great formative period of the European witch craze, left England innocent of both a developed demonological theory and mass persecutions. In 1542, probably as a result of plots against Henry VIII, an Act was passed making conjuration, witchcraft, sorcery and enchantment punishable by death. This, the harshest of the English witchcraft statutes, was repealed along with other Henrician legislation in 1547.

Witchcraft became a felony again in 1563. This Act almost certainly owed much to the influence of returning Marian exiles who had imbibed continental ideas on witchcraft, and were convinced that England needed sound laws against the devil's agents in this as in other respects. The 1563 Act made causing the death of a human being by witchcraft or conjuring spirits punishable by death. Lesser forms of witchcraft, like using magic to search for buried treasure, injuring or attempting to injure people or property, or provoking people to 'unlawful love' by magic, were punishable by a year in prison punctuated by four appearances on the pillory for a first offence, death or, in some circumstances, life imprisonment for the second. This legislation was augmented by a more severe and elaborate Act of 1604, which was connected with the arrival on the English throne of James Stuart, author of a tract against witches. But even this legislation envisaged a year's imprisonment for less serious forms of witchcraft, while minor witchcraft, sorcery and conjuring continued to be tried at the ecclesiastical courts. The laws against witchcraft were repealed in 1736: thus the period in which witchcraft was a crime punishable by secular law roughly coincides with the period covered by this book.

Tracing fluctuations in prosecutions is more difficult than outlining changes in legislation. Witchcraft, as a serious felony, was usually tried at the assizes, but assize records outside the Home Circuit (Essex, Hertfordshire, Kent, Surrey and Sussex) are largely missing before 1650. The one other county for which appropriate records exist, Cheshire, does not seem to have been much troubled by witch prosecutions – oddly, given its proximity to Lancashire, the location of two notorious mass trials. On the evidence of the admittedly incomplete Home Circuit records, the prosecution of witches rose rapidly from 1563 to reach a peak at the end of Elizabeth's reign. Then, despite the 1604 statute and the former interest of the new monarch in such matters, cases fell rapidly at the assizes while, judging by Alan Macfarlane's detailed work on Essex, they were rarely presented before the church courts after that date.

By the 1630s, witchcraft was prosecuted very infrequently on the Home Circuit. Then, in 1645, there came the cluster of trials in Essex associated with Matthew Hopkins, the 'Witch Finder General' (these were, as we shall see, part of the mass trials associated with Hopkins which raged throughout East Anglia) and, a little later, a number of trials in Kent. These two outbreaks created a second peak in the Home Circuit indictments around the middle of the seventeenth century, but trials declined rapidly again after that point. Records from the north and the south-west, which become available after 1650, suggest that witchcraft prosecutions in those areas were similarly running at a very low level by the late seventeenth century.

On the strength of surviving documentation, the last executions definitely known to have been carried out for witchcraft in England occurred in 1682, although a woman was condemned to death and possibly hanged in 1685, and the last assize trial in 1712. The successful prosecution of witches was obviously extremely rare for at least two generations before the repeal of the laws against them.

Overwhelmingly, those accused of witchcraft at the Home Circuit assizes were charged with causing death or injury to people or animals or, more rarely, with damaging property. Accusations of conjuring spirits, or of exhuming dead bodies under the 1604 Act, were almost non-existent. It is also noteworthy that only a small proportion of those accused were actually executed. Figures amassed in 1929 by C.L. Ewen[1] show that indictments against 513 accused witches survive in the records of the Home Circuit, of whom only 112 were hanged: even in the panic atmosphere of the Hopkins era many escaped the noose. A further, and as yet unexplained, peculiarity of these Home Circuit records is the part played by Essex. On Ewen's calculations, of 790 surviving indictments from that circuit, 473 came from Essex, as did 299 of those accused and 82 of those who were hanged. In Sussex, to take the extreme opposite, a mere 17 people were tried for witchcraft and only one was hanged. It is almost tempting to suggest that without Essex, there would have been no English witch craze to discuss.

The Hopkins trials, the nearest known English equivalent to the mass trials experienced in a number of European states, await definitive study. It seems' safe to argue, however, that they were essentially a product of the legal, institutional, religious and perhaps even psychological instability caused by three years of warfare: it is no accident that there were, at a slightly later date, smaller witch-panics in Newcastle and Kent, and a slight rise in prosecutions in Cheshire. Doubtless, loss of trial records has deprived us of details of many other prosecutions from around this time, while even study of the Hopkins episode is obscured by gaps in the documentation. Such documentation and printed sources as survives suggests that 250 witches were tried, or at least underwent preliminary investigation in the Hopkins trials, of which upwards of 100 were executed. The trials began, seemingly at Hopkins's instigation, near his home at Manningtree in Essex, and spread through Suffolk, Norfolk, Cambridgeshire, Bedfordshire, Huntingdonshire and the Isle of Ely. The episode involved, unusually for England, a team of witch-hunters (Hopkins, Stearne, and a woman named Mary Phillips who proved adept at searching for the witch's mark) and a number of dubious pretrial practices. English law did not permit the torturing of felony suspects, but Hopkins and his associates used sleep-deprivation on suspects, forced them to spend long periods walking in their cells, and made extremely crude use of the swimming test: significantly, these irregularities ceased with the arrival of the assize judges. But even at the height of the Hopkins panic opponents were not afraid to speak out, notably John Gaule, a Huntingdonshire clergyman who forcefully voiced his objections to the trials. The Hopkins panic petered out in 1647; nothing remotely like it ever troubled England again.

The background to prosecution in normal periods was much the same throughout the country. Let us consider a typical case of 1646 from Yorkshire. Henry Cockcrofte, a yeoman farmer and clothier of Heptonstall, told how Elizabeth Crossley, a woman already 'in an evill report for witching', came to his house begging for alms. She was seemingly displeased with what she was given, but went away. The next night Cockcrofte's young son, not yet two years of age and in good health, began to suffer fits, and eventually died about three months later. Cockcrofte decided the child had been bewitched and, together with two of his neighbours, went off to confront Mary Midgely, another of the village's reputed witches. She admitted that she could 'witch a little', but told Cockcrofte that Crossley, Crossley's daughter Sarah, and another woman were more potent witches and were responsible for the child's death. Other villagers filled in further details. One recounted how his mother had died seven years previously, attributing her death to witchcraft and accusing Crossley on her deathbed, while another told how his cattle had fallen sick after his wife had denied Midgely some wool she had begged.

The basic elements in this case were the pre-existing suspicions that the accused were witches (Crossley's 'evill report'), and the tensions over giving alms or favours, the typical incident which came to mind when humans or animals fell inexplicably ill and witchcraft was already suspected. This common pattern can be fitted into a wider socioeconomic context. Most cases of this type seem to have involved slightly richer villagers accusing slightly poorer ones, especially those economically marginal old women who would be begging for alms: thus it has been argued that witchcraft accusations were encouraged by the increased social stratification of village society and the development of rural capitalism. An old neighbourly ethic, arguably, was breaking down, while the poor law had not yet established itself as an alternative method for coping, both practically and psychologically, with the local poor. Accusers of witches were uncertain about how to react when confronted by a begging neighbour, and often felt guilty when they refused their request. When an inexplicable illness or accident followed, the guilt was transferred: the breaker of community norms was no longer the refuser of alms, but rather the suspected witch. Thus accusations of witchcraft characteristically alleged concrete harm to neighbours rather than devil worship or attending the sabbat: prosecutors were the witch's 'victims' rather than witch-hunting judges or clergymen.

Less peculiar was the fact that most English witches were women: something like 90 per cent of those accused of witchcraft at the Essex assizes, for example. The exact reasons why the witch stereotype should be female remain elusive. Women have been regarded as more prone to witchcraft than men in cultures far removed in time and space from early modern England, and it is possible that the mysteries of conception, child-bearing and menstruation may have acquired an occult status in the male consciousness. The strong contemporary misogynistic streak also contributed to the notion that witches were likely to be women. Female mental and moral instability, their supposed position as the weaker vessel, made them, it was held, less resistant to Satan's advances. In an early and extremely influential work against witches published after his death in 1608 the celebrated theologian William Perkins declared 'woman being the weaker sex is sooner entangled by the devil's illusions with this damnable art than the man ... in all ages it is found true by experience that the devil hath more easily and oftener prevailed with women than with men'. Yet it is clear that it was not any women, but usually old and helpless ones, who were accused of witchcraft: pamphlet accounts of trials and the works of sceptical authors concur that the archetypal witch was poor, old, frequently confused, and often widowed or socially isolated. This suggests that on the level of village accusations, concern over the economic marginality of the female elderly was probably more significant than any general misogyny.

Indeed, recent research into the connections between women and witch-craft has very much moved the agenda away from any simplistic notion of witchcraft accusations as the direct product of male-generated patriarchy or misogyny. Detailed work on the relevant court records and the pamphlet literature demonstrates that, initially at least, a large proportion of witch-craft accusations arose from disputes between women, disputes which frequently centred around the alleged bewitching of a child. Here we have a clue to how witchcraft might be seen as operating in that most female-dominated of social activities, child-rearing, with the mother of a suppos-edly bewitched child accusing what was often a post-menopausal woman. At the very least, detailed reading of the better-documented witchcraft cases often leads us into the world of female popular culture at a village commu-nity level, with all of the friendships, rivalries, feuds and jealousies which that culture seems to have included. Yet another strand of thinking has begun to apply modern feminist psychiatric theory to the statements of confessing witches and female witnesses, and opened up yet more perspec-tives on how witchcraft operated on a mental level. Without doubt, the women involved in witchcraft cases were living in a male-dominated society, and the court system to which they brought formal accusations was presided over by men. Yet surprisingly often these formal accusations arose after disputes between women: disputes which sometimes led to a number of women voicing their concern over witchcraft in their commu-nity, evaluating the reputation of the supposed witches through gossip networks, and suggesting ways in which witchcraft could be handled.

As we have noted, England had not developed a full-scale witch theory in the fifteenth century, and English witches were always less cosmically menacing than some of their continental counterparts. In 1566, when the first detailed account of an English witch trial was published, the main attributes of the English witch, apart from the ability to harm her neighbours, were the keeping of a familiar demon in animal form and having a mark on the body from which the familiar sucked the witch's blood. As the years passed, the witch figure became more elaborate. The idea of the pact with the devil, although implicit in the notion of the familiar, did not assume central importance until late in Elizabeth's reign, while the image of the devil as a cloven-footed man dressed in black is not found until a little later. Sexual intercourse between witches and demons was only a prominent feature of trials during the Hopkins episode, and that interference with sexual intercourse and the reproductive processes which so exercised continental demonologists was largely absent from English trials. Even the witches' sabbat appeared late in English beliefs, and remained a very tame affair. Nothing like a full-blown sabbat is found until some West-Country trials of the 1650s and 1660s, and even there the witches' activities were fairly decorous. Whereas continental witches indulged in sexual orgies at the sabbat and dined on the bodies of newborn infants there, English witches danced to the devil's piping and consumed 'wine, cakes and roast meat'.

Nevertheless, such beliefs demonstrate wider notions about the nature of witchcraft than the village maleficium which features so prominently in that most limited of sources, the trial indictment. Something like a sophisticated demonology was emerging piecemeal, much as it had done in parts of continental Europe in the fifteenth century. Ironically, but luckily for poor old widows, at the same time as it was developing, the weight of educated opinion was turning against belief in witches. Our accounts of West-Country sabbats are drawn from Joseph Glanvill's *Saducismus Triumphatus*, a book which was essentially an attempt to convince an increasingly sceptical public of the reality of witches and of the wider spirit world of which they were part.

Certainly, by the late seventeenth century educated opinion was becoming receptive to new ideas on the world and the universe which were rendering magic redundant. Yet witch trials were in decline, in the south-east at least, something like two generations before these new theories were making any marked impact. The ending of trials must, therefore, be ascribed to other causes. In 1584, at the height of trials in the south-east, the Kentish justice of the peace Reginald Scot published his *Discoverie of Witchcraft*, a devastating critique of the demonological ideas enshrined in such classics as the *Malleus Maleficarum* or the works of Bodin. Scot's position, pared to its fundamentals, was essentially that of modern common sense: most of what witches were meant to do was plainly nonsensical, and the methods by which they were tried made a mockery of justice. Even the scriptural allusions to witchcraft, upon which so much of the demonologists' arguments rested, were, according to Scot, mostly misconstrued or mistranslated, and anyway had little to do with the old women being accused of witchcraft in Elizabethan England. His opinions foreshadowed those which became common after the middle of the seventeenth century, and were in large measure restated in Sir Robert Filmer's *Advertisement to the Jury-Men of England* of 1653. Filmer, best known for his *Patriarcha*, a defence of absolutist kingship, was another Kentish JP, and his tract on witchcraft added another dimension to the decline in prosecutions. One of his central themes was the problem of how witchcraft was to be legally proved. Judges had always been a little unhappy about the need to suspend normal ideas about evidence when trying witches, and this may well have helped account for the decline in trials in the 1630s. By the late seventeenth century broader changes in cosmology and religion were reinforcing sceptics or those worried about legal proofs. Christianity in 1700 placed less emphasis on a providential God as a force in everyday life, and thus the devil correspondingly became less of a directly active agent and less of a threat.

Although educated opinion may have been changing by about 1700 (and even this process should not be overstated), opinion among the masses was still largely acceptive of the reality of witchcraft. Their world was one where it was more difficult to do without magic as part of the wider belief system. The poor had recourse to white witches, cunning men or women, until well into the nineteenth century, and in some areas belief in maleficium, the old ability of the village witch to harm her neighbours, can be found at least up till then. But it would be dangerous to accept too simplistic a polarity between some notion of an enlightened élite and one of the credulous masses. Scepticism must have existed among the poor, even if evidence of it is difficult to come by. The tensions that preceded the celebrated Lancashire trials of 1612 provide an interesting and unexpected example: John Nutter, one of the accusers at those trials, was cheerfully told by a relative to whom he confided his fears that he was bewitched that 'thou art a foolish ladde, it is not so, it is thy miscarriage [i.e. misfortune]'. Yet the weight of evidence does suggest that the bulk of the population still believed in witches and maleficium. In 1751 Ruth Osborne, a suspected witch, was subjected to the swimming test at Tring, Hertfordshire, and died after the experience. Thomas Colley, a local man who had played a part in the swimming, was later hanged for her murder, a neat demonstration of how the attitudes of the courts had changed. Detailed work on this incident has demonstrated that it was not a simple display of popular brutishness and credulity: there was a complex background of popular attitudes and village conflict. Nevertheless, there is something convincing about the vignette of the crowd who attended Colley's execution standing 'at a distance to see him go, grumbling and muttering that it was a hard case to hang a man for destroying an old wicked woman who had done so much harm by her witchcraft'. Beliefs may have been changing, but they were evidently very slow to do so among the lower orders.

The triumph of natural philosophy

At about the same time as witch trials on the Home Circuit were declining in the 1620s two remarkable men were making a distinctive, and lasting, contribution to scientific development. The first was Francis Bacon. Bacon had been a leading statesman before his disgrace in 1621, but he had also been heavily involved in scientific, philosophical and literary studies. He turned decisively to these after his exclusion from politics. In many respects, his attitudes were still those of the magus: he envisaged what he called a 'Great Instauration', a general reform of the world. More prosaically, his insistence on inductive thinking, on observation of facts and on experimentation did much to establish scientific method (it also led to his death: Bacon died from bronchitis contracted in March 1626 while experimenting with deep-freezing a chicken). It has been argued, perhaps more uncertainly, that his insistence on the practical applicability of scientific work left a distinctively utilitarian streak in English scientific endeavour.

The second major figure was the physician William Harvey. Harvey, who had acquired his medical education at the outstanding medical school at Padua, was Lumleian Lecturer to the London College of Physicians from 1615, and physician extraordinary to James I from 1618. He is best remembered, however, for his discovery of the circulation of the blood, which was made public by his *Exercitatio Anatomica de Motu Cordis et Sanguinis in Animalibus* of 1628. Like Bacon, Harvey was still working within a basically Aristotelian framework, and his contribution was in many ways an indirect one. He too demonstrated the importance of a proper scientific method, and his model investigation of one organ provided a precedent which could be applied to other parts of the body or, indeed, to other areas of scientific investigation. Certainly, Harvey's influence ensured that English anatomy and physiology enjoyed something of a golden age in the mid-seventeenth century. Yet he did not regard himself as representing any major break with the past. His attachment to established ideas was illustrated vividly when John Aubrey asked the great man what works he should read when beginning his own intellectual endeavours. Aubrey remembered, 'he bid me goe to the fountain's head, and read Aristotle, Cicero, Avicenna, and did call the neoteriques [i.e. modern writers] shittbreeches'.

The Civil Wars, despite the disruption which attended them, did not seriously disrupt the burgeoning scientific activity of which Bacon and Harvey were representatives. Harvey, a convinced royalist, went to Oxford with the King, and helped keep intellectual activity alive there. At Cambridge a group of Platonic and Neo-Platonic thinkers remained active throughout the Interregnum, and were to enjoy a lasting formative influence over English natural philosophy. A group of Anglo–Irish intellectuals, sometimes referred to as the 'Invisible College', came together under the aegis of Robert Boyle. Most importantly, scientific advances were made by another group of scholars at Oxford, of which the leading light was John Wilkins, from 1648 warden of Wadham College. In 1649 the 'Philosophical Society of Oxford' was formed, and meetings were held regularly, initially at Wilkins's lodgings in Wadham. The Oxford Society prefigured the later Royal Society, conducted a number of innovative enquiries, and included in its membership a number of individuals who were to be of considerable consequence in intellectual circles after 1660, the most famous being Christopher Wren.

This blossoming of scientific activity over the 1640s and 1650s introduces a problem which has caused considerable controversy among historians: that of the alleged connections between the Scientific Revolution and Puritanism. The Scientific Revolution and Puritanism can both be interpreted as progressive movements, and were chronologically close: those who like their history to be tidy have, accordingly, made claims that the two phenomena were linked causally. Certainly, the large number of scientific works published between 1640 and the Restoration, many of them written from an avowedly Puritan and reformist viewpoint, would seem to support such a contention. But a number of difficulties remain. The first is that of definition: neither 'Puritan' nor 'science' are terms that can be easily defined in the seventeenth-century context, and both phenomena contained different, even irreconcilable, elements. Thus many of the 'scientific' works published by advanced Protestants in the Interregnum were written from a populist position and had a strong millenarial tinge. Many Puritans had a suspicion of natural philosophy, not least those radicals who saw the universities as bastions not only of outdated privilege but also of outdated learning. Moreover, after the purges at the end of the Wars, parliamentarian and Cromwellian authorities showed little regard for the ideological soundness of those whom they placed in the universities and, conversely, many Puritan dons survived the sea-change of 1660. Thus the mathematician Seth Ward, who was deprived of his Cambridge post in 1644 for refusing to take the Covenant and was later to be a hardline episcopalian Bishop of Exeter, was made Savilian Professor of Astronomy at Oxford in 1649 and was a prominent member of the Wilkins circle. Wilkins himself, despite his adherence to Puritanism and the Interregnum regimes, prospered after the Restoration and became Bishop of Chester in 1668. Such careers demonstrate the impossibility of making any simplistic connection between religious affiliation and scientific originality.

Nevertheless, both contemporaries and historians have seen the middle of the seventeenth century as something of a watershed in scientific thought. John Aubrey commented that 'the searching after natural knowledge began but since or about the death of king Charles the First', while, more recently, the historian of science, Charles Webster, has claimed that 'between 1626 and 1660, a philosophical revolution was accomplished in England'.[2] The event which is commonly thought to have symbolized that revolution was the foundation of the Royal Society, which received its first charter in July 1662. The Royal Society had its origins in those groups of natural philosophers who had met in London and the universities over the two previous decades, although it probably owed an additional, if indirect, debt to Gresham College, founded at London in 1597 as a centre for what might be broadly described as scientific studies. The intellectual level of the Royal Society in its early years should not be overestimated: many of its members were dilettantes, amateurs, or simply gentlemen with a vague interest in ideas which were becoming increasingly fashionable. Even so, the Society was founded by a core of dedicated scholars, and maintained an important function in promulgating new ideas, carrying out experiments and, through correspondence, maintaining contact between London-based intellectuals and their colleagues in the provinces.

As the early history of the Royal Society demonstrates, scientific ideas were beginning to attract a broad interest. But this interest came overwhelmingly from the top of society. The scientists themselves, for the most part, were of good family. Michael Hunter has taken a sample of 65 British-born scientists active in England in the later seventeenth century, and investigated their social background. Forty per cent came from landed families, and 23 per cent were sons of Anglican clergy: only 12 per cent were the offspring of merchants, and 14 per cent of yeomen, artisans and other plebeians. Three-quarters of them had been educated at Oxford or Cambridge, while over half had taken a higher degree.[3] Similarly, a high proportion of those attracted to natural philosophy in the provinces were gentry or clergymen. Such men founded the local philosophical societies which flourished in the later seventeenth century in such regional centres as Norwich, York or Exeter. It was the activities of such amateur enthusiasts, many of them extremely learned, which makes it possible not to write the history of the Scientific Revolution simply in terms of a roll-call of famous scientists.

There were, however, a fair number of these about: Robert Boyle the chemist, youngest son of the Earl of Cork, and typical of the gentleman virtuoso of the period; Robert Hooke, a skilled experimenter in both physics and chemistry; the German emigré Henry Oldenburg, appointed, with John Wilkins, secretary of the Royal Society in 1663, and whose correspondence is an important source for historians of science. Most famous was Isaac Newton. Newton is best known for his work on the principles of gravitation, which shattered the Aristotelian idea that the celestial and terrestrial worlds operated under different sets of physical rules. His other work on mechanics, and in particular his three laws of motion, laid the basis for modern physics, while his work on optics was also of prime significance. But even Newton, whose education at Cambridge in the 1650s had exposed him to Neo-Platonist ideas, did not offer a complete break with past thinking. His *Principia* of 1687 was attacked by more thorough-going mechanists as owing too much to the occult tradition, and Newton's interest in alchemy adds some substance to these criticisms. Initially, therefore, Newtonian ideas did not attain unqualified success in Europe. But in England they rapidly achieved the status of a new orthodoxy, and Newton's protégés came to hold key positions in the academic and intellectual establishment. Most importantly, the success of Newton's ideas meant that the thinking of René Descartes did not establish itself strongly in England. Descartes was distrusted by the English as a materialist, and there was probably also some concern that his excessive deductive rationalism might prove to be as stifling an intellectual system as the old scholasticism.

The strong traces of earlier traditions in Newton's thought should remind us that the novelty of the new philosophy was not so great nor was its triumph so rapid or complete as has sometimes been imagined. Certainly, Neo-Platonic influences remained strong long after 1650. Robert Plot, professor of chemistry at Oxford, worked within an alchemic, Hermetic tradition, while the writings of the Low Countries Paracelsian physician Jean Baptista van Helmont were an important influence on medical thinking. Moreover, many of the natural philosophers of the late seventeenth century felt that they, like the Renaissance magus, were working for a higher moral purpose, and the old optimism about acquiring universal knowledge lived on. Above all, the natural philosophers were insistent that the Christian God remained a central part of their scheme of things. There was a general feeling that laying bare the secrets of the universe would inevitably lead to an understanding not only of the natural world, but also of its creator: thus Joseph Glanvill saw one of the objects of natural philosophy as being to 'understand the artifice of the omniscient architect in the composure of the great world'. Ultimately, certain elements of the new science, and particularly its more mechanical elements, would help erode the old notion of a providential God playing an active role in the affairs of the world. A new idea of the Almighty was emerging, perhaps as the great clockmaker rather than the active rewarder of right and wrong. But the Newtonian stand against what were considered to be the overly mechanistic principles of Descartes ensured that God retained a vital position in the new reformulation of the nature of the cosmos.

Despite this, charges of atheism, or at least of a partial denial of the power of the Almighty, were among the criticisms hurled at the new science. To Henry Stubbe, the members of the Royal Society were 'a company of atheists, papists, dunces & other enemies to all learning', while Henry Croft, Bishop of Hereford, declared that 'this way of philosophising all from natural causes, I fear, will make the whole world turn scoffers'. Even those ecclesiastical conservatives who did not share these fears might be hostile to the natural philosophers, for there was an entrenched feeling that the proper purpose of education was instruction in right religion, compared to which scientific experimentation was of very secondary importance. Similarly a number of Neo-Platonists, convinced of the need to keep sights fixed on the higher purposes of intellectual enquiry, thought that much of the new insistence on the experimental method was misplaced. Henry More, a Cambridge Platonist, disparaged 'that more mechanical kind of genius that loves to be tumbling of and trying tricks with the matter (which they call making experiments)'. Criticism, ranging from mild scepticism to outright hostility, came from a number of other quarters and was prompted by a number of considerations: at one end of the spectrum, the College of Physicians was suspicious of the Royal Society as a potential interloper into their field, while at the other wits at the court of Charles II found much to amuse them in the doings of some of the natural philosophers. At the other end of the social scale, as the virtuosi often complained, artisans and tradesmen maintained a healthy scepticism about what they saw as the 'whimsyes of contemplative persons'.

Researches into the realities of scientific culture in the later seventeenth century have continued to question the straightforward model of 'science as progress', and have not only raised questions about how valuable modern concepts of 'science' are when applied to the period, but have also led to a questioning of those very concepts of science themselves. Certainly, the scientific culture of Restoration England was not divorced from the wider cultural values of the society in which it flourished. As we shall see, recent thinking has emphasized the continuities in the mental framework of the major scientific figures of the period, while it has been suggested that even the experimental method, decried by Henry More but seen as of central importance by historians of science, was not as value-free as later myth would have it. Thus Robert Boyle's celebrated experiments with the air pump have been shown to have been carried out not within some abstract intellectual or social context, but rather through the use of an experimental method which was appropriate to Boyle's perceptions of the cultural, religious and political needs of Restoration England. The study of the history of science has been bedevilled by that search for the 'origins of the modern' which has distorted so much of our view of the early modern period, and historians have now become much more sensitive in their attempts to delineate the exact nature of the intellectual changes which were involved in the natural philosophy of the later seventeenth century.

Moreover, change in methods of thought was not restricted to what the modern world would recognize as science. It also affected philosophy, most notably in the writings of John Locke. Locke is most familiar to historians through his *Two Treatises of Government*, a work which was mobilized as an apology for the Glorious Revolution and which is generally regarded as one of the main theoretical bases for liberal politics. Locke's interests, however, furnish yet another demonstration of how the early modern scholar was characteristically engaged in a wide range of studies. As well as his political studies, Locke took an interest in epistemology, philosophy, education and medicine, and his contemporary reputation was based not on the *Treatises* but rather on his *Essay Concerning Human Understanding* (1690), and his *Some Thoughts Concerning Education* (1693). At Oxford, where he took both his BA and MA, Locke was more interested in experimental science than in the traditional curriculum, and was connected with the Wilkins circle. He subsequently maintained an interest in this field, and first came to the attention of the great as a physician. He spent extensive periods in France and Holland, and made a number of contacts with foreign scholars. The last 30 years of his life (he died in 1704) were spent largely in developing his ideas on epistemology. His views on the theory of knowledge, of which an important element was the refutation of the concept of innate knowledge which was central to Descartes' thinking, were to be tremendously influential.

The spread of new attitudes was also reflected in the arrival of 'Political Arithmetic', the forerunner of modern statistically based social enquiry. William Petty, active from the Interregnum onwards, began his career in land-surveying, and became convinced of the need for and possibility of a wide statistical study of society and the economy which might serve as a basis for national planning. John Graunt was responsible, in 1661, for analysing the London Bills of Mortality, foreshadowing the modern notion that the population can be interpreted and analysed quantitatively. Gregory King was responsible for a number of projects, among which the best known is his statistical analysis of late seventeenth-century English society. The drift of much of this political arithmetic, with its incipient modernity, was towards a closer co-operation between men of science and the central government, as was happening in France at that time. Generally, the English government ignored the need for such contacts. Its most important contribution was the foundation of the Royal Observatory at Greenwich, to which John Flamsteed was appointed the first Astronomer Royal in 1676. The Royal Observatory was founded specifically to settle the problem of how to determine longitude at sea, but it became the centre for more general astronomical investigation and scientific instruction. Flamsteed, for example, conducted 20,000 observations between 1676 and 1689, while the need to raise money for new instruments in the face of governmental parsimony led him to instruct 140 private pupils between the date of his employment and 1709.

The Royal Observatory was founded with a very practical end in view, and the connection between astronomical investigation and the realities of maritime navigation was a very real one. But in general, and despite the practical streak which Bacon is supposed to have bequeathed to English science, there is little evidence of direct benefits being passed from the natural philosophers to the more mundane area of practical technology. When, about 1760, that 'wave of great inventions' which heralded the arrival of the Industrial Revolution occurred, the inventors were normally practical men without a theoretical scientific training. Despite the claims which many late seventeenth-century scientists made for the usefulness of their work, its impact on the wider technology was limited: the ideal of the scientist around 1700 was that of the virtuoso, the gentleman or pseudo-gentleman with enough education, money and leisure to follow his bent for natural philosophy. Artisans and tradesmen showing practical interest in the new developments were limited to a few exceptional categories: makers of scientific or navigational instruments, apothecaries, writers of almanacs.

Nevertheless, it is difficult entirely to jettison the notion that the ideas of the new science were being widely diffused in the early eighteenth century. Even if there is little evidence of direct links between the achievements of the Scientific Revolution and practical technological advance, there is undeniable evidence of a broad diffusion of scientific, and especially Newtonian, knowledge. This process owed much to popularizing books, a work entitled *Newtonianism for Ladies* published in 1737 suggesting a very wide interest in such publications. Another medium was the travelling lecturer. Philosophical societies and similar bodies, aspects of the flourishing provincial urban culture of the early eighteenth century, often treated their members to talks by specialists on scientific topics. James Jurin, born in London in 1684, became master of Newcastle-upon-Tyne Grammar School, gave lectures on experimental philosophy in the area, and was able to educate himself as a doctor on the £1000 he made. William Whiston, son of a rector, was a propagandist for Newtonian physics and gave lectures in London, Bath and Tunbridge Wells, although his decline into eccentricity in his later years probably did little to advance the cause of the new science. By his death in 1752, however, interest in scientific matters was clearly widespread. Even John Wesley, who fancied himself as an amateur doctor, was by 1756 using an electrical healing machine which, he asserted, 'by electrifying in the proper manner cures St Anthony's fire, gouts, headache, inflammations, lameness, palpitations of the heart, palsy, rheumatisms, sprain, toothache, sore throat and swelling of all sorts'.

The Scientific Revolution moved Sir Herbert Butterfield to claim that 'since the rise of Christianity, there is no landmark in history that is worthy to be compared with this'.[4] Some years later, Hugh Kearney has described it as 'an extraordinary intellectual leap which had repercussions ultimately upon every aspect of western thought and life'.[5] Reaching this ultimate position was, however, a very lengthy process. Even among the élite, the old alchemic and Neo-Platonic ideas lived on, while the pamphlet war which followed the last English witch trial, that of a Hertfordshire woman named Jane

Wenham, in 1712, shows that witchcraft was still something whose reality was accepted in educated circles. Plotting the spread of scientific ideas among the masses is, however, more difficult than discovering the survival of 'magical' ideas among the élite. The standard interpretation is that they clung to the old beliefs on magic, witchcraft and astrology longer than their betters. In the last analysis such a view will probably prove correct, but popular scepticism about magic, and popular receptiveness to Newtonian science, are problems which are in urgent need of further research

It is clear, however, that the intellectual developments of the later seventeenth century, of which Locke and Newton were the two great symbols, were both the product and a token of that great transition from an unstable world to a stable one that we have noted so often. The thinking of Newton, for all his debts to Neo-Platonism, is recognizably more 'modern' than that of John Dee. It is also more coherent, more ordered, more convinced of the possibility of finding pattern and regularity, and expressed in more measured terms than the ideas of a Renaissance magus. A parallel shift can be traced in philosophy and political theory, away from the *Angst* over order and human nature which fills the pages of Hobbes's *Leviathan* to the massively less fraught tone of Locke's *Treatises*. The change was one away from fear of things falling apart towards a situation where at least a degree of stability and cohesion could be assumed, intellectually as well as socially. The educated Englishman of the early eighteenth century was confident of being closer to understanding the nature of his physical environment, of the capacity of human reason to render comprehensible the complexity of the universe, of the need to argue deductively from general principles, and of the possibility of a break from tradition being made in the intellectual sphere without a collapse of social hierarchy. We should be cautious about trumpeting the impact of the Scientific Revolution, even more so about the arrival of 'modernity': yet the mental world of 1760 was vastly different from that of 1550, its assumptions much like those of the average European of the late twentieth century. Arguably, this mental change marks the most important transition to occur in the early modern period. It also marks an almost unique influence of English ideas on the wider world. From the 1730s, when Voltaire popularized Newton to the French-speaking world, the ideas of English philosophers assumed a new importance in Europe. By the mid-eighteenth century, England's intellectual achievements were recognized as matching her economic and political ones.

Notes

1 C.L. Ewen, *Witch Hunting and Witch Trials: the Indictments from the Records of 1373 Assizes held for the Home Circuit, A.D. 1559–1736* (1929: reprinted 1971), p. 99.

2 Charles Webster, *The Great Instauration: Science, Medicine and Reform 1626–1660* (1975), p. xiii.
3 Michael Hunter, *Science and Society in Restoration England* (Cambridge, 1981), pp. 60–1.
4 Quoted *ibid.*, p. 1.
5 Hugh Kearney, *Science and Change 1500–1700* (1971), p. 12.

EPILOGUE:
STRIFE WITHIN STABILITY

Politics and society, 1653–1760

Little of the transition to a more stable world was apparent in late 1653, when there occurred yet another governmental experiment: a Protectorate, based upon a written constitution, the Instrument of Government. That this experiment proved more durable than the Rump or Barebones was due in large measure to the abilities and standing of the Lord Protector, Oliver Cromwell. Above all, Cromwell was able to manage the army: it was there, as the events of 1647–60 demonstrate, that the key to political survival lay. With Cromwell as Protector the army knew that its interests would be safeguarded, while Cromwell knew he could depend upon accumulated goodwill and respect when dealing with the soldiery. He leant most heavily on military support in 1655 when, after largely abortive royalist risings, he divided the country into a number of groupings of counties, each of them under the supervision of a major general who added a military stiffening to local government. The major generals, although looming large in later gentry folklore, proved to be a very short-lived experiment. By late 1656 they were attracting criticism in parliament, even from the Cromwellian court clique. By that time the Protector was being wooed by civilian supporters anxious to broaden the base of the regime. Early in 1657 these drew up a new constitution, the Humble Petition and Advice, and offered Cromwell the Crown. Personal dislike of the idea on the Protector's part, coupled with a very proper concern over alienating the army, prevented him from accepting the kingship: yet the Humble Petition and Advice, complete with its Upper House which obviously constituted a Cromwellian House of Lords, was accepted. This indicated a desire to civilianize the regime and widen its potential support. At least some of the political nation were coming round to the idea that the Protectorate offered the most likely available guarantee for the preservation of property and social hierarchy.

Protectorate to James II

Perhaps the most puzzling, if most instructive, aspect of Oliver Cromwell's Protectorate was its local dimension. The events of 1649–53 undoubtedly constituted a political revolution, but there is little evidence that they amounted to a social one. By the 1650s, the established county families who had run local affairs before 1642 had largely been eased out, at least in their main lines. Local control now passed to lesser gentry, to some known adherents of the regime from even lower social strata and, to a limited extent, to the military. Yet there was no wholesale attack on social hierarchy. Peers and upper gentry were excluded from political power and social dominance, yet they were not purged as were their equivalents in the later French or Russian Revolutions. Royalists were subjected to fines, penal taxation and the confiscation of land, but most even of these managed to weather the adverse conditions. Indeed, one of the most striking aspects of the Protectorate was the absence of any serious royalist risings. The widespread plotting of 1655 resulted, Penruddock's Rising in Wiltshire apart, in little by way of serious activity. The Sealed Knot, a group of well-born royalists, took their instructions to deter wild risings too far, and in fact attempted to prevent risings of any sort. Further hindrances arose from the personal and faction rivalries which had bedevilled the royalist cause since 1640, while the amateurishness of most royalist plotters made them easy prey to John Thurloe, Cromwell's gifted intelligence chief. But behind all this we sense the sheer improbability of any major rebellion by the political nation in the early modern period. Cromwell's army provided a powerful disincentive to potential rebels but, even allowing for that, peers and gentry were strangely unwilling to take direct action against a regime most of them detested.

The death of Cromwell on 3 September 1658 introduced a bewildering period of rapid political change. It is tempting to regard this as a prologue to the inevitable return of the Stuarts: but many contemporaries, Charles Stuart among them, did not interpret the period in this way, while many participants in the crowded events of September 1658 to May 1660 struggled actively against such an outcome. Certainly the reception given to Richard Cromwell, who followed his father as Protector, was encouraging: both the army and the Protectorate's civilian supporters seemed happy enough with him. Unfortunately Richard failed (and it is doubtful if anyone could have done better) in preventing friction between parliament and army. In April 1659 the troops intervened yet again, dissolved parliament, and in effect ended the Protectorate. The triumvirate of military grandees, Desborough, Fleetwood and Lambert, were anxious to dress military rule in at least the rags of constitutionalism: in May 1659 they recalled the Rump Parliament, thrown out six years previously by the army. This encouraged the Rump's veteran MPs into the delusion that they were indispensable. Royalist plots, which produced a serious rising in Cheshire led by Sir George Booth and suppressed by Lambert, forced a temporary unity on to the regime. But in October the troops, headed by Lambert, took control again. A Committee of Safety was set up, and laboured to concoct a constitutional settlement. Over the winter of 1659–60 support for this Committee, and hence for the army, slackened. On Boxing Day 1659 the Rump Parliament reassembled yet again, the nearest thing to a legitimate ruling body in England, yet obviously not the 'free and full' assembly which a broad spectrum of public opinion was demanding. By this date, however, a new force was poised to enter English politics: General George Monck and Parliament's army of Scotland.

George Monck was the epitome of the professional soldier. He was also, as the fourth of 10 children of a poor Devonshire gentleman, the epitome of a younger son making his way in the world. Monck had been in the English, French and Dutch services on the continent, and had served in Charles I's forces against the Scots, the Irish and the Long Parliament. After capture and three years' imprisonment he decided to place his talents at the disposal of his most recent enemies, and by 1659 was parliament's commander in Scotland. His motives in 1659 are to some extent obscure: it is probable that he was simply anxious to preserve legitimate civilian rule, and may also have been affected by the fears of social upheaval generated by the Quaker scare of that year. Later in 1659 Monck declared for parliament against military rule and began, some desertions notwithstanding, to move his troops towards the border. Lambert came north to meet this threat, concentrating his forces at Newcastle, but moved back to London when news reached him of growing opposition in the south. His army broke up as it marched southwards, and Monck entered England on 2 January 1660. All military forces apart from his dissolved, demands for a free parliament grew, and the political situation became yet more confused. The members excluded by Pride's Purge rejoined the Rump in February. Legislation amounting to an interim settlement was passed, and the Rump then voted for its own dissolution and for elections for a new parliament in which, significantly, royalists would be allowed to vote. By March, Stuart agents were in active communication with Monck, who by now was coming to see a restored monarchy as the most likely guarantee of order. The elections for the Convention Parliament, which witnessed overwhelming support for royalist candidates, buttressed this view. The parliament met on 25 April, and on 1 May Charles Stuart's Declaration of Breda was read to both Houses. They agreed that according to 'fundamental laws' England was to be governed by King, Lords and Commons. Charles II was proclaimed on 8 May, landed at Dover on 25 May and entered London four days later.

The exact significance of the events of 1640–60 remains elusive. Most people in 1660 simply wanted to forget them, and return to some idealized version of what had existed before the wars began. Yet events down to 1688 and beyond were to prove that few of the constitutional issues over which the nation had gone to war had been settled in 1660.

Politically, the most immediate consequence of the Interregnum was the confirmation of that dislike for aggressive central government which had been so strong in the late 1630s. In religion, unity of belief was gone, but toleration of a diversity of beliefs still lay in the distant future. Secular mass politics, which had surfaced precociously with the Levellers, were to disappear for a century and a half. Those who have claimed a relationship between the economic advance of the period and its political upheavals have yet to demonstrate the connections convincingly enough. The limited colonial acquisitions of the Interregnum, notably Cromwell's taking of Jamaica, may have pointed to later developments, although modern historians might view their consequences differently from Victorian celebrants of imperial expansion: indeed, as one has remarked, 'it may now be argued that the complexion of Brixton is the most tangible enduring achievement of the Protectorate'.[1] Less tangible, but perhaps more relevant to our immediate concerns, is the sense that, however much people might have wanted them to be, things would never be quite the same again. The mysteries of kingship had been unravelled, and the state had been run, laws passed, policy formulated and wars declared without a monarch. Charles II, at least, was never to forget that point.

But in May 1660 the greetings of London's City Fathers and the merry-making of the masses provided convincing displays of loyalty, and of relief at the return to normality. The problem was how to convert this loyalty and relief into a practical working settlement. Charles had to accommodate both those who had suffered for their support of the Stuart cause, and those who had previously opposed it, but whose more recent support had been vital in the near past and would remain vital in the foreseeable future. The level of complaint among old cavaliers, although not to be taken fully at its face value, suggests that the second group did better. Certainly, Charles was anxious to avoid a counter-revolutionary terror. Regicides had to be executed, but the King's objective was reconciliation: accordingly, a Bill of Pardon, Indemnity and Oblivion was rushed through parliament. Venner's Rising of January 1661 gave the new regime a nasty shock, but there was, in reality, surprisingly little republican plotting: adherents of the Good Old Cause were shattered by what they interpreted as divine intervention against them. Royalists were correspondingly sure of divine favour, and although Star Chamber, the High Commission, the Court of Wards, and other instruments of prerogative rule were not revived, the Restoration settlement was solidly pro-monarchical. Militia Acts, vesting control of the armed forces in the King, were passed in 1661 and 1662, an Act to preserve the person of the King was passed in 1661, as was legislation against tumultuous petitioning, while the Triennial Act, a guarantee of regular parliaments, was emasculated in 1664. Nowhere was the aggressively royalist mood demonstrated more clearly, however, than in the religious settlement.

On 4 April 1660 Charles, in the Declaration of Breda, had expressed his willingness to leave the settlement of religious matters to parliament: he was anxious that his return should not be delayed by the disagreements which precision over such matters at that stage might have caused. Most knowledgeable observers, Charles among them, thought that the likely form of religious settlement would be a compromise between episcopalianism and presbyterianism. Events proved otherwise. The members of the Cavalier Parliament had been thoroughly frightened by the religious chaos of the two previous decades. They, like the gentry back in the shires, rallied to the cause of an episcopalian Church of England. Its doctrine and government were to be founded on the Thirty-Nine Articles, its liturgy and public service on the Book of Common Prayer. Such a church was seen as the guarantor of the traditional form of English Protestantism, and as a necessary antidote against popular anarchy in both the religious and the social spheres. Aided by Gilbert Sheldon, his capable Archbishop of Canterbury, Charles had hoped to form a broadly based church, while practicalities meant that he was still dependent on clerics from the previous regime. But the religious settlement, grounded as it was on gentry reaction, produced a Church more traditional and authoritarian than Charles had envisaged. In particular, the religious legislation of the Cavalier Parliament, known, a little unfairly, as 'The Clarendon Code', was hostile to the sects. The Act of Uniformity of 1662, with the suppression of faction and schism as its major objective, effectively ended any hopes of an accommodation between episcopacy and presbyterianism. Acts of 1664 and 1670 aimed to suppress conventicles, while an Act of 1665 tried to prevent all ministers who had been ejected under the Act of Uniformity from residing within five miles of the location of that living, or any borough. The Licensing Act of 1662 provided the means of suppressing both dissenting tracts and politically subversive literature. The hopes of the Presbyterians, who had made such a decisive contribution to the process of Restoration, were dashed.

As this legislation demonstrates, more than the Stuart monarchy was restored with the Restoration. Gentry control returned in local government, and both the Lords and Commons were dominated by members of the traditional élite. Parliament now sat more or less annually (1672 and 1676 were exceptions): a successful restoration indeed. Most members of the Cavalier Parliament, in its early stages at least, probably saw their function in traditional terms: they would debate a few matters, vote supplies to the Crown, pass some legislation, and then go home to their wives and foxhounds. But these regular parliamentary sessions broke the familiar pattern, and laid the foundations for later parliamentary politics. Immediately after 1660 the dominant minister was the veteran constitutional royalist, Edward Hyde, Earl of Clarendon. But his ascendancy waned, and in 1667 he was impeached and fled abroad. The next 'ministry' was known as the Cabal, after the initials of its principal members (Clifford, Arlington, Buckingham, Ashley and Lauderdale). In so far as the Cabal followed coherent policies, they were broadly in line with supporting greater royal powers and greater religious toleration, but the ministry collapsed in 1674, mainly because of royal religious and foreign policy. It was followed in turn by the ascendancy of Sir Thomas Osborne, later Earl of Danby. Danby's great contribution to English political life was his realization of the possibilities of managing parliament through royal patronage. This need for management demonstrated how parliament was now a regular feature of politics: yet there was still little about the two Houses which would have been incomprehensible to a parliamentarian of the 1620s. Above all, events in parliament were still intimately connected with the ebb and flow of faction-fighting at court.

Domestic politics were complicated by new developments in foreign affairs. The reign of Charles II saw two main trends in foreign policy: warfare against the Dutch, and the King's desire for an alliance with France. The First Dutch War of 1652–54 had not broken the economic ascendancy of the United Provinces, and in 1665 a second war was launched against them. Initially all went well, but this war ended badly when the Dutch burnt ships and naval installations in the Medway in June 1667: it was this disaster which precipitated the fall of Clarendon, blamed for the misconduct of a war to which he was opposed. The Third Dutch War of 1672–74 was a less traumatic affair militarily, but it did augment fears that England was simply becoming a satellite of France. Charles himself was pro-French, regarding Louis XIV as a model of monarchy. In 1670 he signed the secret Treaty of Dover with Louis, promising, in return for a French subsidy, to declare himself a Catholic when events in England allowed. This secret treaty was directly opposite to official foreign policy, which in 1668 had produced the Triple Alliance of England, the Dutch and Sweden, a treaty which was popularly regarded as being anti-French. The end of the Third Dutch War in February 1674 not only demonstrated the futility of warfare against the United Provinces, but also left many Englishmen convinced of the need to protect Protestantism, and in particular English Protestantism, against the Catholic absolutism of Louis XIV. Many of Charles II's subjects were deeply concerned at his obvious sympathy for a monarch whom they regarded as a threat to their liberties and their religion.

Domestic politics, however, were still mainly enmeshed in the problems unleashed by the crisis of 1640–42: the powers of the monarchy, the rights of parliament, the freedom of elections, the rights of the judiciary, the continuing issue of religion, and now the succession. These problems, and even more the nature of parliamentary politics, show broad continuities back to, and beyond, the calling of the Long Parliament. But, in the autumn of 1678, a series of events began which were, albeit temporarily, to disrupt these familiar patterns. One of the constants of the Restoration political scene was fear of Catholicism, and in the 1670s much had happened to heighten this fear. James, Duke of York, successor to the Crown, absented himself from Anglican services, resigned his English offices, and allowed his second wife, Mary of Modena, to use their household as a haven for Catholics. As in the late 1630s, the court was widely regarded as a convivial environment for papists, a suspicion which Charles's evident affection for things French did little to assuage. There was, therefore, a ready reception when a popish plot, aiming to murder Charles, massacre Protestants, and introduce a Catholic army into the realm was 'discovered' in September 1678. Titus Oates, a principal witness to the plot, swore his information to Sir Edmund Berry Godfrey, who disappeared and was found murdered some three weeks subsequently. Hysteria swept London, a number of alleged plotters were executed, and stringent measures were initiated against Catholics. Fears died down in the summer of 1679, and Oates and his fellows were later convicted of perjury and severely punished. The political temperature, however, had been raised alarmingly.

Danby fell as a result of the plot, and on 24 January 1679 the Cavalier Parliament was finally prorogued, and elections planned for its successor. Conditions for the emergence of new political alignments now existed, not least because the passions generated by the Popish Plot had already created political flux. Anthony Ashley Cooper, Earl of Shaftesbury, a former royal minister who had broken with Charles in 1673, now headed a backlash against royal policy. This focused on the question of the succession. On 27 April the Commons voted that James, Duke of York, being a papist, was a leading figure in the Popish Plot, and Shaftesbury and his supporters brought in a bill to exclude him from the succession. Charles dissolved parliament on 12 July, but the issue would not go away, and he had to prorogue the parliament which followed it seven times between October 1679 and October 1680. During this period of agitation over exclusion there emerged, under Shaftesbury's leadership, the first Whigs: the first political party in anything like the modern sense to be seen in England. This, despite its intrinsic interest, proved to be a precocious and ineffectual development. The last parliament of the reign, meeting at Oxford in March 1681, was dissolved when yet another Exclusion Bill was brought in. The Exclusion Crisis had seen two years of political turmoil and the prefiguration of the modern political party: yet its most significant outcome was that Charles achieved a position of strength which was rarely rivalled in seventeenth-century England. He had emerged triumphant from two years of opposition over a matter which touched a fundamental chord in English prejudices, and weathered a turmoil which many thought would inaugurate a new civil war.

The last four years of Charles II's reign entered later Whig legend as the period of the 'Stuart Revenge'. This was a bad time to be a known Whig or dissenter. A handful of prominent Whigs suffered trial for treason, especially after the Rye House Plot of 1683, while many others were deprived of local, and especially municipal, office. The laws against dissent were put into effect more stringently, and in many areas troops were brought in to suppress dissenters, a practice all too reminiscent of Louis XIV's *dragonnades* against his Huguenot subjects. Parliament did not sit in this period, despite the Triennial Act, while Charles's standing army was built up in strength and publicized by royal propagandists as a bulwark against the social subversion held to be inherent in Whiggery and dissent. Financial retrenchment and modest French subsidies meant that money was not a problem. Above all, Charles avoided that alienation of the political nation which his father had achieved by 1640 and which his brother was to achieve by 1688. Taxes were light and legal, and the contemporary upsurge in trade added to national prosperity and, via indirect taxation, to the royal revenues. If ever Stuart absolutism was to be a possibility it was in the early 1680s, when Charles had a full treasury, an adequate standing army, and the support of the bulk of the political nation. But his death, on 6 February 1685, paved the way for renewed instability.

The event which many had feared and some had tried to prevent came to pass: James, Duke of York, a professed Roman Catholic, came to the throne. Yet his regime seemed secure enough initially. There were none of the immediate Protestant risings which many had predicted. Parliament, which James called rapidly, was loyal, and overwhelmingly Tory. A rebellion broke out in June when the Duke of Monmouth, Charles II's illegitimate son, landed at Lyme in Dorset and declared himself for the Protestant Cause, yet it was defeated within a month at Sedgemoor (6 July). Many artisans and small-holding farmers rallied to Monmouth's cause, but the gentry did not, and there was little overt support outside the south-west. The military defeat of the rebellion was followed by a savage repression and a rallying of the Tories behind James. At this time James seemed willing to work with, and able to retain the support of, both traditionally minded gentry and the Anglican church. But signs of future trouble rapidly showed themselves. Both Houses of Parliament had, by the autumn of 1685, slid into opposition to James's desire to maintain a sizeable standing army, and to his policy of favouring Catholics. On 20 November he prorogued parliament, and dismissed MPs who had opposed the court from any offices they held. He entered into the main drift of his policy over the next two years, a dependence on Catholic (and, later, on Protestant nonconformist) office-holders, and an attack on existing privilege.

The roll-call of James's iniquities is well known, and needs only be repeated briefly here. He offended local élites by remodelling borough charters to ensure the election of MPs favourable to royal policy, and by replacing Anglican gentry JPs with Catholics and dissenters. He not only maintained what was, by English standards, a large standing army (some 40,000 strong in the summer of 1688) but also officered it, although to a lesser extent in reality than in Protestant myth, with Catholics. He attacked the privileges of Magdalen College, Oxford, by interfering with the election of its president and attempting to foist a papist one on it. The deprivation of the fellows who resisted, and their subsequent replacement with yet more papists, was seen not only as an attempt to subvert an Anglican institution, but also as an attack on property rights, a college fellowship being regarded as a type of freehold. James alienated the Anglican establishment further by prosecuting seven bishops, headed by Sancroft, the Archbishop of Canterbury, for refusing to read a Declaration of Indulgence accepting the legality of the Crown's dispensing powers. Their trial, which ended in acquittal, was a triumph for James's opponents. By the summer of 1688 much of the political nation was united in its opposition to James's policies. But the problem, as in the 1630s or the 1650s, was that there was little that could actually be *done*. As with Cromwell's Protectorate, the presence of a standing army probably acted as a disincentive to rebellion, but the causes of quiescence went much deeper: once more, we encounter the traditional dislike of rebellion, reinforced as it now was by memories of what rebellion and its consequences had brought on in the years after 1642. The political nation had immense psychological difficulties in envisaging armed resistance to a monarch even as inimical as James II.

Fortunately, somebody in the Dutch Republic had rather fewer reservations about such matters. William of Orange, husband of James's daughter Mary, had long taken an interest in English affairs. William's main object in life was to frustrate Louis XIV's plans to achieve French hegemony in western Europe, and developments in England were obviously very relevant. With the accession of a Catholic King, English Protestants began to think of William as a potential saviour of English liberties and of the Protestant religion. Negotiations between Englishmen alienated by James's policies and William's agents accelerated in 1688, while the birth of a son to James on 10 June of that year, threatening a Catholic succession, lent an added urgency to matters. A formal invitation to William to intervene in English affairs was made by Compton, the Bishop of London, and six influential laymen. Despite the critical nature of European affairs, William decided to invade, managed to get the support of the Dutch government for the venture, and gathered an army and a fleet. After a false start when the expedition had to turn back because of adverse winds, William sailed down the Channel and landed at Torbay in Devon on 5 November, a propitious date for the Protestant Cause. He advanced to the regional capital, Exeter, where he received little support from the local clergy or Tory corporation, but a great deal from the populace and gentry. He then advanced on London. James concentrated his forces, on paper twice as numerous as William's, at Salisbury, but they began to fall apart, especially when the monarch, discouraged by the earliest desertions, decided to retreat to the capital. By that time a number of provincial centres, notably Chester, Hull, Norwich, Nottingham and York had fallen to William's supporters. After unsuccessful attempts to rally support in London, James decided to flee the country, but was inconveniently captured by some Kentish fishermen, who apparently thought he was a Jesuit agent. Fortunately, he decided to make another attempt at escape, and on 22 December left for France, hoping perhaps that the political chaos created by his actions would lead to his speedy recall.

James's decision to escape abroad prevented any outbreak of civil warfare, but it left Lords and Commons wondering how best to fill the political vacuum which had been created. The basic problem, as so often in the seventeenth century, was how to address the realities of the current political crisis while maintaining at least a pretence of political propriety. A group of peers and influential MPs asked William to take control of the government provisionally and to call for a parliamentary election. The resulting Convention Parliament met on 22 January 1689. Its members envisaged a number of solutions to the constitutional crisis. A small number, who could be safely disregarded, were for recalling James on terms. Many (particularly in the House of Lords) wanted some form of regency, with William governing on behalf of James, who would retain the title of monarch, or Mary. The first alternative was clearly unworkable, the second was scotched by William's refusal to be subordinate to his wife. The only way out was to ignore the rules of succession and strict constitutional legality, and offer the Crown jointly to William and Mary. The Whigs cooked up the happy fiction that James's flight amounted to an abdication, that the throne was now vacant, and that the Crown, despite England's being an hereditary monarchy, was in a sense more or less elective. The stirring of Stuart support in Scotland and Ireland, fear of an early French intervention on behalf of James, and rumblings among his supporters in England dictated prompt action, and those unhappy with the constitutional position swallowed their reservations. On 13 February William and Mary became King and Queen. The actions of James's opponents were justified and the Protestant religion and the liberties of the subject were confirmed by the Bill of Rights: a document which catches the reality of what had happened by reading more like a medieval charter of liberties than a modern constitution. Essentially, the political nation had been alienated by their monarch, and sought to preserve their liberties by exchanging him for another one along lines which would have been perfectly comprehensible to a medieval baron. The social and local aspects of the events of 1688–89 have not been subjected to the same scrutiny as those of 1640–42, and such detailed work as has been carried out, notably on London, suggests that the Glorious Revolution did have its popular dimension, especially when the role of dissent is considered. Yet it is difficult not to conclude that this was the most conservative of revolutions: above all, it defies any Marxist or neo-Marxist attempt to be connected with major socioeconomic changes.

Glorious Revolution to Treaty of Utrecht

The unity of purpose which allowed the Revolution settlement to be cobbled up died away soon after the passing of the Bill of Rights. William himself was by inclination an autocratic monarch, although his experience of politics in the United Provinces had familiarized him with the arts of political manoeuvre. That these acts were necessary became obvious when he realized, to his distaste, that English parliamentarians were even more bloody-minded, short-sighted and slippery than republican Dutch regents. There were a number of other complications. Mary was popular, but William was a difficult man to get on with and not likely to win friends easily. His unfavourable initial impression of English politicians led him to rely heavily on his trusted Dutch advisers, few of whom bothered to establish close contacts with English grandees. Accordingly, there was considerable resentment against the Dutch interest. Moreover, William was abroad for at least half of most years in his reign, and the need to keep things running in his absence (especially after the death of Mary in 1694) created additional strains, although these were in large measure met by the development of the Cabinet. The underlying problem was that the settlement of 1688–89 still left many things unsettled. Everybody was agreed, and most people were very contented, that England was a limited monarchy. But where exactly the limits lay remained a very imprecise matter. Long-term political problems were not solved overnight by the Glorious Revolution.

Additional strains were created by the ramifications of England's involvement in continental warfare. William's main motive in invading England was the harnessing of that nation's resources to the defeat of Louis XIV. The English political nation, hostile to heavy taxation, to a large and aggressive central government, and to a large standing army, now found itself having to countenance all these things. One of the major themes of the 1690s was the growth of war taxation, and of the administrative and financial institutions needed to manage that taxation and the military machine it supported. The growth was small by modern standards, and even by those of some contemporary European states, but it was enough to cause dismay. The 1690s also witnessed a concomitant growth in the executive and in government bureaucracy. A number of government departments, notably the Principal Secretaries' Office, the Treasury and the Navy Office (which had been expanded in the period 1660–88) were still small, and the court and the royal household actually contracted under William and his successor, Queen Anne. But some, among them the Post Office, the Customs and Excise, and others created to administer warfare or which emerged after the Union with Scotland of 1707, grew rapidly. Backwoods gentry were alarmed at the proliferation of the costs and personnel of government, although for those at the top the opportunities to dispense patronage, and thus expand the number of MPs and others with a stake in the new regime, increased massively.

A more celebrated innovation of the years after 1688 was the emergence of party politics. Obviously, the parties which arrived in that period were not as coherent or disciplined as their modern equivalents. Both 'Whig' and 'Tory' comprehended different groupings and alliances, and these tended to shift their positions and alter their alignments in response to various stimuli, whether over political principle or personal faction politics. Similarly, it was as difficult as ever to ensure that MPs attended sessions regularly: in William III's reign, an average division of the House would be attended by 238 members, less than half the total. At times, moreover, the Whig–Tory dichotomy would be replaced by, or subsumed in, the older court–country divide: the old 'country' distaste for big government, big finance, placemen and standing armies never went away, and on occasion could assert itself decisively. Even so, during the 1690s two distinct parties, each with an acknowledged leadership, a party organization, clubs, propagandists, and distinctive sets of attitudes did emerge. Over most of the period 1689–1714 observers of and participants in politics, from heads of administration down to electors casting their votes, viewed political life and political culture in terms of party.

The basic shift of William's reign was that the Tories, associated with the court under James II, now identified themselves with those country attitudes which the first Whigs had appropriated at the time of the Exclusion Crisis. Although they numbered industrialists and merchants in their midst, Tory rhetoric now harped on the virtues and interests of country gentlemen, a group which felt increasingly that post-1689 developments had little to offer them. They became hostile to the growth of the executive and of bureaucracy; to the growth of the monied interest, regarded not only as the natural support of a swollen government, but also, with its credit transactions and other incomprehensible financial devices, as unnatural and corrupting; and to dissent, which they identified with demagogy and the socially subversive sectaries of the 1650s. These attitudes, reinforced by traditional xenophobia and dislike of high taxes, meant that the Tories formed a natural majority of the political nation. The Whigs, on the other hand, claimed to stand for English liberties and English Protestantism against the tyranny of James II and of the French monarch whom he and his brother so admired. The typical Whig of Tory propaganda was either a financier or a dissenter, although in reality the party included members of many other groups, including gentry. Indeed, the Whigs suffered from comprehending a variety of groupings and sectional interests, as well as from being, under normal circumstances, a minority of the political nation. They were, however, better led and better organized than the Tories.

By 1695 William's regime was an increasingly unpopular one. The political nation had welcomed William and Mary in 1688 as preservers of English liberties, but had not envisaged being embroiled in continual warfare against the French. Tory country gentlemen were obviously disillusioned, and those merchants outside the circles who were involved in financing or supplying the armed forces were alienated by the disruption of trade that warfare entailed. Criticisms of William's policies, notably of his maintaining a standing army in peacetime, grew after hostilities were ended with the Treaty of Rijswijk in 1697. The elections of 1698 accordingly returned a solid body of MPs hostile to royal policy, disaffected country Whigs and independents lining up with Tories. The Act of Settlement of 1701, which ensured the succession of the House of Hanover, can be read as much as a critique of William III's government as a barrier against a Stuart restoration. Clauses asserted the primacy of England's interests over those of the continental possessions of any future monarch, insisted that any such monarch should be a communicating member of the Church of England, made it impossible for them to leave England without parliament's permission, and tried to ban foreigners from the Privy Council and placemen from the House of Commons. Yet, strangely, the ramshackle settlement put together in three working weeks early in 1689 had continued to function: deep in their hearts, even Tory gentlemen fulminating against the land tax, Dutchmen and parasitic financiers knew that the only real alternative, Catholic absolutism on the French model, would be even more distasteful.

William died in the spring of 1702, and was followed by Anne, second daughter of James II. By that time it was evident that Europe was on the brink of renewed warfare. On his deathbed in 1700 Charles II of Spain had attempted to frustrate plans among the western powers to carve up the Spanish Empire by leaving his possessions to Philip of Anjou, second son of Louis XIV's heir. Europe was now faced with the prospect of a France dynastically connected with what was still a massive empire. The reign of Anne was dominated by the ensuing War of the Spanish Succession (1702–13). Until 1710 political control was vested in a ministry headed by Sidney, Earl of Godolphin, at home, and John, Duke of Marlborough, abroad. The ministry was under constant pressure, from high Tories before about 1705, and from the Whigs after that date: yet its achievements were formidable. Marlborough, the first English military commander of European reputation for quite some time, was victorious at Blenheim (1704), Ramillies (1706) and, less decisively, at Oudenarde (1708) and Malplaquet (1709), and also showed considerable diplomatic skills in dealing with allied politicians and generals. At home, Godolphin engineered the Regency Act of 1706, which helped buttress the Protestant succession, and the Act of Union with Scotland of 1707, as well as defeating a challenge for power from an up-and-coming Tory, Robert Harley. But by 1709, as in the mid-1690s, country opinion was growing hostile to a war which seemed to be going nowhere, yet which was becoming ever more costly. The Second Dutch War had cost £1,600,000 or thereabouts a year: the War of the Spanish Succession cost five times that amount annually.

As the manoeuvrings against Marlborough and Godolphin suggest, party was still a dominant issue in English politics during Anne's reign. The Triennial Act of 1694, which owed its existence to the belief that regular parliaments would ensure uncorrupt government, inaugurated a period of frequent general elections, nine of them being held between 1695 and 1713. These elections were contested in many constituencies, which meant that the electorate was kept in a permanent state of agitation over these years. The electorate was, moreover, growing in size, reaching 300,000 by 1713. As ever, a split between court and country along traditional lines might supplant party divisions: something very much like this seems to have occurred in the last five years of the seventeenth century. Yet over most of Anne's reign it was party which counted. With Addison, Swift, Steele and Defoe all writing on current issues, it was also a reign that witnessed a remarkable flowering of that polemical literature which had been a feature of English life since the 1640s. Party politics were no longer the concern merely of the great at Westminster, but also regularly informed political opinion in the nation at large. Yet at its highest the rage of party demonstrated that its most important function was the containment of political conflict. The polemics of hack writers or the actions of a mob at an election might appear distasteful, but they took place essentially within a set of political conventions which had been operating tacitly since 1688. These ensured that any political inconveniences engendered by the new political system would be far less disruptive than a civil war or the regular impeachment of ministers. Party strife now clearly operated in a context of political stability.

Religion, although a less explosive element than it had been in 1640-42, 1679-81 or 1688-89, was still of prime importance. William III was a Calvinist of the old school, firmly attached to the notion of a providential God: apparently the only joke he is recorded as having made was when he landed at Torbay, and asked Gilbert Burnet, 'Well, Doctor, what do you think of predestination now?' He was probably very happy to be described in the Bill of Rights as 'the glorious instrument appointed by God' for 'delivering this kingdom from popery and arbitrary power'. Anne, conversely, was a dedicated Anglican. Unfortunately, the Church of England was badly split in her reign. The drift among educated clergy and laity was towards latitudinarianism, a more inclusive style of Anglicanism which envisaged the possibility of coexistence with Protestant dissent and took an attitude towards Christianity which was more in keeping with the Age of Reason than with the harsher theology of old-style Puritanism. The lower clergy, and the Tory gentry, took a more robust view. Encouraged by an over-optimistic view of Anne's attitudes, the lower clergy and their gentry allies attempted to implement a clerical reaction. 'Occasional conformists', dissenters who made token attendances at Anglican services in order to be formally entitled to hold governmental or municipal office, were made the subject of hostile legislation. Calvinist refugees from Germany, a few thousand of whom were granted a general naturalization when they entered the country in 1708-9, became a political football between Whig and Tory. Tensions were brought to a head when, on 5

November 1709, Dr Henry Sacheverell preached an ultra-Tory sermon before an appreciative Lord Mayor of London, in which he lambasted the familiar objects of high-church and Tory loathing. The government attempted to impeach him, but the trial misfired badly. His counsel conducted a brilliant defence, and Sacheverell was found guilty by only a narrow majority of the Lords, receiving the token punishment of being debarred from preaching for three years. Nevertheless, the high-church triumph which was expected to follow this disaster for the Whigs failed to materialize. Anne, and Robert Harley, who founded a new ministry in 1710, were determined not to put themselves under the influence of factious clergymen or Tory extremists. High-church agitation was still fierce, but Anne was able to pass over high-churchmen, such as Francis Atterbury, in favour of milder Tories when appointing bishops. Her death ended any hopes of a high-church ascendancy.

Religion continued to exercise a wider influence over political and social attitudes. Anne's Anglican convictions allowed the development of that Anglican revival which had begun in the 1690s, while more generally, a non-secular view of the social order and the monarchy which preserved it was still current. Notions of divine-right monarchy may have been less obtrusive after 1688, but they were still present: the accession of both William III and George I were publicized as examples of divine providence, and the adherents of both these monarchs were unlikely to discard what remained in many ways the most convincing justification for royal authority. Queen Anne was the last English monarch to touch for scrofula, the 'King's Evil': evidence of the lingering belief in the thaumaturgic properties which were attached to the sacred office of monarchy. The social order continued to be seen in terms of a fixed hierarchy appointed by God, its social inequities immutable. Isaac Watts, in his *Essay Towards the Encouragement of Charity Schools*, noted that God had ordained that in all ages there should be rich and poor, and that He 'hath alloted to the poor the meaner services, and hath given the rich the more honorable business of life. Nor is it possible according to the present course of nature and human affairs to alter this constitution of things.' Most educated contemporaries were convinced that the social hierarchies of the period were created by God, not by man.

It was, however, the perennially earthly machinations of career politicians which determined the course of day-to-day politics. The reputation of Godolphin and Marlborough waned, and Robert Harley intrigued against them with politicians and disgruntled army officers. The general election of 1710, held against a background of war-weariness and high-church agitation, resulted in a resounding Tory victory and was followed by a solidly Tory ministry. The surprising resiliency of the French fuelled the growing conviction that the war had gone on long enough, and the Tory ascendancy provided a congenial atmosphere for complaints that English interests were being sacrificed to those of the Dutch, the Austrians or other allied powers. Harley, who became Lord Treasurer and Earl of Oxford in 1711, set about negotiating with the French. His efforts bore fruit in the Treaty of Utrecht (1713), which saw the emergence of Britain as a world power. But any feelings of Tory triumph at the ending of the war were quickly overtaken by events. Queen Anne died on 1 August 1714. The English, having brought in a Dutch monarch to protect their liberties in 1688, now turned to a German one to perform the same task. The Elector of Hanover became King George I of England, leaving the Tories even more confused over their attitudes to the succession.

The Whig ascendancy

The political environment in which George I found himself was a complex one. Ultimately, the constitution appeared to give power to parliament. By the Bill of Rights of 1689 and the Act of Settlement of 1701 parliament had placed severe restrictions on any future monarch, George included. He could not be a Roman Catholic, or be married to one. He could not intrude his countrymen too blatantly into positions of power. He could not suspend the laws of the realm. Parliament supplied him with his armed forces and the taxes which supported them, while the King's ministers were, in the last resort, answerable to parliament. Yet royal support was still vital for any ministry. The goodwill of the monarch could protect a minister from unpopularity, while the withdrawal of that goodwill ensured that a political career would be blocked or terminated. Certainly George I and the German advisers he brought with him were willing to exercise power and play an active role in politics. Although he was not over-endowed intellectually, the tradition that he was stupid and incapable of forming or following a policy is overdrawn. Most immediately, the Peace of Utrecht, by which, he felt, Britain had let down Hanover and her other allies, left him determined to remove the Tory leaders who had engineered it.

Almost from the start, therefore, George I's reign saw a transition from the Tory hegemony of 1710–14 to the beginnings of the Whig ascendancy. Despite Utrecht, George probably initially envisaged including Tories in the government, but he was alienated by a violent Tory propaganda campaign against him. Tory propagandists used his foreignness (he could speak little English) and his German advisers to stir up country xenophobia against him, and also launched more exotic smears against him – notably that he used two Turkish servants, Mohamed and Mustapha, for 'abominable purposes'. Moreover, the leaders of the Tories had shown little initiative in preparing for the Hanoverian succession, while the estrangement between Oxford and Bolingbroke left that leadership divided. The Jacobite rising of 1715, although not as threatening as was feared at the time, finally discredited the Tories in George's eyes: for the remainder of the reign Whigs were able to buttress their position by reminding the monarch of the links between the Tories and the Stuart cause. Yet even before the 1715 rising it was obvious that the Tories were on their way out. There had been a massive purge of Tories in the administration in 1714, with the Cabinet cleared of them, their places being taken by senior Whigs. The Privy Council had its membership reduced from 80 to 32, one member being a young Whig named Robert Walpole, now made paymaster of the forces despite having been imprisoned for corruption under the previous regime. The Jacobite scare of 1715 had allowed the Whigs to suspend Habeas Corpus and pass a Riot Act which cleared the way for the use of the standing army against popular demonstrations. They also passed a Septennial Act in 1716, by which parliaments could last for seven years rather than for three. For the traditional defenders of English liberties and parliamentary rights, this was a striking performance. The radical tendencies of the first Whigs were now far distant.

But within a year the Whigs were suffering badly from internal factional strife. The old guard, led by James, Earl of Stanhope, and Charles, Earl of Sunderland, were challenged by the younger Whigs, notably Walpole, and Charles, Viscount Townshend. Walpole, in particular, was an excellent politician. He consolidated his reputation among the parliamentarian gentry by his opposition to the Peerage Bill of 1719, and by adroit footwork managed to emerge unscathed from the wreckage when the South Sea Bubble burst in 1720. From then until 1742 Walpole was able to dominate politics. His success was attributable to a number of factors. He had an excellent understanding of the House of Commons, in which he was to sit for a total of 41 years. He had a comprehensive grasp of parliamentary tactics and of the workings of patronage and faction. He was also a superb speaker, as the debates of 1719 demonstrated. Above all, he realized that the key to success in being a parliamentary leader in early Hanoverian England lay in not doing very much. Those seeking bold new political schemes and innovatory legislation will find little to satisfy them in Walpole's ascendancy. Both he and the rest of the political nation would have agreed with the writer who in 1723 declared in the *Northampton Mercury* that 'the first safety of princes and states lies in avoiding all councils or designs of innovation, in ancient and established forms and laws, especially those concerning liberty and property, and religion'. The events of the seventeenth century, thought most Hanoverians, were proof enough of the dangers of innovation. Walpole was, by and large, content simply to exercise and enjoy power: his one major departure from this position, the excise scheme, was, instructively enough, a disaster.

Walpole, as J.H. Plumb and his pupils have convinced us, conferred one-party government, peace abroad, stability at home, and executive efficiency on Britain. These were the golden days of oligarchic politics, with Whigs unassailably in control, the legislature subordinated to the executive, a sense of common identity among those in power, and the population at large effectively excluded from the processes of political decision-making. The maintenance of this situation depended overwhelmingly upon placemen in the House of Commons, of whom there were some 260 by 1761. Their votes could never be taken entirely for granted, but their presence, and the patronage upon which the working of the system depended, were essential to the working of politics. The management of the elections which returned them was also of prime importance. Under the existing electoral system, 40 English counties with an electorate of some 160,000 voters returned 80 MPs, while 205 boroughs with an electorate of 101,000 returned 409. Wales, with 21,000 electors, and Scotland, with 2700, returned 24 and 45 members respectively. Since the Exclusion Crisis it had been obvious that the crucial problem in any general election was the control of borough seats, especially those with small and pliable electorates. Some boroughs had a very wide franchise, comprehending all adult males in a few favoured centres. Others were more restricted: one-third of boroughs had less than 100 voters, some had very few indeed. In 1690 perhaps one-third of borough seats were under private or government control, by 1761 well over half, only 20 of which were firmly Tory. Over the same period, the rising costs of electioneering confirmed the trend towards oligarchy implicit in these figures. Viscount Perceval spent £900 wooing the 32 voters of Harwich in 1727, an exercise which had cost Samuel Pepys a mere £8 5s 6d in 1689. County elections, in which influence had to be exercised over thousands of voters, could be hideously expensive: the most celebrated example, the Oxfordshire election of 1754, cost the Tory promoters and their supporters £20,000. Understandably, elections were less frequently contested in the mid-eighteenth century than they had been 50 years before. In 1705 65 per cent of counties went to the poll, a proportion which had dropped to 7.5 per cent by 1747. Increasingly, parliamentary politics were the monopoly of landed aristocrats: nobody else could afford the costs of participation.

Yet the strength of the Hanoverian settlement and of Walpole should not lead us to ignore their opponents entirely. When George I came to the throne there were reckoned to be 58 individuals living with a better claim to it than his. James Francis Edward, the son of James II, was the most obvious and by far the most dangerous of them. Throughout the period 1689–1745 English regimes regarded a Stuart restoration as their greatest danger: certainly Walpole was almost paranoid about the Jacobite menace. But, as the events of 1715 and 1745 proved, there was a wide gap between desultory plotting or loose alehouse talk and actually risking one's neck for the future James III or Charles III. When disgruntled Tories toasted The King Over The Water, they were generally motivated by country frustrations rather than by any deep affection for the Stuart cause. Indeed, by 1720 most Tory politicians had recognized the bankruptcy of Jacobitism, and applied themselves to working within the framework of the Hanoverian state. The years 1725–35 saw the emergence of a 'patriot' alliance of country Whigs, independents and Tories, their collective views being represented from 1726 in a journal called *The Craftsman*. In the event this alliance, like later attempts to combine against Walpole, failed to prosper. Personal ambition and personal animosities, as well as the unreality of any long-term alliance between even disgruntled Whigs and Tory backbenchers, made any cross-party opposition alliance impossible.

The Whig monopoly of power at the centre did not prevent the continued development of extra-parliamentary political culture and political action, much of it anti-Walpolean. There were ample opportunities for obtaining and discussing political information. Men met together to read newspapers and argue over their contents in the alehouse, in local debating societies and, above all, in the coffee house. The coffee house, that great innovation of the mid-seventeenth century, rapidly became central not only to the sociability and leisure time of the middling orders, but also to their political culture. By 1739 there were 551 coffee houses in central London, and by 1763 even a small market-town like Knaresborough in North Yorkshire could boast a coffee house taking four London newspapers. Satirical prints, ballads and the theatre all combined to help keep an extra-parliamentary political culture going. The introduction of stage licensing in 1737 and the eight writs for libel issued against *The Craftsman* help demonstrate just how seriously government took the criticism of this wider political world. Local conflicts helped to maintain an interest in party even if Walpole's hegemony was making it redundant in parliament. At Norwich, for example, there were no contested parliamentary elections over the period 1715–27: yet the years between 1721 and 1729 witnessed 21 elections for municipal office, all of them contested along party lines. Party politics now bit deep into society: local office-holders – mayors, justices of the peace, even churchwardens and poor-law officials – all had coercive and other powers, and were prepared to use them to further party interest. Mob action, while perhaps best taken as the lowest common denominator of politics, demonstrated the breadth of the political culture of the period, and also had a tendency to follow party lines. The common people may not yet have developed a comprehensive critique of society or a political programme for its restructuring but, here as elsewhere, they showed that they had a strong sense of corporate identity and a capacity for collective action. If the eighteenth century was a period of oligarchy, it was an oligarchy modified by riot.

But the political culture, and the conflicts it encompassed, existed within, and was essentially limited by, an almost universal acceptance that the post-1688 constitution was a Good Thing. Everybody from an election rioter to Walpole was convinced that they were singularly lucky in living under the settlement as established at the time of the Glorious Revolution: it was this, they felt, which made England different, especially from continental absolutist regimes. This settlement did not imply popular sovereignty or a vision of a society based upon political equality. Rather, its main benefit was that it protected the subject from the arbitrary will of an absolute monarch. It converted natural rights to civil liberties, not to political participation, which was the prerogative of the propertied. Apparently a large proportion of the unenfranchised felt that the constitution offered them rights and liberties, these being protected by that great shibboleth of eighteenth-century political debate, the rule of law. Englishmen, even the four-fifths of them who could not vote, felt that the Glorious Revolution had guaranteed civil liberties and legal rights for themselves and their families. By the early eighteenth century growing national prosperity was also seen as a benefit derived from the constitution: political prints of the period showed the freeborn Englishman, prosperous, quaffing ale and dining off roast beef, in contrast to his French counterpart, living off black bread and frogs' legs, oppressed by Catholic clergy and the agents of the absolutist state.

Concentration on events at Westminster has led not only to a failure to realize the importance of this wider political culture, but also to a downgrading of the importance of religion. Religion was, however, still fundamental to most analyses of politics. Their views may have received a more critical response than those of their pre-1642 counterparts, but churchmen were still willing to attribute dramatic events to divine intervention, and to derive moral lessons from them. The South Sea Bubble crisis of 1720, the Jacobite Atterbury's Plot of 1722 and the Jacobite Rebellions of 1715 and 1745, bad harvests in 1727, 1740 and 1756, the outbreak of plague in France in 1721 and the earthquake which destroyed Lisbon in 1755, all served for this purpose. Ideas of the divine right of monarchy and of the divine basis for social hierarchy had survived 1688, and were certainly still current, if a little threadbare, in 1760.

The church continued to enjoy a political power which matched its ideological influence. In certain respects the Church of England might feel itself bound to suffer under a Whig oligarchy: the Whig tradition was an anti-clerical one. Hence Convocation, a brief revival in 1741 apart, did not meet between 1717 and the nineteenth century, and high-churchmen tended not to be favoured with high ecclesiastical office early in Walpole's ascendancy. Yet Walpole was as aware of the need to avoid conflict and controversy in religious matters as in all others. He was not a great friend of dissent, and the cry of 'The Church in Danger', which had proved so potent at the time of the Sacheverell affair and which was to revive in the 1750s, was not invoked while he was prime minister. Despite some posing and a little crypto-Jacobitism, the Anglican clergy were able to adapt to a Whig regime which looked increasingly unthreatening. By 1720, indeed, Anglican polemicists were becoming worried by a new set of enemies. Having battled against Protestant nonconformity and the adherents of Rome in the seventeenth century, they now found themselves confronting deism, freethinking and even atheism. Their fears were exaggerated, but the strength with which they entered into theological debate with these novel challengers points to the continued vitality of Anglicanism. The Church of England was still a tremendously powerful force, intellectually, culturally, economically and, not least, politically.

Although at times Walpole must have looked as permanent a feature of the English scene as the established church, even he could not last for ever. In the 1741 general election his ministry suffered badly, while his parliamentary opponents achieved unity by attaching themselves to the interest of the Prince of Wales. Newcastle and Hardwicke, former allies of Walpole, became increasingly unhappy with his running of the war into which Britain had entered in 1739 against Walpole's wishes, and declared themselves ready to run a rival administration. Walpole resigned on 1 February 1742, and went to the Upper House as Lord Orford. Effective control passed to John, Lord Carteret, later Earl of Granville, who was in turn ousted in 1746 by Thomas Pelham-Hollis, Duke of Newcastle, and his brother Henry Pelham. This administration, which lasted until Pelham's death in 1754, created an alliance between the 'Old Corps' of Whigs and some new allies: the most noteworthy individual to achieve office at this stage was William Pitt, the future Earl of Chatham. On Pelham's death Newcastle became prime minister, but failed to maintain momentum, not least because, after Walpole, a prime minister operating from the House of Lords faced severe difficulties. In 1757 matters were set on a sounder footing when he founded a joint ministry with Pitt. The renewal of European warfare in 1756 made the formation of a viable regime essential, and Pitt was to steer the country through this conflict, the Seven Years War, until 1761. By that time the new monarch, George III, had spent a year listening to Pitt's critics, and set out to inhibit his policy. The ensuing peace, which was signed in 1763, although marking another step in the formation of the British Empire, was a disappointment to Pitt.

The accession of George III is normally regarded as an important watershed in British political history. His long reign was to see the arrival of John Wilkes and radical politics, the shock of the American and French Revolutions and, from the 1790s, the first stirrings of mass political consciousness since the Levellers. All this seems very far away when the situation in 1760 is assessed without recourse to hindsight. At that date political stability, in the sense that politics was a game played by great men, and that this situation was accepted by the population at large, seemed assured. The politics of the Exclusion Crisis and the Glorious Revolution, the rage of party and the frequent elections of 1695–1715, the alarums caused by the rebellions of 1715 and 1745, the nagging worry about the Protestant succession, were all very distant. That most famous historian of eighteenth-century English politics, Sir Lewis Namier, argued that the very notion of party itself was redundant in parliamentary politics at the time of George III's accession. Politics as a matter of ideology or principle had come to something of a full stop.

Certainly, the school of thought currently dominating our interpretation of mid-eighteenth-century politics stresses the political stability of the period. The doyen of that school, J.H. Plumb, made the point forcefully in 1965 in his Ford Lectures at Oxford, which were published in book form two years later. Plumb contrasted the Stuart and the Hanoverian periods thus:

> In the seventeenth century men killed, tortured and executed each other for political beliefs; they sacked towns and brutalized the countryside; they were subjected to conspiracy, plot and invasion. This uncertain political world lasted until 1715, and then began rapidly to vanish. By comparison, the political structure of eighteenth-century England possesses adamantine strength and profound inertia.[2]

This thesis can, perhaps, be criticized in detail: yet its basic validity seems irreproachable. Such strife as there was in the period 1689–1760, Jacobite invasions apart, was essentially the strife of faction or party, containable within the existing political system and offering no challenge to it. The 'rage of party' between Whig and Tory, even at its most bitter, had much of the character of a safety valve. But Plumb, turning briefly from the purely political arena, also sensed an underlying shift linking his preoccupations with those which have concerned us in this book. He postulated the existence of 'deep social causes of which contemporaries are usually unaware'[3] which made political stability of the type he delineated possible. It is to the implications of this deeper stability that we will now turn.

Plumb wrote of the stability he found being the product of 'profound inertia'. More fruitfully, another historian of eighteenth century England, Dorothy Marshall, has pointed out that 'stability comes from the balancing of tensions, not from inertia'.[4] English society in the first half of the eighteenth century was far from inert. It combined intellectual inventiveness, economic enterprise, a burgeoning consumer society and a relatively advanced political culture. It was, nevertheless, stable, and that stability owed much to the resolution of a number of those tensions inherent in early modern England. Most fundamentally of all, the economy was able, except in the worst of bad years, to feed the population adequately, and even the labouring poor were free from the spectre of starvation. A related problem, the tension between an economy which fluctuated on an annual basis and a social structure which changed at a much slower pace, had achieved equilibrium. Religion, although still a fertile field of intellectual speculation and debate, and although still vital both to the individual believer and to the broader concepts of authority, morality and social hierarchy, was no longer a cause for armed struggle or a vehicle for revolutionary ideologies. Among the élite, the landed orders had learnt to accommodate the growth of commercial wealth, and the politically active gentry

– the bane of Charles I, Cromwell and James II – had been tamed by the Whig aristocracy.

There is a massive contrast between this situation and the ethos of the century which preceded 1650. As we have seen at various points, the second third of the seventeenth century saw a marked historical discontinuity on a number of levels. The century up to about 1650 was a period of steady population growth: the one following it one of relative demographic stability. The first century was a period of mounting pressure on resources, of rising food prices, of declining real wages: the second one in which all these trends stabilized or were reversed. The first saw an increase in social mobility: the second the development of oligarchy and of a more restricted recruitment into many sections of the élite. The first saw a boom in the traditional institutions of education, the universities and the grammar schools: the second their stagnation. The first saw Christianity, both official and unofficial, as a dynamic force: in the second official Christianity at least did much to adjust to the more measured mood of the Age of Reason. The first century ended in civil warfare: the second with Pitt and Newcastle. The basic transition was one from a society which was, and thought itself to be, under pressure, to one which was, although by no means free of problems, much more assured. Despite occasional periods of panic, the mid-eighteenth century was largely free of that cosmic *Angst* which characterizes so much of the social and political comment of the years between 1550 and 1650.

The change, it must be stressed, was a relative one: there were still people, in 1760, worried about threats to social stability, about popery, and about the consequences of mankind's fall from divine grace. Even so, the general mood was not one of impending social collapse. England was sharing that new equilibrium in social, cultural and political affairs which had obtained in Europe from the turn of the seventeenth and eighteenth centuries. On a European level, it has been claimed that 'the years around 1700 appear more ordered, more assured about accepted conventions, less divided, less prone to vast and uncontrolled strivings in new directions, and less passionate about commitments – in sum, more settled and relaxed – than the preceding years'.[5] The pathological gloom about humanity's chances of survival, so marked before 1650, was now largely absent. Generally, then, England in 1760 was stable, its social fabric based firmly on familiar and solidly established structures, hegemonies and ideologies. The landed aristocracy was socially dominant, as much so as in 1550. Economic production was still based overwhelmingly on agriculture and handicraft industry. The Church of England, essentially as set up in 1559, was the dominant religious presence, with vital functions in government and in the maintenance of social discipline, its communicants the only group of believers in England who could aspire to full political citizenship. As we have emphasized continually, those deep and rapid economic, social and, ultimately, political changes which set in after about 1780 would not have been easy to predict in 1760. English society had changed since 1550, but these changes were not such as to make later developments inevitable. We should be suspicious, again as has been emphasized throughout this book, of interpretations of history which constantly seek for the 'origins of modernity' in the early modern period, and try to trace some more or less linear development in which the seeds of twentieth-century Britain can be seen in the Age of the Tudors. As we have seen, developments over the two centuries which we have studied were simply not like that: change in one area and advances in another were often separated chronologically, and were often so disparate in their origins that a direct causal connection is difficult to trace.

Such a conclusion does imply a certain obligation to discuss a little more fully such changes as did occur. Obviously, there were a number of important transitions over the early modern period, although, if we may return to a theme touched upon in the previous paragraph, these transitions are perhaps not at their most obvious if we limit ourselves to an examination of social structures. As historians of late medieval England never tire of pointing out, a number of the 'new' features of English society whose arrival has traditionally been located in the sixteenth and seventeenth centuries were, if sometimes only in the more economically advanced parts of the country, already in place by 1500. Many working people were wholly or mainly dependent upon wage labour rather than subsistence farming. Social stratification in the village community was already marked, and some historians have claimed that the century of demographic expansion which was ended by the Black Death in 1348 created similar tendencies in rural society to those traced for the century of demographic expansion which ended about 1640. The 'rise of the gentry', once seen as one of the most fundamental features of the social history of the 100 years before the Civil Wars, looks less remarkable in the light of what we now know about the fourteenth- and fifteenth-century gentry. As we have noted in the previous paragraph, the dominance of the landed aristocracy continued, even if that dominance was exercised in different ways in the mid-eighteenth century from those which had characterized it in the fifteenth. Even the structures of family life seemed to have changed little over the same sort of timespan. If the once generally accepted distinctions between the medieval and early modern periods now seem uncertain, arguably, those traditionally drawn between the early modern and modern periods are still sustainable: the arrival of large-scale urbanization and factory production, mass politics, something like the modern state, political and social discourses based on the concept of class, although perhaps even here some of the distinctions look more questionable than they may have done to historians two generations ago. Certainly there were changes over the two centuries covered by this book: but if the transitions of traditional historiography now look less convincing than before, what can be put in their place?

One of the most important changes in this period was in the relation-ship between the localities and central power. Superficiallly, this change might seem to lie outside 'social history', but even the briefest analysis demonstrates the falseness of such an assumption: the implications for society in this realignment were massive. As we have argued, before the later seventeenth century the English state was, compared to the situation in a number of other western and central European states, underdevel-oped. From that point, however, the logic of raising and funding a large army and navy, as well as the logic of a developing ideology based on patriotism and xenophobia, heightened the sense of England (and indeed Britain) as a distinct entity. But even before the late seventeenth century, the steady development of central government meant that the provinces were gradually enmeshed in a web of information-gathering, taxation and law enforcement. We have only to look at the minutes of a late Elizabethan Privy Council meeting to see how these processes looked from the centre. And, for the perspective from local society, we have only to consider how the gentry in county élites became involved in the state system as ever more active justices of the peace and militia officers, and how parish élites, differentiated more sharply from the village poor by the broader socioeconomic changes of the period, became involved in the state system as parish constables, churchwardens and overseers of the poor. Gentlemen had served as justices before 1550, and yeomen as parish constables: but the intensification of the demands of central government from the mid-sixteenth century interacted with broader social and economic changes to provide something new. This development was uncertain in some places, and always subject to local or regional varia-tions, yet, in total, it was significant enough. England has many histories: that of the nation, but also those of each individual within that nation, and of such intervening phenomena as villages, towns and counties, trades and colleges, guilds and families. These various histories were becoming more closely enmeshed, and more interdependent, as the sixteenth, seven-teenth and eighteenth centuries progressed.

The second major shift, or set of shifts, was cultural. The most obvious aspect here was, perhaps, the implications of the growth in literacy and education. Again, research by medievalists is challenging the old stereo-types, and revealing that many of the laity were literate in the fifteenth century. Yet it is difficult to argue that, whereas in the late middle ages illiteracy was seen as characteristic of lay society, by 1760 it was seen as characteristic of the poor. Changes in educational demand and educational provisions over the period 1550–1760 meant that, whatever else the English had in common by the latter date, their upper, middle and middling ranks shared a distinctive literate culture, which helped both to help define their Englishness and help distinguish them from the labour-ing poor. To this marked cleavage based on literacy was added, perhaps a little less certainly, the socially selective nature of that retreat from magical and occult culture which we have noted. Belief in witchcraft and cunning men was now largely restricted to the poor and lower elements of the middling sort. The religious changes of the period reinforced these developments and these divisions. We accept that religious beliefs can be held at least as fervently by the poor as by the comfortably-off, and here as elsewhere any general statement involves the risk of oversimplification. Yet it remains clear that the Reformation and the religious developments which followed it had created a religiosity of a more intellectualized and internalized nature, a religiosity which depended upon reading and reflection rather than looking at those doctrinal strip cartoons which were medieval church wall paintings. In sum, these cultural and religious changes helped make England a very different place in 1760 from what it had been at the end of the middle ages.

What these changes added up to was, first, that English society was more self-conscious and, second, that the English had made the transition from being the remote offshore islanders of 1550 to 'polite and commercial people' of the mid-eighteenth century. It is here, perhaps, that we tread upon more contentious and more speculative ground. Measuring changes in manners and sensibility is always difficult, and we have every right to be cautious about any schema dependent upon any overarching concept of a 'civilizing process' or 'revolution in sentiment'. What we return to, in effect, are those questions, still terribly under-researched, not least when dealing with the common people, of how individuals interacted, of what were thought to be appropriate ways of presenting onself, of what was thought of as proper human conduct, of what was thought to be a decent human being. The situation here remains uncertain, yet it has been argued that those broad cultural changes of the period, allied to greater material comfort and the arrival of the early stages of the consumer society, did make England an appreciably more 'modern' place in 1760 than it had been in 1550. By the later date we find ourselves in a world of a burgeoning material culture, of a well-developed urban sector, of clubs and associations, of models of genteel sociability. The impact of these phenomena doubtlessly varied between social groups, while for all social strata the uncertainties created by disease or sudden economic disaster were real enough. Yet, sometimes in very subtle ways, social alignments and social identities had changed and become more complex.

There remain some basic questions about how the social history of the early modern period should be approached. What I hope to have done in this book is to explore what emerges when simplistic models of socio-economic development are abandoned. The limitations inherent in uncritical attachment to such models are all too obvious. They are neatly illustrated in attitudes expressed by Christopher Hill in a work covering much the same period and confronting many of the same problems as this one. Hill declared that he was 'concerned with the making of modern English society. We shall be looking for those elements of the new which are emerging.' This, he felt, was 'the only possible historical attitude: anything else involves the dangers of sentimental antiquarianism'.[6] I would contend that concentrating on 'the elements of the new which are emerging', not least in hands less sensitive than Hill's, tends to produce distortions as damaging as those he seeks to avoid. We may accept that one of the main functions of history is to help explain why and how we are in the peculiar situation in which we find ourselves. Yet a concentration on 'the making of modern English society', on the 'elements of the new', or the superficially 'relevant' can lead to the writing of very bad history. This problem seems to be especially acute when it is the early modern period which is under consideration.

Readers of this book will have encountered a Somerset woman complaining about her husband's sexual performance; the Durham widow Margaret Smith trying to marry her daughter off; Sir Richard Cholmely advising his successors to keep up traditional standards of hospitality; the London tailor John Reeve having a face-to-face conversation with the Almighty; William Stout having his education disrupted by the demands of agricultural production; the Yorkshire villager Henry Cockcrofte, convinced that his son was bewitched; and the Duchess of Marlborough, arguing with Sir John Vanbrugh about the design of Blenheim Palace. Arguably, none of these microcosms of the human condition tell us very much about those emergent 'elements of the new' which have been so eagerly sought by Hill and other historians of the period. Perhaps dwelling on such episodes and individuals is merely a display of that 'sentimental antiquarianism' of which Hill is so rightly suspicious. But I would contend that one of the things history, and especially social history, has to do, is to attempt, however imperfectly, to understand people as they were. Margaret Smith, Henry Cockcrofte, the Duchess of Marlborough and the rest were real people facing what were to them real problems as they tried to get through life as they were living it. Most of the inhabitants of the late twentieth-century world, professional historians included, are real people trying to get through life. Those pondering the 'relevance' of early modern social history need look no further.

One of the things which historians can legitimately do is help make our world intelligible, and hence the search for origins or for the seeds of new developments can be justified. But this is not the only facet of that process of 'understanding ourselves in time' which is one of the main reasons for studying history. We will understand ourselves most fully if we realize that the society in which we live, and the assumptions upon which we arrange our lives, are not the only ways in which human beings have gone (and in fact do go) about organizing their existence. Grappling with the realities of the world that existed before factories, before mass politics, before rapid communications and before effective medicine, is a salutary experience. It stretches our imagination. It also deepens us in our humanity. But it is best done if we leave behind our models of long-term change, if we discard the assumptions of historical or sociological preconceptions, if we cease to look merely for the origins of our present condition. Obviously, we must begin any historical enquiry by asking questions, questions which must be formulated in the light of our current conceptualizations, and then go back to refine and refashion those conceptualizations in the light of the answers to those questions. But our main responsibility when studying people in the past, including the early modern English, is to try to understand them in their own terms.

In this book I have set out to practise what I have been preaching here. Writing it has been a peculiar exercise: the arguments of long and complex monographs based on years of research have been compressed into a sentence; intellectual or theological points which occupied the best minds of the period for over half a lifetime have been mentioned in passing; social changes which affected the life of generations summed up in a paragraph or two. What has resulted from this process will, I hope, stimulate many of its readers to dip more deeply into the large recent output of writing on early modern English society, and perhaps even encourage a number of them to get to grips with the thousands of printed works and millions of documents which survive from the period. For, despite the efforts of so many labourers in this section of Clio's vineyard, there is still much work to be done.

Notes

1 Ronald Hutton, *The Restoration: a Political and Religious History of England and Wales 1658–1667* (Oxford, 1985), p. 191.
2 J.H. Plumb, *The Growth of Political Stability in England 1675–1725* (1967; Harmondsworth, 1969, 1973), p. 13.
3 *Ibid.*
4 Dorothy Marshall, *Eighteenth Century England* (1962), p. 3.
5 Theodore K. Rabb, *The Struggle for Stability in Early Modern Europe* (Oxford, 1975), p. 4.
6 Christopher Hill, *Reformation to Industrial Revolution: A Social and Economic History of Britain 1530–1780* (1967; Harmondsworth, 1973), p. 8.

Further reading

Where not otherwise specified, place of publication is London.

General

Christopher Hill, *Reformation to Industrial Revolution: A Social and Economic History of Britain 1530–1780* (1967; Harmondsworth, 1973) is the only work confronting social developments over the whole of our period, but has been overtaken by more recent research. Joyce Youings, *Sixteenth-Century England* (Harmondsworth, 1984), and Roy Porter, *English Society in the Eighteenth Century* (Harmondsworth, 1982) are useful introductions: Penguin have yet to publish a seventeenth-century volume in their social history series. Keith Wrightson, *English Society 1580–1680* (1982), is excellent in many respects, but is weak in its treatment of élites and hampered by a peculiar timespan. R.W. Malcolmson, *Life and Labour in England 1700–1780* (1981), is less inspiring. Paul Langford, *A Polite and Commercial People, 1727–1783* (Oxford, 1989), is an excellent guide to eighteenth-century England. Keith Thomas, *Religion and the Decline of Magic* (1971; Harmondsworth, 1973), a study of popular beliefs in the sixteenth and seventeenth centuries, is one of those rare books leaving the reader with a new view of what history might be about. Similarly, Peter Laslett, *The World We Have Lost* (3rd edn, 1983), although now rather dated, is still a stimulating introduction to the dimensions of social history.

Politics 1550–1653

The best general book covering this topic is Conrad Russell, *The Crisis of Parliaments: English History, 1509–1660* (Oxford, 1971). For the period

1550–1603, see: Penry Williams, *The Tudor Regime* (Oxford, 1979); D.M. Palliser, *The Age of Elizabeth: England under the later Tudors, 1547–1603* (1985); Jennifer Loach and Robert Tittler (eds), *The Mid-Tudor Polity, c.1540–1560* (1980); and Christopher Haigh (ed.), *The Reign of Elizabeth I* (1984). A.G.R. Smith, *The Government of Elizabethan England* (1967), is an excellent short introduction to that subject, while the interplay between central and local institutions has been examined in a series of articles by G.R. Elton: 'Tudor Government: The Points of Contact. I. Parliament', *Transactions of the Royal Historical Society*, 5th series, 24 (1974), pp. 183–200; 'Tudor Government: The Points of Contact. II. The Council', *ibid.*, 25 (1975), pp. 195–211; 'Tudor Government: The Points of Contact. III. The Court', *ibid.*, 26 (1976), pp. 211–28. Professor Elton's analysis of the workings of Tudor parliaments, including their legislative role, was taken further in his *The Parliament of England, 1559–1581* (Cambridge, 1986).

The early Stuart period is currently undergoing a ferment of revisionism. Derek Hirst, *Authority and Conflict: England 1603–1658* (1986), is a judicious guide to the outcome of the early first stages of this rethinking. Work in progress by Jenny Wormald will provide a reinterpretation of James I: for some of her initial thoughts, see her 'James VI and I: Two Kings or One?', *History*, 68 (1983), pp. 187–200. Conrad Russell, *Parliaments and English Politics 1621–1629* (Oxford, 1979) is a magisterial study: readers with little time to spare could read his 'Parliamentary History in Perspective', *History*, 62 (1976), pp. 1–27, with profit. Proponents of the long-term causes of the English Civil War include: Christopher Hill (ed.), *The English Revolution of 1640: Three Essays* (1940); and Lawrence Stone, *Social Change and Revolution in England, 1540–1640* (1963). For more recent views, see: Howard Tomlinson (ed.), *Before the Civil War, 1603–1642: Essays in Early Stuart Politics and Government* (1983); and Anthony Fletcher, *The Outbreak of the English Civil War* (1981). Kevin Sharpe, *The Personal Rule of Charles I* (New Haven, etc., 1992) is massive and masterly, while the impact of warfare in the 1640s is discussed in Charles Carlton, *Going to the Wars: the Experience of the British Civil Wars 1638–1651* (1992), which includes estimates for the casualties suffered. David Underdown, *Riot, Revel and Rebellion: Popular Politics and Culture in England, 1605–1660* (Oxford, 1985), opens up the possibility of a history of the politics of the period 'from below'.

Ivan Roots, *The Great Rebellion 1642–1660* (1966), is still the best general introduction, a masterpiece of compression. Newer perspectives are provided by John Morrill, *The Revolt of the Provinces: Conservatives and Radicals in the English Civil War, 1630–1650* (1976); and John Morrill (ed.), *Reactions to the English Civil War 1642–1649* (1982). Specific episodes receive detailed treatment in: David Underdown, *Pride's*

Purge: Politics in the English Revolution (Oxford, 1971); Blair Worden, *The Rump Parliament* (Cambridge, 1974); Austin Woolrych, *Commonwealth to Protectorate* (Oxford, 1982). G.E. Aylmer, *The Levellers in the English Revolution* (1975), is the best short introduction to the subject.

Those wishing to explore the notion of a General Crisis should read: Trevor Aston (ed.), *Crisis in Europe, 1560–1660* (1965); and Geoffrey Parker and Lesley M. Smith (eds), *The General Crisis of the Seventeenth Century* (1978).

Population

E.A. Wrigley and R.S. Schofield, *The Population History of England 1541–1871: A Reconstruction* (1981), is fundamental, but daunting in its size and technicality. Those wanting a brief guide to the subject could do worse than read E.A. Wrigley, *Population and History* (1969).

G.R. Quaife, *Wanton Wenches and Wayward Wives: Peasants and Illicit Sex in Early Seventeenth-Century England* (1979), although not entirely satisfactory, is the best exploration of sexual behaviour for the period. Some indications of the directions of ongoing research into the history of prostitution is provided by Paul Griffiths, 'The Structure of Prostitution in Elizabethan England', *Continuity and Change*, 8 (1993), pp. 39–64. Other studies of sexuality and its consequences are: J.A. Sharpe, *Defamation and Sexual Slander in Early Modern England: the Church Courts at York* (Borthwick Paper, 58, York, 1980); Alan Bray, *Homosexuality in Renaissance England* (1982); Peter Laslett and Karla Oosterveen (eds), *Bastardy and its Comparative History* (1980); and N.E. Hull and P.C. Hoffer, *Murdering Mothers: Infanticide in England and New England, 1558–1803* (New York, 1981).

Andrew B. Appleby, *Famine in Tudor and Stuart England* (Liverpool, 1978), is the standard introduction. Paul Slack, *The Impact of Plague in Tudor and Stuart England* (1985), replaces earlier work, although J.F.D. Shrewsbury, *A History of the Bubonic Plague in the British Isles* (Cambridge, 1970), can still be read with profit. Charles Creighton, *A History of Epidemics in Britain*, 2 vols (2nd edn, 1965), is also useful.

The family

Despite its many defects, Lawrence Stone, *The Family, Sex and Marriage in England, 1500–1800* (1977; Harmondsworth, 1979), will probably be most people's starting point. It should be read in conjunction with Alan Macfarlane's review article in _History and Theory_, 18 (1979), pp. 103–26. Ralph A. Houlbrooke, _The English Family 1450–1700_ (1984), provides a more balanced view, while a number of detailed studies, including one by Kathleen Davies, can be found in R.B. Outhwaite (ed.), _Marriage and Society; Studies in the Social History of Marriage_ (1981). Jack Goody, Joan Thirsk and E.P. Thompson (eds), _Family and Inheritance: Rural Society in Western Europe 1200–1800_ (Cambridge, 1976), stresses the family's importance in economic life and property transference; while Michael Anderson, _Approaches to the History of the Western Family 1500–1914_ (1980), is an excellent short introduction to the topic of family history as a whole. For some local evidence, see Miranda Chaytor, 'Household and Kinship: Ryton in the late sixteenth and early seventeenth centuries', _History Workshop_, 10 (1980), pp. 25–60. Stone has followed his 1977 overview with a trilogy of works on marriage which contain much vivid material, most of it drawn from ecclesiastical court records: _The Road to Divorce: England 1530–1987_ (Oxford, 1990); _Uncertain Unions: Marriage in England, 1660–1753_ (Oxford, 1992); _Broken Lives: Separation and Divorce in England, 1660–1857_ (Oxford, 1993). Philippe Aries, _Centuries of Childhood_ (New York, 1965; Harmondsworth, 1973), has proved influential, but its conclusions have been challenged by Linda A. Pollock, _Forgotten Children: Parent–Child Relations from 1500 to 1900_ (Cambridge, 1983).

Towns and villages

The urban history of the period is best approached via a number of collections of essays: Peter Clark and Paul Slack (eds), _Crisis and Order in English Towns 1500–1700: Essays in Urban History_ (1972); A.M. Everitt (ed.), _Perspectives in English Urban History_ (1973); Peter Clark and Paul Slack (eds), _English Towns in Transition 1500–1700_ (Oxford, 1976); Peter Clark (ed.), _The Transformation of English Provincial Towns 1600–1800_ (1984). P.J. Corfield, _The Impact of English Towns 1700–1800_ (Oxford, 1982) is good on the eighteenth century. Civic ritual is a subject currently attracting considerable attention: the most useful introduction is M.E. James, 'Ritual, Drama and Social Body in the Late Medieval English Town', _Past and Present_, 98 (1983), pp. 3–29. For the subject's significance at a later date see P. Borsay, ' "All the Town's a Stage": Urban Ritual and Ceremony 1660–1800', in Peter Clark (ed.), _The Transformation of English Provincial Towns 1600–1800_ (1984). Dr Borsay's _The English Urban Renaissance: Culture and Society in the English Provincial Town, 1660–1770_ (Oxford, 1989), is also of crucial importance. David Underdown, _Fire from Heaven: the Life of an English Town in the Seventeenth Century_ (1992) is a vivid portrayal of one fragment of the urban experience of the period.

A.L. Beier and Roger Finlay (eds), *London 1500–1700: the Making of the Metropolis* (1986) provides an invaluable introduction to recent work on the capital's history. Three excellent detailed studies have deepened our understanding of life in the capital: Steve Rappaport, *Worlds within Worlds: Structures and Life in Sixteenth-Century London* (Cambridge, 1989); Ian W. Archer, *The Pursuit of Stability: Social Relations in Elizabethan London* (Cambridge, 1991); and Jeremy Boulton, *Neighbourhood and Society: a London Suburb in the Seventeenth Century* (Cambridge, 1987). Two older works which are still worth reading are: Norman G. Brett-James, *The Growth of Stuart London* (1935); and Dorothy George, *London Life in the Eighteenth Century* (1925; Harmondsworth, 1966).

The sources and methods involved in studying rural communities in this period are discussed in Alan Macfarlane, Sarah Harrison and Charles Jardine, *Reconstructing Historical Communities* (Cambridge, 1977), although the general reader will probably find David Hey, *The Oxford Companion to Local and Family History* (Oxford, 1996) more accessible. Individual village studies include: W.G. Hoskins, *The Midland Peasant* (1957); Margaret Spufford, *Contrasting Communities: English Villages in the Sixteenth and Seventeenth Centuries* (Cambridge, 1974); David G. Hey, *An English Rural Community: Myddle under the Tudors and Stuarts* (Leicester, 1974); Keith Wrightson and David Levine, *Poverty and Piety in an English Village: Terling, 1525–1700* (2nd edn, Oxford, 1994); and Cicely Howell, *Land, Family and Inheritance in Transition: Knibworth Harcourt 1280–1700* (Cambridge, 1983). Perhaps the best avenue into the world of the early modern community, however, is Richard Gough, *The History of Myddle*, ed. David G. Hey (Harmondsworth, 1981). Conflict in the community is now a much-studied theme: an excellent introduction to many of the issues involved is provided by Martin Ingram, 'Ridings, Rough Music and the "Reform of Popular Culture" in Early Modern England', *Past and Present*, 105 (1985), pp. 80–113, while Keith Wrightson, 'The Politics of the Parish in Early Modern England', in Paul Griffiths, Adam Fox and Steve Hindle (eds), *The Experience of Authority in Early Modern England* (1996), is an excellent guide to the current thinking on the problem. Laura Gowing, *Domestic Dangers: Women, Words and Sex in Early Modern London* (Oxford, 1996) is the fullest discussion yet published on an important area of inter-neighbourly dispute.

The national community and the problem of order

Works discussing the theory and development of the state include: J.H. Shennan, *The Origins of the Modern European State 1450–1725* (1974); Kenneth H.F. Dyson, *The State Tradition in Western Europe: A Study of an Idea and Institution* (Oxford, 1980); and Norbert Elias, *State Formation and Civilization* (Oxford, 1982). For a study focused specifically on England, see John Brewer, *The Sinews of Power: War, Money and the English State 1688–1783* (1989). For the development of an important bureaucratic department to set beside these more generalized works, see Henry Roseveare, *The Treasury: The Evolution of a British Institution* (1969).

Paul Slack (ed.), *Rebellion, Popular Protest and Social Change in Early Modern England* (Cambridge, 1984), is an excellent introduction to the theme of popular disturbance; while Anthony Fletcher, *Tudor Rebellions* (1968) examines a wider spectrum. On crime, see: J.S. Cockburn (ed.), *Crime in England 1550–1800* (1977); J.A. Sharpe, *Crime in Early Modern England 1550–1750* (1985); and J.M. Beattie, *Crime and the Courts in England 1660–1800* (Oxford, 1986). Paul Griffiths, Adam Fox and Steve Hindle (eds), *The Experience of Authority in Early Modern England* (1996) is an important collection of essays dealing with various aspects of order and authority.

Gender is one of the variables discussed in Susan Dwyer Amussen, *An Ordered Society: Gender and Class in Early Modern England* (Oxford, 1988). The topic enjoys fuller coverage in Anthony Fletcher, *Gender, Sex and Subordination in England, 1500–1800* (New Haven, 1995). For an exploration of the importance of age hierarchies, see Paul Griffiths, *Youth and Authority: Formative Experiences in England 1560–1640* (Oxford, 1996), and the earlier essay by Keith Thomas, 'Age and Authority in Early Modern England', *Proceedings of the British Academy*, 62 (1976), pp. 205–48. Suicide is studied sensitively in Michael MacDonald and Terence R. Murphy, *Sleepless Souls: Suicide in Early Modern England* (Oxford, 1990). There is a growing literature on the history of madness: Roy Porter, *Mind Forg'd Manacles: a History of Madness in England from the Restoration to the Regency* (1987), is a characteristically lively introduction.

Our appreciation of the importance of county and regional history was sharpened by Alan Everitt and his *Change in the Provinces: the Seventeenth Century* (Leicester, 1969) states his position clearly. Good county studies include: T.G. Barnes, *Somerset 1625–1640, A County's Government during the 'Personal Rule'* (1961); A. Hassell Smith, *County and Court: Government and Politics in Norfolk, 1558–1603* (Oxford, 1974); and Anthony Fletcher, *A County Community in Peace and War: Sussex, 1600–1660* (1975). Clive Holmes, 'The County Community in Stuart Historiography', *Journal of British Studies*, 19.ii (1980), pp. 54–73, offers a critique of the emphasis placed on the county, while Anthony Fletcher, *Reform in the Provinces: the Government of Stuart England*

(Princeton and London, 1986) examines the interplay between local and central government.

Keith Wrightson, 'The Social Order of Early Modern England: Three Approaches', in Lloyd Bonfield, Richard M. Smith and Keith Wrightson (eds), *The World we have Gained: Histories of Population and Social Structure* (Oxford, 1986) is the best introduction of how to analyse society at this date.

The economy

Useful introductions are: J.D. Chambers, *Population, Economy and Society in Pre-Industrial England* (Oxford, 1972); B.A. Holderness, *Pre-Industrial England: Economy and Society 1500 to 1750* (1976); D.C. Coleman, *The Economy of England, 1450–1750* (Oxford, 1977); and Charles Wilson, *England's Apprenticeship, 1603–1763* (2nd edn, 1984). Those seeking more detail should read C.G.A. Clay, *Economic Expansion and Social Change: England 1500–1700*, 2 vols. (Cambridge, 1984).

Agriculture is best approached via Joan Thirsk (ed.), *The Agrarian History of England and Wales* (Cambridge: in progress 1967–), of which volumes IV and V cover our period. R.H. Tawney, *The Agrarian Problem in the Sixteenth Century* (1912; reprinted New York, 1967) is a classic, but should be read with Eric Kerridge, *Agrarian Problems in the Sixteenth Century and After* (1969). Kerridge's *The Agricultural Revolution* (1967) argues strongly for decisive changes in agriculture over the seventeenth century. For another approach to the agricultural history of the period see Ann Kussmaul, *A General View of the Rural Economy of England, 1538–1840* (Cambridge, 1990).

On commerce, see: Ralph Davis, *A Commercial Revolution: English Overseas Trade in the Seventeenth and Eighteenth Centuries* (Historical Association Pamphlets, General Series, 64, 1967); W.E. Minchinton (ed.), *English Overseas Trade in the Seventeenth and Eighteenth Centuries* (1969); and Ralph Davis, *English Overseas Trade 1500–1700* (1973). My ideas on industry owe much to: D.C. Coleman, *Industry in Tudor and Stuart England* (1975); Maxine Berg, Pat Hudson and Michael Sonescher (eds), *Manufacture in Town and Country before the Factories* (Cambridge 1983); and Maxine Berg, *The Age of Manufactures 1700–1820* (1985). A once-fashionable concept is discussed in L.A. Clarkson, 'Proto-Industrialization': The First Phase of Industralization?* (1985). The significance of developments in the Tyneside coalfield is emphasized in David Levine and Keith Wrightson, *The Making of an Industrial Society: Whickham, 1560–1765* (Oxford, 1991).

On the growth of consumerism, see: Joan Thirsk, *Economic Policy and Projects: the Development of a Consumer Society in Early Modern England* (Oxford, 1978); N. McKendrick, J. Brewer and J.H. Plumb, *The Birth of a Consumer Society: the Commercialization of Eighteenth-Century England* (Bloomington, Indiana, 1982); Margaret Spufford, *The Great Reclothing of Rural England: Petty Chapmen and their Wares in the Seventeenth Century* (1984); and Lorna Weatherill, *Consumer Behaviour and Material Culture in Britain, 1660–1760* (1988). Alan Macfarlane, *The Origins of English Individualism* (Oxford, 1978), argues strongly for the long-term existence of capitalist economic attitudes in English society.

The landed orders

Lawrence Stone, *The Crisis of the Aristocracy 1558–1641* (Oxford, 1965) is the essential starting point. The story is taken further by: Lawrence Stone and Jeanne C. Fawtier Stone, *An Open Elite? England 1540–1880* (Oxford, 1984); John Cannon, *Aristocratic Century: the Peerage of Eighteenth-Century England* (Cambridge, 1984); J.V. Beckett, *The Aristocracy in England, 1660–1714* (Oxford, 1986); and M.L. Bush, *The English Aristocracy: a Comparative Synthesis* (Manchester, 1984). Many of the essays in J.H. Hexter, *Reappraisals in History* (1961) have a bearing on the subject.

For an excellent analysis of the gentry see Felicity Heal and Clive Holmes, *The Gentry in England and Wales 1500–1700* (1994). The importance of this social group was signposted by R.H. Tawney, 'The Rise of the Gentry, 1558–1640', *Economic History Review*, 9 (1941), pp. 1–38. The subsequent 'Gentry Controversy' is summed up by J.H. Hexter, 'Storm over the Gentry', in *Reappraisals*. J.T. Cliffe, *The Yorkshire Gentry: from the Reformation to the Civil War* (1969), is first rate, and his later *The Puritan Gentry: the Great Puritan Families of Early Stuart England* (1984) is well worth reading. Peter Roebuck, *Yorkshire Baronets 1640–1760: Families, Estates and Fortunes* (1980), is another good regional study, while more general information on this later period can be found in G.E. Mingay, *English Landed Society in the Eighteenth Century* (1956). Jonathan Powis, *Aristocracy* (Oxford, 1984) is a stimulating and wide-ranging discussion of the subject.

Non-landed élites

Everybody should read J.H. Hexter, 'The Myth of the Middle Class in Tudor England', in *Reappraisals in History* (1961). Curiously, good local studies of the commercial bourgeoisie in early modern England are hard to come by. I have leant heavily on R.G. Wilson, *Gentlemen Merchants: The Merchant Community in Leeds 1700–1830* (Manchester and New York, 1971), and gleaned what I could from the urban histories of the period. John Smail, *The Origins of Middle Class Culture: Halifax, Yorkshire, 1660–1780* (Ithaca and London, 1994), is an important study of developments in one provincial town, while Peter Earle, *The Making of the English Middle Class: Business, Society and Family Life in London, 1660–1730* (1989), outlines the fortunes of the middle class in the capital, although the book's subtitle is a more accurate indication of its contents than its main title.

The best introduction to the professions in our period (although again a little late in its focus) is G.S. Holmes, *Augustan England: Professions, State and Society, 1680–1730* (1982), from which I have in particular drawn for my discussion of doctors and army and navy officers. This can be read in conjunction with Wilfrid Prest (ed.), *The Professions in Early Modern England* (London, New York and Sydney, 1987). For the clergy, see: Rosemary O'Day, *The English Clergy: the Emergence and Consolidation of a Profession 1558–1642* (Leicester, 1979); Felicity Heal, *Of Prelates and Princes: a Study of the Economic and Social Position of the Tudor Episcopate* (Cambridge, 1980); Rosemary O'Day and Felicity Heal, *Princes and Paupers in the English Church 1500–1800* (Leicester, 1981); and, for a good local study, John H. Pruett, *The Parish Clergy under the Later Stuarts: The Leicestershire Experience* (Urbane, Chicago and London, 1978). The two fullest analyses of the legal profession come from the first half of our period: C.W. Brooks, *Pettyfoggers and Vipers of the Commonwealth: The 'Lower Branch' of the Legal Profession in Early Modern England* (Cambridge, 1986); and Wilfrid R. Prest, *The Rise of the Barristers: A Social History of the English Bar 1590–1640* (Oxford, 1986). These should be read with Wilfrid R. Prest (ed.), *Lawyers in Early Modern Europe and America* (New York, 1981), a number of the essays in which deal with English developments. Our knowledge of the medical profession has been increased by the massive recent growth in the history of medicine, much of which has taken the form of books written or edited by Roy Porter: his *Disease, Medicine and Society in England, 1550–1860* (1987), is a good introduction. For a rather different view of medical provision in the period, see Lucinda McCray Beier, *Sufferers and Healers: the Experience of Illness in Seventeenth-Century England* (1987).

The common people

Mildred Campbell, *The English Yeoman under Elizabeth and the Early Stuarts* (1960) remains the standard introduction: see also Gordon Batho,

'The Yeomanry and the Opportunities for the Capable', in Joan Thirsk (ed.), *The Agrarian History of England and Wales* (Cambridge: in progress, 1967–), vol. IV. On urban masters, those with a taste for original documents should read *The Autobiography of William Stout of Lancaster, 1665–1772*, ed. J.D. Marshall (Chetham Society, 3rd series, 14, 1967). Claims for the importance and cohesion of the middling orders of society are made by Jonathan Barry and Christopher Brooks (eds), *The Middling Sort of People: Culture, Society and Politics in England, 1550–1800* (1994).

The fullest accounts of labouring life are centred on the eighteenth century: C.R. Dobson, *Masters and Journeymen: a Prehistory of Industrial Relations* (1980); John Rule, *The Experience of Labour in Eighteenth-Century Industry* (1981); Ann Kussmaul, *Servants in Husbandry in Early Modern England* (Cambridge, 1981); and Keith Snell, *Annals of the Labouring Poor: Social Change in Agrarian England, 1660–1900* (Cambridge, 1985). D.C. Coleman, 'Labour in the Economy of the Seventeenth Century', *Economic History Review*, 2nd series, 8 (1956), pp. 280–95, is still vital reading, while Steven R. Smith, 'The London Apprentices as Seventeenth-Century Adolescents', *Past and Present*, 61 (1973), pp. 149–61, is suggestive of the importance of apprentice culture. Alan Everitt, 'Farm Labourers', in Thirsk (ed.), *Agrarian History*, vol. IV, is an early attempt to get at a difficult subject. Much fascinating work on migration is brought together in Peter Clark and David Souden (eds), *Migration and Society in Early Modern England* (1987). For an early exploration of Black History, see James Walvin, *The Black Presence: a Documentary History of the Negro in England, 1555–1860* (1971).

Alice Clark, *The Working Life of Women in the Seventeenth Century* (2nd edn, 1969) is a classic, but is inevitably being overtaken by research in progress. Much of this is summarized in Pamela Sharpe, 'Continuity and Change: Women's History and Economic History in Britain', *Economic History Review*, 2nd Series, 48 (1995), pp. 353–69, which includes a comprehensive bibliograhy. On this subject, see also Lindsey Charles and Lorna Duffin (eds), *Women and Work in Pre-Industrial England* (1985). Mary Prior, 'Women and the Urban Economy: Oxford 1500–1800', in Mary Prior (ed.), *Women in English Society 1500–1800* (1985) is a good local study.

On the poor, see: Dorothy Marshall's old but still unreplaced *The English Poor in the Eighteenth Century* (1926); E. Melling (ed.) *Kentish Sources, IV, The Poor* (Maidstone, 1964); and J.F. Pound, *Poverty and Vagrancy in Tudor England* (1971). My account of vagrants is based largely on: Paul Slack, 'Vagrants and Vagrancy in England, 1598–1668', *Economic History Review*, 2nd Series, 27 (1974), pp. 360–79; and A.L. Beier, *Masterless Men:*

the Vagrancy Problem in Britain 1560–1640 (1985). Paul Slack's earlier researches into poverty and vagrancy have now developed into his *Poverty and Policy in Tudor and Stuart England* (1988), an excellent overview of the subject. Social problems in the latter part of our period are discussed in Lee Davison, Timothy Hitchcock, Tim Keirn and Robert Shoemaker (eds), *Stilling the Grumbling Hive: the Response to Social and Economic Problems in England, 1689–1750* (Stroud, etc., 1992).

The importance of custom in the life of the lower orders in the eighteenth century is made clear in E.P. Thompson, *Customs in Common* (1991). The Derbyshire lead-miners have been the subject of an important doctoral thesis by Andy Wood: for a preliminary impression of his findings, see his 'Social Conflict and Change in the Mining Communities of North West Derbyshire, *c.* 1600–1700', *International Review of Social History*, 38 (1993), pp. 31–51.

Religion

There is no really satisfactory introduction to this subject. For the earlier period, Felicity Heal and Rosemary O'Day (eds), *Church and Society in England: Henry VIII to James I* (1977), gives a good impression of current preoccupations, while Patrick Collinson, *The Religion of Protestants: The Church in English Society 1559–1625* (Oxford, 1982) is superb, as is his *The Birthpangs of Protestant England: Religious and Cultural Change in the Sixteenth and Seventeenth Century* (Houndmills, Basingstoke, 1988). Christopher Hill, *Society and Puritanism in Pre-Revolutionary England* (1964) is still worth reading, but the best access to what Puritanism was about comes from reading P.S. Seaver, *Wallington's World: A Puritan Artisan in Seventeenth-Century London* (1985). John Bossy, *The English Catholic Community* (1975) replaced all previous work on the subject, but is beginning to be challenged. The importance of Arminianism was suggested by N. Tyacke, *Anti-Calvinists: the Rise of English Arminianism, c. 1590–1640* (Oxford, 1987).

Two introductions to the post-1642 sects are: Christopher Hill, *The World Turned Upside Down: Radical Ideology in the English Revolution* (1972; Harmondsworth, 1975); and J.F. McGregor and Barry Reay (eds), *Radical Religion in the English Revolution* (Oxford, 1984). More specific studies include: A.L. Morton, *The World of the Ranters: Religious Radicalism in the English Revolution* (1970); B.S. Capp, *The Fifth Monarchy Men: a Study in Seventeenth-Century Millenarianism* (1972); and Barry Reay, *The Quakers and the English Revolution* (1985). For a reassessment of religious radicalism among parliamentarian troops, see Mark A. Kishlansky, *The Rise of the New Model Army* (Cambridge, 1979).

The restored Church of England is described in: I.M. Green, *The Re-Establishment of the Church of England 1660–1663* (Oxford, 1978); Norman Sykes, *Church and State in England in the Eighteenth Century* (Cambridge, 1934); and *idem, From Sheldon to Secker: Aspects of English Church History 1660–1768* (Cambridge, 1958). G.V. Bennett, *White Kennett 1660–1728, Bishop of Peterborough: a Study in the Political and Ecclesiastical History of the Early Eighteenth Century* (1957) describes an outstanding but representative Anglican, while Arthur Wane, *Church and Society in Eighteenth-Century Devon* (Newton Abbot, 1969) provides a welcome local dimension. Wesley F. Baker, *John Wesley and the Church of England* (1970), and A. Armstrong, *The Church in England, The Methodists and Society, 1700–1850* (1973) offer a basic introduction to eighteenth-century Methodism.

Neither E.D. Bebb, *Nonconformity and Social-Economic Life* (1935), nor Cecil Roth, *A History of the Jews in England* (Oxford, 1941) have been replaced as general overviews.

Education and literacy

Rosemary O'Day, *Education and Society 1500–1800: The Social Foundations of Education in Early Modern England* (1982) is the best general introduction, although Joan Simon, *Education and Society in Tudor England* (Cambridge, 1966; reprinted 1979) is an excellent study for the earlier part of our period. David Cressy, *Education in Tudor and Stuart England* (1975), marshals a number of extracts from contemporary sources. Older studies include Kenneth Charlton, *Education in Renaissance England* (London and Toronto, 1965), and Nicholas Hans, *New Trends in Education in the Eighteenth Century* (1951). On higher education, see: Lawrence Stone (ed.), *The University in Society*, 2 vols (Princeton and London, 1975); Hugh Kearney, *Scholars and Gentlemen: Universities and Society in Pre-Industrial Britain 1500–1700* (1970); and Wifrid R. Prest, *The Inns of Court 1590–1640* (1972). The history of the grammar schools is charted in Foster Watson, *The Grammar Schools to 1660: their Curriculum and Practice* (Cambridge, 1908), and W.A.L. Vincent, *The Grammar Schools: their Continuing Tradition, 1660–1714* (1969). Barring-out and related problems are described in Keith Thomas, *Rule and Misrule in the Schools of Early Modern England* (Stenton Lectures, 9, Reading, 1976).

David Cressy, *Literacy and the Social Order: Reading and Writing in Tudor and Stuart England* (Cambridge, 1980) is an excellent book, but should be read in conjunction with Margaret Spufford, 'First Steps in Literacy: the Reading and Writing Experiences of the humblest

Seventeenth Century Spiritual Autobiographers', *Social History*, 4 (1979), pp. 407–36. The general trends in education over the first half of our period and their connection with other phenomena are discussed in Lawrence Stone, 'The Educational Revolution in England, 1560–1640', *Past and Present*, 28 (1964), pp. 41–80.

Culture, popular and élite

There is no work of synthesis on the subject of popular culture in this period, although Barry Reay (ed.), *Popular Culture in Seventeenth-Century England* (1985) is an excellent introduction. Tim Harris (ed.), *Popular Culture in England, c. 1500–1850* (1995), while not doing much to help solve the conceptual difficulties inherent in the subject, also contains some first-rate essays, including a stimulating contribution by Susan Dwyer Amussen on 'The Gendering of Popular Culture in Early Modern England'. Two good discussions of particular themes are: R.W. Malcolmson, *Popular Recreations in English Society 1700–1850* (Cambridge, 1973); and Margaret Spufford, *Small Books and Pleasant Histories: Popular Fiction and its Readership in Seventeenth-Century England* (1981). P. Burke, *Popular Culture in Early Modern Europe* (1978), remains the standard introduction to the subject. New approaches to cultural history are described in Lynn Hunt (ed.), *The New Cultural History* (Berkeley, Los Angeles and London, 1989), while those interested in this subject might also read a pioneering book by one of its French practitioners, Roger Chartier, *Cultural History: Between Practices and Representations* (Oxford, 1988).

Developments in painting are given in considerable detail in the 'Oxford History of English Art' series. Relevant volumes are: Eric Mercer, *English Art 1553–1625* (Oxford, 1962); Margaret Whinney and Oliver Millar, *English Art 1625–1714* (Oxford, 1957); and Joseph Burke, *English Art 1714–1800* (Oxford, 1976). A good one-volume introduction is Ellis Waterhouse, *Painting in Britain 1538 to 1790* (4th edn, Harmondsworth, 1978). An accessible guide to the history of the literature of the period is provided by the New Pelican Guide to English Literature, edited by Boris Ford. Relevant volumes are: 2, *The Age of Shakespeare* (1982); 3, *From Donne to Marvell* (1982); 4, *From Dryden to Johnson* (1982). The standard introduction to the music of the period is Ernest Walker, *A History of Music in England* (3rd edn, Oxford, 1952), while J. Summerson, *Architecture in Britain 1530–1830* (Harmondsworth, 1966) provides a useful overview of the subject. Two books indicating links between the artistic and the social worlds are Michael Foss, *The Age of Patronage: The Arts in Society 1660–1750* (1971); and Judith Hook, *The Baroque Age in England* (1976). Roy Strong's work has been significant in emphasizing the role of the court as a centre of culture and as a focus for wider cultural values: see, in particular, his *Henry Prince of Wales and England's lost Renaissance* (1986).

Magic, witchcraft and natural philosophy

Keith Thomas, *Religion and the Decline of Magic* (1971; Harmondsworth, 1973) is the best introduction to magic and related beliefs. Alan Macfarlane, *Witchcraft in Tudor and Stuart England: a Regional and Comparative Study* (1970) is excellent on the experience of village witchcraft, while John Stearne, *A Confirmation and Discovery of Witchcraft* (1648; reprinted Exeter, 1973) is a remarkable insight into how witchcraft prosecutions looked to a witch-finder. James Sharpe, *Instruments of Darkness: Witchcraft in England 1550–1750* (1996) is a recent overview of the subject.

F.A. Yates, *The Occult Tradition in the Elizabethan Age* (1979), is good on the impact of Neo-Platonism, and the next episode in the story is recounted masterfully in Charles Webster, *The Great Instauration: Science, Medicine and Reform 1626–1660* (1975). Michael Hunter, *Science and Society in Restoration England* (Cambridge, 1981) is excellent, while Derek Parker, *Familiar to All: William Lilly and Astrology in the Seventeenth Century* (1975) is a lively account of the leading popular astrologer of the time. Robert K. Merton, *Science, Technology and Society in Seventeenth-Century England* (1938; 2nd edn, New York, 1970) makes what would now be considered as oversimplistic connections between scientific, economic and religious change. More recent general introductions include: Hugh Kearney, *Science and Change 1500–1700* (1971); R.S. Westfall, *The Construction of Modern Science* (Cambridge, 1977); and A.R. Hall, *The Revolution in Science* (1983). For a recent reappraisal of a major scientific debate of the period, which puts late seventeenth century 'science' firmly in its contemporary context, see Steven Shapin and Simon Schaffer, *Leviathan and the Air-Pump: Hobbes, Boyle, and the Experimental Life* (Princeton, 1985).

Politics 1653–1760

The period is covered by two good recent textbooks: J.R. Jones, *County and Court: England 1658–1714* (1978); and W.A. Speck, *Stability and Strife: England 1714–1760* (1977). For the 1650s, see Ivan Roots, *The Great Rebellion 1642–1660* (1966). Oliver Cromwell has attracted his fair share of biographers, yet he still remains elusive: Christopher Hill, *God's Englishman: Oliver Cromwell and the English Revolution* (1970;

Harmondsworth, 1972), probably gets nearer to his subject than most. The limitations of his opponents' activities are explored in David Underdown, *Royalist Conspiracy in England 1649–1660* (New Haven, 1960).

A good introduction to events around 1660 is Ronald Hutton, *The Restoration: A Political and Religious History of England and Wales 1658–1667* (Oxford, 1985). Later episodes in Charles II's reign are dealt with by John Kenyon, *The Popish Plot* (1972), and J.R. Jones, *The First Whigs: the Politics of the Exclusion Crisis 1678–1683* (1961).

Good accounts of the Glorious Revolution are J.R. Jones, *The Revolution of 1688 in England* (1972), and J. Carswell, *The Descent on England* (1969), the latter being especially interesting on the European context. Gary Stuart de Krey, *A Fractured Society: The Politics of London in the First Age of Party 1688–1715* (Oxford, 1985), adds an important local dimension which emphasizes the importance of popular and dissenting politics. Two thought-provoking pieces on the later Stuarts are: J.H. Plumb, *The Growth of Political Stability in England 1675–1725* (1967; Harmondsworth, 1969, 1973); and John Miller 'The Potential for "Absolutism" in Later Stuart England', *History*, 69 (1984), pp. 187–207. See also Geoffrey Holmes (ed.), *Britain after the Glorious Revolution 1689–1714* (1969). D.W. Jones, *War and Economy in the Age of William III and Marlborough* (1989) is a richly detailed analysis of how England managed to finance its war effort and how near financial disaster was in those years.

Sir Lewis Namier, *The Structure of Politics at the Accession of George III* (1957), is the classic account of how politics stood at the end of the period covered by this book. My account of the political life of the generation before 1760 is based on: B.W. Hill, *The Growth of Parliamentary Parties, 1698–1742* (1970); John Brewer, *Party Ideology and Popular Politics at the Accession of George III* (Cambridge, 1976); John Cannon (ed.), *The Whig Ascendancy: Colloquies on Hanoverian England* (1981); Linda Colley, *In Defiance of Oligarchy: the Tory party, 1714–1760* (Cambridge, 1982); and Jeremy Black (ed.), *Britain in the Age of Walpole* (Basingstoke, 1984). Reading E.P. Thompson, *Whigs and Hunters: the Origin of the Black Act* (1975), and J.C.D. Clark, *English Society 1688–1832* (Cambridge, 1985) should convince students that the interplay between society and politics in early Hanoverian England is a subject open to varying interpretations.

Index